AN INTRODUCTION
TO THE SCIENCE OF PHONETICS

AN INTRODUCTION
TO THE SCIENCE OF PHONETICS

Nigel Hewlett
Janet Beck
Queen Margaret University College, Edinburgh

LAWRENCE ERLBAUM ASSOCIATES, PUBLISHERS

2006   Mahwah, New Jersey   London

Senior Acquisitions Editor:	Emily Wilkinson
Executive Assistant:	Bonita D'Amil
Cover Artwork:	Janet Beck
Cover Layout:	Kathryn Houghtaling Lacey
Composition:	LEA Book Production
Text and Cover Printer:	Hamilton Printing Company

This book was typeset in 10 pt. BookmanITC Lt BT Roman, Bold, and Italic.
The heads were typeset in Swiss 721Cn BT, Roman, Bold, and Italic.

Lawrence Erlbaum Associates, Inc., Publishers
10 Industrial Avenue
Mahwah, New Jersey 07430
www.erlbaum.com

Library of Congress Cataloging-in-Publication Data

Hewlett, Nigel.
An introduction to the science of phonetics / by Nigel Hewlett, Janet Beck.
    p. cm.
Includes bibliographical references and index.
ISBN 0-8058-3868-6 (alk. paper)
1. Phonetics.   I. Beck, J. Mackenzie (Janet Mackenzie)   II.Title.
P221.H48 2006
414'.8—dc22   2005042042
                                                          CIP

Books published by Lawrence Erlbaum Associates are printed on acid-free paper, and their bindings are chosen for strength and durability.

Printed in the United States of America
10 9 8 7 6 5 4 3 2 1

Contents

PART III Auditory Phonetics

PART IV Speech Production

Foreword

Those who dare to write books on phonetics face an uphill task. They have to take a subject which is by its nature auditory, dynamic, and transient and manipulate it so that it works in a medium which is visual, static, and permanent. Writing for professionals is not so bad, for the authors can at least assume a common background which—apart perhaps from the occasional obscure voice quality—will make descriptions of sounds immediately recognizable.

No such assumption can be made with the new student. There is no harder task, in the world of language study, than to write an introductory book on phonetics. Grammarians and lexicographers, even phonologists, have it easy, by comparison. They have no need to maintain a synergy between three worlds of sound—production, transmission, and reception. Nor do they need to master concepts in three worlds of intellect—anatomy, physiology, and physics—four, even, if we include the limited but necessary mathematics. Indeed, which other subject demands, at its initial encounter, a readiness to cope with the concepts, methods, and terminology of four sciences?

Success can only come from years of experience of having to teach the subject from scratch, and it is a sense of pedagogical awareness and realism that pervades the present book. The authors have heard it all. They know which sounds are difficult and which aren't. They know which teaching strategies work and which don't. They know what motivates a student and what doesn't. The proof of the phonetics pudding is always in the exercises. The exercises in this book are among the best you will ever see.

But the ingredients for the pudding also have to be right. And the chief ingredient is top-quality descriptions. All phonetics textbooks describe, but some are more descriptive than others. The real strength of the present book is the meticulous account it gives of the articulation (and associated acoustics) of individual sounds—and not just of the obvious vowels and consonants, which have been presented a thousand times over, but of the unobvious ones, which many phonetics books never mention at all. Indeed, it would have been difficult to handle them before 1999, when the International Phonetics Alphabet was extended to cope with unusual sounds. This is the first account I have seen which devotes proper attention to the aim and range of that extension.

It is an essential broadening of the scope of phonetics. The developmental and the deviant are established dimensions of enquiry in several other subjects, such as psychology, and they are no less important here. As the authors put it, at the beginning of chapter 6, this extension "is partly for the benefit of readers who may have a specific interest in speech disorder or development of speech in children and partly because it seems useful for any phonetician to have some awareness of the full potential range of speech production." Quite so. The only surprising thing is that, in 2006, the latter point still needs to be made. But it does, for most phonetics texts have passed over the developmental and pathological areas in silence.

It is the world of speech pathology which drives and unifies this book. Speech pathology is a subject that generates good phoneticians, because it makes them more broad-minded—less likely to think along predetermined phonological lines. All speech pathologists know that anything that *can* go wrong, *will*, sooner or later, and they need to be prepared for it. In phonetics, it has not been easy, until now, to find the required preparatory detail.

And, much more than in other applied fields, speech pathology makes you listen, really listen, to the fine distinctions which emerge, as speech vacillates between the deviant and the normal. Any phonetics textbook which claims to be of practical value, in relation to speech therpautics and management, has therefore to ensure that speech production does not swamp the much less well charted domain of speech reception. A glance at the contents of this book will show that this consideration has been at the forefront of the authors' minds.

In an introductory textbook, when the going gets tough, students are apt to complain "why study all this?" The speech pathologist can provide an answer that goes well beyond the usual intellectual "because it's there." They can say, with a level of confidence that can only come from accumulated clinical experience: "because it helps." And that would be my answer, too, to anyone who asked me why they should use this new introduction, when beginning their course in phonetics.

—*David Crystal*

Preface

This book grew out of courses we teach in practical phonetics, speech acoustics, speech production, and hearing. It is hard to find a single text containing all these topics, which was the original motivation for writing the book. We would like to express our gratitude to several generations of students, on whom we have tried out earlier versions of many chapters and who have contributed useful observations and suggestions. Their help was particularly appreciated with the practice boxes and the exercises that we have included. We would also like to thank those whose influences have shaped our own interest in phonetics. For example, chapters 3, 4, and 5 are strongly influenced by the teaching approach and materials used by Sandy Hutcheson in her excellent Practical Phonetics classes at the University of Edinburgh, and chapter 18 draws on many years of mentoring from John Laver.

We have endeavored to support the text with plentiful figures and tables. All the anatomical illustrations are from original drawings by Janet Beck, except where otherwise indicated.

Brian Moore made many helpful and detailed comments on drafts of chapters 13 to 15. Simon Shemilt made valuable and encouraging comments on these same chapters. Stephen Cowen's technical support and advice was, as always, greatly appreciated. We would like to thank Bill Hardcastle for his support throughout this enterprise and for reading and reviewing the entire manuscript. However, we take full responsibility for all errors in the book and we would be grateful to be informed of any errors that readers detect. We would also like to thank Emily Wilkinson, of Lawrence Erlbaum Associates, for her encouragement and her patience. Finally, we would like to thank our respective families for their support and forbearance, particularly in the latter stages of the preparation of the manuscript.

—*Nigel Hewlett*
—*Janet Beck*

1 Introduction

In attempting to choose a title that would accurately cover the broad range of topics in the book, we eventually decided on *An Introduction to the Science of Phonetics*. Much of the material in the book could go by the name of speech and hearing science. However, phonetics is a more inclusive name. It allows us to include a chapter on speech perception, the stage beyond hearing. It also implies a link to other aspects of language (phonology, syntax, semantics, and pragmatics). Most important, it includes the tradition of systematic, trained auditory observation, which is the concern of the first section of this book. Even where this technique is not used alone (as it still is in many applications—in many applications in speech pathology, for example), it remains an important ingredient of the most successful work in phonetics/speech and hearing science.

Phonetics is the scientific study of the sounds of speech, including their production and their perception. Like eating and walking, speech comes naturally and so for the most part we don't consciously consider what the process involves. Studying phonetics requires a systematic, conscious consideration of how speech sounds are made, what they sound like, and how they compare with each other. Beyond the present chapter, the book is divided into four sections. The system of description and analysis that has become established is described in Part I. It includes phonetic transcription, which is a very useful tool in all branches of phonetics. Part II, on acoustics, describes the physical nature of speech sounds during their fleeting existence in the air between speaker and hearer. In one sense, this acoustic signal *is* speech. It is what the speaker produces and the hearer hears. A large and well-established body of knowledge is now available on the acoustic structure of speech. Part III deals with hearing and perceiving speech. Of course, there are other things to be heard besides speech (music, for example, and environmental noises like thunder and traffic noise, the hearing of which can be very useful to us) and hearing science is wider than a study of the hearing of speech, although for humans speech is surely the most important noise around. Likewise, on the production side, the subject of Part IV, humans can produce other sounds besides speech. But in this case there can be even less doubt that the other sounds that can be produced by the human vocal tract, like crying and laughing and moaning and whistling, take second place to speech.

This book attempts a fairly comprehensive introduction to the subject and some readers may wish to read selectively. Much of the material in Part I will ease the way to an understanding of later sections, particularly Parts II and IV. Certainly, some knowledge of phonetic transcription would be essential for these later sections. Parts III and IV assume an understanding of material in Part II. However, Parts III and IV can be read independently of each other. We have tried to make the text as simple as it can be, while (hopefully) avoiding misleading oversimplifications. Some chapters will be found more difficult than others, depending on the prior knowledge of the reader, although no previous knowledge of phonetics is assumed nor is any specialist knowledge of anatomy, physiology, or mathematics. For the most part, applying the rules of arithmetic is all that will be demanded of the reader, so far as mathematics is concerned (although, admittedly, there is a square root or two in chap. 17). The only real exception is logarithms, which are needed for understanding the semitone scale (chap. 9), the decibel scale (chap. 10), and some graphs related to hearing (in Part III). Logarithms are explained in the text and the reader is not expected to have prior knowledge of them. Many readers will find chapters 10 and 17 the most difficult in the book. A detailed understanding of chapter 10 is not necessary for understanding chapters 11 and 12, but it is important for understanding some of the content of Part III, on hearing. Chapter 17 could be omitted, without causing difficulties in reading chapters 18 and 19, the final chapters of the book.

Most chapters contain practice boxes at intervals in the text. They describe articulatory activities to be carried out by the reader or straightforward test questions to be answered. Many chapters also have a set of exercises at the end. All these activities and exercises are focused on the acquisition or improvement of phonetic skills (transcribing speech, interpreting spectrograms, specifying hearing thresholds, and so forth) and we urge readers not to skip them.

Phonetics, (the Rest of) Linguistics, and Psychology

Linguistics is the scientific study of language, including, notably, the areas of semantics, syntax, and phonology. Whether phonetics should be counted as part of linguistics or as a separate discipline is an argument too obscure to be of much interest here (or anywhere else, possibly). However, there are obviously connections and overlap in the study of different areas of language. Modern linguistics is much concerned with the nature of mental representations, including mental representations of the phonetic forms of words, and ultimately with answering the question: What is the nature of human language? Many linguists assert that linguistics itself is situated within the field of psychology.

In the production of speech, in real time, a sentence is formulated in the brain and is transformed into a sequence of movements of the speech organs, so speech is the result of both mental and physical activity. In the comprehension of speech, a listener hears an acoustic signal, which is transformed into a sentence in their brain. Explaining the processes of production and comprehension is the province of phonetics in combination with (the rest of) linguistics and psychology. The relationship between the mental activity and the physical activity that are involved in speech is a complex and unusual one. The physical movements of the tongue, lips, and so on are goal-oriented actions, like walking and eating. The physical forces to be overcome may vary according to the context: for example, producing a "b" sound, while lying down, involves overcoming different physical forces from producing a "b" sound while standing up. Similar things can be said of a physical activity like swallowing. However, the goal of swallowing is relatively easy to define: to get a bolus of food or liquid traveling down toward the stomach, without choking. The goals of the movements made in speaking are not so easy to define. They communicate meanings, by means of words, so the need to define relationships between physical events and mental phenomena soon arises. Also, the word goal implies the possibility of success or failure. How do we measure the success or failure of a speech utterance? Speech communication requires, in addition to the speaker, at least one listener, and the success or otherwise of an utterance lies with whether or to what extent it has successfully transmitted intended meanings to a listener, or listeners. A little thought around this issue will soon produce some interesting complications with judging whether or not a particular piece of speech has achieved its goal. Although it is not directly addressed to such questions, which trespass into other areas of linguistics and psychology, this book aims to give the reader the phonetic knowledge that is required in order to pursue them.

Speech Sounds, Phonemes and Pronunciational Variants

We referred to "speech sounds," which gives an impression that speech consists of sequences of separate sounds, just like the writing on this page consists of sequences of separate letters. However, unlike the letters on this page, speech sounds do not come separated, because a speech utterance is a continuous stream of sound. Nevertheless, it is common to record and analyze such a stream as if it arises from a number of discrete sounds put together. This is the approach taken, for the most part, in this book. A pronunciation of the word "bun," for example, is treated as a sequence of three individual speech sounds: a "b" followed by a "u" ("ʌ" in phonetic transcription) followed by a "n." This approach probably seems convincing, even obvious. It may indeed be the correct one but it does become less, rather than more, obvious with increasing knowledge of phonetics.

When a speech sound (or a sequence of speech sounds) is referred to in writing, by a letter, it is either written between slashes or between square brackets: for example, either /p/ or [p]. Roughly, /p/ stands for all instances of "p." It stands for a sound category that functions as a contrastive unit in the language in question, the name for which is a *phoneme*.[1] When, on the other hand, the letter is used to denote an actual utterance of the phoneme, on one particular occasion, it is enclosed in square brackets. Square brackets are also used to denote systematic pronunciational variants: For example, the phoneme /p/ in English has (at least) two systematic variations in its pronunciation, according to whether it occurs at the beginning of a syllable or elsewhere. The reasons behind the distinction should become clearer after a reading of the first few chapters of this book.

A proper exploration of the issues raised in the preceding paragraph is the domain of *phonology*, which is the study of speech sound systems in different languages, how they are represented mentally, and how they function in distinguishing one word from another. A good introduction to phonology is Carr (1999). Understanding phonology requires some prior knowledge of phonetics. A knowledge of the material in Part I of this book would suffice for much of the phonological literature. However, more and more in recent years, research in phonology has used, as evidence, findings from experimental phonetics, in which case it requires a knowledge of material in Parts II to IV.

Accents of English

Where possible, illustrations of speech sounds in this book are taken from English. However, there are many varieties of English. Although differences in syntax and vocabulary are not an issue in a book on phonetics, differences in pronunciation certainly are. A group of people who pronounce their language in approximately the same way are said to speak with the same *accent*. Accents may be defined more or less narrowly. Accent differences are associated with geographical and sociological factors. The normal orthography does not change according to accent. The word "where," for example, is pronounced in quite different ways, according to accent, but it is always spelled the same.

We make most frequent reference to three (broadly defined) standard accents: General American, RP, and Scottish English. *General American* is spoken widely across the whole of the United States. *RP* (sometimes also called BBC English or Southern British Standard English) is the accent of most upper-class English people (and some Welsh, Irish, and Scottish, too). RP stands for Received Pronunciation, the meaning of which is obscure. *Scottish English* (more precisely, Standard Scottish English) is the accent of most middle-class speakers in Scotland. There are some radical differences among these accents. Scottish English has a rather different vowel system from most other accents; for example, the words "look" and "Luke" share the same pronunciation, but the words "heard" and "herd" are pronounced differently. Both General American and Scottish English pronounce the "r" sound in words like "floor" and "horse." They share this feature with, for example, Irish English and Canadian English. In RP, there is no "r" sound after a vowel, so the words "flaw" and "floor" are pronounced the same. It shares this feature with, for example, Australian English and New Zealand English.

No attempt is made here to give a systematic description of accent variation. The standard work on accents of English, from a phonetic point of view,

---

[1]Where a technical term is defined, it may be written in italics. The words chosen for this treatment are those that are essential phonetic terms or necessary for an understanding of subsequent material.

is Wells (1982). Wells could be read comfortably by anyone who has worked through Part I of this book. The study of associations between phonetic variables and sociological variables goes by the name of sociophonetics.

Applications of Phonetics

This book is focused on what might be called the core of phonetic science but phonetics finds applications in many related fields. This section gives an idea of the range of applications of phonetics.

Psychology of Communication. From one point of view, phonetics is situated within the broad field of communication. Most of the time, even in the modern technological age, speech occurs in the context of people taking turns to be speaker and listener in a face-to-face conversation. In such a situation, many other factors (visual signals of one sort or another, for example) interact with the phonetic signal in complex ways. For example, it may be possible to convey sarcasm entirely by tone of voice. Alternatively, it may be conveyed by facial or other gestures or by some combination of the phonetic and the visual. In any case, whether or not sarcasm is conveyed depends on the listener as well as the speaker (cf. the remarks made in the introductory section of this chapter, about speech communication). What one person perceives as sarcasm, another may not. Phonetics forms an important part of the complex study of face-to-face communication.

Speech Technology. Speech technology is a large and growing field with, by now, quite a long history. For many years we have been able to make a permanent recording of speech and other sounds, either by mechanical or electrical means, and play it back. Nowadays, most recordings are in digital form. Digital recordings tend to be better quality and they are more convenient for editing and storage. Speech can now be produced by machine (speech synthesis) and recognized by machine (speech recognition), although, at the time of writing, there remains substantial room for improvement, especially in the case of speech recognition. Phonetic science contributes in all sorts of ways to such developments. For example, economies can be made with playback systems if it is known how the ear responds to sound. Perceptual encoding, as it is called, is a technique in which certain features are deleted from the recorded material in the knowledge that the human ear will not detect any difference.

Speech synthesis must contend with contextual variation. The "b" in "bun" is phonetically different from the "b" in "nub." So it is no good just telling the machine to "produce a b"; speech synthesis systems have to find ways of taking account of context and taking account of the fact that a speech utterance is a continuous stream of sound. A problem for speech recognition (greatly underestimated in the early days) is the sheer amount of variability in speech, which human listeners cope with but that easily confounds machines. Sources of variability include the identity of the speaker (factors like sex, age, and health, as well as accent), the topic under discussion, and the degree of informality of the occasion.

Forensic Phonetics. Suppose, for example, that in a criminal trial the prosecution presents evidence in the form of a tape recording of a threatening phone call. The prosecution claims that the voice on the recording belongs to the defendant. The defendant claims it is not his voice. Phoneticians have given evidence as expert witnesses in a number of cases of this sort. The techniques of analysis that are involved in such work include both trained listening skills (described in Part I of this book) and acoustic analysis (described in Part II).

Clinical Phonetics.   Last, but not least (considering it is both authors' main interest!), we should mention clinical phonetics. Disorders of speech and of hearing, although not usually life threatening, or even obviously disabling at first sight, nevertheless have catastrophic effects on people's ability to participate normally in social and economic life. The disorders cover a wide spectrum. They differ according to the nature of the syndrome and the age of the affected person. For example, a difficulty with producing speech requires a different form of intervention from a difficulty with hearing it; abnormal structure of the speech apparatus (a cleft palate, for example) creates different problems from a reduced precision of control over the movements of the speech organs; being deaf from birth produces quite a different situation from that of acquiring deafness late in life; and so on. In wealthier countries, at least, a specialist profession, or professions, supplies a service of diagnosis and treatment for people suffering from speech, language, or hearing disorders. In the United States, audiologists and speech pathologists undergo a common basic training. In Britain, training for audiologists and speech and language therapists is separate. In some parts of Europe, there is a distinction between logopaedists (community-based practitioners concerned mainly with developmental disorders) and phoniatrists (hospital-based practitioners concerned mainly with voice problems). Nowadays, it is almost certainly the case that the largest number of users of phonetics comes from these clinical professions. Practitioners in all such professions should be familiar with all or most of the knowledge on normal speech and hearing that is contained in this book.

Basic Principles

2 Principles of Phonetic Analysis and Transcription

In order to understand the nature and function of speech, we need first to be able to describe and analyze speech sounds in a systematic and scientific manner. In addition, sharing of knowledge about phonetics relies on unambiguous systems of transcription, allowing speech to be represented in a written form so that a reader can understand exactly what sound is represented by each phonetic symbol. As the introduction has indicated, speech is a complex and dynamic process, and analysis and representation of speech needs to take this into account. A useful framework for analysis is to remember the sequential process involved in speech production and interpretation by the listener. Figure 2.1 is a very simplified representation of this chain of events, whereby speech is programmed and produced by a speaker, passes through the air in the form of acoustic energy, and is heard and processed by the listener. It is also, of course, heard and processed by the speaker so that he or she is able to monitor speech production both by listening to the output and by monitoring the physical processes of speech production. As the figure shows, analysis of speech sounds can tap into any part of this chain, so that it is possible to use a variety of approaches to phonetic analysis. For example, we can investigate speech by measuring physiological aspects of speech production, such as the movements of the lips, tongue, and so on. Some techniques for physiological measurement are considered in Part IV. Another approach is to sample speech output, using analogue or digital recordings, and to analyze the patterns of acoustic energy as described in Part II. It is probably true to say, however, that the most widespread approach to speech analysis is to tap into listeners' perceptual judgments about the speech they hear. Auditory perceptual approaches to speech analysis require no special equipment, and draw on the highly developed skills in producing, listening to and interpreting spoken language that most people develop naturally during childhood.

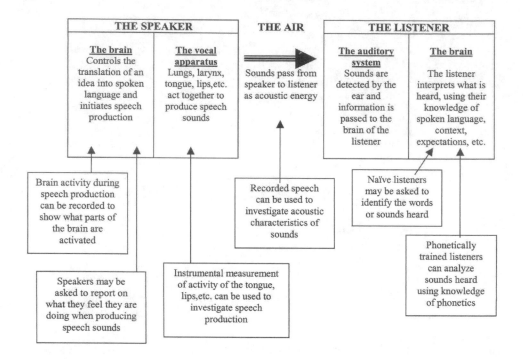

FIG. 2.1.   A diagrammatic view of the speech process, to illustrate possible approaches to speech analysis.

DEVELOPING SKILLS IN PRACTICAL PHONETICS

The traditional approach to phonetics teaching, especially within the United Kingdom, places a lot of emphasis on the development of skills in "practical phonetics." Essentially, these are the skills that phoneticians apply when investigating speech without the aid of technical instrumentation. Practical phonetics includes not only listening skills, but also skills in transcribing what is heard and the ability to produce a full range of speech sounds accurately from transcription or phonetic description. Phoneticians need to take a more conscious and analytical approach to listening and speaking than is normally required for spoken communication, so that any speech sound, whether or not it is familiar from a listener's native language, can be described and transcribed in a systematic manner. This requires a significant shift in focus: Whereas the primary motivation for listening to speech is usually to decode the message conveyed by the speaker, a phonetic approach to listening requires more attention to detail.

The emphasis on developing phonetic performance skills stems from a widespread belief that these support and enhance skills in auditory perceptual analysis. Although the scientific evidence for this is sparse, experience and anecdotal evidence strongly support the value of performance in learning phonetics, and many of the activities included in the following chapters are aimed at encouraging phonetic performance and experimentation with your own speech output. It is not reasonable to expect that practical phonetic skills can be learned entirely from a book, but the following chapters are designed to offer as much self-help as possible within the context of a textbook. The ideal source of training is someone who is themselves an able phonetician and who has the teaching skills required to help other people learn. Failing that, a range of audio-, video-, and web-based teaching and learning resources for phonetics is available. Some good resources are listed at the end of this chapter, but readers should be aware that availability is changing all the time. Whenever audio recordings are being used, it is also essential that playback quality is as good as possible, as any distortion of recording quality will impede auditory training.

Experience suggests that some people find it very much easier to develop skills in practical phonetics than others. People who find phonetics really easy can cause considerable frustration for those of their peers who have to work harder, and it may be worth speculating on what makes a "natural" phonetician. Some preliminary research suggests that people who score well on musical aptitude tests (without necessarily having musical training) and who have high levels of awareness of their own articulatory movements, seem to do better in practical phonetics than others (Mackenzie Beck, 2003). The good news is that, given appropriate motivation, support, and training, almost all learners develop more than adequate skills in practical phonetics. It appears that some people just have to make more adjustments to their habitual listening style.

Identification of speech sounds may involve a number of strategies. For familiar sounds, it may be possible simply to match the sound heard against templates stored in the auditory memory. For less familiar sounds, a more complex approach may be needed. Most unfamiliar sounds will include some phonetic characteristics that are familiar as auditory components of better known sounds. In this case, the sound may be analyzed through a process of disentangling the auditory features that characterize it. This is explained further in chapters 4 and 5, but it is really just a slightly more analytical way of doing what foreign language learners often do at a relatively intuitive level. For example, a native speaker of English, when learning how to produce the sound in the middle of the French word for lamb ("agneau") or the Spanish "Señor," may think of the sound as combining some of the characteristics of English /n/ with those of the sound at the beginning of the word "yes."

An alternative approach is simply to imitate the sound as accurately as possible, and then to analyze how the imitated sound is produced. Although this often appears simple, it involves a complex set of interlinking processes. The listener/imitator needs to be able to manipulate his or her own speech output so as to produce an accurate imitation, to monitor the auditory quality of the sound produced in order to decide when it matches the target sound, and then to have sufficient awareness of how the structures involved in speech production are behaving during the imitated sound production to allow a full analysis of the sound. All of these skills fall within the realm of practical phonetics.

TRANSCRIPTION

As we have already indicated, transcription is only one strand of practical phonetics, but it warrants a more extended discussion. The question of how best to

represent speech in written form has exercised many generations of phoneticians. It is clear that few written forms of language come close to a true representation of speech sounds. Even in alphabetic systems of writing, where there
is generally some relationship between letters and speech sounds, it is seldom
possible to confidently predict the phonetic form of all words in a language
from the written form. English is notorious in this respect, and there are many
instances where the "same" sound is written in a number of different ways. For
example, in most accents of English the words "fleece," "piece," and "peace"
have the same vowel sound, but it is spelled in three different ways. Conversely,
the same sequence of letters may be pronounced differently in different contexts. An obvious illustration of this is the "-ed" sequence that signals the past
tense in English. In words such as "fried," "banned," or "sneezed," this is pronounced as something we can loosely describe as a /d/-sound, whereas in
words like "passed," "coughed," and "pushed" it is produced as a /t/-sound. In
another set of words, including "pointed," "padded," and "pitied," a vowel is inserted before the /d/-sound. If we can't rely on the orthographic form to tell us
how a word is spoken, and if we want to represent the speech of languages that
are not written down, then we need other ways of representing speech. There is
a long history of phonetic transcription systems, dating back more than three
centuries (Abercrombie, 1967). These systems vary widely; some represent
speech production in a very iconic way, whereas others use an alphabetic approach. The International Phonetic Alphabet, which is now accepted as a standard across the world, has evolved during the last century as a means of
representing speech sounds from all the languages of the world. It includes a
wide range of symbols for individual sounds, as well as diacritics for adding
phonetic detail, and it also offers conventions for the transcription of continuous features such as voice quality and intonation. The current version of the International Phonetic Alphabet (IPA), agreed by the International Phonetic
Association in 1993 and updated in 1996, is shown in Appendix A (The International Phonetic Association, 1999). The phonetic principles that dictate the
layout of the IPA chart are outlined in the following chapters, but it may be helpful at this stage to illustrate how transcription can be used to describe speech,
by comparison with standard forms of writing.

Consider the English word "brought." The orthographic form includes seven
letters, but most English speakers would agree that this word consists of a sequence of only four sounds: two consonants, followed by a vowel, and then a
word-final consonant. The sequence of phonemes in this word (that is, the linguistic sound units), for most British English accents, is transcribed as /brɔt/.
Although this transcription is more useful than the standard spelling as an indicator of standard pronunciation, it still falls short of a detailed transcription
of a particular individual's pronunciation on any given occasion. The way in
which each of these sound units is actually produced may vary quite considerably, depending on such factors as the speaker's accent background, age, and
gender, the position of the word within an utterance, and the style of speech
used (formal vs. casual). A more detailed phonetic transcription needs to reflect this variation. The second consonant, /r/, for example, may be produced in
a number of ways. Some Scottish speakers might use a trilled /r/ (transcribed
phonetically as [r]), whereas speakers from Southern England are more likely
to use a smoother sounding /r/ produced by movement of either the tip of the

tongue (transcribed as [ɹ]) or the lower lip (transcribed as [ʋ]). Remember the convention mentioned in chapter 1, that slanting brackets indicate phonemes, whereas square brackets indicate the actual phonetic realizations of these phonemes. The other phonemes in this word may be subject to similar variation. The vowel may vary in duration, for example. There is a general tendency for Scottish speakers to have a shorter vowel than speakers from the United States or Southern England, for example, and the length will also be affected by the position and stress of the word within an utterance. Finally, the /t/ may be produced as a standard [t] or as a glottal stop [ʔ]. It may also be realized as dental [t̪] (where the tongue is pushed forward against the teeth), especially if this word is followed by a word like "the" or "this."

In summary, we have at least three ways of representing this word, as shown below.

1. The standard written form: *brought*
2. A phonemic transcription, showing the linguistic sound units: /brɔt/. This does not differentiate between minor differences in pronunciation.
3. A phonetic transcription, indicating the precise way in which the word is spoken. Each phoneme may have a number of phonetic variants, including:

/r/ → [r], [ɹ], [ʋ]
/ɔ/ → [ɔ] (short) or [ɔ:] (long)
/t/ → [t], [t̪] or [ʔ].

Possible phonetic realizations of this word thus include [bɹɔt], [brɔʔ] and [bʋɔ:ʔ]. The main source of confusion here is that the same symbol may be used either to represent a phoneme or to represent a phonetic realization, and it may also occur in the orthography. It is therefore important to pay attention to the brackets used. From the given example it can be seen that /r/, in slanted brackets, represents any type of production of this phoneme, whereas [r], in square brackets, refers specifically to a trilled realization of the phoneme. When a symbol is enclosed within square brackets, then, this conveys some very precise information about the auditory characteristics of the sound and about the way in which it is produced. A phonetician, on seeing the symbol [t], will immediately know not only what the corresponding sound is, but also what configuration of the tongue, larynx, soft palate, and so on is involved in its production. Among the information encoded by this particular symbol is the fact that this sound is produced when the tip or blade of the tongue makes contact with the roof of the mouth immediately behind the upper incisor teeth. Addition of a diacritic to make [t̪], indicates a slightly different sound, where the tongue makes contact with the back of the upper incisors. This is an example of the way in which transcription can capture phonetic detail and show quite subtle differences between sounds.

SEGMENTAL AND PARAMETRIC APPROACHES TO ANALYSIS

The use of phonetic symbols to represent speech in transcription reinforces a view of speech as a string of discrete sounds. We might expect that physiological and acoustic measurements would show each sound as a period when all measurements were in a steady state, interspersed with rapid adjustments at the boundaries between sounds. In fact, when we look at measurements of speech production in detail, things look more complicated, and it becomes clear that speech sounds do not exist as clearly separable items. Nonetheless, as long as we don't lose sight of the fact that speech is really a continuously varying process, it is often convenient and useful to analyze speech as if it did consist of strings of separate sounds.

In a segmental approach to speech analysis, the first task of the listener is to identify the separate sounds that make up an utterance. Each separate sound is called a *segment*, or *phone*, and the process of deciding where the boundaries are between separate sounds is known as *segmentation*. Most people, for most of the time, find that they can intuitively segment speech, and there tend to be relatively few disagreements between listeners about how many segments there are in any given utterance. The real skill then comes in identifying the phonetic characteristics of each sound, so that it can be properly classified and labeled. As we have already explained, the auditory quality of each segment is a direct consequence of the configuration and function of the speech production mechanism. Phonetic labeling draws on a set of conventional and precise terminology as a means of making explicit our understanding of the speech production mechanisms associated with particular auditory qualities. Segmental analysis, then, involves the perceptual equivalent of chopping speech into segment-sized pieces, and then using the auditory quality to make judgments about the state of the tongue, lips, larynx, and so on. As we have seen, phonetic transcription is simply a shorthand means of representing that information.

Speech segments have been likened to beads on a string, but a more useful analogy is to think of each utterance as being somewhat like a length of woven ribbon, made up of a number of strands that change in color or texture at intervals, so that the pattern varies along its length. Segmental analysis is akin to cutting the ribbon at each point where there is an obvious change in pattern, so that you end up with a lot of short pieces, and then looking to see what strands are in each piece. Parametric analysis is more like taking single strands and tracking any changes in color or texture along their whole length. Strands, or parameters, tracked during speech analysis might include movements of the tongue or lips or vocal fold activity within the larynx. Segmental analysis is valuable when the focus of interest is on the exact phonetic realization of the linguistic sound units, and on the ways in which phonetic differences signal differences in meaning. Parametric analysis may be of more value where the focus of attention is on the phonetic relationships between segments. It can also throw light on the nature of transitions between one segment and the next. While it is true that boundaries between segments can generally be fairly easily identified, because all the phonetic features that change at the boundary between one segment to another are typically quite closely coordinated, parametric analysis shows that the changes are often not completely simultaneous.

This first section follows traditional approaches to phonetics, in that the emphasis is on the application of practical phonetic skills in segmental analysis of speech, but it is important to be aware that utterances are produced as continuously varying streams of sound and that the process of segmentation imposes artificial divisions. It is also important to remember that phones do not exist in isolation and that the production of each one will be affected by its neighbors and by the context and style of speech.

List of Resources for Practical Phonetics

Wells, J., & House, J. (1995). *The sounds of the International Phonetic Alphabet.* London: University College London. (This recording of all the sounds of the IPA is available in cassette, CD, or CD-ROM format, from The Listening Centre, Department of Phonetics and Linguistics, University College London, Wolfson House, 4 Stevenson Way, London NW1 2HE.)

http://hctv.humnet.ucla.edu/departments/linguistics/VowelsandConsonants/index.html (This is a very useful site, including audio demonstrations of most IPA sounds.)

http://uk.cambridge.org/linguistics/resources/ipahandbook (This has downloadable audio files of a range of languages, illustrating IPA sounds. It supports the Handbook of the International Phonetic Association [1999].)

3 An Introduction to the Vocal Apparatus

When people begin to learn phonetics for the first time, most are very unfamiliar with the insides of their own mouths. Given how much we all use our mouths, for eating, talking, and facial expression, and how familiar we are with the sensations produced by our tongues, it is remarkable how seldom most people consider the nature of the internal structures of the mouth and throat. This may be partly to do with cultural inhibitions about displaying the inside of the mouth, as exemplified by the convention of covering the mouth when yawning. A necessary first stage in studying phonetics is to be thoroughly familiar with the oral cavity, and the other structures involved in speech production. The practice activities in this chapter are designed to encourage you to explore your own speech production mechanisms and, if possible, those of friends. Comparing the individual characteristics of two or more people may help to raise awareness about how much variation there is inside the mouth and throat. Casual observation of any group of people makes it clear that the basic blueprint for the human face, with two eyes above a centrally placed nose and a mouth, allows for enormous variation in the detailed configuration of these features. Just as much variation is evident in the internal structures.

It is not important at this stage to be able to describe the muscles and tissues of the vocal apparatus in great detail, so this chapter aims to provide a fairly simple overview of the anatomical features that are most important for speech production. This should be sufficient to allow an understanding of the general phonetic principles that are introduced in the following chapter, but for anyone wanting to extend their knowledge, more detailed descriptions of relevant anatomy and physiology can be found in Part III of this volume.

Figure 3.1 shows a very schematic diagram of the whole of the *vocal apparatus.* The term "vocal apparatus" is used here to include all of the structures that are involved in production of speech. It is worth remembering that for most of these structures, their involvement in speech production is secondary

16

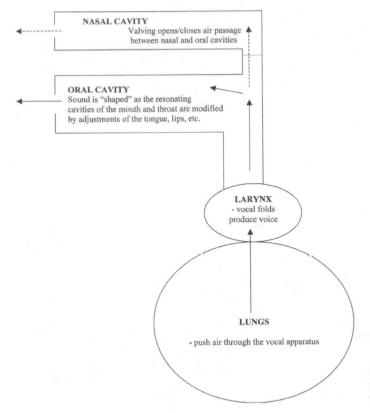

FIG. 3.1. A schematic representation of the vocal apparatus.

to other functions that may be more important in terms of maintenance of life. These primary functions are generally to do with respiration and/or eating and swallowing. For example, it is probably obvious that the tongue is an essential part of the speech production apparatus, but it is also essential for moving food around the mouth when chewing and for the control of swallowing. The vocal apparatus can be subdivided into three key elements:

1. the *lungs* and associated structures, which are responsible for moving air in and out of the system. As we will see, movement of air through the vocal apparatus is an essential part of speech production;
2. the *larynx*, which is responsible for creating the main sound source for speech production;
3. the *vocal tract*, defined here as the airways above the larynx, within which sound is "shaped" and amplified. The vocal tract consists of a branching tube. From the larynx, the airway passes up through the pharynx, behind the tongue, and then divides into two branches. The main branch of the vocal tract for sound production goes forward through the mouth, but a side branch leads up through the nose.

A slightly more realistic diagram of the vocal apparatus is shown in Fig. 3.2.
   The following description, together with the practice activities, is intended to guide you through an examination of the structures that can be observed without

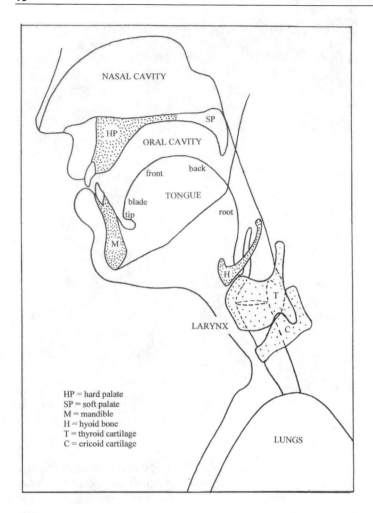

NASAL CAVITY

SP

HP

ORAL CAVITY

back

front

TONGUE

blade

tip

root

M

H

T

LARYNX

C

HP = hard palate
SP = soft palate
M = mandible
H = hyoid bone
T = thyroid cartilage
C = cricoid cartilage

LUNGS

FIG. 3.2. A dia-
grammatic view of
the vocal apparatus.

any invasive equipment, and to give you some idea of the hidden internal structures. To get the most out of this chapter you will need at least one pocket mirror
and a small flashlight. Note that the use of two mirrors at an angle (see Fig. 3.3)
allows the roof of the mouth to be seen without having to tilt the head at an un-
comfortable angle. It is often useful to use fingers to feel the texture and shape of
each structure, but hygienic considerations obviously make this inadvisable
when examining someone else's mouth, unless protective gloves are worn.

It is probably easiest to start by examining the most easily visible structures, so we will start with the lips, and then move progressively inward and
downward. As you work through the activities suggested in the practice boxes,
you may find it helpful to sketch what you see, so that you have some record of
your own observations.

THE LIPS

People are generally very familiar with the external appearance of the lips.
They are capable of a considerable range of movement, which is used in eating, in signaling facial expression, and in speech. Their movements allow the

entrance to the mouth to be expanded or constricted both vertically and horizontally, and they can be protruded forward or (to a lesser extent) pulled back against the teeth and gums. At the center of the lips, the back surface of the lower lips extends downward to attach at the bottom of the lower gum, while the back surface of the upper lip attaches at the top of the upper gum. At the sides, the inner surface of the lips merges with the inner surface of the cheeks.

Practice 3.1: Lips

First observe the external appearance of your lips, using a mirror. When your face is at rest, do the upper and lower lips make contact along their full width? Now consider the inner surfaces of your lips. Using your fingers, feel the thickness of your lips (from the inner to the outer surface) and note how the inner surface of the lip connects with the gum and jaw bone. People are often surprised by how much vertical space there is behind the lips and by how much thickness there is between the inner and the outer surfaces. Experiment with changing your lip position. For example, push your lips as far forward as they will go, as if making an exaggerated "oo" sound, and then spread them as far as you can, in an exaggerated "ee" sound. Notice changes in the shape of your lips, and in the size and shape of the opening into the mouth, as you do this.

THE TEETH AND JAWS

The teeth are rooted in two horseshoe-shaped arches of bone, which are parts of the upper and lower jaws. The upper jaw (*maxilla*) is an integral part of the facial skeleton and fused with the main part of the skull. The lower jaw (*mandible*) is jointed with the skull close to the ear, and pivots vertically from this attachment to open and close the mouth. It is also capable of some lateral and forward movement. In most people (though not all) the upper arch of teeth is slightly larger than the lower one, so that the upper teeth overlap the lower ones both at the sides and at the front. Although

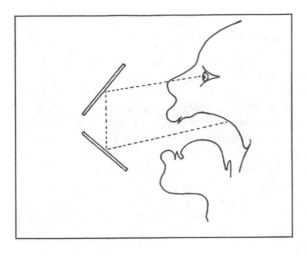

FIG. 3.3. The use of two mirrors to view the inside of the oral cavity.

we can define a typical number and arrangement of teeth for humans, many people will have lost one or more teeth by the time they reach adulthood, as a result of disease, accidental damage, or planned removal. There is considerable individual variation in details of dentition and in the relationship between the upper and lower sets of teeth, and this may have some influence on details of speech production.

Practice 3.2: Teeth

Open your mouth wide, and look at your teeth, so that you can observe the overall shape of the upper and lower dental arches. Notice the differing shapes of teeth at the front and sides of the dental arch. Are upper and lower sets of teeth similar? Now bite your teeth together and check to see whether the upper central teeth (incisors) are in front of the lower incisors or behind. If the upper incisors are further forward, are they nearly touching the lower incisors or is there a space between the upper and lower incisors?

THE ALVEOLAR RIDGE

Behind the upper teeth the arch of bone supporting the teeth forms a horizontal bony shelf, known as the *alveolar ridge*. The width of this shelf is greatest in the center, behind the central upper teeth (incisors), and narrows toward the sides and back of the dental arch. The alveolar ridge is an important landmark in speech production.

THE HARD PALATE

Behind the alveolar ridge, the roof of the mouth arches up, so that the front part of the roof of the mouth is shaped somewhat like half an inverted bowl. This part of the roof of the mouth is described as the *hard palate* because it is, like the alveolar ridge, formed from bone with an overlying layer of mucosal tissue. As a result it is fairly rigid and feels hard to the touch. Again, there is a lot of variability in the width, length, height, and contours of the hard palate.

Practice 3.3: Alveolar Ridge and Hard Palate

Use your fingers or tongue to explore the roof of your mouth behind the upper teeth. The horizontal shelf just behind the upper incisors is the alveolar ridge. If you run your tongue or fingers from side to side along the alveolar ridge, notice whether it is smooth or corrugated. For most people the alveolar ridge is easy to identify at the front of the dental arch. If you follow the ridge round to the sides and back of the dental arch, does it get narrower or disappear completely?
Now examine the shape of the roof of the mouth behind the alveolar ridge. For most people there is a fairly steeply curved arch behind the alveolar ridge, leading to the highest point of the roof of the mouth. If possible, compare your own hard palate with that of other willing people, and note the degree of similarity or difference in size and shape. To what extent can

you dent or distort the tissue in this area if you press firmly with a finger
or your tongue?

THE SOFT PALATE (VELUM) AND UVULA

The bony hard palate extends back about as far as the back of the upper
dental arch. Behind that the roof of the mouth consists of an arched muscular sheet, curving down toward the back of the oral cavity. This part of
the roof of the mouth is known as the *soft palate*, or *velum*. The back edge
of the soft palate curves down to a projecting piece of tissue, which hangs
down from the center of the velum. This is the uvula. When seen from the
front, as in Fig. 3.4, two arches of muscle are visible, extending downward
and outward from the sides of the velum. The upper, outer arch of muscle
runs from the velum to the walls of the pharynx (the airway at the back of
the mouth), whereas the lower, inner arch runs from the velum to the sides
of the tongue. These muscles, together with the muscles within the velum
itself, control the position of the velum and uvula. At rest, the back of the
velum and uvula hang down at the back of the oral cavity, but the velum is
able to move upward and backward so that it blocks the airway into the
nose. It therefore acts as a valve, controlling the flow of air through the nose
and preventing food and liquid from passing into the nasal cavity when eating and swallowing. Its function in speech production is discussed further
in chapter 4.

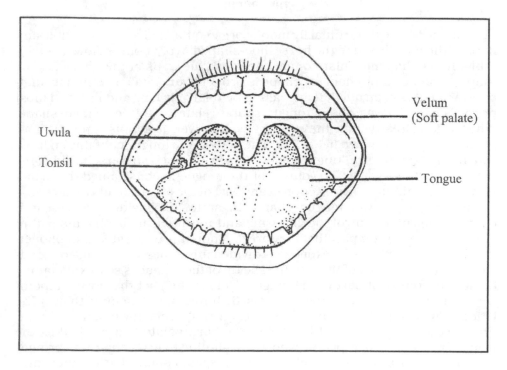

FIG. 3.4.   A view of the oral cavity from the front.

Practice 3.4: Velum and Pharynx

If you gently probe the roof of your mouth with a finger or your tongue, moving backward from the hard palate, you will reach a point at which the hard, rigid nature of the arch changes to a softer and more pliant texture. The area of softer tissue is the soft palate, or velum. Be careful, as touching too far back may trigger a gag reflex. Look into your mouth, relating what you see to the structures labeled in Fig. 3.4. If it is difficult to see past your tongue, open the jaw a little wider and say a long "ah" sound. This should cause the tongue to move downward, making it easier to see to the back of the oral cavity. Identify the uvula, which protrudes downward from the center of the back border of the velum, and look beyond it, if you can, to see the back wall of the pharynx.

Describe the texture and color of the pharyngeal wall.

Now try saying a series of short "ah" sounds and notice what happens to the velum and uvula.

Identify the faucal pillars, curving down from the sides of the velum. The tonsils are situated between the faucal pillars, and may appear as irregular masses of tissue protruding between them. They are sometimes visible, although in many adults the tonsils are so small that they do not protrude enough to be visible. Note whether your tonsils are visible and, if they are, note what color they are. They are usually relatively pale, and a red or dark pink coloration usually indicates some degree of inflammation.

THE TONGUE

The tongue is an extraordinarily mobile organ, attached to the mandible and floor of the mouth and to the horseshoe-shaped hyoid bone, below the mandible. It also has muscular connections with the walls of the pharynx. The tongue's capacity for changing shape is probably unequaled in human anatomy. When it is protruded, it appears to be relatively long and flat, and most people's perceptions about tongue shape relate to this extended shape. When it is at rest within the oral cavity, however, it adopts a much more rounded form, as shown in Fig. 3.2. The body of the tongue contains an intricate network of interlinking muscles, some running transversely and some longitudinally. Because the volume of the tongue is constrained, deformation brought about by contraction of any part of the tongue tends to have consequences for overall tongue shape. In spite of considerable research efforts, muscular control mechanisms and mechanical constraints within the tongue are so complex that they are still not fully understood. In phonetics, the upper surface of the tongue is divided into zones, according to the adjacent part of the roof of the mouth. The tip of the tongue is self-explanatory, being the frontmost part of the tongue. This is the part that forms a point when the tongue is protruded or raised. Immediately behind that is the blade, which typically lies below the alveolar ridge when the tongue is at rest. The part of the tongue that lies below the hard palate is described as the front of the tongue. For people who are beginning to learn their way around the vocal apparatus, this label sometimes seems somewhat counter-intuitive, as this part of the tongue surface actually looks quite far back when viewed from the outside world. If you look again at the diagram in Fig. 3.2, however, you will see that this is still a large part of the tongue behind and below this zone. The part of the tongue that lies below the velum and uvula is the back of the tongue, and the part of the tongue that faces backward, within the pharynx, is described as the root of the tongue.

The distribution of nerve endings within the tongue is much more dense around the tip and blade. This means that people have a much greater awareness of touch in this area of the tongue, and find it much easier to feel speech movements involving the tip and blade.

It is not possible to view the structures described from here on without specialized mirror techniques or fiberoptic endoscopes, so readers will need to refer to the diagrams provided.

Practice 3.5: Tongue

Opening your mouth wide, and letting your tongue relax, observe the shape and texture of the upper surface of the tongue.

If you close your mouth, can you feel any contact between the upper surface of your tongue and the roof of the mouth? If so, is the contact at the sides, the alveolar ridge, the palate, or some combination of these? This will vary from person to person, with some people feeling very little contact and others much more.

Now open your mouth again and observe how your tongue changes shape if you stick it out, point it up toward your nose, down toward your chin, and move it from side to side.

Point your tongue tip up again so that you can observe the under-surface of the tongue. Compare the texture of the under-surface with the upper-surface of the tongue. Note the narrow web of tissue in the center of the under-surface, extending to the midpoint of the back of the lower dental arch. This is the lingual frenulum.

THE EPIGLOTTIS

The *epiglottis* is a relatively rigid projection from the root of the tongue. It is often described as being leaf-shaped, but could equally well be compared to the blade of a rounded canoe paddle. Its rigidity derives from cartilage, and it behaves as if it were attached by a horizontal hinge fixed toward the lower part of the root of the tongue. If it swings down, it therefore blocks the airway. Its function is primarily to prevent food from passing into the lungs during swallowing, and it does not seem to play a very important role in speech production. However, the epiglottis may be involved in the production of some rather rare speech sounds (Ladefoged & Maddieson, 1996) and probably underlies certain distinctive singing styles, such as the "growl" used by certain jazz and blues singers (Esling, 1999).

THE PHARYNX

The airway running from the back of the oral and nasal cavities down to the larynx is called the *pharynx*. It is sometimes subdivided into three approximate zones: the *nasopharynx* (behind the nasal cavity) the *oropharynx* (behind the oral cavity and tongue), and the *laryngopharynx* (above the larynx), but such subdivision is probably not important at this stage.

THE LARYNX

The *larynx* acts as a kind of valve, opening and closing the airway. It consists of a skeletal framework of cartilages, and a complex set of muscles that support and control the position of two adjustable ledges or folds of tissue, which protrude into the airway. These folds of tissue can either be pulled back against the walls of the airway, as shown in Fig. 3.5a, or brought together as in Fig. 3.5b so as to prevent the passage of air, liquid, or solid in or out of the lungs. Although the primary biological function of this valving system is to prevent anything other than air from entering the lungs, the human larynx has evolved in such a way as to play an important role in speech production. When the tissue folds are brought together, and air is pushed past them from the lungs, they vibrate rapidly and create a noise. It is because of this that they are known as the *vocal folds* or, more colloquially, as vocal cords. The term "vocal fold" is generally preferred in phonetics, because it reflects the structure more accurately. The function of the vocal folds in speech production is described further in chapter 4, and again, in more detail, in chapter 18.

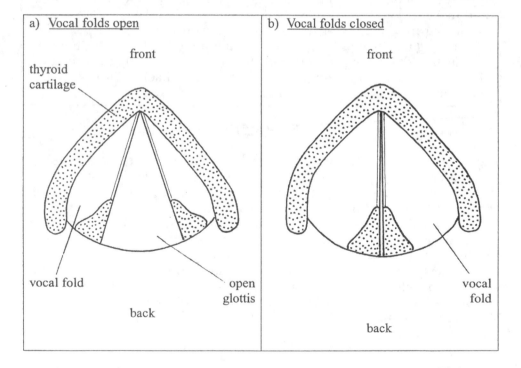

FIG. 3.5.   A diagrammatic view of the larynx, as viewed from above: (a) the position of the vocal folds during breathing; (b) the vocal folds closing the airway.

THE RESPIRATORY SYSTEM BELOW THE LARYNX

Below the larynx, the airway passes through the *trachea*, and then divides into two *bronchi*, which lead down into the lungs, dividing and subdividing into the airways and airspaces of the lungs. The lungs and chest are involved in moving air in and out of the body. Their primary role is in the process of respiration, bringing oxygen-rich air into the body, and expelling carbon dioxide, but they are also essential for speech production, in controlling the movement of air through the vocal apparatus. The lungs have a broad base, more or less like a semi-oval in shape, and they then taper toward the top. The tissue of the lungs is very rich in blood and consists of a network of airsacs and air tubes. This gives them a spongy structure, so that they absorb air when they are expanded, and squeeze it out when they are contracted. The rib cage encircles the lungs and the muscular *diaphragm* separates the thoracic (chest) cavity from the abdomen. The lungs are enclosed in an airtight membrane, so that when the space around them expands, air is sucked into the lungs until the air pressure is the same as that outside the body. When the space around the lungs is reduced, air pressure inside the lungs increases and air is squeezed out. The expansion and contraction of the lungs is controlled by muscles in the chest walls and diaphragm, as shown in Fig. 3.6.

Practice 3.6: Chest and Lungs

Place the back of the fingers of one hand on the side of your rib cage and the palm of the other one on the center of your abdomen. Breathe in and out in an easy, relaxed way, without tensing your shoulders or your abdominal muscles. The movements of your hands will reflect the movements of the chest wall and abdomen, and you will probably notice both hands moving outward as you breathe in, and inward as you breathe out. The reason for the abdomen moving out as you breathe in is that as the diaphragm is pulled downward it displaces the contents of the abdomen. Still using your hands to monitor chest wall and abdominal movement, take a deep breath in and then start speaking. Is the pattern of movement the same as when breathing out when not speaking?

THE NASAL CAVITY

The structures described so far can be thought of as a tube, or series of connected cavities, leading from the lungs to the outside through the mouth. There is, of course, another route between the lungs and the outside air, leading through the *nasal cavity.* The airway from the lungs branches at the back of the oral cavity, with one branch leading directly forward through the oral cavity and the other leading up behind the soft palate (velum) and then forward into the nasal cavity. The side walls of the nasal cavity are rather convoluted, and the airway is divided into two channels by a vertical sheet of tissue running from the bridge to the floor of the nose, known as the nasal septum.

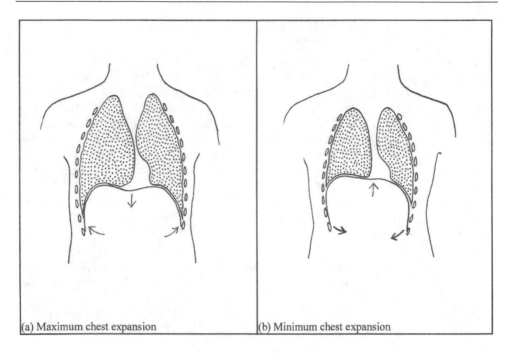

(a) Maximum chest expansion | (b) Minimum chest expansion

FIG. 3.6.   A diagrammatic view of the lungs and associated structures: (a) at the point of maximum chest expansion; (b) at the point of maximum chest contraction.

Later chapters build on this introduction and a wide range of textbooks offer more detailed information about the anatomy and physiology of the vocal apparatus. Among these are some useful sources written specifically with the needs and interests of phoneticians in mind, including Dickson and Maue-Dickson (1982), Perkins and Kent (1986), Kahane (1988), Borden, Harris, and Raphael (2003), and Seikel, King, and Drumright (2000).

Before moving on, it may be useful to say a little about some standard anatomical terms that are used later in this book. So far, the orientation of the diagrams shown is probably fairly clear, but this may not always be the case when the vocal apparatus is considered in more detail. Wherever possible we use easily understood descriptors (e.g., "as seen from the front"), but sometimes the use of conventional anatomical terminology allows a more concise description of the orientation of illustrative diagrams. The structures involved in speech production and hearing are shown typically either as if the body has been cut in a particular way (i.e., along an anatomical plane), or as viewed from a given direction. The following list of common anatomical terms may be useful when interpreting figure legends:

- Frontal or anterior view: as seen from the front
- Posterior view: as seen from behind
- Lateral view: as seen from the side
- Section = a representation of what the structures would look like if the body was cut along a particular plane. The orientation of anatomical planes is shown in Fig. 3.7.

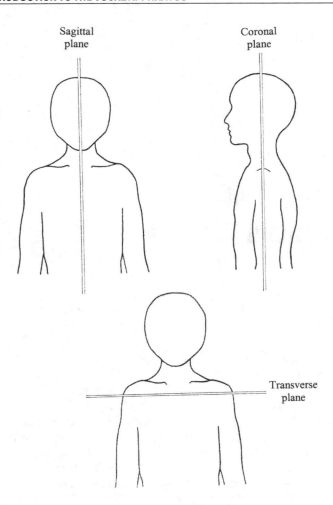

FIG. 3.7. A diagrammatic view of the human body illustrating the orientation of conventional anatomical planes.

4 Basic Principles of Consonant Description

It is convenient to think of speech production as involving a number of different processes, which may be varied independently, and combined in various ways to produce discriminable speech sounds. The four main processes involved in speech production are the airstream mechanism, phonation, articulation and the oro–nasal process. This chapter considers how these processes are involved in production of consonants. Chapter 2 discussed some common approaches to phonetic analysis, including the use of symbols from the International Phonetic Alphabet (IPA) to transcribe particular speech sounds. This chapter aims to increase readers' familiarity with the IPA by using phonetic symbols wherever speech sounds are referred to, and the IPA chart is included as Appendix A. You need not be concerned, however, if you do not immediately remember the symbols, as speech sounds are also described in terms of speech production and illustrated by examples of words in which they occur wherever this is appropriate.

THE AIRSTREAM MECHANISM

As we have seen, the vocal tract takes the form of a bent tube, extending from the larynx to the lips, with a side branch leading up from behind the oral cavity and out through the nose. In order to produce any speech sound, the column of air in the vocal tract tube must be made to move in some way. The need for moving air can be demonstrated quite simply by trying to say any sequence of words in English while holding your breath. As long as no air is coming either in or out of the vocal tract, it will be impossible to produce very much in the way of audible speech. It may be possible to produce one or two isolated and unusual speech sounds, but generally the result is silence. This is because the vast majority of speech sounds are produced using what is known as a *pulmonic egressive* airstream. This simply means that air is pushed outward through the vocal tract from the lungs as the volume of the chest cavity is reduced through downward and inward movement of the ribs. It is possible to speak on a *pulmonic ingressive* airstream, that is, talking while breathing in, but this is generally much less efficient. This is largely due to the shape of the vocal folds, which are not adapted to vibrate efficiently on an ingressive airstream, but is also due to habitual patterns of controlling air flow from the lungs. The respiratory system in humans is characterized by the potential for very precise control of the gradations of relatively slow egressive air flow that are required for speech. The level of respiratory control of ingressive airstreams seems to be much less exact, and inspiration (breathing in) is typically faster than the patterns of expiration (breathing out) that are used for speech. Ingressive pulmonic airstreams are used occasionally in speech production, in spite of the lower efficiency mentioned earlier. In normal speech this may occur when a speaker is running out of breath, or speaking while laughing. Use of an ingressive airstream may also serve to disguise the voice or to signal particular meanings of words. This latter usage, applied to the words meaning "yes" and "no," seems to be common in a variety of languages, including Norwegian and Danish (Laver, 1994). In speech disorder, intermittent use of an ingressive pulmonic airstream may be observed in any person who has difficulty in coordinating respiration with other aspects of speech production, or who has inadequate respiratory support for speech. It may thus occur in speakers with cerebral palsy or those with chronic respiratory problems, for example.

It may be noted that this section began by pointing out that no sequence of words from the English language could be produced in a normal manner without breathing either in or out. In some other languages of the world there are, in fact, a few speech sounds that can be produced while holding the breath. This is because airflow within the vocal tract can be initiated by movements of the larynx or the tongue rather than by respiratory effort. Such sounds are relatively rare, however, and are considered in more detail in chapter 6. For the rest of this chapter, it may be assumed that all sounds are produced using a pulmonic egressive airstream.

Practice 4.1

Take a breath and count slowly and clearly until you run out of breath. Notice what happens as you begin to run short of air. You will probably become increasingly aware of the way in which pulses of air are actively pushed out of the lungs using a combination of downward and inward movement of the ribs. Note how far you are able to count before you are forced to stop by lack of air. Try the same counting task while breathing in. Note any changes in the quality of your voice. Are you able to count as far on one breath?

PHONATION

A major classificatory distinction in phonetics relates to what is happening as the air stream passes through the larynx. A fuller discussion of this process is given in chapter 18, but the brief description that follows should allow an adequate level of understanding for the early stages of phonetic analysis.

The larynx is situated within the neck, just above the top of the trachea. It is a surprisingly complex structure of muscle and other soft tissues within a protective framework of cartilages, and it probably evolved primarily as a mechanism for protecting the airway. The larynx is usually easily located by identifying the thyroid cartilage. This is the largest cartilage of the larynx and forms a protective and supporting girdle around the front of the airway. It can be felt, and often seen, as a protuberance at the midline of the neck. It tends to be more prominent in men than in women, and is hence often known as the Adam's apple. Where the airway passes through the thyroid cartilage, two flexible folds of tissue, known as the vocal folds (or vocal cords) protrude from its side walls. As Fig. 4.1 shows, the vocal folds can either be drawn back so as not to interfere with airflow in and out of the lungs, or they can be brought together to close off the airway. In normal, quiet breathing they are drawn apart.

For many speech sounds, the main sound source is produced by vibration of the vocal folds. The vocal folds are brought together into the midline of the airway (see Fig. 4.1) so that air is prevented from passing through the larynx. As air is pushed out of the lungs, air pressure below the vocal folds builds up until the pressure is enough to force the vocal folds upward and apart. As a burst of air escapes into the vocal tract, air pressure below the vocal folds immediately decreases, the folds snap back together again, the airway is once more blocked, and the sequence of events is repeated. This process is described in more detail in chapter 18. The vibratory sequence

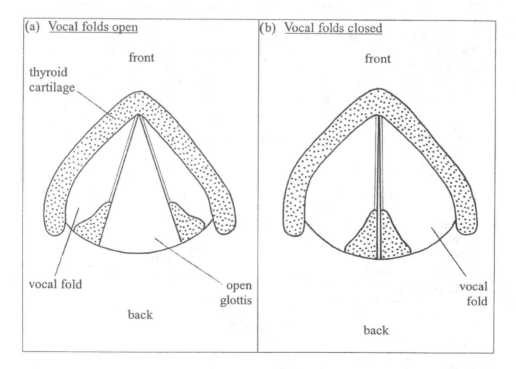

FIG. 4.1.　A schematic view of the vocal folds as seen from above: (a) vocal folds open (as in breathing or during voiceless sounds); (b) vocal folds closed, blocking the airway.

is very rapid, typically occurring somewhere in the region of 200 times per second in women or 100 times per second in men. This process of vocal fold vibration is called *voicing*, and gives much of the audibility and carrying power to speech. The term *phonation*, which is used in the title of this section, has a wider meaning than voicing, in that it encompasses whisper as well.

Any speech sound that involves vocal fold vibration is described as a voiced sound. Voiced sounds include most vowels and consonants such as those at the beginning of the words "my" or "leg." Some sounds, however, are produced with the vocal folds pulled apart so that there is no vibration, and these are described as voiceless sounds. Examples of voiceless sounds include the consonant sounds at the beginning of the words "sea" and "feel."

The approach suggested in Practice 4.2 for deciding on the voicing state works reasonably well for sounds that can be prolonged for long enough to feel whether or not there is any sensation of vibration. It is less useful for sounds such as [g], which are by their nature too short for the vibration to be felt. A more detailed discussion of the voicing state in such sounds is given in chapter 6.

Practice 4.2

Locate the thyroid cartilage and place your fingers firmly but lightly on the flat surface of the cartilage, just to one side of the midline. When you are confident that you have identified the thyroid cartilage, try producing a long "mmmm." It is usually possible to feel a faint vibration through the surface of the neck, especially if the sound is at a fairly low pitch. If you find it difficult to feel the vibration, try increasing the volume of the sound, and experiment with slightly different finger positions or vary the pitch of the note until you can feel the vibration most easily. When the vocal folds are vibrating there should be a clearly audible pitch or tone. If you try making a prolonged voiceless sound like "sssssssss," you should be able to feel that this time there is no vibratory sensation.

Once you are sure that you can identify the vibration and/or the sound quality that is associated with voicing, try prolonging the following sounds, and decide whether they are voiced or voiceless.

(a) the sound that is written as "n" at the beginning of "no" (= [n])
(b) the sound that is written as "sh" at the beginning of "she" (= [ʃ])
(c) the sound that is written as "v" at the beginning of "van" (= [v])
(d) the sound that is written as "ge" at the end of the word "beige" (= [ʒ])
(e) the sound that is written as "th" in the word "think" (= [θ])

Answers. (a) voiced, (b) voiceless, (c) voiced, (d) voiced, (e) voiceless

---

THE ARTICULATORY PROCESS IN CONSONANT PRODUCTION

The role of the phonatory system in the production of voiced sounds is to produce a basic sound source that, if unmodified, would be heard as a simple buzzing sound, bearing little resemblance to any of the speech sounds we hear around us. This relatively simple sound is modified and amplified as it passes through the vocal tract. The characteristic auditory quality of any sound depends on the configuration of the cavities above the larynx. Adjustments of the lips, jaw, and tongue alter the shape and size of the resonating spaces within the vocal tract and may cause points of constriction within the vocal tract tube. In voiceless sounds there is, of course, no significant sound produced within the larynx, as the air passes between the vocal folds relatively unimpeded. The audibility of these sounds generally arises higher up the vocal tract, from friction created by the passage of air through constrictions of the vocal tract tube. The process of adjusting the configuration of the vocal tract through movements of the tongue, jaw, and lips is known as *articulation*. When considering consonant production, it is convenient to differentiate between two features of articulation: the position of greatest vocal tract constriction (place of articulation) and the amount of constriction or obstruction of the airflow (degree of stricture).

Place of Articulation

The vocal tract can be constricted at any point along its length, from pharynx to lips, through individual or concerted movements of the lips, jaw, and tongue and (to a lesser extent) the pharyngeal walls. Any consonant production will entail active movement of at least one of these articulators, which we may call the active articulator. In many consonant sounds the active articulator will be creating a constriction (stricture) by moving toward a static or immovable part of the vocal tract, which we may call the passive articulator. To give an example, the production of [s] (as at the beginning of the English word "sea") involves the tip or blade of the tongue (the active articulator) creating a constriction at the front of the oral cavity by moving up toward the alveolar ridge, just behind the teeth. As with all speech processes, the place of articulation varies from moment to moment during speech.

Although, as we have said, the vocal tract consists of a continuous tube, which may be constricted at virtually any point along its length, it is convenient, and conventional, to classify the location of articulatory strictures according to specified zones or *places of articulation*. Figure 4.2 summarizes the key places of articulation, and indicates the active and passive articulators that would normally be involved in creating a stricture each place. Figure 4.3 illustrates the actual tongue positions for two places of articulation: alveolar and velar. Both of these figures are two-dimensional representations of the vocal tract, in sagittal section (i.e., as if cut vertically from front to back, along the midline). This type of representation is used frequently in the following chapters. Table 4.1 shows some examples of consonants from RP that are produced at each place of articulation.

The following description of the conventional categories of place of articulation is designed to guide the reader in his or her own production, and we recommend that you read it in conjunction with Practice 4.3.

All the sounds described in the following text are voiceless and fricative (see "Degrees of Stricture," following). This means that air passes freely through the larynx, but that somewhere higher up the vocal tract there is a constriction caused by an adjustment of one or more of the articulators. As air is pushed out from the lungs, the airflow becomes turbulent at the point of greatest constriction, giving a characteristic "hissy" quality. This group of sounds has been cho-

	Active articulator	Passive articulator
1. Bilabial	Upper and lower lips (both active)	
2. Labiodental	Lower lip	Upper teeth
3. Dental	Tip or blade of tongue	Upper teeth
4. Alveolar	Tip or blade of tongue	Alveolar ridge
5. Postalveolar	Tip or blade of tongue	Behind alveolar ridge
6. Palatal	Front of tongue	Hard palate
7. Velar	Back of tongue	Soft palate (velum)
8. Uvular	Back of tongue	Uvula
9. Glottal	Vocal folds	

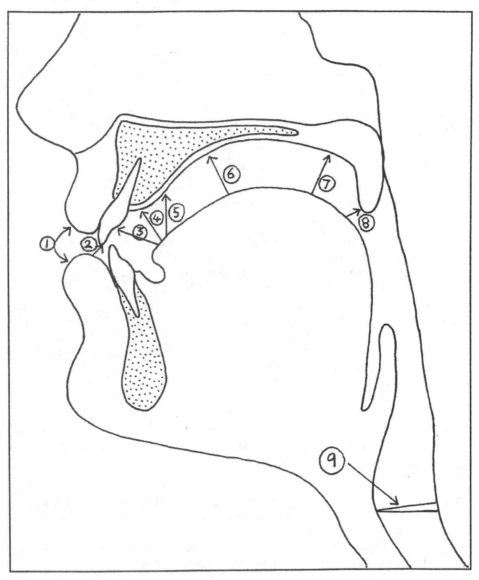

FIG. 4.2. A schematic representation of the articulators involved in the principal places of articulation.

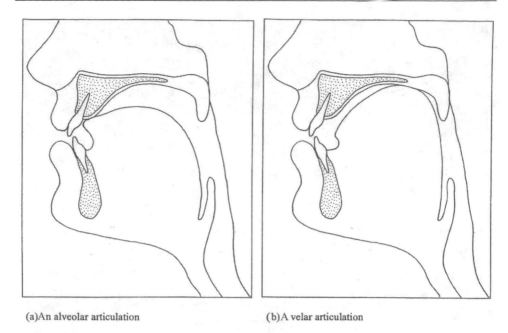

(a)An alveolar articulation   (b)A velar articulation

FIG. 4.3.   Diagrams showing tongue positions involved in articulation of (a) an alveolar consonant, and (b) a velar consonant.

Practice 4.3

The aim of this activity is for you to experiment by producing a series of
similar sounds, which differ only in the place of articulation. Your task is
to follow the descriptions in the following text, manipulating your own
articulators so as to vary the place of articulation, while developing an
awareness both of the position of your own articulators and of the sounds
produced. It may be useful to observe yourself in a mirror, so that you can
observe any visible changes in lip, jaw, and tongue position. Try making
each sound in isolation, and then between vowels. A useful exercise is to
take a word like "sassy," but then replace the two [s] sounds with each of
the sounds described in turn. When you come to the alveolar place of articulation, note whether you use apical or laminar articulation (as explained
in the text). Once you are confident that you can produce sounds at all
places of articulation, try saying palatal, then velar, and then uvular
sounds in sequence. Notice what happens to the apparent "pitch" of the
sounds as you change place of articulation.

---

sen for two reasons. First, these sounds can be prolonged, thus allowing time for
readers who are attempting Practice 4.3 to develop an awareness of their
articulatory placement. Second, small shifts in place of articulation result in
quite clear differences in auditory quality. Examples of words in which these
sounds occur are taken from English unless stated otherwise.

A Voiceless Bilabial Fricative [ɸ].   To make this sound, simply purse your lips
slightly and blow, as if blowing out a candle. If you make the gap between the up-

per and lower lip small enough, a clearly audible sound should emerge. This is a bilabial fricative. This sound does not occur in most accents of English, but it is found in a wide variety of other languages, including some from the Niger-Congo family of languages spoken in the southern half of Africa (Laver, 1994).

A Voiceless Labiodental Fricative [f].   This is familiar to speakers of English as the sound at the beginning of the word "fin." Bring the lower lip (the active articulator) slightly back toward the upper teeth (the passive articulator), and blow air between the articulators.

A Voiceless Dental Fricative [θ].   This is the sound that occurs at the beginning of the word "thin" in most accents of English. The tip or blade of the tongue (the active articulator) is pushed slightly forward so that airflow is constricted between it and the upper teeth (the passive articulator). Note that some accents of English, such as the Cockney accent of London, do not differentiate between voiceless dental and labiodental fricatives in pairs of words like "fin" and "thin." Cockney speakers would produce these words identically, beginning with a voiceless labiodental fricative as described earlier (Hughes & Trudgill, 1996).

A Voiceless Alveolar Fricative [s].   [s] occurs at the beginning of words like "sun" and "cease." The constriction in this case is formed by the tip or blade of the tongue (active articulator) being held close to the alveolar ridge (passive articulator) so that air passes through a narrow channel between the two. Speakers tend to separate into at least two distinct groups in terms of the precise manner in which they produce this alveolar constriction. Some speakers produce [s] and other alveolar sounds by raising the tip of the tongue toward the alveolar ridge. This is known as an apical articulation. Others produce this sound by anchoring the tip of the tongue behind the lower teeth and raising the blade of the tongue toward the alveolar ridge (laminar articulation). Informal surveys of successive cohorts of U.K. Speech and Language Therapy students with a range of accent backgrounds support the view that laminar articulation of alveolar consonants is far more common than apical articulation, if the accents of English spoken in the United Kingdom are taken as a whole.

A Voiceless Postalveolar Fricative [ʃ].   This sound occurs at the start of words such as "short" and "sugar." The blade of the tongue (active articulator) is displaced backward slightly so that a constriction is created between the tongue and the roof of the mouth just behind the alveolar ridge (passive articulator). English speakers producing this sound may notice a tendency to round their lips as they make the postalveolar articulation. This lip rounding, which is discussed further in chapter 6, is not an essential co-requisite of postalveolar articulations, as will be obvious if you hold the tongue articulation constant but gradually spread the lips as in a smile.

A Voiceless Palatal Fricative [ç].   Palatal sounds involve raising of the front of the tongue (that is, the part of the tongue that normally lies beneath the hard palate) toward the hard palate. In other words, the front of the tongue is the active articulator, and the hard palate is the passive articulator. This is a sound that does not appear in standard inventories of English sounds, and the easiest way for English speakers to produce it may be to take a familiar vowel sound as a starting point. Prolong the vowel that most English speakers would produce at the beginning of the word "ease." You may be able to feel that as the tongue moves from a rest position at the start of the vowel, it moves upward and forward toward the hard palate. Now hold the tongue in the position used for the vowel, but instead of voicing the sound, just push air out from the lungs and through the mouth in the same way as for the previous sounds. This should result in a voiceless palatal fricative, which sound sounds more consonant-like. Voiceless palatal fricatives are used in a wide range of languages, including German. Examples of German words ending in [ç] include "Mich" ("me") and "Licht" ("light"). Although we have just indicated that this sound is not usually described as a "sound of English," there are some words in which it may be produced by some speakers, at least in some contexts. It may, for instance, occur at the start of the words "huge" or "human" for many U.K. speakers of English, although this is less likely in American English. It may also occur following the [p] at the start of "pure."

A Voiceless Velar Fricative [x].   This is sound that is not utilized at all by most accents of English, although it occurs in Scottish accents of English in words like "loch." The active articulator is the back of the tongue (that is, the part of the tongue which normally lies beneath the soft palate) and this is raised so as to articulate with the soft palate or velum (the passive articulator). This is another sound that occurs in German, at the end of words like "Buch" ("book"). For English speakers who are unfamiliar with the sound, the simplest approach to production of [x] is probably to put the tongue in the position for the consonant [k], as at the start of "caught," and then to lower it very slightly, so that air can just pass between the articulators.

A Voiceless Uvular Fricative [χ].   To make a uvular fricative, the back of the tongue (active articulator) must be pulled up and slightly backward toward the uvula (passive articulator). As this is another sound that will be unfamiliar to many speakers of English, the best approach to its production may be to produce [x] again, and then slide the tongue backward. Although velar and uvular fricatives may initially be hard to differentiate for speakers of English, they are used contrastively in a number of Amerindian and Caucasian languages (Ladefoged & Maddieson, 1996).

A Voiceless Glottal Fricative [h].   A glottal fricative does not involve the tongue, teeth or lips, but is made by bringing the vocal folds close enough to produce a hissy sound, without vibrating as they would for a voiced sound. To make a glottal fricative, try producing a vowel sound (e.g., the vowel in "at"), in a fairly loud whisper. The word "hat" in English usually starts with a voiceless glottal fricative.

This section has focused on nine key places of articulation. Finer subdivisions of these categories may be used by some authors. For example, Laver (1994) followed many earlier phoneticians in differentiating between postalveolar and palatoalveolar places of articulation. Both fall between alveolar and palatal zones, with palatoalveolar being slightly further back than postalveolar, but for anyone beginning phonetics this is quite a subtle distinction, and one that does not appear on the standard table of consonant symbols produced by the Handbook of the International Phonetic Association (1999). Some further places of articulation (e.g., retroflex and pharyngeal) are introduced in chapter 6.

TABLE 4.1   **Some Consonants of English Produced at Each Place of Articulation**

Place of Articulation	Phonetic Symbol	Examples of Words That May Contain Each Sound
Bilabial	[p]	pat, upper, tap
	[b]	bat, robin, cab
	[m]	mat, timing, rum
Labiodental	[f]	fat, coffee, stiff
	[v]	vat, over, give
Dental	[θ]	think, ether, bath
	[ð]	these, breathing, bathe
Alveolar	[s]	sat, bossy, hiss
	[d]	doe, meadow, mad
	[n]	no, any, own
Postalveolar	[ʃ]	she, ashore, ash
	[ʒ]	beige
Palatal	[j]	yellow
Velar	[k]	cat, packing, ark
	[g]	go, bigger, sag
Uvular		The uvular place of articulation is not used in most accents of English
Glottal	[h]	hat, behind
	[ʔ]	Some speakers may use this as a form of /t/ in the middle or at the end of words, for example, butter, bat

Note. This does not include all sounds of English, but gives a number of examples of sounds used in most standard varieties of English at each place of articulation. While in many cases the phonetic symbol is similar to the orthographic form (i.e., the spelling), this is not always the case.

Manner of Articulation

For each place of articulation, it is possible to produce different patterns of constriction, which vary in terms of the degree of constriction and/or the tongue configuration. The dynamic pattern of constriction and release used in articulation can be described as the *manner of articulation.*

Degrees of Stricture

It is possible to constrict the vocal tract to varying degrees at any given place of articulation. Like other variables in speech production, the degree of stricture varies continually during speech. Consonants are generally classified in relation to three *degrees of stricture,* which can be ranked according to the extent to which they impede the flow of air through the vocal tract. These three degrees of stricture are described here and illustrated in Fig. 4.4.

The schematic representations show the degrees of stricture associated with the three main classes of sound; stops, fricatives, approximants.

	Degree of stricture	Class of sound
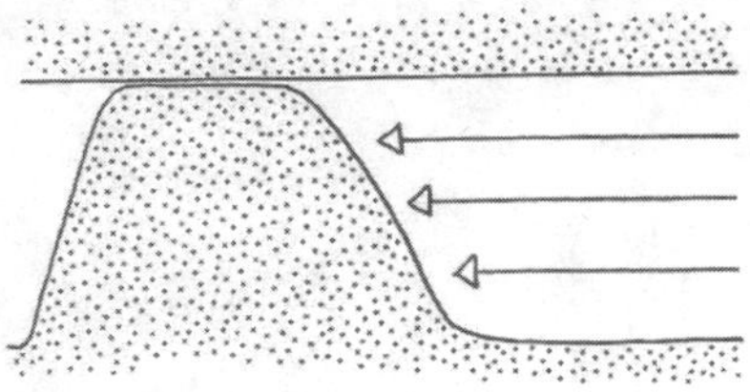	Complete closure	Stop
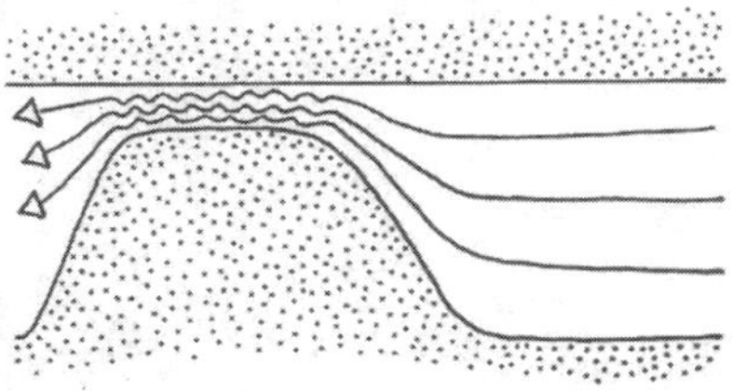	Close approximation	Fricative
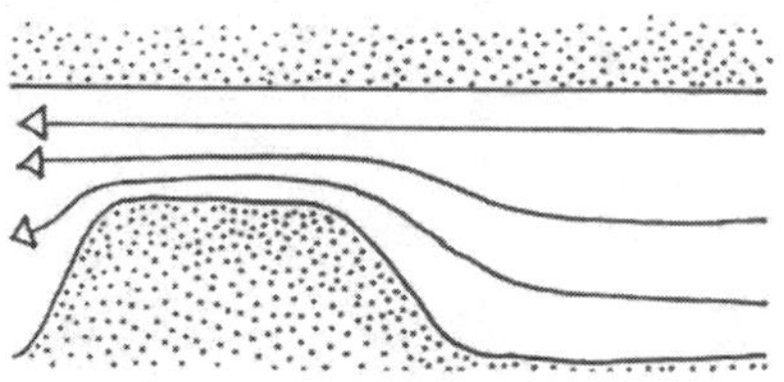	Open approximation	Approximant

FIG. 4.4.   A schematic representation of the degrees of stricture associated with stops, fricatives, and approximants.

Complete Closure.   In articulations that involve complete closure the articulators create an airtight seal, so that the airstream is completely obstructed at that point. Sounds that are produced with a stricture of complete closure are called *stops*, a name that captures the fact that air is "stopped" from moving past the point of articulatory closure. Examples of stops include [t], as at the start of "tie" and [b] as at the start of "buy." Note that while the articulatory closure is maintained, no air is able to pass out of the mouth and the sound cannot be prolonged. Another example of a sound involving a stricture of complete closure is [m] as at the start of "my." This may seem somewhat different from the others, as it is a sound that can be prolonged, but visual inspection should confirm that there is, in fact, a complete closure between the two lips, as in [b]. The difference here is that air is passing through the nose, a fact that can be confirmed by the observation that holding the nostrils closed immediately prevents the sound from being sustained. The difference between [b] and [m] is explained further later in this chapter.

Close Approximation.   In a stricture of close approximation, the articulators come close enough to each other to impede the flow of air through the vocal tract without stopping it altogether. As air passes through the narrow gap between the articulators it becomes turbulent, producing local audible friction, giving a characteristic auditory quality. Sounds produced in this way are known as *fricatives*, reflecting the characteristic fricative airflow. The "hissy" quality of the sounds used to illustrate place of articulation has already been mentioned; these are all voiceless fricatives. Where fricative airflow is associated with voicing, the auditory impression is more aptly described as "buzzy." Examples of voiced fricatives include [z] as at the start of "zoo" and [v] as at the start of "van."

Open Approximation. Open approximation describes a degree of stricture in which the articulators move sufficiently close to one another to cause some narrowing of the vocal tract, but without impeding the airflow enough to produce turbulence and audible friction. Laminar airflow between the articulators is maintained, giving sounds a smooth auditory quality. Such sounds are known as *approximants*. Although this term does reflect the fact that the articulators are approximated (that is, brought toward each other without touching) the convention that both fricatives and approximants are described as having degrees of stricture including "approximation" in the descriptor can cause some confusion for students on initial exposure to this terminology. An example of an approximant from English is the consonant at the start of "yes," which is assigned the symbol [j].

To summarize, we can divide consonants into three main classes (stops, fricatives, and approximants) according to the degree of stricture created by the articulators (complete closure, close approximation, and open approximation). There are a few sounds that are difficult to fit within the three-way classification described so far. For these we need to introduce three further categories of stricture, all of which are somewhat different in nature from the categories just described, in that they are characterized by a rapid change or alternation in the degree of stricture.

Intermittent Closure. The active articulator is held in such a way that the airstream flowing past it causes it to vibrate rapidly. In this way there is a rapid alternation between a stricture of complete closure and one of some degree of approximation. Segments produced in this way are known as *trills*. Many speakers of English never use trills, but in some regional accents an alveolar trill is sometimes used as a form of /r/. The places of articulation where trills may be made are limited to those where there is sufficient elasticity of the articulator(s) involved for rapid alternation of closure and open approximation to occur. In normal speech, therefore, trills are confined to labial, alveolar, and uvular places of articulation.

Complete Closure Followed by Close Approximation. Some languages utilize speech segments that consist of a fricative preceded by a brief stop closure at the same place of articulation. Such a segment is, in effect, a rapid sequence of a stop and a fricative, but because they behave linguistically as single units and have somewhat different durational characteristics from other sequences of stop + fricative, it is conventional to treat them as a distinct class of speech sounds known as *affricates*. Most accents of English include two affricate sounds, both of which involve a postalveolar place of articulation; [tʃ], as at the start of "chain" and [dʒ], as at the start of Jane."

Percussive Sounds. Percussive sounds are, as the name implies, produced by the impact of one articulator striking another. The commonest percussive

Practice 4.4

The aim of this activity is for you to produce consonants with differing degrees of stricture at at least two places of articulation. Start with the bilabial place of articulation, because this is clearly visible and you should be able to observe the varying degrees of stricture quite clearly using a mirror.

- Put your lips into the position for [b] as in "bee." Hold this position, and note the complete closure of the articulators (upper and lower lips), which prevents any air from escaping between the lips. [b] is a voiced bilabial stop.
- Now put your lips in the position for [b] again, start producing [b], but open the lips just enough to let air leak out a little. Try to make sure that the sound is voiced and that the lips are close enough, in a stricture of close approximation, to produce "buzzy" audible local friction. This is a voiced bilabial fricative [β].
- Make [β] again, but this time do not bring the lips close enough together to produce friction. The sound should be "smoother" in quality. This is the voiced labial approximant [β̞]. *N.B.* When the same symbol is used to represent both a fricative and an approximant, they may be distinguished by using the diacritic shown here [̞] to represent the approximant. Try putting these three sounds between vowel sounds.
- Take a deep breath, put your lips loosely in the position for [b] as for the stop just mentioned, and then try to push air between your lips. Experiment until you are able to produce a bilabial trill, [ʙ]. Both lips may be involved in the rapid alternation between complete closure and open approximation. This sound is not usually used as a speech sound in English, but may be used paralinguistically as a signal of being cold.
- Form a complete closure between the lips again, as in [b], and release the closure slowly so that you produce a sequence of a bilabial stop followed by a fricative [bβ]. This is a bilabial affricate.

Now produce the same progression at an alveolar place of articulation. [d], as at the start of "do," is a voiced alveolar stop; [z], as at the start of "zoo," is a voiced alveolar fricative. If you prolong [z] and gradually let the tongue fall a bit until you hear the sound become smooth in quality, somewhat like an "r" sound, this will be a voiced alveolar approximant. Then try making an alveolar trill [r], an alveolar tap [ɾ], and a voiced alveolar affricate [dz]. For the affricate, just aim at making a smooth sequence of [d] + [z]. Compare this alveolar affricate with the familiar postalveolar affricate, [dʒ], as used in English at the beginning of the word "jump." Notice how place of articulation for the whole stop + fricative sequence is further back for [dʒ].

sounds are taps, which occur primarily at an alveolar place of articulation. They are characterized by very rapid movement of the tip of the tongue, so that it touches the alveolar ridge only momentarily, before "bouncing" away again. This produces a sound that is perceptually distinct from an alveolar stop, having an auditory quality a little like that of an interrupted trill. The IPA symbol for a tap is [ɾ]. Taps occur quite commonly in a number of varieties of English, but may represent different phonemes. In North American accents, for example, taps commonly occur as a realization of /t/ in word medial position, in words such as "butter," whereas for many speakers of Scottish English taps are used to represent the /r/ phoneme in words such as "bridge" or "girl."

Direction of Airflow: Central Versus Lateral.   All consonants except stops involve passage of an airstream through the oral cavity. If the articulation involves the tongue, then the configuration of the tongue surface can be varied so as to allow airflow either over the center or the sides of the tongue. Fricatives and approximants may thus be described as being either central or lateral.

For *central* passage of the airstream through the oral cavity, a closure is formed between the side rims of the tongue and the upper molar teeth and gums, so that the airstream is directed over the center of the tongue. For some sounds, such as the fricative [θ] (as at the start of "thin"), or the approximant [j] (as at the start of "yes"), the tongue is fairly flat, so that the air passes through a broad central channel. The fricative [s], while also having central airflow, has the tongue grooved along its length, so that the air flows through a much narrower channel. For *lateral* passage of the airstream through the oral cavity a closure is formed at some point in the center of the vocal tract, and the air is directed around this obstruction so that it flows over the sides of the tongue. For [l], as at the start of "lie," there is contact between the tip/blade of the tongue and the center of the alveolar ridge, but the sides of the tongue are lowered so that air passes freely between the sides of the tongue and the roof of the mouth. This is an alveolar lateral approximant. Figure 4.5 shows a schematic representation of the difference between central and lateral airflow in fricatives and approximants. All the fricatives discussed earlier in this chapter are central fricatives, and conventional phonetic labeling is based on an assumption that all fricatives and approximants are central unless stated otherwise. Central fricatives occur in the consonant systems of all known languages, but lateral fricatives are much rarer. Examples include [ɬ] in Welsh, and [ɮ] in Zulu (see Practice 4.5).

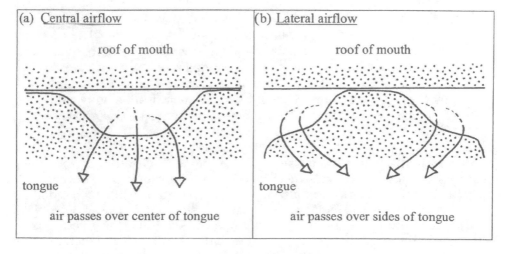

FIG. 4.5.   A schematic view of a cross section of the vocal tract showing tongue configurations during (a) a central fricative or approximant, and (b) a lateral fricative of approximant.

Practice 4.5

The aim of this activity is to develop awareness of the articulatory and auditory characteristics of central and lateral approximants and fricatives.
Approximants:
Compare the sound [ɹ] as at the beginning of some speakers' pronunciation of "ray" with [l] as in "lay." Put your tongue in the position for [ɹ] and note the contact between the sides of the tongue and the teeth and gums. Change the tongue position to that for [l], and you should now notice that there is firm contact between the tip/blade of the tongue and the center of the alveolar ridge, but that the sides of the tongue are lowered away from the roof of the mouth. Both these sounds are approximants, and should be produced without audible friction. Although it is likely that the place of articulation will be slightly further back for [ɹ] (postalveolar) than for [l] (alveolar), both are voiced and the key difference between them is that the first is a central approximant and the second a lateral approximant.
Fricatives:
Try producing the following voiceless fricatives, first of all in isolation and then between vowelsounds:

(a) Voiceless alveolar (central) fricative [s]: Put your tongue in the position for [s] and prolong the sound. Note the contact between the sides of the tongue and the upper teeth. Say a long [s], alternating between a pulmonic egressive airstream (as normal) and a pulmonic ingressive airstream (i.e., breathing in), and feel where the cold incoming air passes over your tongue as you breathe in.

(b) Voiceless alveolar lateral fricative [ɬ]: Put your tongue in the position for [l] as in "lay." Remember that now you should be able to feel contact between the tip/blade of the tongue and the center of the alveolar ridge. Make a voiceless [l] and try to produce audible friction. Now alternate a pulmonic ingressive and egressive airstream as you make the sound. On the ingressive airstream you should be able to feel cold air passing over the side(s) of the tongue. Does it pass equally over both sides of the tongue, more on one side than the other or only over one side? There is considerable individual variation in how symmetrical the lateral airflow is, but you should be able to feel a clear difference between the central and lateral fricatives. Try alternating [s] and [ɬ] while maintaining a constant egressive airflow, concentrating on the sensation associated with the change in tongue configuration and the contact you can feel between the tongue and the roof of the mouth.

Lateral fricatives can, of course, be voiced as well as voiceless, so you can repeat the same exercise contrasting voiced alveolar central versus lateral fricatives. The voiced alveolar central fricative is [z], as in "zoo." To produce a voiced alveolar lateral fricative, start with [ɬ] and add voicing while maintaining the audible friction. The symbol for this sound is [ɮ]. An alternative approach is to start with the familiar [l] and then raise the sides of the tongue slightly so as to restrict the airflow enough to produce friction.

THE ORO–NASAL PROCESS IN CONSONANT PRODUCTION

In chapter 3 we described the way in which the velum acts as a valve at the opening between the nasal cavity and the rest of the vocal tract. Depending on the position of the velum, the nasal cavity may either be shut off from the rest of the vocal tract, or coupled to it. It is this valving action of the velum that forms the basis of the oro–nasal process in speech production. The velum has two alternative positions, which determine whether or not the nasal cavity is linked to the rest of the vocal tract: (a) It can be raised up and back to form a velic closure with the back and side walls of the pharynx, thus closing off the nasal cavity. The airstream must therefore pass through the oral cavity. Any segment of speech produced in this way is called *oral.* (b) The velum may be lowered, so that there is no velic closure. The airstream is then free to pass through the nasal cavity. If there is simultaneous voicing, then nasal resonance may be clearly audible. Any segment produced in this way is called *nasal* or *nasalized.* Generally, the term *nasal* is used if the airstream passes *only* through the nasal cavity, and not through the oral cavity. The term *nasalized* is used if air passes simultaneously through the oral and nasal cavities. Examples of nasal and nasalized segments are discussed further later. Figure 4.6 compares the velic positions and airflow in alveolar oral and nasal stops.

Oral and Nasal Stops

Oral and nasal stops both involve a stricture of complete closure between the articulators, but differ in terms of velic position. For example, [d] and [n] are both voiced alveolar stops, but [d] is oral, and [n] is nasal.

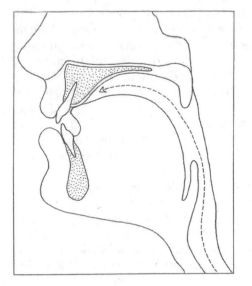
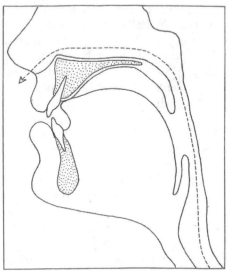

<table>
<tr><td>(a) An alveolar oral stop (or plosive).
Air coming from the lungs is
trapped within the oral cavity.</td><td>(b) An alveolar nasal stop.
Air coming from the lungs passes
freely through the nasal cavity.</td></tr>
</table>

FIG. 4.6.   The vocal tract showing the position of the articulators and the velum during (a) an alveolar oral stop, and (b) an alveolar nasal stop.

Oral Stop [d].   As well as the articulatory stricture of complete closure, there is also a velic closure. The two closures prevent an egressive airstream from escaping, so that the air is trapped in the vocal tract and compressed. When the articulators separate, the trapped air explodes out of the oral cavity with an audible noise, known as *plosion*. For this reason, [d] may be called either an *oral stop*, or a *plosive*.

Nasal Stop [n].   There is no velic closure, and therefore the airstream, being prevented by the articulatory closure from escaping through the oral cavity, flows through the nasal cavity. [n] is a *nasal stop.*

Labial, alveolar, and velar nasal stops occur in English. Palatal nasal stops occur in French (For example, in "a*gn*eau") and uvular nasal stops occur in Japanese. Nasal stops can usually be assumed to be voiced, but voiceless nasal stops do occur in a number of languages. For example, the phonetic difference between voiced and voiceless nasal stops functions linguistically in Burmese. Some English-speaking children may also produce voiceless nasal stops in early stages of speech development, in words starting with an /s/ + nasal stop cluster, where the adult production would involve a sequence of a voiceless fricative followed by a voiced nasal stop. For example, the word "snap" may be produced as [n̥ap], instead of the adult form [snap].

Practice 4.6

Look into a mirror and locate the velum and uvula. Try to raise and lower the velum. Most people find that they cannot do this intentionally, but that it will raise automatically if you either yawn or say the vowel [ɑ] (usually represented orthographically as "ah"), and then relax to lower it again. Try this several times, concentrating on the sensation as it moves. Compare [d] and [n]. Note the stricture of complete closure between the tip and blade of the tongue and the alveolar ridge, and between the rims of the tongue and the upper molar teeth and gums. Try to prolong a [d]. Feel the build-up of air pressure behind the articulatory closure, and note the slight explosion as you release the articulatory closure. You can feel the exploding air if you put your hand just in front of your mouth. If you make a voiceless oral stop, like [t], the explosion of air will be even easier to feel. Why should this be?
Make a long [n]. Use your hand to feel the airstream escaping nasally, and note that there is no air escaping orally. What happens if you hold your nose while producing [n]?
Try to produce nasal stops at other places of articulation, for example, labial [m], velar [ŋ], dental [n̪], palatal [ɲ] and uvular [N].
Can you make a voiceless nasal stop? Using [n], alternate voicing and voicelessness: [n n̥ n n̥ n n̥ n n̥]. [n̥] is a voiceless nasal stop. Try making [n̥] between vowels. Try making voiced and voiceless nasal stops at other places of articulation, for example, labial [m] and [m̥]; velar [ŋ] and [ŋ̥]. Make these between vowels.

Nasalization of Other Segments

For all segment types other than stops, it is customary to assume that the segment is oral, that is, produced with velic closure so that air is only directed through the oral cavity. Because the position of the velum can be varied independently of the action of any of the other speech production processes, it is, however, possible for any sound that does not involve a stricture of complete closure to be produced with simultaneous nasal and oral airflow. In such a situation the sound is described as being nasalized. Thus the sound [j], as in "you," is described simply as a voiced palatal approximant, but we can assume that it is an oral sound. If the velum is lowered to allow air to pass into the nasal cavity as well as through the oral cavity, it will be called a nasalized voiced palatal approximant [j̃]. The diacritic [˜] is used to indicate nasalization.

Nasalization may be associated with specific segments; for example, nasalized vowels form part of the sound systems of many languages, including French, Burmese, Portuguese, and Yoruba. In most varieties of British English, nasalization is a feature of vowels that are adjacent to, or between, nasal stops. Nasalization may also be present in some speakers as a pervasive background coloring to their speech, being audible on all vowels and some consonants. This is especially marked in some accents of North American English, and indeed it is one of the key features that is manipulated by British people when they imitate U.S. accents. In lay terms, when the background level of nasalization used by a speaker is higher than is usual for that speaker's sociolinguistic group, they are often described as "speaking through their nose." Excessive nasalization may also occur in certain types of speech disorder, either when there is impaired muscular control of velic closure (e.g., in certain types of neurological disorder), or where there is some abnormality of the structure of the palate, as in cleft palate.

PHONETIC LABELING CONVENTIONS FOR CONSONANTS OF ENGLISH

Throughout this chapter, standard conventions for phonetic labeling have been gradually introduced, but it may be useful at this stage to make the links between

---

Practice 4.7

This activity involves vowels as well as consonants, as a way of encouraging general awareness of nasalization.

Produce an oral vowel [a] as in "hat," then lower your velum to produce a nasalized vowel [ã]. Just think of it as "speaking through your nose." Alternate [a ã a ã a ã a ã], watching in a mirror. Try to feel the sensation of your velum moving. Make a series of other vowels, for example, [i] as in "bee" or [ɔ] as in "paw" both oral and nasalized. Say the oral sequence [awa]. Now make the whole sequence nasalized to produce [ãw̃ã]. Do the same with [ij i] and [ɔzɔ]. You may notice that the consonants sound somewhat weaker when they are nasalized, as the airflow through the mouth is reduced.

Compare the vowels in the English words "bead," "been," and "mean." Most readers will notice a progressive increase in nasality. Say the utterance "One man went far away." Which parts do you think may be nasalized? Now try making the utterance nasalized throughout.

Answer. The vowels in the word "one" and "man" and the "wen" sequence in "went" are likely to be nasalized for most speakers of English.

standard labels and the speech production processes involved in consonant production more explicit. Consonants are conventionally given labels that indicate three phonetic parameters: voicing, place, and manner. Voicing refers to the phonatory process, so the first part of the phonetic label will answer the question: Is this consonant voiced or voiceless? The place part of the label indicates place of articulation, whereas manner refers to all other aspects of articulation. Primary among these is the category of sound associated with degree of stricture, that is, stop (or plosive), fricative, approximant, trill. The term "manner" also covers the central/lateral distinction in fricatives and approximants and the oronasal process. For anyone who understands the conventions of phonetic analysis and labeling, it should thus be possible to label any sound, whether it is familiar or unfamiliar, in such a way that another phonetician will be able to understand quite precisely what sound is being described and, indeed, be able to perform it. The conventional approach to labeling involves a number of "defaults," and the flow chart in Fig. 4.7 indicates the decisions that are made in arriving at a standard three part label. Some examples of labels are:

[b] as in "bed" = a voiced bilabial oral stop (or a voiced bilabial plosive, as oral stops are also known as plosives).
[m] as in "man" = a voiced bilabial nasal stop.
[s] as in "sun" = a voiceless alveolar fricative.
[v] as in "van" = a voiced labiodental fricative.
[j] as in "yes" = a voiced palatal approximant.
[l] as in "less" = a voiced alveolar lateral approximant.

The IPA symbols for the most common consonant sounds of English, as spoken by speakers with standard accents of Britain, North America, and Australia, are shown in Table 4.2. Figure 4.8 shows the same sounds tabulated so as to reflect the speech production processes described in the main body of this chapter. By using the general principles previously outlined, and working systematically through the decisions involved in phonetic labeling, readers should be able to describe almost any consonant sound they might come across, from any language in the world, even if they have never heard such a sound before. There are a few more places and manners of articulation to be introduced in chapter 6, but they are really only extensions of the approach outlined in this chapter.

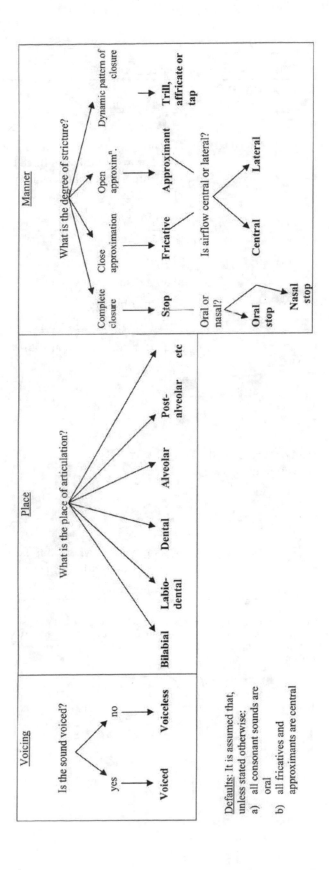

FIG. 4.7. A flow chart showing the decision-making process underlying phonetic labeling.

TABLE 4.2   **The Most Common Consonant Sounds of English**

Phonetic Symbols	Phonetic Symbols
[b] as in "**b**ale"	[p] as in "**p**ale"
[d] as in "**d**ale"	[t] as in "**t**ail" (some speakers may use a glottal stop [ʔ] in words like "bu**tt**er" or "ba**t**." American speakers may use a tap [ɾ] in words like "bu**tt**er")
[g] as in "**g**ale"	[k] as in "**k**ale"
[v] as in "**v**ale"	[f] as in "**f**ail"
[ð] as in "**th**is"	[θ] as in "**th**ink"
[z] as in "**z**oo"	[s] as in "**s**ue"
[ʒ] as in "bei**ge**"	[ʃ] as in "**sh**e"
	[ç] as (sometimes) in "**h**uge"
	[x] as (for some speakers) in "lo**ch**"
	[h] as in "**h**at"
[m] as in "**m**ail"	
[n] as in "**n**ail"	
[ŋ] as in "si**ng**"	
[ɹ], [ɾ], or [r] as in "**r**ail," or "b**r**ead" ([ɹ] is the commoner approximant; [ɾ] is a tap; [r] is a trill)	
[l] as in "**l**eg"	
[j] as in "**y**ell"	
[w] as in "**w**itch"	[ʍ] as in **wh**ich (where this is pronounced differently from "witch")
[dʒ] as in "**j**ump"	[tʃ] as in "**ch**op"

Note. This is a preliminary list of useful phonetic symbols. The examples of words in which they occur may not be entirely accurate for all speakers of English. The aim is to show the commonest phonetic representations of the orthographic forms shown, and this set of symbols should allow you to make a start at phonetic transcription.

	Bilabial	Labiodental	Dental	Alveolar	Post-alveolar	Palatal	Velar	Glottal
oral stops (plosives)	p b			t d			k g	ʔ
nasal stops (nasals)	m			n			ŋ	
Trills and taps				r ɾ				
fricatives	** ʍ	f v	θ ð	s z	ʃ ʒ	ç	x	h
affricates					tʃ dʒ			
(central) approximants	** w				ɹ	j		
lateral approximants				l				

Symbols to the left hand side of the boxes indicate voiceless sounds; those on the right hand side of the boxes represent voiced sounds.
** [w] and [ʍ] are both articulations involving two simultaneous places of articulation (labial + velar).
[w] is a voiced labial velar approximant, [ʍ] is a voiceless labial velar fricative.

FIG. 4.8.   A chart of the consonant symbols used in the transcription of English (adapted from the International Phonetic Alphabet).

Practice 4.8

1. Name (a) the active articulator and (b) the passive articulator for the following sounds.

   [θ], as at the start of "*th*ink"
   [t], as at the start of "*t*in"
   [k], as at the start of "*k*ing"
   [p], as at the start of "*p*in"
   [f], as at the start of "*f*at"

2. Which of the following sounds have a stricture of close approximation?

   (a) [v]
   (b) [k]
   (c) [j]
   (d) [θ]
   (e) [w]
   (f) [m]
   (g) [s]

3. Which of the following sounds are produced with velic closure?

   (a) [ŋ]
   (b) [k]
   (c) [d]
   (d) [v]
   (e) [n]
   (f) [m]
   (g) [ʃ]

4. Label the following sounds, using a standard phonetic label, that is, voiced/voiceless, place of articulation, manner.

   (a) [z]   (f) [ð]
   (b) [g]   (g) [n]
   (c) [ŋ]   (h) [f]
   (d) [ʃ]   (l) [dʒ]
   (e) [l]   (j) [r]

5. Assign a symbol to each sound described here:

   (a) The vocal folds are closed and vibrating. There is velic closure. The front of the tongue has moved toward the hard palate to form a stricture of open approximation, with the sides of the tongue making contact with back teeth.
   (b) The vocal folds are open and not vibrating. There is velic closure. The lips are closed to form a stricture of complete closure.

(c) The vocal folds are closed and vibrating. There is no velic closure. The back of the tongue forms a stricture of complete closure with the soft palate (velum).

(d) The vocal folds are open and not vibrating. There is velic closure. The blade of the tongue forms a stricture of close approximation with the alveolar ridge, with air being channeled over the middle of the tongue.

6. Complete the following, making sure that you can explain your reasoning.

[m] is to [n] as [b] is to [...]
[t] is to [s] as [d] is to [...]
[f] is to [v] as [t] is to [...]
[g] is to [d] as [...] is to [n]
[p] is to [m] as [k] is to [...]

Answers.

1. (Note that some speakers with non-standard varieties of English may not produce the sounds in these words exactly as indicated.)

   (a) tip/blade of tongue; upper teeth
   (b) tip/blade of tongue; alveolar ridge
   (c) back of tongue; velum (soft palate)
   (d) lower lip; upper teeth

2. (a), (d), and (g). (i.e., all the fricatives)
3. (b), (c), (d), (g) (i.e. all the oral sounds)
4. (a) voiced alveolar fricative
   (b) voiced velar oral stop (or plosive)
   (c) voiced velar nasal stop
   (d) voiceless postalveolar fricative
   (e) voiced alveolar lateral approximant
   (f) voiced dental fricative
   (g) voiced alveolar nasal stop
   (h) voiceless labiodental fricative
   (i) voiced postalveolar affricate
   (j) voiced alveolar trill

5. (a) [j], (b) [p], (c) [ŋ], (d) [s]
6. [m] is to [n] as [b] is to [d]
   The first member of each pair is bilabial, and the second is alveolar. Voicing and manner of articulation are otherwise the same within each pair.

   [t] is to [s] as [d] is to [z]
   The first member of each pair is an oral stop and the second is a fricative. Voicing and place of articulation are the same within each pair.

[f] is to [v] as [t] is to [d]
The first member of each pair is voiceless and the second is voiced.
Place of articulation and manner of articulation are the same within
each pair.

[g] is to [d] as [ŋ] is to [n]
The first member of each pair is velar and the second is alveolar.
Voicing and manner of articulation are the same within each pair.

[p] is to [m] as [k] is to [ŋ]
The first member of each pair is a voiceless oral stop (plosive) and
the second is a voiced nasal stop. Place of articulation is the same
within each pair.

5 Basic Principles of Vowel Description

Although most people have quite clear intuitions about which sounds in spoken language are consonants and which are vowels, it is much harder to give a clear description of the precise phonetic factors underlying these judgments. For example, most speakers of English would agree that the sound [j] at the start of the word "yes" is a consonant, whereas the sound represented by the letters "ee" in "feet" is a vowel, but the phonetic difference between these two sounds may actually be very small. In terms of voicing and articulatory posture, these two sounds may be, in fact, virtually equivalent. The differentiation between vowels and consonants is very closely tied up with the concept of the syllable as either a phonological or a phonetic unit. The nature of the phonological syllable is somewhat abstract, and continues to be the focus of lively debate, which is too extensive to be considered in any detail here. The simplest approach is to follow Laver (1994, p. 114) in defining the phonological syllable as "a complex unit, made up of nuclear and marginal elements." Marginal elements correspond to what are generally called consonants, and nuclear elements are generally described as vowels. For any given language, we can formulate rules about permitted combinations of marginal and nuclear elements, but the nuclear element is a basic requirement of any syllable.

As Laver (1994) pointed out, the notion of the syllable as a phonetic unit is even more difficult to define, as attempts to provide physiological, acoustic, or auditory definitions have failed to demonstrate physically measurable correlates of a phonetic unit that correspond to the phonological syllable. Similar difficulties arise if we try to identify phonetic factors that delineate the phonetic representations of marginal elements (consonants) from those that represent nuclear elements (vowels). There are some general tendencies that can be identified, in that duration of vowels is usually longer than that of consonants and the articulation of vowels involves less constriction of the vocal tract. The problem is that these are just tendencies, and there may be instances where listeners, when asked to listen to two sounds, may unanimously and confidently agree that one is a vowel and one is a consonant, but where a detailed phonetic analysis shows no difference in duration, articulatory features, or acoustic output. For some speakers, in certain contexts, this may be true of the sounds in "yes" and "feet," described earlier. This difficulty in drawing a clear phonetic boundary between vowels and consonants led Laver (1994) to suggest that the terms "vowel" and "consonant" should not be applied as phonetic labels, preferring to use the term "syllabic vocoid" to describe sounds that have a degree of stricture that is no greater than open approximation and that carry the weight of a syllable. We nonetheless, continue to use the terms "vowel" and "consonant," on the basis that they are in wide usage and that intuitive judgments about what is a vowel and what is a consonant are generally fairly stable. We draw on the general tendencies, mentioned earlier, that vowels are characterized by a relative lack of constriction of the vocal tract and are typically longer in duration than consonants. They can also be assumed to be voiced, although voiceless vowels do occur occasionally, and these are discussed later in this chapter.

This relative lack of vocal tract constriction means that the conventional approach to phonetic description that is used for consonants, and that focuses on the point of greatest constriction (place of articulation), is not easily applicable to vowels. Instead, phoneticians have tended to use a combination of approaches, based partly on articulatory placement of the tongue, jaw, and lips, and partly on more abstract judgments about auditory perceptual characteristics of vowels. The approach to learning about vowels taken here places the emphasis on the articulatory characteristics of vowels. The development of high levels of auditory perceptual skill in identifying and differentiating between vowels requires extensive exposure to live or recorded models of vowel production. There are a number of useful multimedia resources available, including an increasing range of web-based material such as that provided by the University of California in Los Angeles (UCLA). Before embarking on a description of vowel production, it may be useful to point out that there are some valid reasons why production and perception of vowels may initially be harder than for consonants. During consonant production, the tactile sensations that result from contact between the tongue and the roof of the mouth are important factors in giving speakers an awareness of tongue position. In vowel production, however, the more open vocal tract means that there is relatively little contact between the tongue and the roof of the mouth. The more limited tactile feedback may cause some problems for some people as they begin to develop awareness of articulatory positions in their own vowel production. With practice, however, other cues can be used to develop awareness of articulatory postures. A further difficulty in writing about vowels, when readers are likely to come from a wide range of geographical backgrounds, stems from the fact that vowel quality varies between accents. This means that it is harder to select appropriate examples of words from the English language that illustrate a particular vowel quality in a way that is accessible by readers from different accent backgrounds.

A basic concept underpinning this section, which is expanded in the discussion of vowel formants in chapter 17, is that the acoustic characteristics of a vowel (and hence its auditory quality) depend on the shape and volume of the resonating spaces within the vocal tract between the larynx and the lips. The shape and volume of these spaces is determined partly by an individual's physical characteristics (e.g., vocal tract length, height and width of the hard palate) and partly by articulatory adjustments of the lips, tongue, and pharynx. The following discussion of vowel description is based on the assumption that all readers will have approximately equivalent physical characteristics, and hence that all speakers do the same thing when they produce equivalent vowel sounds. This convenient assumption, which is not always made explicit in phonetics teaching, generally holds well enough, but it is a little simplistic and there may be times when it needs to be questioned. Consider, for example, two speakers who are aiming to produce a vowel quality that is associated with an expanded oral cavity. A speaker who has a very high palatal arch may be able to produce this kind of vowel quality with much less active lowering of the tongue and jaw than will be needed by a speaker with a smaller palatal arch. For the moment, however, we will ignore such differences.

THE ARTICULATORY PROCESS IN VOWEL PRODUCTION

Different vowel qualities arise from different shapes of the vocal tract and different lip positions. Articulatory classification of vowels draws on three aspects of vowel production: vertical adjustments of the tongue, horizontal (front–back) adjustments of the tongue, and lip position.

Tongue Position: Height of the Tongue

All vowels are produced with no more constriction than is involved in the production of approximant consonants, so the tongue is not close enough to the roof of the mouth to produce audible friction. The relationship between the tongue and the roof of the mouth varies along a scale from relative closeness to extreme opening. Vowels may be classed as *close, close-mid* (also known as half-close), *open-mid* (or half-open), or *open*, depending on the degree of oral cavity opening involved. Because of the wide variation in vowel pronunciation in different accents of English, the following examples are only possible suggestions, and may not apply for all speakers. Close vowels involve some constriction of the vocal tract, being produced with relatively little jaw opening and the tongue body raised so the upper surface of the tongue is close to the roof of the mouth. In most accents of English, the vowels in "peep," (usually [i]), and in "poop" (usually [u] or [ʉ]), are close vowels. At the other end of the scale, open vowels are characterized by a lack of constriction in the oral cavity, as the tongue body is lowered. This tongue lowering is typically associated with (and facilitated by) a lower jaw position. The vowel in the word "map" is, for most accents, an open vowel. Figure 5.1 compares the tongue positions for a close vowel [i] and an open vowel [a], as in RP realizations of the words "peep" and "map," respectively. Close-mid and open-mid vowels have intermediate tongue positions, and some examples are given later in this chapter.

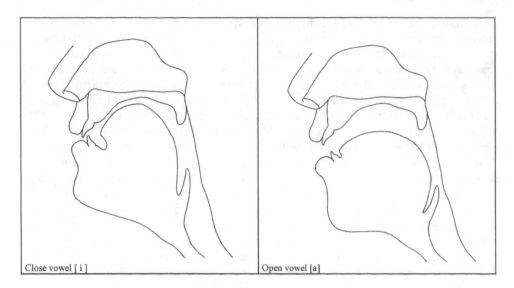

Close vowel [i]

Open vowel [a]

FIG. 5.1. A sagittal section of the vocal tract showing tongue positions for the close vowel [i] and open vowel [a].

Tongue Position: Front Versus Back

The position of the body of the tongue within the oral cavity can also be adjusted in the horizontal plane, from a more fronted to a more backed position. Vowels are usually classified fairly simply, as being front, central, or back. For close vowels, where there is some degree of oral cavity constriction, it is possible to describe front and back vowels in terms of the point of greatest constriction. For close front vowels, the constriction is between the front of the tongue and the hard palate, whereas for close back vowels, the point of greatest constriction is between the back of the tongue and the velum or uvula. In other words, the categories front and back in vowel production correspond to the categories palatal and velar (or uvular) in consonant classification. The close vowel [i], shown in Fig. 5.1, is a front vowel, and can be contrasted with the vowel [u], used by RP speakers in "moon." Close central vowels are, as you might expect, intermediate between front and back, so the point of greatest stricture is near the junction of the hard palate and velum.

It is less appropriate to describe more open vowels in terms of place of constriction, and it may be better to focus on the effects of front-back adjustments of the tongue body on the size of the resonating spaces. Retraction of the tongue body for back vowels will reduce the volume of the pharynx and expand the resonating volume at the front of the oral cavity, whereas forward adjustments of the tongue for front vowels will expand the pharyngeal space. For accents that have different vowels in the words "Pam" and "palm," both are usually open vowels, but the first is a front vowel and the second a back vowel. Similarly, a comparison of the tongue positions for the vowels in "bed" and "bought" will typically show that the first of these has a front and the second a back vowel, although both are a little less open than the previous pair of vowels. For speakers who do not pronounce the /r/ in words such as "bird" and "word," the vowel in these words will usually be central.

Practice 5.1: Height of the Tongue

Compare close and open vowels. [i], as in English "bead," is a close vowel. The tongue is fairly close to the roof of the mouth, and you should be able to feel some contact between the sides of the tongue and the upper teeth and gums. [a], as in British English "bad," is an open vowel. If you move from [i] to [a], you should notice that the jaw drops and the tongue moves away from the roof of the mouth so that the contact between the sides of the tongue and the teeth is lost.

Try saying the vowels in the words "bead," "bid," "bed," and "bad." For most people, there will be a step-wise progression from close to open vowels. Use a mirror to observe the progressive opening of the mouth, and feel the gradual loss of contact between the tongue and the roof of the mouth.

Practice 5.2: Front Versus Back Vowels

Hold a long close front vowel [i], as in "bee," and note the amount and place of any contact between the sides of the tongue and the roof of the mouth. Now produce a close back vowel [u], as in some English pronunciations of the word "two" (e.g., RP—aim for a BBC English pronunciation). Two techniques may help you to find the right tongue position if you are not sure about this vowel. One is to prolong the labial-velar approximant at the start of a word like "water." The other is to whistle the lowest note you can manage, hold your tongue and lips in that position, and then produce a vowel sound. Alternate [i] and [u], noting how the contact position of contact between the sides of your tongue and the roof of the mouth changes as you move from one vowel to the other. Feel how the whole body of the tongue moves forward and back as you produce these vowels.

Contrast the vowels in "bed" and "bought," prolonging the vowels so that you can focus on the tongue position. In most accents, the vowel in "bed" will be a front vowel (often an open-mid vowel [ɛ]) and the vowel in "bought" will be a back vowel (open-mid or more open). Alternate these two vowels. You will probably notice that there is little or no contact between the tongue and the roof of the mouth for either vowel. For the front vowel in "bed," you may notice some contact between the tip of the tongue and the lower teeth. If you move to the back vowel in "bought," you should be able to feel the whole of the tongue body move backward. Can you still feel contact between the tip of the tongue and the lower teeth?

Compare your production of the vowels in "Sam" and "psalm." Are they the same or different? For some speakers these will be similar, but if you do have a difference, the vowel in the second is likely to be further back. Both will probably be open vowels, so there will be little or no contact between the tongue and the roof of the mouth, but you may be able to feel the body of the tongue move backward and forward as you alternate the vowels, as with the last pair.

Lip Posture: Rounded Versus Unrounded

The third key factor to be considered in vowel description is lip position, as this has a considerable influence on vowel quality. Changing the posture of the lips not only alters the size of the opening at the outer end of the vocal tract, but it may also affect the length of the vocal tract. The lengthening of the vocal tract that can be produced by protruding the lips can have a marked effect on vocal tract resonance and hence the perceived quality of a sound. This potential for complex three-dimensional adjustment of the lips in vertical, lateral, and front–back directions is difficult to capture in a simple analytical framework, and it is often adequate to use a simplified set of categories. At a most basic level, vowels may be classified into those that are *rounded* and those that are *unrounded.* The vowels that typically occur in most varieties of British English in the words "bee" [bit], "bet" [bet] and "bat" [bat] would be described as unrounded, whereas the vowels in the words "boot" and "bought" would be described as rounded. This binary distinction works reasonably well as a starting point, but is a little crude, and it may be useful to make slightly finer distinctions. For example, it may be important to differentiate between vowels like that in "bet," where the lip position is fairly neutral, with no significant adjustment away from a rest position other than an opening of the mouth that results from lowering of the jaw, and the vowel used in most varieties of English in "bee." In this latter vowel, the lips are typically actively spread, so that the lip opening is expanded sideways. The [ɛ] of "bet" would then be described having a *neutral* lip position, whereas the [i] of "bee" would be described as having a *spread* lip position. It is also often useful to differentiate between degrees of lip rounding. In many varieties of English, the vowel [u] in "boot" is produced with a relatively extreme form of lip rounding, so that the lip opening is significantly reduced and the lips are protruded forward. This type of lip rounding may be described as *close rounding.* The vowel [ɔ] in "bought," by comparison, has a much less marked degree of rounding, which is described as *open rounding.*

    Classification of vowels into four categories (spread, neutral, open rounded, close rounded), as shown in Fig. 5.2, is perfectly acceptable for most types of phonetic analysis, but there may be some occasions when more detail is needed; this may be the case when fine articulatory differences between different accents, languages, or speakers are the focus of interest. There is no widespread convention to draw on in such situations, but Laver (1980, p. 37; 1994, p. 279) suggested a framework that allows classification of lip posture in terms of vertical and horizontal adjustments relative to neutral. This framework provides a terminology for more detailed description of lip position and it also highlights the range of lip movement that is potentially available for speech production. Figure 5.2 does not indicate variations in the amount of lip protrusion and it is important to remember that lip protrusion can be manipulated to some extent independently of the lateral and vertical adjustments of the lips. It is, for example, possible to adopt a close rounded lip position either with or without forward protrusion of the lips. Rounded vowels, such as those in many people's production of "boot" or "bought," typically have lip rounding in combination with some degree of lip protrusion. As a general rule, it seems that open rounding is associated with more forward protrusion than is close rounding

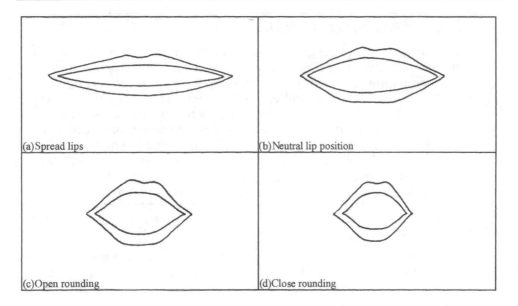

FIG. 5.2.   A schematic front view of labial settings: (a) spread lips; (b) neutral lip position; (c) open rounding; (d) close rounding.

(Laver, 1994, p. 279). Lip rounding without protrusion does occur, however, and people who adopt a non-protruded type of lip rounding as a habitual pattern of speech are sometimes described as speaking with "pursed lips."

Monophthong Versus Diphthong

Vowels that show a relatively constant articulatory configuration throughout their duration, apart from the rapid transitions to and from adjacent sound segments, are described as monophthongs, which translates literally as single sounds. In most accents of English, the majority of vowels that occur in stressed syllables are typically produced as monophthongs. There are, however, a number of vowels in English that are characterized by quite marked movement of the articulatory configuration of either the tongue, the lips, or both. Consider, for example, the vowel in the word "voice." Most speakers of English will start this vowel with a tongue position that is relatively back and a rounded lip posture, and will then move the tongue forward and upward while releasing the lip rounding. Such a vowel is described as a diphthong, literally a "two-sound" vowel. The terms monophthong and diphthong are often seen as designating discrete categories but, as so often in phonetics, these categories really just represent different parts of a continuum. When we start to look at spectrograms of vowels (see chap. 12), it becomes obvious that even where vowels are perceived as being steady-state monophthongs, the acoustic representation often indicates some articulatory movement. Similarly, although diphthongs typically show very marked shifts in the spectrographic pattern, this does vary depending on the accent, the speaker, and the context and style of speech. As a result, it is not always easy to make a categorical phonetic distinction between monophthongs and diphthongs.

Practice 5.3: Lip Position in Vowel Production

Try adopting a range of lip positions, using a mirror. Start with a neutral position, relaxing your lips as they would be at rest, allowing them to fall open loosely as you open your jaw. For most people it is enough to open the jaw just far enough to see a small vertical gap between the upper and lower incisor teeth. Now try moving your lips into each of the positions shown in Figure 5.2, noting whether you naturally adjust the degree of forward protrusion as you modify the shape and size of the lip opening. Now try producing the vowels in the words "bee," "bed," "bad," "bought," and "boot," and notice how the lip positions change. Referring back to Fig. 5.2, decide how you would classify your own lip position during production of these vowels.

Practice 5.4: Monophthong and Diphthong

Try producing a range of vowels from your own accent or language, and decide whether they seem to be most like monophthongs or diphthongs. For speakers of English, the following list of words may be useful: bead, bid, boot, bud, book, bite, voice, bait, bout, bet, bat, palm, bob, bought.

In a monophthong the vowel should be recognizable if you prolong it without any movement of the tongue or lips. In a diphthong, the vowel will only be clearly recognizable if you move the articulatory position (i.e., lips and/or tongue).

For the majority of speakers of English the vowels in the words "bat" and "bead," for example, are monophthongs, whereas the vowels in "bout" and "voice" are diphthongs, but this is not universal. Use a mirror to decide whether the articulatory change in your own diphthong production involves the lips, tongue, or both.

Voicing in Vowels

Looking at the languages of the world as a whole, the great majority of vowels are voiced, and it is reasonable to assume that vowels will be voiced unless it is stated otherwise. Phonetically voiceless vowels do, however, occur. In a minority of languages, there is a phonological contrast between voiced vowels and those that are either completely voiceless or that have some glottal friction (whisperiness). Laver (1994) cited a number of examples taken from a range of Amerindian and Australian languages. Partially voiced or voiceless vowels may sometimes also be observed in languages that have no phonological voicing contrast. In English, for example, vowels may be whispered or voiceless either at the end of an utterance, or where they are relatively unstressed and adjacent to voiceless consonants. Many speakers would thus produce the vowel in the word "to" without voicing, when it occurs in an utterance like "Come to tea," where it is unstressed and between two voiceless plosives. Another common example from English, which is commonly voiceless for similar contextual reasons, is the first, unstressed vowel in the word "potato." In whispered speech, of course, neither vowels nor consonants will be voiced in the usual sense of the word.

MAPPING VOWELS

Classification and description of vowels has been one of the major challenges facing phoneticians, as it is difficult to identify clear criteria that can be used to delineate one category of vowel from another. If we take the three articulatory parameters outlined above, close–open, front–back, and lip spread–lip rounded, it is clear that we are dealing with a complex situation. Each of these three parameters is a continuum, and they can coexist in any combination. We therefore have the potential for continuous variation along three intersecting dimensions, and no clear articulatory boundaries that can be used for classification. A large number of strategies have been used in attempts to address this difficulty, but one of the most useful is the notion of mapping vowels. This involves plotting vowels onto a vowel area, by reference to standard vowel qualities.

The Vowel Area

Vowel area is a term used to identify the potential range of vowel qualities that can be produced by speakers with fairly standard vocal tracts, and it can be seen either as a rather abstract representation of the range of auditory perceptual qualities, or as a more concrete representation of tongue position. The vowel area is usually represented by a quadrilateral, as shown in Fig. 5.3. This shape has evolved over the last 100 years or so and is derived partly from attempts to plot the highest point of the tongue during vowel production across a full range of vowels. These plots show that the highest point of the tongue always falls within a slanted ovoid shape, which has been modified to give a simpler shape that can be more easily reproduced. The standard vowel quadrilateral can be interpreted quite straightforwardly in relation to the articulatory features already described. Vowels to the left-hand side of the space are front vowels whereas vowels to the right-hand side of the space are back vowels; vowels at the top of the space are close vowels and vowels at the bottom of the space are open vowels. The vowel quadrilaterals shown in Fig. 5.3 show the relative positions of some stressed vowels from RP, General American English, and Standard Scottish English accents. The vowel symbols used correspond to the vowels used in the words listed. It can be seen that all three accents have similar close front vowels in words like "bee," but that the vowels in words like "fast" and "moon" differ more significantly. For example, the Scottish vowel in "moon" is further to the left than the equivalent vowel in RP, showing that it is typically produced with the tongue further forward than in RP.

One shortcoming of the vowel area is that it is a two-dimensional space, reflecting vertical and horizontal dimensions of tongue adjustment, but it does not allow for variations in lip position. It is therefore possible for two vowels with quite different auditory qualities to occupy the same point within the vowel area, if the quality difference is due to lip position.

Reference Vowel Qualities: The Cardinal Vowel System.   The mapping of vowels shown in Figure 5.3 is based on what is probably the most widely used approach to vowel analysis. The *Cardinal Vowel* system, developed by Daniel

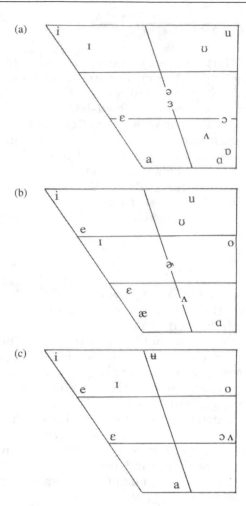

FIG. 5.3.   Charts of selected stressed vowels from: (a) RP; (b) General American; (c) Scottish English.

Jones during the early decades of the 20th century (see Abercrombie, 1967, pp. 176–177), provides a framework of reference vowel qualities, so that any given vowel quality can be related to the cardinal qualities. Although the technique relies largely on learned auditory qualities, there is a clear association between these and the articulatory characteristics of the vowels. Jones gave very explicit articulatory descriptions for two contrasting "hinge" vowels, which represent extremes of vowel production, and that really act as the linchpins for the whole system. He described the first of these, Cardinal Vowel No. 1, as "the sound in which the raising of the tongue is as far forward as possible and as high as possible consistently with its being a vowel" (Jones, 1947, p. 31) and he specified that the lips should be spread. In other words, this is a close front vowel, in which the front of the tongue is so close to the hard palate that if it were any closer there would be audible friction, and it is an extreme form of the vowel [i] illustrated in Fig. 5.1. The second, Cardinal Vowel No. 5, is "a sound in which the back of the tongue is lowered as far as possible and retracted as far as possible consistently with the sound being a vowel" (Jones, 1947, p. 31) and he indicated that this should be produced with unrounded lips. This, then, is an extreme version of an open back unrounded vowel, and is given the symbol [ɑ]. Jones then specified a set of further peripheral vowels (i.e., vowels around the edge of the vowel space), which are intended to be perceptually equidistant from each other. This gives a set of eight vowel qualities, which Jones classified as the Primary Cardinal Vowels. Figure 5.4 shows the positions of these eight Cardinal Vowels plotted on the standard vowel quadrilateral.

The cardinal auditory qualities of these vowels are associated with characteristic tongue and lip postures and these are shown in Fig. 5.5. It can be seen from this figure that as the tongue moves around the peripheral positions, from close front [i] to open front [a], and thence through open back [ɑ] to close back [u], there is a corresponding progression of lip position from spread to neutral and then to increasing degrees of rounding.

One danger in focusing too much on these eight vowel qualities as a basis for vowel analysis is a tendency to view these particular combinations of tongue and lip positions as being usual and inevitable. In fact, tongue and lip position can be controlled quite independently, which greatly extends the potential range of vowel qualities available to speakers. Daniel Jones proposed a secondary set of Cardinal Vowels to allow for this independence of tongue and lip articulation and they are a very valuable tool for increasing awareness of the range of auditory qualities that result from independent adjustments of either tongue or lip position. A rather imprecise articulatory description of the secondary set of eight Cardinal Vowels, which are numbered from 9 to 16, is to say that the while the tongue positions of the secondary set are equivalent to those of the primary set, each secondary vowel is associated with a lip position "opposite" to that of the

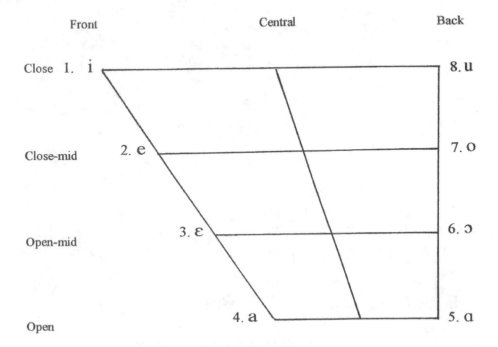

FIG. 5.4.   A vowel chart showing placement of Primary Cardinal Vowels 1 to 8.

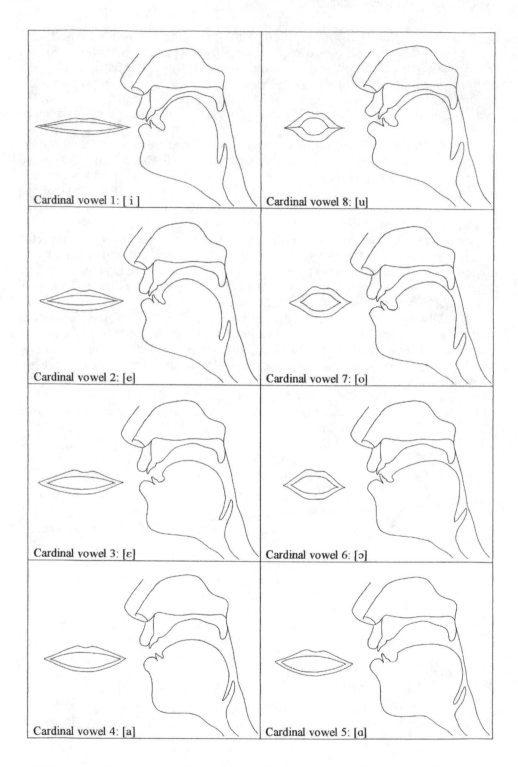

FIG. 5.5.   A diagrammatic representation of tongue and lip positions for the Primary Cardinal Vowels 1 to 8.

equivalent primary vowel. The word "opposite" is used rather loosely here, but the following description should make the meaning clearer.

Figure 5.6 illustrates approximate lip positions for Cardinal Vowels 1 to 8 and 9 to 16. Taking the close front vowels first, readers should already be familiar with Cardinal Vowel 1, [i], which is produced with a spread lip position. The equivalent secondary Cardinal Vowel 9, [y] is produced using the same tongue position, but with a close rounded lip position, similar to the one associated with Cardinal Vowel 8, [u]. In simple terms, an articulatory description for Cardinal Vowel 9 = the tongue position for Cardinal Vowel 1 + the lip position for Cardinal Vowel 8.

A similar transposition applies to the relationship between the two close back Cardinal Vowels, 8 and 16. The Primary Cardinal Vowel 8, [u], is produced with a close rounded lip position, whereas the secondary equivalent, [ɯ], is produced with a spread lip position, similar to that involved in the production of Cardinal Vowel 1.

Exactly the same process can be applied to the close mid and open mid vowels. The front close-mid Cardinal Vowel 10, [ø], is produced with a similar tongue position to Cardinal Vowel 2, [e], but a rounded lip position as for Cardinal Vowel 7, [o], whereas Cardinal Vowel 15 combines the tongue position of Cardinal Vowel 7 with the slightly spread lip position of Cardinal Vowel 2. The front open-mid Cardinal Vowel 11, [œ], shares a tongue position with Cardinal Vowel 3, [ɛ], and the open rounded lip position of Cardinal Vowel 6, [ɔ].

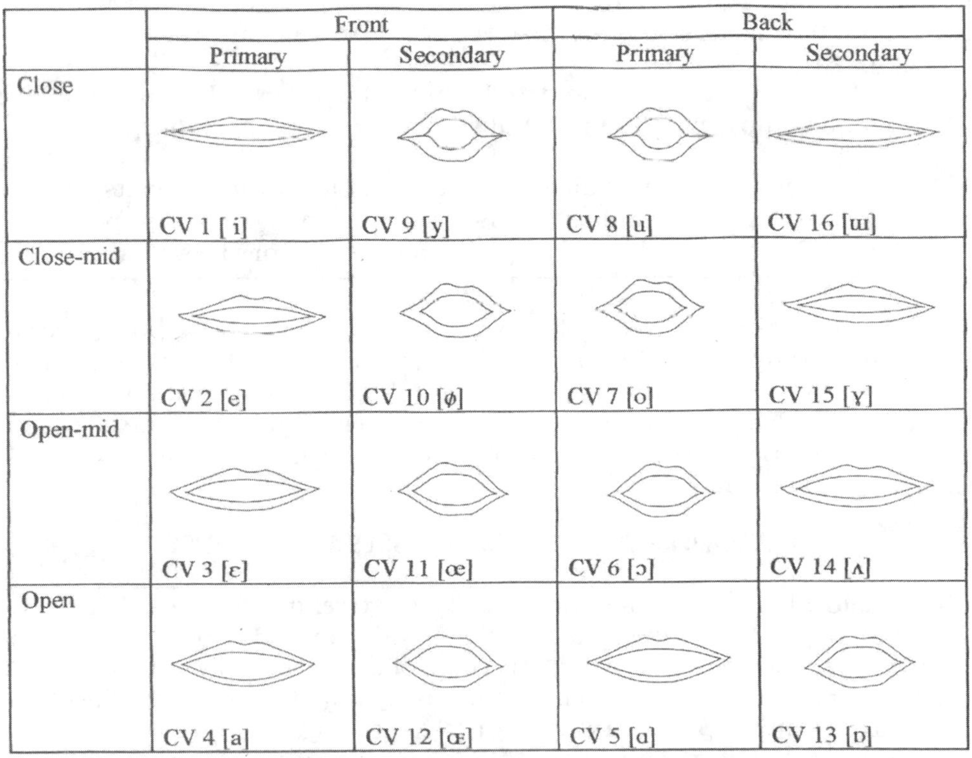

	Front		Back	
	Primary	Secondary	Primary	Secondary
Close	CV 1 [i]	CV 9 [y]	CV 8 [u]	CV 16 [ɯ]
Close-mid	CV 2 [e]	CV 10 [ø]	CV 7 [o]	CV 15 [ɣ]
Open-mid	CV 3 [ɛ]	CV 11 [œ]	CV 6 [ɔ]	CV 14 [ʌ]
Open	CV 4 [a]	CV 12 [œ]	CV 5 [ɑ]	CV 13 [ɒ]

FIG. 5.6. Lip positions for Cardinal Vowels 1 to 16.

Practice 5.5: Independent Lip and Tongue Adjustment

The aim of this activity is to encourage independent adjustments of the tongue and lips. This is the basis of the transposition from primary to secondary Cardinal Vowels.

1. Hold tongue position constant and vary lip position.

   (a) Prolong a close front vowel [i], noting the spread lip position. Keeping the tongue in the same position, gradually move the lips to a rounded lip position, as for the close back rounded vowel [u] (see Practice 5.2). You should then be producing the close front rounded vowel, [y]. Focus carefully on the tongue-to-palate contact pattern for [i], to ensure that you maintain this as you adopt the rounded lip position, and don't allow the tongue to move back. Note the change in vowel quality as the lip position changes.
   (b) Produce a prolonged close back rounded vowel [u], again focusing on tactile feedback to ensure that you maintain the tongue position, and gradually unround and then spread your lips as for [i]. This should result in a close front unrounded vowel [ɯ].

2. Hold lip position constant and vary tongue position.

   (a) Alternate between [y] and [u]. Both have close rounding of the lips, but the tongue should move between a close front and a close back position.
   (b) Alternate between [i] and [ɯ]; this involves exactly the same tongue movement as in (a), but with a spread lip position.

3. Experiment further with independent lip and tongue movements, by starting with other familiar vowels and either changing the lip position while you hold the tongue position constant, or vice versa.

Readers may be able to predict, by now, that Cardinal Vowel 14, [ʌ], is a combination of the tongue position for Cardinal Vowel 6, [ɔ], with the fairly neutral lip position associated with Cardinal Vowel 3, [ɛ]. Both the front and back Primary Cardinal Vowels, number 4, [a], and number 5, [ɑ], are produced with a fairly neutral lip positions. Their secondary equivalents both have lip rounding (and protrusion).

TRANSCRIBING VOWELS: USING SYMBOLS AND DIACRITICS

The IPA alphabet provides a set of symbols for vowel transcription that correspond to the cardinal vowels just described, with some additional symbols for more central vowels (see Appendix A). These offer a reasonably extensive set of symbols for a broad transcription of vowel quality, but there are some difficulties associated with vowel transcription. Strictly speaking, the IPA vowel symbols represent Cardinal Vowel qualities, which map onto the vowel area precisely as shown in Fig. 5.4. True Cardinal Vowel qualities seldom occur in "real" speech, however, and so the transcriber must decide how best to assign a symbol to a vowel that is somewhat different from any of the Cardinal Vowel qualities. The usual phonetic approach is to decide where in the vowel area a given vowel lies, and then to use the symbol to which it is closest. In practice, therefore, vowel symbols are best thought of as representing an area within the vowel space rather than a specific point on the vowel quadrilateral. As illustration of this, it can be seen from Fig. 5.3 that the RP vowel in the word "bad" is given the same symbol as that used in the same word by Scottish speakers, but these two vowels do not occupy quite the same position within the vowel area. RP speakers typically use a vowel that is more fronted than that used by Scottish speakers. If further detail is required in transcription, diacritics may be used to indicate the relationship between the vowel heard and the Cardinal Vowel that is represented by the symbol chosen. For example, in the vowels just described, the Scottish version is significantly further back than Cardinal Vowel 4, and this can be shown by modifying the symbol with the backing diacritic, to give [a̠]. The IPA chart offers a number of useful diacritics for vowel transcription, including those for fronting, backing, raising, and lowering. There are also diacritics indicating that a vowel is more central than the symbol would normally suggest (i.e., intermediate between front and back) or more mid-centralized (i.e., more toward the center of the vowel area). Uncertainty about choice of symbol may arise if a vowel is intermediate between two Cardinal vowels, and it is not uncommon for different listeners to use different symbols for the same vowel, even when they agree

---

Practice 5.6: Integration of Vowel and Consonant Performance

The aim of this activity is to integrate your production of vowels and consonants by practicing unusual sequences of sounds. You may find that some of the sound sequences suggested here feel a little awkward initially, especially where a sequence of consonants does not typically occur within the words of your own language(s), but all should be possible with a little practice.

1. Produce the following nonsense words as exactly as you can from the transcriptions given:

(a) [θimatʃ]	(c) [gwadjɔp]	(e) [vlumbiʃɹɔ]
(b) [ʃnuflɛskt]	(d) [byðaŋ]	(f) [jadʒɛzi]

2. Design and produce at least four of your own nonsense words. Each word should have 5 segments, selected to fit the criteria described here.

   - an alveolar consonant; a close vowel; a voiced fricative; a front vowel; a nasal stop
   - a voiceless plosive; a back vowel; an approximant; an open vowel; a voiceless fricative
   - a nasal stop; a rounded vowel; a voiced plosive; a back vowel; an affricate
   - a voiceless fricative; a nasal stop; an unrounded vowel; an approximant; a voiceless plosive

about where to map them on the vowel area. If, for example, a vowel is judged to be halfway between Cardinal Vowels 2 and 3, either [ẹ] (i.e., more open than [e]) or [ɛ̣] (i.e., closer than [ɛ]) could be used.

Diphthongs, because of their dynamic nature, are not amenable to transcription using a single symbol, so the usual approach here is to use a sequence of two symbols that represent, as closely as possible, the start and end points of the vowel. In RP, production of the vowel in "how" would thus be transcribed as [au], as it moves from an open front unrounded vowel to a close back rounded vowel. In the same accent, the vowel in the word "voice" would be transcribed as [ɔi], as it moves from an open-mid back rounded vowel to a close front unrounded vowel.

Although this chapter has introduced some general principles for vowel analysis and description, vowels do pose very complex issues for phonetics (and phonology) and a fuller discussion is not possible in this text. A useful description of accent-related variations in the vowels of English can be found in Wells (1982) and more extended discussions of the phonetic characteristics of vowels in general can be found in texts such as Laver (1994) or Ladefoged and Maddieson (1996).

6

Extending the Set of Speech Sounds

Chapter 4 provided a set of classificatory categories, relating to voicing, place, and manner of articulation, as an introduction to the general principles of phonetic analysis and description of consonants. The selection of speech sounds was explicitly anglocentric, in order to allow speakers of most varieties of English to identify the sounds under discussion. The aim of this chapter is to present a fuller range of speech sounds, extending the set beyond those that commonly occur in English to include sounds that occur across the whole range of the world's languages, as well as sounds that are more likely to occur in developing speech or in speech disorder. By the end of this chapter, you should have some familiarity with almost all the sounds represented by symbols in the IPA consonant chart (see Appendix A). In addition, we introduce some of the sounds represented by symbols on the extIPA chart, shown in Appendix B (International Phonetic Association, 1999). This chart is an extension of the standard IPA chart and is designed to include sounds that are not typical of normal adult speech, but that may be seen during early stages of development or in disordered speech. You should refer to both these charts as you read this chapter, with a view to learning a full inventory of symbols for use in segmental transcription. The inclusion of sounds from the extIPA chart is partly for the benefit of readers who may have a specific interest in speech disorder or development of speech in children and partly because it seems useful for any phonetician to have some awareness of the full potential range of speech production. The following sections introduce some new classificatory categories, relating to place of articulation, manner of articulation, and airstream initiation.

MORE PLACES OF ARTICULATION

Figure 4.2 in chapter 4 shows some key places of articulation, but is not exhaustive. The IPA chart includes two places of articulation that we have not yet described, and the extIPA chart includes some additional places of articulation that, though rarer in normal adult speech, may nonetheless occur in minority languages, in normally developing speech, or in speech disorder.

Retroflex

Retroflex is included on the IPA chart as a place of articulation, but the term also implies a very specific type of tongue configuration. The place of greatest constriction in retroflex consonants is generally near the pre-palatal region (i.e., at the very front of the hard palate), but it may be slightly further forward. The defining feature of retroflex sounds is that the tongue is curled back, so that the stricture involves the undersurface of the tongue and the roof of the mouth, as shown in Fig. 6.1. The auditory quality of retroflex sounds is very much colored by the tendency for the tongue body to be drawn back and down in order to facilitate this tongue tip curling. The effect of this is often quite clearly audible during the transitions to and from a retroflex sound. These tend to have the characteristic "dark" quality that derives from constriction in the pharyngeal area and expansion at the front of the oral cavity.

The IPA chart includes specific symbols for retroflex plosives [ʈɖ], a nasal stop [ɳ], fricatives [ʂʐ], a central approximant [ɻ] and a lateral approximant [ɭ]. All these symbols share the element of a descending line, curving to the right, added to the appropriate alveolar symbol. The remaining retroflex symbol on the chart, for a flap, is dealt with later in this chapter. Retroflex sounds are found in a wide range of languages and Laver (1994) reviewed a number of sources to illustrate the high incidence of retroflexion among the language groups of the Indian subcontinent and in the languages of Australia. One example, taken from Ladefoged

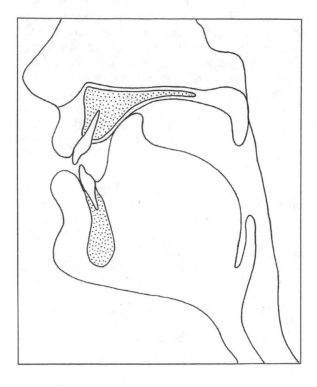

FIG. 6.1. A diagrammatic view of the vocal organs during articulation of a retroflex plosive.

(1972, p. 9) is Malayalam, which is spoken in Southern India. This has a three-way phonemic contrast between dental, alveolar and retroflex plosives:

[kuṯːi] "stabbed" [kutːi] "peg" [kuṭːi] "child"

The auditory quality of retroflexion is so distinctive that retroflex realizations of the phonemes /t/ and /d/ are, in fact, often one of the key phonetic features used in crude radio and television portrayals of the English spoken by people originating from the Indian subcontinent.

Practice 6.1: Retroflex Sounds

Produce a voiced plosive, between vowels, using a retroflex place of articulation [aḍa]. Think of this simply as producing a /d/ with the tongue tip curled up and back so that the under-surface of the tongue contacts the roof of the mouth. Use a mirror to check that the under-surface of the tongue is articulating with the roof of the mouth, behind the alveolar ridge, and just in front of the hard palate. Observe the difference in articulatory placement and auditory quality when you alternate a voiced retroflex plosive with a voiced alveolar plosive, for example, [aḍa] and [ada]. Note that a more complex tongue adjustment is involved in moving from the open front vowel to the retroflex plosive than in moving to the alveolar plosive.

Now try producing each of the other retroflex sounds just listed, putting them between vowels and noting that they all share a similar "dark" auditory quality.

Produce the phrase "**Da**dd**y** took **Lizz**ie **d**ow**n** **t**o the **d**en**t**is**t**," using alveolar realizations of the phonemes /d/, /t/, /n/, /l/, /z/, and /s/, which are italicized in the orthographic version. Now try replacing all of these with the retroflex equivalents, and notice the change in overall quality.

Practice producing the words from Malayalam listed previously, focusing on the articulatory and auditory differences between them.

Pharyngeal

The pharyngeal place of articulation involves the back or root of the tongue as the active articulator, creating a constriction of the pharynx, as shown in Fig. 6.2. Describing the pharyngeal walls as the passive articulator may not always be completely accurate, as the muscles within the walls of the pharynx may also be involved in constricting the vocal tract. Pharyngeal fricatives occur in a number of languages, including Somali, as shown in the following illustration, taken from Laver (1994, p. 254). Arabic and Hebrew are often described as having pharyngeal fricatives, but there is some debate about the nature of these (Ladefoged & Maddieson, 1996). The auditory characteristics of pharyngeal fricatives are somewhat variable, depending on whereabouts within the pharynx the greatest constriction occurs. The voiceless pharyngeal fricative is represented by the symbol [ħ], and the voiced equivalent by [ʕ]. Examples of pharyngeal fricatives in Somali are:

[saʕ] "cow" [sɔʕɔtɔ] "traveler" [sɛːħɔ] go to sleep [libæħ] lion

Although pharyngeal plosives sometimes occur in disordered speech, they are not generally included in descriptions of the sounds of the languages of the world and the IPA chart does not therefore include distinct symbols for these sounds. They can be transcribed using the appropriate uvular symbols modified by the backing diacritic, that is, [q̠] and [ɢ̠]. Pharyngeal nasal stops are obviously not possible, because the point at which airflow is blocked for pharyngeal stops is below the point at which the oral and nasal cavities divide.

Transcription conventions for the following places of articulation are included in the extIPA set of symbols, but not on the standard IPA symbol chart. This is because they occur only rarely within normal adult speech. They are included here because they do fall within the potential range of phonetic performance by anyone with a normal vocal tract, and may occur either in normally developing speech of young children or in people with speech disorder.

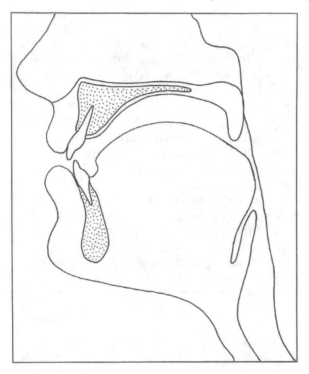

FIG. 6.2. A diagrammatic view of the vocal organs during articulation of pharyngeal fricative.

Practice 6.2: Pharyngeal Sounds

Review the fricatives covered in chapter 4 (Place of Articulation section). Produce a voiceless uvular fricative [χ]. Prolong the fricative while rotating the tongue back and down slightly. You should notice a fall in the apparent pitch as you do so, as the point of greatest constriction moves back to the pharyngeal area, until you are producing a voiceless pharyngeal fricative [ħ]. Production of a uvular fricative involves the back of the tongue articulating with the uvula, which is itself pulled up and back toward the back wall of the pharynx to produce velic closure, preventing nasal airflow. It does not, therefore, need a very great tongue movement to change the place of articulation from uvular to pharyngeal.

Now try alternating the voiceless pharyngeal fricative with a voiced pharyngeal fricative [ʕ]. Try producing the Somali words shown, noting how far the tongue has to move between the front vowel and the word final fricative in the first example.

Pharyngeal plosives have already been mentioned. Why were pharyngeal nasal stops not discussed?

Try making voiced and voiceless pharyngeal plosives [ɢ] and [q] by pulling the tongue further back to make a stricture of complete closure between the back or root of the tongue and the pharynx. Practice making these plosives between vowels.

Dentolabial

Dentolabial sounds are produced by the lower incisors articulating with the upper lip. This is the converse of labiodental sounds (upper incisors and lower lip), and they are sometimes, for this reason, described as reversed labiodentals. The auditory quality of sounds produced in this way is quite similar to that of labiodentals, although when visual cues are used, the labiodental versus dentolabial distinction is unambiguous, as indicated in Fig. 6.3. For anyone with a normal relationship between the lower and upper jaws, production of dentolabials may require a muscular adjustment to protrude the mandible (lower jaw). For speakers who have a naturally protruding lower jaw, however, dentolabials may be easier to produce than labiodentals, and may be used as alternative realizations for phonemes that are usually realized as labiodental. Dentolabial sounds are transcribed using the equivalent labiodental symbol, modified by a dental diacritic over the symbol. A voiced dentolabial fricative would thus be transcribed as [v̪].

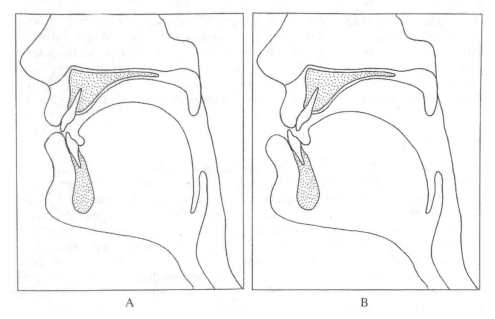

A   B

FIG. 6.3. A diagrammatic view of the vocal organs during articulation (a) a labiodental fricative and (b) a dentolabial fricative.

Labioalveolar

Labioalveolar sounds involve the lower lip, as the active articulator, and the alveolar ridge as the passive articulator. It is probably immediately apparent that such sounds are somewhat awkward to produce for speakers who have a full upper dentition. They are more likely to be used by speakers who are missing at least the central teeth of the upper dental arch. For example, children who lose both of their upper incisors simultaneously may, for a short period, realize labiodental fricatives as labioalveolar fricatives. Transcription of labioalveolar sounds uses the equivalent bilabial or labiodental symbol with parallel horizontal lines (as in an "equals" sign) underneath. A labioalveolar nasal stop would thus be transcribed as [m̳]. The use of this diacritic for labioalveolar sounds may make better sense if you think of it as a double backing diacritic (i.e., two minus symbols). This is because the lower lip is displaced backward by two places of articulation, if we take articulation between upper and lower lips as being the most natural or neutral pattern of articulation. Labiodental sounds are often described as being displaced articulations, because the lower lip is actively retracted toward the passive articulator just behind the upper lip, that is, the upper teeth. In labioalveolar sounds, the lower lip is retracted even further, so it can be thought of as having a double displacement.

Bidental

This is a rather rare place of articulation, where the upper and lower teeth act as the articulators. Unusually, therefore, neither lips nor tongue are involved in creating the stricture. The Standard IPA chart does not include any symbols for transcribing such sounds, even though Ladefoged and Maddieson (1996) cited two reports of bidental fricatives occurring in a dialect of Adyghe spoken in the Black Sea area. Bidental fricatives may also occur in speech pathologies where the speaker is unable to control the tongue sufficiently to constrict the vocal tract. The convention for transcribing bidental fricatives, suggested in the extIPA chart, uses the appropriate glottal fricative symbol with a dental diacritic both above and below the symbol. A further symbol, for a bidental percussive, is discussed later. It is noticeable that the auditory quality of bidental fricatives is quite variable, as the precise pattern of constriction is very much dependent on the speaker's individual pattern of dentition.

Linguolabial

Linguolabial articulations involve an extreme forward displacement of the tongue so that the tip or blade of the tongue (active articulator) articulates with the upper lip, as in Fig. 6.4. It is reported to occur in some languages of the Pacific (Laver, 1994) and may occur in young children where there is any exaggeration of the common tendency to front the tongue during speech. Again, this place of articulation is sufficiently rare that the standard IPA chart does not provide symbols for transcription. The extIPA chart does, however, offer a convention for transcribing such sounds, whereby the appropriate dental (where available) or alveolar symbol is modified by a specific diacritic underneath the symbol, which looks somewhat like a stylized flying seagull. It is possible to produce a full range of manners of articulation at a linguolabial place of articulation, including plosives [t̼] [d̼], fricatives [θ̼] [ð̼], a nasal [n̼], approximants, for example [l̼], and a trill, [r̼].

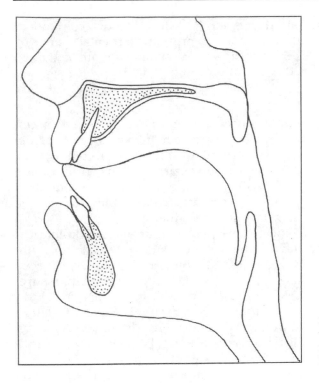

FIG. 6.4. A diagrammatic view of the vocal organs during articulation of a linguolabial plosive.

Interdental

Interdental articulations are produced with the tongue tip or blade displaced a bit further forward than for dental articulations, so that the tip protrudes between the upper and lower teeth. Where the typical realizations of the word initial phonemes in the words "think" and "these" are dental fricatives in Southern British English speakers, they are more likely to be interdental in Californian English (Ladefoged, 2000). There is obviously a continuum of tongue placement between dental and interdental places of articulation, with extreme (usually disordered) interdental articulations involving protrusion of the blade of the tongue as well as the tip. It is not easy to specify a precise cut-off point between dental and interdental places of articulation, but markedly interdental articulations are typically associated with immature or disordered patterns of articulation and the auditory quality may be described as "imprecise" or "muffled." A wide range of interdental sounds may occur in developing speech, or in speech disorders that are characterized by a generalized fronting of the tongue relative to the roof of the mouth. This type of articulation may occur, for example, in Down syndrome (Mackenzie Beck, 1988).

At least two different conventions have been suggested for transcription of interdental sounds. Laver (1994) followed Ladefoged and Maddieson (1996) in transcribing interdental fricatives by adding the advanced diacritic [₊] to the dental fricative symbols. This convention becomes a little more cumbersome for manners of articulation for which there is no dental symbol, as two diacritics then need to be used underneath the symbol. For example, because there are no IPA symbols for dental plosives, transcription of a voiced interdental plosive would require the voiced alveolar plosive symbol [d] to be modified with both the dental diacritic [ ] and the advanced diacritic [ ]. An alternative convention, which is incorporated into the extIPA chart, is to represent interdental sounds by either the dental symbol (for fricatives) or the alveolar symbol (for other sounds) with the addition of dental diacritics drawn both above and below the symbol.

Velopharyngeal

Velopharyngeal sounds are generally only encountered in disordered speech production, and are usually fricatives or trills. They involve a stricture between the soft palate, acting as the active articulator, and the walls of the pharynx in the region where velic closure occurs during production of oral sounds (see Fig. 6.5). When velopharyngeal fricatives occur during speech production they are most often involuntary sounds, resulting from a failure to achieve complete velic closure. If a speaker is able to produce only partial velic closure, then under some circumstances there may be unwanted audible fricative airflow between the velum and the walls of the pharynx. Such sounds are sometimes also described as "nasal snorts," and they are most likely to occur during, or adjacent to, segments that require high intra-oral air pressure, such as plosives or fricatives. Velopharyngeal fricatives may therefore indicate difficulties with velic closure resulting from congenital disorders such as cleft palate or certain types of neurological impairment. Under conditions of high airflow, velopharyngeal trills may occur, presumably involving intermittent closure between the uvula and the back wall of the pharynx.

The extIPA conventions suggest two different ways of transcribing velopharyngeal frication. Where it occurs simultaneously with another, usually oral, sound, it is viewed as a secondary articulation and a diacritic [≈] is superimposed on the appropriate symbol. Velopharyngeal frication accompanying a voiceless alveolar frica-

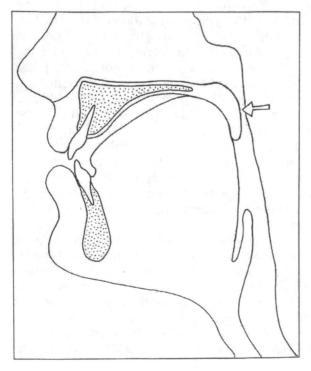

FIG. 6.5. A diagrammatic view of the vocal organs showing the source of velopharyngeal frication when produced with a simultaneous velar articulation.

tive would thus be transcribed as [s̃]. Where velopharyngeal frication occurs in isolation, as a primary articulation, it is transcribed as [fŋ].Velopharyngeal trills are so rare that there is no accepted symbol for them.

Practice 6.3 should help to consolidate the new places of articulation, although velopharyngeal consonants are excluded from the practice activities, on the basis that many speakers with normal vocal tracts find them difficult to produce.

Practice 6.3: New Places of Articulation

Practice making a series of sounds using the newly introduced places of articulation. Produce each sound both in isolation and between vowels, using a mirror to confirm the articulatory placements and noting the auditory qualities.

1. Retroflex sounds. See Practice 6.1.
2. Pharyngeal sounds. See Practice 6.2.
3. Dentolabial sounds. Most people will have to protrude the jaw a little in order to bring the lower teeth into contact with the upper lip. Compare labiodental and dentolabial fricatives and notice that although the articulatory movements are markedly different, they sound quite similar. Try making dentolabial plosives and nasal stops. Don't worry if you find it difficult to produce these without a bit of air leakage and/or audible frication, as many people find it difficult to achieve complete closure because of irregular or widely spaced teeth.
4. Labioalveolar fricatives. Pull your lower lip back toward your alveolar ridge and try making voiced and voiceless fricatives. Note that these, too, sound somewhat similar to labiodental fricatives.
5. Bidental fricatives. Produce bidental fricatives by simply biting the teeth together, keeping the tongue low within the oral cavity and the lips well apart, and push air between the teeth so that you get a fricative sound. Try this with and without voicing.
6. Linguolabial sounds. All you need to do to form a linguolabial articulation is place the tip of the tongue against the upper lip. Try producing the following linguolabial sounds between vowels: (a) a voiceless linguolabial plosive; (b) a voiced linguolabial nasal stop; (c) a voiceless linguolabial fricative; and (d) a voiced linguolabial lateral approximant. Compare the auditory quality of these sounds with their alveolar counterparts.
7. Interdental sounds. Produce a voiceless dental fricative, making sure that the tip/blade articulates with the back surface of the upper teeth. Then make an interdental fricative by pushing the tongue forward, so that the tip of the tongue protrudes between the upper and lower teeth. Try making a voiced fricative, a nasal stop, and plosives at the same place of articulation.
   Produce a sequence of voiceless fricatives as follows, noting how the quality of the friction changes with place of articulation:
   bilabial; labiodental; dentolabial; linguolabial; interdental; dental; bidental; alveolar; postalveolar; retroflex; palatal; velar; uvular; pharyngeal.

MORE MANNERS OF ARTICULATION

Percussive Sounds

One percussive sound was introduced in chapter 4, but we need to look more broadly at percussive articulations as a class. These sounds are, as the name implies, produced by the impact of one articulator striking another. The commonest percussive sounds are taps and flaps, so these are discussed first. Taps have already been described in chapter 4, and flaps are somewhat similar, except that the tongue tip starts its trajectory toward the alveolar ridge from a retroflex position. As the tongue rapidly uncurls, the tip strikes the roof of the mouth just behind the alveolar ridge. The auditory effect of a flap is very similar to that of a tap, except that the "dark" coloring associated with a retroflex tongue position is usually detectable at the onset of the sound. The IPA symbol for flaps, [ɽ], highlights the retroflex starting point for flap production by incorporating the characteristic retroflex curve below the line. The r-like remainder of the symbol reflects the fact that in English, at least, flaps usually represent the /r/ phoneme.

Two additional, and much rarer, percussive articulations are represented by symbols in the extIPA chart. Their exclusion from the main IPA chart is an indication that they do not seem to occur as typical forms of adult speech in any part of the world, although they may have some communicative function. The symbol, [ʘ̬], is used to transcribe a bilabial percussive sound, which might be described in lay terms as lip-smacking. This is simply a sound produced by the percussive contact between tense upper and lower lips. The final percussive sound to be considered here is the bidental percussive [ʭ], which results from the upper and lower teeth striking each other to produce an audible sound. This is not generally viewed as a normal feature of speech, and probably occurs most often as an intrusive, involuntary sound in speakers who have poor control of jaw movements or who have poorly fitting dentures.

MORE AIRSTREAM MECHANISMS

As indicated in chapter 4, most speech sounds involve an egressive pulmonic airstream, but many languages in the world also include sounds that use other mechanisms to initiate movement of air through the vocal tract. These nonpulmonic airstream mechanisms, and the sounds that utilize them, are described in the following.

Glottalic Airstream Mechanism

The glottalic airstream mechanism may be used to initiate either ingressive or egressive airflow through the vocal tract. In either case, a column of air is trapped between closed (or nearly closed) vocal folds and an articulatory closure further up the vocal tract. The whole larynx then moves vertically, acting somewhat like a piston, so that the column of air is either compressed or rarefied. Release of the articulatory closure then allows rapid movement of air either in or out, so as to equalize the air pressure within the vocal tract and in the atmosphere. The following descriptions of egressive and ingressive glottalic airstreams should make this clearer.

Sounds Made on a Glottalic Egressive Airstream: Ejectives.   In ejective stops, the vocal folds are brought together to block any airflow through the glottis, and articulatory activity of the tongue or lips produces a simultaneous complete closure of the vocal tract at some point along its length. The velum is raised to prevent air from passing into the nasal cavity. The larynx is then pulled upward by the laryngeal elevator muscles, thus contracting the vocal tract and compressing the enclosed air column. When the articulatory closure is released, the compressed air escapes from the vocal tract with a sharply audible burst of sound. This sequence of events is shown schematically in Fig. 6.6.

Ejective fricatives and affricates may also occur, if the articulatory closure is not quite complete or if it is released gradually. Ejectives are found in languages from a wide variety of geographical locations, including North Central and South America, Africa, the Caucasian area, and parts of Asia, and examples of language data can be found in Laver (1994), Ladefoged and Maddieson (1996), and in the Handbook of the IPA (1999). Ejectives are transcribed by adding an apostrophe to the symbol for the equivalent pulmonic sound. For example, the symbol for a velar ejective stop is [k'], whereas that for an alveolar ejective fricative is [s'].

Sounds Made on a Glottalic Ingressive Airstream: Implosives.   Implosive stops start with a column of air being trapped between the vocal folds and an articulatory closure in just the same way as ejective stops. The larynx is then pulled down, however, using the laryngeal depressor muscles, so that the column containing the trapped air is expanded. The air is thus rarefied, so that when the articulatory closure is released, air rushes into the vocal tract until atmospheric pressure within the vocal tract is restored. This is shown in Fig. 6.7. Voiceless implosives, made with the glottis completely closed as previously described, are not, in fact, at all common. Much more common are voiced implosives. These are produced by bringing the vocal folds together, but leaving them sufficiently relaxed that as the larynx is lowered against the pulmonic air pressure, they vi-

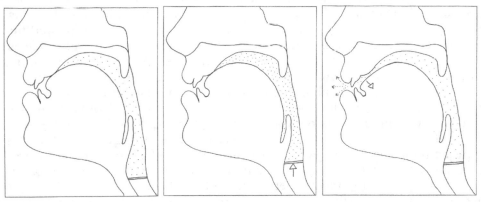

1. A column of air is trapped between the closed glottis and an articulatory closure (shown here as alveolar).

2. The larynx moved upward, compressing the trapped air.

3. Air bursts out at high pressure as the articulatory closure is released.

FIG. 6.6.   A diagrammatic representation of the sequence of events involved in production of a voiceless alveolar ejective stop.

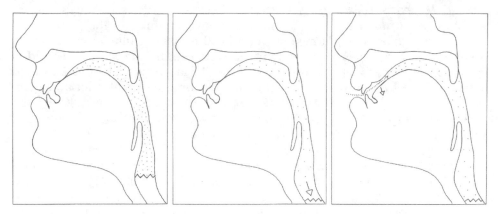

1. A column of air is trapped between the closed, vibrating vocal folds and an articulatory closure (shown here as alveolar).

2. The larynx is lowered, so that the trapped air becomes rarefied.

3. As the articulatory closure is released, air rushes into the oral cavity to restore atmospheric air pressure.

FIG. 6.7. A diagrammatic representation of the sequence of events involved in production of a voiced alveolar implosive stop.

brate, producing voicing. The pulmonic air that enters the vocal tract during the phase of double closure is not sufficient to overcome the rarefaction caused by lowering the larynx, so air still implodes into the vocal tract when the articulatory closure is released. Voiced implosives are transcribed by using the symbol for the equivalent pulmonic plosive with a right-hand curl added to the top corner of the symbol, making [ɓ], [ɗ], [ɠ], and so on.

Voiced implosives of this kind occur in many languages, including Sindhi, and may contrast with voiced plosives produced on a pulmonic airstream (Ladefoged & Maddieson, 1996). Wells (1982, p. 489) commented on the occasional use of the bilabial implosive [ɓ] as a realization of word-initial /b/ in some parts of North America. Voiced implosives may also occur in some speakers as disordered realizations of voiced pulmonic plosives. This may happen, for example, in deaf speakers who are striving, with little auditory feedback, to maintain a clear distinction between voiced and voiceless plosives, and hence "over-voice" the voiced plosives. A little experimentation with one's own performance makes it easy to see how this pattern might develop. Any attempt to sustain voicing while maintaining a stop closure higher up the vocal tract is likely to be short-lived, because the vocal fold vibration involved in voicing depends on a pressure gradient. In other words, the vocal folds will only vibrate if pressure is higher below the larynx. If air cannot escape from the vocal tract because of an articulatory closure, then the air pressure above the larynx rises rapidly, until it is very difficult to maintain voicing. One strategy for temporarily overcoming this difficulty is to lower the larynx in opposition to the pulmonic airstream, thus reducing the air pressure above the larynx. This is, in fact, what most people will do unconsciously if asked to prolong a voiced stop without releasing it, and can be observed in oneself by either looking in a mirror or feeling the position of the laryngeal cartilage while doing this maneuver.

Practice 6.4: Glottalic Airstream

1. Ejectives. Hold your breath, keeping a slightly tense vocal tract, and try making a very sharp "t" sound. Notice that as long as you are continuing to hold your breath during production, no pulmonic airstream will be involved in the sound production, and the sound produced will almost certainly be a voiceless alveolar ejective [t']. If so, you should be able to notice the larynx moving upward momentarily, either by using a mirror or by placing your fingers lightly on your larynx. Try producing ejectives at some other places of articulation, including bilabial [p'], palatal [c'], and velar [k'] ejectives. If you try producing these between vowels, you may notice that there is a barely perceptible break between the ejective and the following vowel, as the glottal closure is released to allow continuation of the pulmonic egressive airstream.

2. Voiced implosives. Make the articulatory closure for a bilabial stop and try to produce voicing while maintaining the complete closure. You will find that it is not possible to maintain voicing for very long, but as you do so the larynx will move downward. This is the first phase of implosive production. Repeat the exercise, but this time release the stop closure as you are voicing. Air should implode into the oral cavity, and you should notice that the sound has a "darker" quality than the familiar egressive bilabial plosive. This is a voiced bilabial implosive [ɓ]. Repeat this with some other places of articulation to produce alveolar [ɗ], velar [ɠ], and uvular [ɗ] implosives. Practice producing these before, after, and between vowels.

Velaric Airstream Mechanism

This is somewhat similar to the glottalic airstream, in that a column of air is trapped within the vocal tract and then expanded so that the trapped air is rarefied before the outermost articulatory closure is released. In this case, however, the innermost closure is produced by the back of the tongue articulating with the velum. A second, simultaneous, articulatory closure is made further forward in the mouth. The body of the tongue is then pulled back and down to expand the cavity within which the air is trapped. The consequent reduction in air pressure within the oral cavity causes an ingressive rush of air as soon as the outermost articulation is released. Sounds produced in this way are described as clicks and the sequence of events involved in production of an alveolar click is shown in Fig. 6.8.

Clicks are common in languages of Southern Africa and also occur in some North American languages. In English and other European and Western cultures, clicks often fulfill a paralinguistic function. For example, the voiceless labial click, produced with lip protrusion, is very widely used in some cultures to represent the noise of kissing. Alveolar or dental clicks often indicate disapproval or exasperation, and are often shown in written form as "tut tut." A traditional way of encouraging horses to move on is to

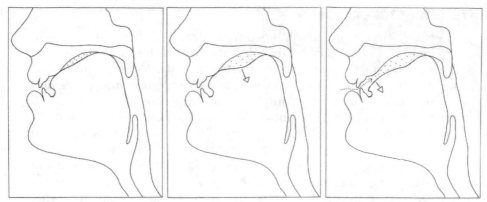

1. Air is trapped between a complete velar closure and a more anterior articulatory closure (shown here as alveolar).

2. Both closures are maintained while the body of the tongue pulls downward, so that the trapped air is rarefied.

3. As the anterior articulatory closure is released, air rushes into the oral cavity to restore atmospheric air pressure.

FIG. 6.8. A diagrammatic representation of the sequence of events involved in production of an alveolar click.

use an encouraging alveolar lateral click, and the sound of the horses hooves is sometimes imitated by using a sharply resonant retroflex or postalveolar click, using secondary adjustments of lip position to vary the apparent pitch.

An important feature of clicks is that the whole process of click production takes place in the oral cavity, in front of a complete closure at a velar place of articulation. This means that clicks may occur simultaneously with a pulmonic airstream below and behind the velum. The velum itself may either be raised, so that air is unable to pass through the nasal cavity, or lowered, so as to allow nasal airflow. Assume, for the moment, that there is velic closure preventing nasal airflow. Laver (1994, pp. 177–178) pointed out that where clicks occur in connected speech, it is likely that the egressive pulmonic airstream will continue so that air pressure will build up below the velar closure in just the same way as for pulmonic velar plosives. This may occur with or without voicing, and Laver therefore suggested that clicks most often occur in running speech as double articulations, represented as [k͡ʘ], [g͡ʘ], and so on. The auditory perceptual difference between clicks occurring in isolation and double click + velar plosive articulations is, however, subtle enough that we probably do not need to be too concerned about it here.

A further, and perhaps more easily identified, possibility for simultaneous pulmonic and velaric airstreams arises if there is no velic closure and nasal airflow can continue. It is perfectly possible to produce any click while simultaneously producing a velar nasal stop. Clicks produced with this type of nasal component are described as nasal clicks, and may be either voiced or voiceless. Such sounds can be transcribed in such a way as to highlight the double mechanism of production by linking a velar nasal symbol with the click symbol, as in [ŋ͡ʘ], [ŋ͡!], and so on.

Practice 6.5: Velaric Airstream

Make a bilabial click [ʘ] in isolation, aiming for the sound that is often used to represent a kiss. Feel how the back of the tongue raises towards the velum in preparation for production of this click. Now try putting this in a fluent sequence between vowels. Note that you do not need to use as much protrusion of the lips as is often used for the "kiss" variant of this click. Try varying the place of articulation, so that you produce clicks at dental [ǀ], alveolar [!], and palatoalveolar (a bit further back than postalveolar) [ǂ] places of articulation. For the lateral alveolar click [ǁ] you need to make an alveolar closure and then release the closure by lowering the sides of the tongue. Try a series of vowel-click-vowel-click sequences: [aʘaǃ],[ɛǂɛʘ], [ɔǁɔǀ], and so on.

Now try the same sequence of exercises but create the clicks simultaneously with [ŋ], so that you are using simultaneous pulmonic egressive and velaric airstreams.

FILLING IN THE GAPS

We have now covered all the main categories of place and manner of articulation, but have not made specific reference to every sound represented on the IPA chart. It may be useful for you now to look at the chart and identify all the symbols for sounds that have not been mentioned so far. Full descriptions and discussion of all of these sounds can be found in texts such as Laver (1994) and Ladefoged and Maddieson (1996), and it is probably not necessary to consider each one in detail. Given a reasonable understanding of the general principles of phonetics given earlier, it should be possible to work out how all of the less familiar sounds are produced by looking at their placement on the chart. Practice 6.6 gives some guidance about how to extend phonetic performance skills to less familiar sounds.

CONCLUSION

Apart from one or two sounds involving double articulation, which are described in chapter 7, you should now be able to interpret all the symbols included in the main IPA chart, as well as many of those from the extIPA chart, and have some idea of what they sound like and how they are produced. Both charts offer conventions for transcribing additional detail about segment production through the use of diacritics to modify symbols. Some of these diacritics are introduced in the following chapter, whereas others are concerned with details of production that are beyond the scope of this book.

Practice 6.6: Filling in Some Gaps

The following activities are intended to show how you can begin to generalize what you already know to unfamiliar sounds.

1. Produce a sequence of voiceless fricatives at the full range of places of articulation, as you did at the end of Practice 6.3. Now produce each one with voicing, to make the voiced counterparts, noting any unfamiliar symbols from the IPA chart. You may be aware that the production of the voiced fricatives is slightly more effortful. Notice whether or not you bring the articulators slightly closer together for the voiced fricatives. Production of audible frication in association with voicing typically requires either a slightly greater degree of articulatory constriction or a slightly greater respiratory effort than is needed when the vocal folds are open.

2. Take other manners of articulation and practice making the same class of sound at different places of articulation. For example, you could produce a full set of nasal stops, or a full set of approximants.

3. Take each place of articulation and work through all the possible manners of articulation as shown on the IPA chart. Speakers of English may find it easiest to start with alveolars, as English includes a wide range of alveolar sounds and many will be familiar. Concentrate your attention on the articulatory differences and similarities between sounds. For example, note that the degree of stricture is similar for the plosives and nasal stops, but that the tongue moves away from the alveolar ridge for the fricatives. Make a voiced alveolar fricative and gradually reduce the amount of constriction until the sound becomes smooth (i.e., it becomes an approximant). Do the same at other places of articulation. Note that production of sounds at some places of articulation may be facilitated by saying them between appropriate vowels. For example, palatal sounds are easiest to produce between close front vowels. If you are not familiar with palatal plosives or nasals, for instance, then try saying them first between [i] vowels. During the vowel, the front of the tongue is already raised toward the hard palate, so it only needs to be raised a little more, without moving the body of the tongue forward or backward, to create the correct articulatory closure. Practice saying them like this a few times, until you are confident about how it feels, and then try varying the vowel, but notice that there may still be a clearly audible [j] off-glide. A similar manipulation of the vowel context may be helpful when practicing uvular and pharyngeal sounds, but in this case use the open back vowel [ɑ] so the tongue is already pulled back within the oral cavity. Given that many people initially lack confidence in differentiating between palatal, velar, and uvular sounds, it may be useful to try these first in sequences as follows: [ici]; [aka]; [ɑqɑ]; [iɲi]; [aŋa]· [ɑɴɑ]; and so on. The vowel contexts should help guide you to the correct tongue placement.

EXERCISES

These questions draw on information both from this chapter and from chapter 4. You may also need to refer to the IPA and extIPA charts.

1. For each place of articulation, state the active articulator and the passive articulator.

   (a) Labiodental (b) Pharyngeal (c) Linguolabial (d) Dentolabial (e) Retroflex (f) Labioalveolar (g) Bidental.

2. Which of the following statements (a–c) is true during production of the sounds listed:

   (a) the larynx must move up; (b) the larynx must move down; or (c) the larynx is not involved?

   a. [ɓ]
   b. [t']
   c. [ǂ]
   d. [ɗ]
   e. [ʘ]
   f. [c']

3. Write down the symbol for each of the following sounds:
   a. a voiced linguolabial lateral approximant
   b. a voiceless retroflex fricative
   c. a voiced bilabial trill
   d. a voiceless pharyngeal fricative
   e. a voiced labiodental plosive (or oral stop)
   f. a voiced dental nasal (or nasal stop)
   g. a voiced uvular fricative
   h. a voiced retroflex flap

4. Write a full phonetic label for each of the following sounds:
   a. [ɦ]
   b. [ɗ]
   c. [ʘ]
   d. [ɢ]
   e. [n̪]
   f. [c']
   g. [β]
   h. [ɲ]

7 Further Exploration of Speech Complexity

The previous chapters have taken a somewhat simplistic approach to phonetic performance and analysis, focusing on what we might think of as the "core" characteristics of each sound in isolation. As we stressed at the start, this is a rather artificial, if convenient, way of thinking about speech. When we look at real connected speech, it rapidly becomes clear that it is not always easy to define clear-cut boundaries between segments and that the precise pattern of production of the "same" segment (i.e., something that can be represented by one label and symbol) may actually vary quite significantly. This subtle variation may be caused by a range of factors, including differences between speakers and the influence of adjacent segments. This chapter introduces some additional features of speech production that may be useful for anyone trying to record and understand the way in which phonetic segments vary, or how different parts of the speech production process are coordinated. This leads in to a brief discussion about some alternative approaches to phonetic analysis, which may be prompted by an interest in such detail. The richness and variety to be found in speech performance is such that we cannot hope to provide a comprehensive coverage, but we hope that the examples selected here will give a flavor of the intricacies that can be revealed by careful phonetic analysis.

FEATURES OF PLOSIVE PRODUCTION

Plosives have so far been treated in a fairly simplistic manner, with a simple binary distinction between voiced and voiceless plosives. A closer examination of plosive production shows a complex range of possibilities for the integration of articulatory closure with voicing and other aspects of speech production. This section describes some of the details of plosive performance, which illustrate very clearly the importance of coordination of the timing of different aspects of speech performance and the influence of adjacent segments on the detail of plosive production. The diagrams here draw heavily on Abercrombie's representations of the ways in which the phases of stop closure relate to voicing features (Abercrombie, 1967). Abercrombie described three phases of stop closure: the closing phase, during which the articulators are moving toward each other; the closed phase, during which the articulators form a stricture of complete closure and air is unable to pass between them; and the opening phase, during which the articulators move away from each other. These phases are shown schematically at the top of Fig. 7.1.

Voicing and Aspiration in Plosives

The most straightforward interpretation of the terms voiced and voiceless would be to assume that in voiced plosives the vocal fold vibration would continue through all phases of stop production, whereas in voiceless plosives, vocal fold vibration would cease during the closed phase and resume at the point of release of articulatory closure. In fact, in many lan-

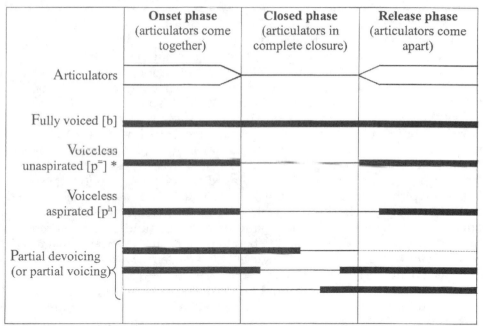

*This may also be described as a devoiced [b̥]

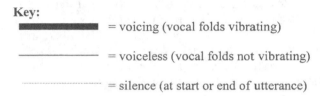

FIG. 7.1.   A diagrammatic representation of the coordination of voicing and articulation in plosive production.

guages the phonological distinction between so-called voiced and voiceless plosive phonemes is signaled by rather more complex timing relationships between voicing and articulation.

One phonetic feature that is often associated with voiceless plosive production, and that is certainly an important perceptual cue for voiceless plosives in English, is aspiration. Aspiration is a feature of coordination between a plosive and a following voiced segment, where there is an audible delay in the onset of voicing after the release of the stop closure. For aspiration to be clearly audible the delay in onset of voicing, commonly known as voice onset time or VOT, must be longer than about one fortieth of a second (see chap. 8 for more on this). It also appears likely that for any given VOT, higher levels of respiratory effort (and hence airflow) will be associated with more audible aspiration. Figure 7.1 is a schematic representation of various patterns of coordination between articulatory closure and vocal fold vibration in the production of plosives. When a fully voiced plosive is produced between voiced segments such as vowels, vocal fold vibration will continue throughout the vocal fold closure. From this, there is a continuum of possibilities through partial voicing, to strongly aspirated plosives.

The use of different patterns of coordination between voicing and articulatory closure to signal linguistic contrasts between "voiced" and "voiceless" does show considerable variation between languages, and may depend on the phonetic context. In many varieties of English, for example, word-initial voiceless plosives are typically realized with clearly audible aspiration, but when they occur as part of a word-initial cluster (/sp-/, /st-/, or /sk-/) they are usually voiceless but unaspirated. "Voiced" plosives in English may, in reality, have little or no voicing, but have a short enough voice onset time that there is no audible aspiration. This means that the voiceless plosives in /s + plosive/ clusters may, in fact, be identical to the so-called "voiced" plosives in other contexts. In French and some other Romance languages, by contrast, "voiced" plosives typically have more voicing than in English, and voiceless plosives may be recognized as such with less aspiration and a shorter voice onset time. Acquisition of language-appropriate patterns of voicing and aspiration requires very precise control of coordination between articulatory movement and vocal fold activity, and children who are developing language within a bilingual setting face particularly interesting challenges (Yavas, 2002).

The need for precise coordination of voicing with articulation is not, of course, confined to plosives, and varying voicing patterns are found in other classes of sound. Fricatives, too, are very prone to intermediate states of voicing, and partial devoicing of "voiced" fricatives is a common finding in English. As with voiced plosives, devoicing is most likely when the fricative is adjacent either to silence or to a voiceless segment, and it can be seen as a partial phonetic accommodation to the voiceless environment. The word-initial fricatives in "van" or "zoo" and the word final fricatives in "save" or "freeze" are therefore more likely to be devoiced than the word-medial fricatives in "heavy" or "fizzy," assuming that these words are produced in isolation.

Affricated Release of Plosives

The preceding discussion of plosives refers to plosives in which the release of the stop closure involves a very rapid opening of the articulators so that there

---

Practice 7.1: Aspiration and Voicing of Plosives

Observe your own production of bilabial plosives in the utterances
"a pear" and "a bear," pronounced fairly emphatically. Place your hand
close to your mouth and note whether there is any difference in the burst
of air released when the words initial plosives are released. Compare
these with the bilabial plosive in "a spare." Is this more like the /p/ in
"pear" or the /b/ in "bear?"

Try producing different degrees of aspiration and voicing of plosives between vowels, as follows:

[apʰa]: Pause momentarily so that there is complete silence between the
vowels, and release the stop closure with a clear burst of air

[ap˭a]: Two strategies may help you to produce unaspirated voiceless
plosives. One is to pause momentarily as before (this will ensure a break
in voicing) and then release the stop so that is sounds more like a /b/. Another approach is to start by saying [aspa]. This will often automatically
result in an unaspirated plosive, and you can then try to repeat the same
type of plosive without the fricative.

[aba]: To ensure full voicing, produce the sequence [aba] fairly emphatically, aiming to maintain continuous voicing throughout the sequence.

Try manipulating aspiration and voicing with alveolar and velar plosives.

---

is a very sudden transition from complete closure to a relatively unconstricted
vocal tract. If, instead, the articulators come apart more slowly, there may be a
relatively long phase during which the vocal tract is sufficiently constricted for
audible friction to be heard. In other words, the plosive is followed by a brief
fricative at the same place of articulation. This is described as affrication of
the stop and is shown diagrammatically in Fig. 7.2. Affricated stops, which
may also be termed affricates, may be transcribed in either of two ways. One
option is to use the symbol for the homorganic (i.e., produced at the same
place of articulation) fricative as a superscript following the plosive symbol,
as in [tˢ], [kˣ], and so on. An alternative is to write both symbols at full size,
with a linking diacritic, as in [t͡s], [k͡x], and so on. A decision about which is
most appropriate probably depends on a judgment about the relative perceptual weighting of the fricative component.

   It is possible to affricate oral stops at any place of articulation, but the most
familiar affricates for speakers of English are probably the postalveolar (or
palatoalveolar) affricates, [t͡ʃ] and [d͡ʒ] (see page 34). These are the sounds
that are usually represented in the spelling by "ch-" or "-tch," as in "chip" [t͡ʃɪp]
or "witch" [wɪt͡ʃ], and by "j-," "g-," "ge," or "dge," as in "jam" [d͡ʒam], "gentle"
[d͡ʒɛntl̩], or "badge" [bad͡ʒ]. In English, postalveolar affricates form part of the
phonology of the language, and there is a phonemic contrast between these
and both the postalveolar fricatives and the alveolar plosives. Similar situations are seen in a wide range of other languages (see Laver, 1994, pp.
364–365 for examples), and postalveolar affricates seem to be particularly
common. Affrication of plosives purely as a phonetic feature of realization is
also quite common, either as an accent-related feature or as an individual id-
iosyncrasy. For example, in some urban accents of British English, notably
Birmingham and the Cockney accent of London, voiceless alveolar plosives

are quite commonly affricated, and this may be especially marked in the context of following close vowels. In Cockney the word "tea" might thus be realized as [t͡səi] (Wells, 1982, p. 323). Given that avoidance of affrication on stop release requires a very rapid opening movement of the articulators, it should not be surprising that affricated stops quite often occur in speakers with motor speech disorders, where speed and coordination of articulatory movement is impaired and they may be unable to produce the rapid articulatory movement needed for a "clean" plosive release.

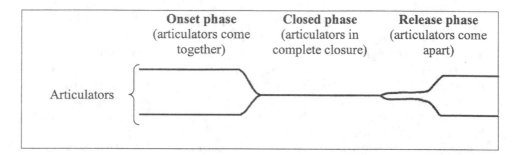

FIG. 7.2. A diagrammatic representation of affricated release of a plosive.

Practice 7.2: Affricated Release of Plosives

Try producing plosives with affricated release at different places of articulation. Think of releasing the plosive in slow motion, so that there is clear frication as the articulators come apart.
Practice voiced and voiceless affricated stops before vowels, for example, [tˢi]; [dᶻi]; [kˣa]; [gˠa];
[pᶲɔ]; [bᵝɔ]; and so on.

Nasal Release of Plosives

Nasal release of plosives is an option that may occur in a phonetic sequence where a plosive (i.e., an oral stop) is followed by a homorganic nasal stop. In such sequences, because the oral stop and the nasal stop share exactly the same articulatory closure, the air pressure that builds up in the oral cavity during the oral stop can be released through the nose at the onset of the nasal stop simply by lowering the velum. Nasal release of plosives in this type of context is a common feature in English, and may occur within words or across word-boundaries. Nasal release in some contexts is, in fact, so common in English that it is often taken as implicit in the transcription of a sequence of an oral stop followed by a homorganic nasal stop. If it is important to be explicit in the transcription, then the superscript [ⁿ] is used after the nasal stop. Thus, the usual realization of the word "sadness" in many accents of English would be [sadⁿəs]. Other examples that might occur in connected speech are:

[sʌdⁿn̩]   "sudden" (where the nasal stop is syllabic)

[bʌtⁿn̩]   "button" (where the nasal stop is syllabic)
[tɒpⁿmɑst]   "top-mast"
[bapⁿman]   "Batman" (where the /t/ assimilates to a bilabial place of
               articulation)
[səbⁿmɪt]   "submit"
[wagⁿŋwil]   "wagon wheel" (where the nasal is syllabic and assimi-
               lates to a velar place of articulation)

In all of these contexts it is, of course, possible to release the plosive concerned orally before the stop closure is formed again for the nasal stop. This
can be indicated in the transcription by using a schwa symbol as a superscript, as in [sʌdᵊn]. Nasal release (also called nasal plosion) is shown diagrammatically in Fig. 7.3, together with lateral release (see next).

Lateral Release of Plosives

Where a plosive is followed by a lateral segment at the same place of articulation, the plosive may be released simply by lowering the sides of the tongue,
while maintaining contact in the center of the oral cavity. The air that has been
trapped within the oral cavity thus escapes laterally. This is known as lateral

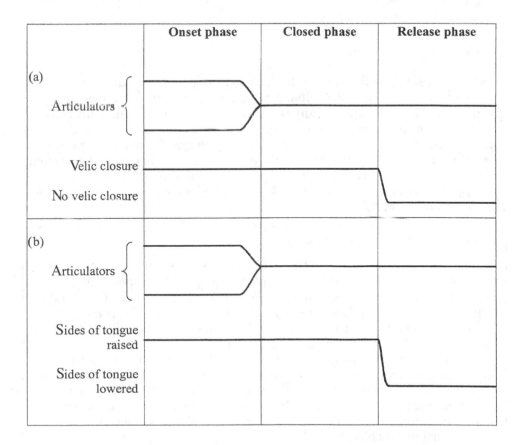

FIG. 7.3.   A diagrammatic representation of (a) nasal, and (b) lateral release of a plosive.

Practice 7.3: Nasal Release of Plosives

Try producing the examples given on page 91, first with oral release of the plosives and then with nasal release. For oral release, you will need to release the relevant plosive, allowing air to escape through the mouth, before you produce the nasal stop. For nasal release, hold the articulatory closure throughout the sequence and allow air to escape through the nose. You may be aware of some sensation associated with the velic opening as nasal release occurs.

Decide whether oral release or nasal release feels and sounds more natural to you in these contexts.

---

release or lateral plosion, and is represented in transcription by use of a superscript [ˡ] after the symbol for the plosive. Lateral release may be heard in many accents of English when alveolar plosives are followed by an alveolar lateral approximant, even across word boundaries. Examples include:

[mɪdˡl̩]	"middle" (where there is a syllabic lateral)
[batˡl̩]	"battle" (where there is a syllabic lateral)
[atˡləs]	"atlas"
[fɹɛndˡli]	"friendly"
[fatˡleɪdi]	"fat lady"
[bɛdˡlɪnɪn]	"bed linen"

As with nasal release, lateral release is an option rather than a necessity, although for many accents of English it can generally be assumed to occur in the given contexts unless specifically indicated otherwise. The alternative is for the tongue contact to be completely released before the lateral articulation is formed. This is indicated in transcription by using a schwa as a superscript. If, in the first example, the tongue tip/blade loses contact with the alveolar ridge completely before the lateral, this would therefore be transcribed as [mɪdᵊl]. This complete release of the stop may be described as central plosion (Laver, 1994, p. 361).

Practice 7.4: Lateral Release of Plosives

Try saying the words given in the foregoing examples, first with lateral release and then with complete or central release. When using lateral release, be aware of the continuing contact between the center of the tongue and the alveolar ridge. When using central release, concentrate on making sure that there is complete release of the alveolar articulation prior to making contact for the lateral approximant.

Try to decide whether or not you would usually use lateral release in these contexts, and whether lateral or central release sounds most natural to you. This will vary from speaker to speaker and from accent to accent.

Try the same process with the following utterance, where the plosives that are highlighted in the orthographic form could all be produced with either central or lateral release.

"a ba**d** lot of co**d** liver oil ma**de** Larry's li**tt**le frien**d** Lucy ill"

Unreleased and Overlapping Plosives

The patterns of plosive release described previously have all involved audible plosion of some sort, but it is not uncommon for plosives to be unreleased, or to be released with no audible escape of air. This can be indicated in a transcription by the use of the diacritic [˺] following the plosive symbol. If, for example the alveolar plosive at the end of the utterance "help" is unreleased, with the lip closure being maintained after the end of the utterance, it can thus be transcribed as [hɛlp˺]. This lack of audible plosive release in utterance-final position is not uncommon in English and is sometimes associated with supplementary glottal closure (see following section on double articulation). Another context in which many speakers of English produce no audible plosive release is where there are two adjacent plosives in a sequence of speech. In this situation, the articulatory closure for the second plosive in the sequence may be created before the articulatory closure of the first plosive is released, so that there is no audible release of the first plosive. This overlapping of the articulatory closures is shown schematically in Fig. 7.4, and is typical of many varieties of English. This tendency to overlap the closure phases of adjacent plosives is not, however,

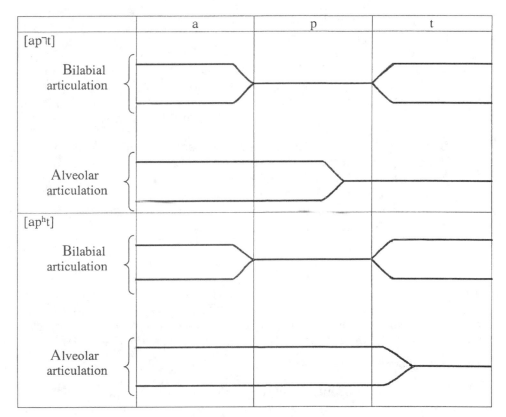

FIG. 7.4. A diagrammatic representation of alternative patterns of coordination of plosive articulation in the phonetic sequence [apt]: (a) with overlapping articulatory closure, and (b) with release of the first stop before articulatory closure of the second.

universal. In French, for example, speakers typically maintain a clear separation of adjacent plosives, releasing the first articulatory closure before the second is created. Although the auditory difference between overlapping and separate release of adjacent plosives is quite subtle, it may nonetheless be one of the cues that differentiates between native and non-native speakers of English. Failure to use language-appropriate patterns of plosive release may also be associated with some types of speech disorder.

Practice 7.5: Incomplete or Inaudible Release of Plosives

1. Say the phrase "Call a cab," first of all with clear audible release of the final bilabial plosive, and then keeping the lips closed for a brief period after you finish speaking so that there is no audible release. Which feels most like your normal pattern of speech? Do you think a lack of audible release has a significant effect on intelligibility? Now think about the following utterances, which all have a word-final plosive:

    She's still asleep
    She's in her crib
    She's not bad
    Did you feed the cat?
    He's not back
    Where's my bag?

    Try saying each of these in a fairly casual style of speech. Do you produce audible release of the final consonant in all/some/none of these? Is there any tendency for voicing or place of articulation to determine whether or not the plosive is audibly released?

2. Say the word "napkin," focusing on the word-medial sequence of a bilabial plosive followed by a velar plosive. Notice whether or not you release the bilabial articulation before the back of the tongue makes contact with the velum. Try producing the word with and without audible release between the two plosives, and think about which sounds and feels more natural to you.

DOUBLE AND SECONDARY ARTICULATION

In most consonant sounds, an adequate description of place of articulation is achieved by identifying the single point of greatest constriction. It is not, however, uncommon for a sound to be characterized by the fact that its production involves a constriction at more than one point along the vocal tract.

Double Articulations

A double articulation occurs when there are simultaneous constrictions of equivalent degrees of stricture at two places of articulation. Double articulations may involve any degree of stricture, and the languages of the world provide a range of double articulations involving complete closure, close approximation, and open approximation.

Double Articulations Involving a Stricture of Open Approximation.   Most speakers of English will be familiar with at least one double articulation. The approximant [w], as in the typical production of "water" or "wind," is typically a double articulation, involving simultaneous constrictions at the lips and in the velar region. It is thus described as a labial velar approximant. Phonetically naïve speakers of English sometimes find this surprising, as most people are much more aware of the visible labial articulation than they are of the velar component. Most people can, however, feel an upward and backward movement of the tongue and a loss of contact between the tip of the tongue and the lower teeth as they move from a "rest" position to the prolonged [w]. The other double approximant articulation for which the IPA provides a specific symbol is the labial palatal approximant [ɥ], produced as [j] + constriction at the lips. Young children acquiring English may use this sound as a realization of /w/, because of a tendency to use a more fronted tongue position than adults.

Double Articulations Involving a Stricture of Close Approximation.   Some speakers of English will have a phonological contrast (i.e., a contrast that signals a difference in meaning) between the double approximant [w] mentioned earlier and the word initial consonant that is represented in the spelling as "wh." Such speakers are likely to use the labial velar approximant described earlier in the word "witch," but will use a voiceless labial velar fricative in words such as "which." The fricative is transcribed as [ʍ]. Note that the double articulations mentioned so far are sufficiently widespread across the languages of the world to merit distinct symbols. The IPA chart includes a separate symbol for a sound described as a voiceless postalveolar velar fricative [ɧ] (that is, simultaneous [ʃ] + [x]). Some reports suggest that this occurs in some varieties of Swedish (Abercrombie, 1967), but this has been questioned (Ladefoged & Maddieson, 1996).

Double Articulations Involving Complete Closure.   Double articulations involving complete closure are fairly common. Some languages exploit double articulations within their phonological systems. This is true for some of the languages of West Africa, such as Igbo, Yoruba, and Idoma, where labial velar plosives contrast with single velar and labial plosives.

Yoruba: [k͡pe] "to call" [ke] "to cry" (Bamgbose, 1969, cited in
             Laver, 1994, p. 314)
Idoma: [ak͡pa] "bridge" [apa] "lizard" [aka] "wheel" (Ladefoged,
             1971, p. 59)

Double nasal stop articulations are less often exploited in signaling phonological contrast, possibly because the nasality masks the subtle auditory perceptual cues that are involved in the distinctions just illustrated. Laver (1994) did, however, cite a report of a labial velar nasal stop and an alveolar velar nasal stop occurring in the minority Provençal language. In other languages, such as English, where double stop articulations do not play a phonological role, they may occur as phonetic variants or as features of connected speech. For example, voiceless oral stops, when in utterance-final or word-final position, are often produced with a simultaneous glottal stop. The words "bap," "bat," or "back" may thus be realized as [bap͡ʔ], [bat͡ʔ] and [bak͡ʔ], respectively. Double articulation as a connected speech feature may be seen as an extreme version of the type of overlapping of adjacent stop closures discussed in the previous section. It is not always easy to identify double stop articulations purely on the basis of auditory perceptual cues, but instrumental techniques for tracking articulatory movement, such as electropalatography (see chap. 19), have shown that double articulations may be quite common in connected speech. Particular patterns of double articulation may also be characteristic of developing speech in children and of certain types of speech disorder, such as cleft palate (Gibbon & Crampin, 2002).

Practice 7.6: Double Articulation

Most readers will use a double labial velar approximant [w] in words like "**w**ater" and "a**w**ay." Produce this sound between vowels, noting that the back of the tongue raises simultaneously with the labial articulation.
Now try producing a labial palatal approximation [ɥ], by producing [j] or [i] with the same kind of lip rounding involved in production of [w]. It is easiest to produce this sound between close front vowels, [iɥi]. The tongue can be kept in more or less the same position throughout the utterance, while the lips round and protrude for the double articulation. This may be easier if you imagine a small child saying "weewee," with the front of the tongue raised toward the palate throughout.
Try some double articulations involving fricative and stop articulations, for example,

  • voiceless postalveolar + velar fricative. Prolong the velar fricative, and then add a postalveolar fricative so that the two are produced simultaneously.
  • voiceless labiodental + alveolar fricative.
  • voiced bilabial + velar plosive.
  • voiced bilabial + alveolar nasal stop.

Secondary Articulation

Where a segment involves two simultaneous articulations with differing degrees of stricture, then the one with the greatest degree of stricture is described as the primary articulation, and the one with the lesser degree of stricture is described as the secondary articulation.

Labialization.   The use of lip rounding as a secondary articulation is very widespread and is, according to Laver (1994, p. 321), found in virtually all languages. When segments requiring lip rounding, such as rounded vowels, occur in connected speech, it is usual for preceding segments to become labialized. It is, in fact, quite common for the labialization to extend over stretches of two or more segments. For example, the English utterance "Susan pushed June" would normally be produced with labialization of all the consonant segments and the unstressed vowel, under the influence of the rounded vowels. Labialization is indicated by use of the superscript [ʷ], so the utterance could thus be transcribed as [sʷusʷəʷnʷpʷʊʃʷtʷd͡ʒʷunʷ].

For many speakers of English, labialization habitually accompanies [ʃ] and [ɹ], whatever the phonetic context in which they appear. The most obvious auditory effect of labialization on fricatives is a marked decrease in the apparent "pitch" of the fricative, and habitual labialization of [ʃ] probably serves a useful purpose in helping to increase the perceptual distance between /s/ and /ʃ/.

Practice 7.7: Labialization

Try producing the utterance "Sarah *thinks* Sam is be**s**t at expre**ss**ing him**s**el*f*," first as you would normally say it, and then adding labialization (i.e., rounding and protruding your lips) to the voiceless fricatives [s], [θ], [f] (see letters in italics). Notice what happens to the quality of these fricatives.

Labiodentalization. Labiodentalization is the adoption of slight retraction of the lower lip toward the upper incisors, creating a secondary constriction that modifies a primary articulation elsewhere within the vocal tract In English, labiodentalization is perhaps most commonly associated with the production of [ɹ]. It may also be heard as an idiosyncratic setting, coloring the whole of an individual's spoken performance, especially in people whose jaw relationship is such that the mandible is slightly retracted relative to the upper dental arch.

Labialization is indicated by use of the superscript [ᵛ], as in some speakers' production of "rabbit" as [ɹᵛabɪt].

Palatalization. In palatalization, the secondary constriction is formed by the front of the tongue being raised toward the hard palate, simultaneously with a primary articulation elsewhere. The auditory effect of palatalization is usually heard as a [j] like off-glide to the palatalized segment, and it is indicated in transcription by use of the superscript [ʲ]. Palatalization functions linguistically to differentiate phonemes in a number of languages, including several Slavic languages, such as Polish. In English, palatalization may occur as part of the allophonic variation of the /l/ phoneme. In many accents, /l/ is realized as a palatalized alveolar lateral approximant [lʲ] when it occurs in syllable initial position, although the extent to which this "clear" or "light" /l/ is used varies considerably between accents.

Velarization. In velarization, the secondary articulation is created by the back of the tongue moving up toward the soft palate. This gives a characteristically "dark" auditory quality to the affected segment, with a [ɯ]-like onset and offset. The general convention for transcription is to modify the relevant symbol with the superscript [ˠ]. In English, many accents that use palatalized [lʲ] in syllable initial position use "dark" or velarized [lˠ] in syllable final position. Some accents, such as urban accents of New York and Glasgow, may velarize the /l/ phoneme wherever it occurs. Velarization may also act contrastively and Laver (1994) cited a nice example from Marshallese (spoken on the Marshall Islands), where the use of velarization acts contrastively to differentiate between male and female titles:

[lˠe] "Mr, Sir" [le] "Ms, Madam" (Harris, cited in Laver, 1994, p. 326)

Pharyngealization. Secondary constriction of the pharynx, either by retraction of the tongue root or constriction of the pharyngeal walls themselves, is also described as adding a "dark" quality to affected segments, but it is qualitatively a little different from the "darkness" of velarization. It could reasonably be described as being somewhat more "strangulated." Impressionistically, in languages that use pharyngealization contrastively, its auditory effect appears to extend further into adjacent segments, often affecting the whole syllable. Transcription utilizes the superscript [ˤ], as in [zˤ].

Practice 7.8: Other Secondary Articulations

Practice palatalizing the following sounds between vowels: [zʲ], [lʲ], [dʲ]. One way to approach this is to produce [i] or [j] simultaneously with the primary articulation. If you produce them first between close front unrounded vowels, that is [i zʲi], and the like, you will probably find that they are automatically palatalized because of the context. Next, try producing them between open front vowels, [azʲ a] and so on. This time, as you move toward the primary articulation from the vowel, you need also to actively move the front of the tongue up toward the palate. Remember that your target is to produce [z] + [j]; [l] + [j]; [d] + [j]. In the context of the more open vowel, you may be able to hear a clear [j]-like off glide after the palatalized segment.

Now try producing the same sounds with velarization, so that the back of the tongue is raised toward the soft palate as it is for [w]. This should give a noticeably darker quality to the sounds, especially for [lˠ].

Say the words "*leaf*" and "*feel*." Focus on the italicized lateral approximants, and notice whether they differ in terms of secondary articulation. If they are different, try to describe the difference in terms of the relative position of the body of the tongue. You could also try swapping the sounds around, so that you start the word "leaf" with the type of /l/ you normally use at the end of "feel," and then say the word "feel" with the type of /l/ you normally use in "leaf." Notice how this changes the sound of the whole word.

PHONETIC RELATIONSHIPS BETWEEN VOWELS AND CONSONANTS

As earlier sections have shown, it is not easy to formulate a phonetic definition that categorically differentiates between close vowels and approximant consonant sounds. One result of this blurred phonetic boundary between consonants and vowels is that a number of IPA symbols for close vowels are, in terms of the articulatory configuration they represent, virtually equivalent to consonant symbols. It is useful to be aware of this equivalence, so Table 7.1 makes some of these relationships explicit. It is worth noting that for some (though not all) equivalent pairs there are obvious similarities between the symbol pairs.

Close front vowels, where the body of the tongue adopts a forward and raised position, involve a constriction in the palatal region and so are more or less equivalent to palatal approximants. Similarly, close back vowels, where the body of the tongue is pulled up and back, are roughly equivalent to velar approximants. If the lips are rounded, this adds a further bilabial constriction, so that the close rounded vowels are equivalent to approximants with double labial + lingual articulations. Decisions about which symbol to use are likely to depend on a variety of factors, but factors such as duration

TABLE 7.1	Correspondences Between Vowels and Approximant Consonants
Vowel Symbol and Phonetic Label	Near-Equivalent Consonant Symbol and Phonetic Label
[i] Close front unrounded vowel	[j] Palatal approximant
[ɯ] Close back unrounded vowel	[ɰ] Velar approximant
[y] Close front rounded vowel	[ɥ] Labial palatal approximant
[u] Close back rounded vowel	[w] Labial velar approximant

and stress may be more pertinent than the precise degree of constriction. Consider, for example, the words "eon" and "yon," as spoken by an RP speaker. These would usually be transcribed as [iɒn] and [jɒn], respectively, but the articulatory configuration at the start of these two words is likely to be very similar. There may be a minimal difference in degree of stricture, and the lip position may be marginally more spread in the first example, but the main phonetic difference is likely to be the relatively longer duration of the constriction in the first word. Although listeners generally show fairly high levels of agreement when asked to decide whether a given sound in a given context is a vowel or a consonant, such decisions often seem to be based more on knowledge of the phonology and orthography of a language than on phonetic factors.

PHONETIC RELATIONSHIPS BETWEEN SEGMENTS

In chapters 4, 5, and 6, there has been little to disturb the convenient assumption that speech sounds can, to some extent, be analyzed and transcribed as if they existed as discrete entities. The physical reality of speech is, however, continuous and dynamic, and the preceding discussion of patterns of plosive release and double and secondary articulation should have alerted readers to some of the complex interactions that may occur between adjacent phonetic segments. It is probably clear, by now, that phonetic segments may vary according to their phonetic context, and this seems a good point to stress the importance of extending phonetic skills to look at aspects of speech that extend beyond single segments.

Coordination of Articulation Between Segments

In connected speech, we observe a wide range of phenomena that arise as the result of interactions between segments, particularly between adjacent segments. Examples mentioned earlier in this chapter include the labialization of consonant segments adjacent to rounded vowels, and the use of nasal plosion when a plosive is followed by homorganic nasal stop. Many connected speech processes seem to be explicable in terms of phonetic expediency or efficiency, in that they result in simpler sequences of speech movement being needed to produce an utterance, but other factors may also be involved. The nature of inter-segmental coordination is discussed further in chapter 19, but the following example may serve to alert readers to some of the processes that are common in every day speech.

Consider the utterance "it came out of her hand bag," as spoken by an RP speaker. The citation forms of the individual words would typically be: [ɪt] [keɪm] [aut] [ɒv] [hɜ] [hand] [bag], but when produced as a whole utterance we may observe something quite different:

[ɪkˈkeɪm aʉt əˣvˣ əɹ hamˣbag]

1. The word-final alveolar plosive in "it" becomes velar in the context of the following velar plosive. This is known as assimilation.
2. The vowel in "of" weakens to [ə].
3. The word-initial glottal fricative in "her" is omitted and the vowel is weakened to [ə].
4. The alveolar plosive at the end of "hand" is omitted and the remaining word-final alveolar nasal becomes bilabial in the context of the following bilabial plosive.

Articulatory modifications of this sort are very common, and it is interesting to listen carefully to casual, connected speech and to notice how what actually happens may differ markedly from expectations.

Suprasegmental Features of Speech

The second broad class of phonetic phenomena that requires us to look beyond the segment includes phonetic features that by their nature extend over whole utterances or longer stretches of speech. These suprasegmental features of speech include the intonational contours of pitch and loudness that are used, for example, to differentiate questions from statements; these will be considered further in chapter 9. Also within this category come the medium-term modifications of voice quality that are used to express mood and emotion, and the longer-term variations in voice quality that signal speaker identity. Some further discussion of the phonetic description of voice quality can be found later in this chapter and in chapter 18.

ALTERNATIVE APPROACHES TO PHONETIC ANALYSIS

Traditional segmental transcription tends to obscure the types of inter-segmental interactions described earlier, and it is often useful to use rather different approaches to phonetic analysis and representation of speech. The two alternative approaches described here are both based on the same phonetic principles as segmental analysis, but use rather different approaches.

Parametric Analysis

In a parametric analysis, individual strands of speech production are tracked throughout an utterance. Figure 7.5 compares a segmental transcription of the word "candle" with a somewhat idealized example of a parametric analysis. This type of analysis relates more directly to the physical process of speech production and allows us to look more closely at the relationships between segments. In the illustration shown here, it is clear that the boundaries between segments are not as clear cut as we might expect, and that adjacent

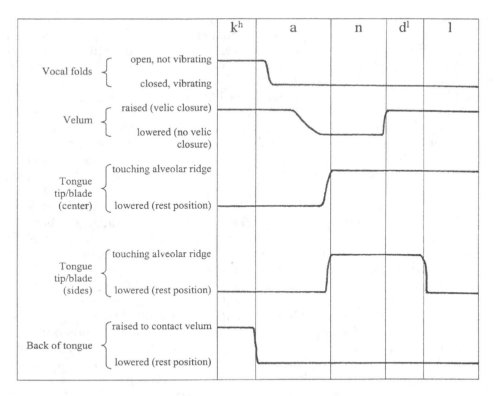

FIG. 7.5.   A parametric analysis of the utternace [kʰandˡ] ("candle").

segments affect each other. For example, the articulatory release of the utter-ance initial velar plosive occurs before the onset of voicing for the following vowel, causing aspiration. Similarly, the transition from the open vowel [a] to the nasal stop [n] involves at least two significant actions. The tongue tip/blade has to rise toward the alveolar ridge and create an airtight seal (a stricture of complete closure) and the velum has to lower so as to allow airflow through the nasal cavity. In this context, it is highly unlikely that these two ac-tions will occur simultaneously. It is more usual for the velic closure to be re-leased before the alveolar stop closure is created, so that the latter part of the vowel becomes nasalized. Parametric analysis makes this type of inter-seg-mental influence much more explicit than is usually the case with segmental transcription. It may also provide insights into the kinds of individual varia-tions of speech production that allow us to identify individual speakers. This is discussed further in the following section.

Analysis of Long Term Voice Quality Settings

One virtue of both segmental and parametric analysis is that it allows us to differentiate between speech sounds on the basis of their particular phonetic characteristics. In other words, it helps us to specify what changes between one segment and another. There may be some situations where the focus of in-terest is not on the phonetic features that differ between speech segments, but

on those features that are shared in common by a wide range of speech segments. This might be the case if we wish to identify the speech characteristics
that are typical of an individual speaker and that differentiate his or her overall speech quality from that of other people. There are, for example, people
who habitually protrude and round their lips more or less throughout speech,
regardless of the phonetic context. This kind of speaker-specific tendency
might emerge from a careful segmental transcription, if consistent
labialization resulting from habitual lip-rounding is represented by extensive
use of the labialization diacritic. It is often simpler as a perceptual strategy,
and more efficient as a descriptive approach, to abstract the long-term tendencies from the segmental analysis and describe these separately as habitual voice quality settings. This approach forms the basis for Vocal Profile
Analysis (Laver, Wirz, Mackenzie, & Hiller, 1981), following Laver's work on
phonetic description of voice quality (Laver, 1980). A setting, then, is not a
static position, but rather a long-term-average adjustment of some part of the
vocal tract, which then acts as a background for segmental articulations. In
the example of habitual lip rounding and protrusion just given, for example,
speakers with this type of setting will usually still differentiate between
rounded and unrounded segments. The long-term-average position results
from a tendency to make rounded segments more rounded than usual, to use
slight lip rounding for segments that typically have a neutral lip position, and
to use less lip spreading than usual on segments like [i], which typically have
spread lips. Habitual setting adjustments may involve the larynx and/or the
vocal tract, and a few examples are given in the following.

Larynx Settings. The position of the larynx in the neck may be habitually
raised or lowered. This affects the length of the resonating cavities. The type of
phonation used for voiced segments may vary. For example, it might be habitually creaky or whispery.

Vocal Tract Settings. Background levels of nasal resonance may vary. For example, many speakers of English produce vowels with audible nasality. The
long-term-average position of the tongue may vary. For example, many speakers of RP use a slightly backed and lowered tongue body setting. Habitual lip
and jaw postures may also color the quality of speech produced.

Much fuller accounts are available, in the references given earlier, for anyone who is interested in finding out more about this approach. It is probably
obvious that several identifiable settings may coexist in the same speaker, so
that a speaker could, for instance, be described as having a whispery voice
with a backed and lowered tongue body and a rounded and protruded lip
setting. When we recognize a voice as belonging to someone we know, it is
largely on the basis of a characteristic combination of habitual speech production settings.

II
Acoustic Phonetics

8
Waveforms and Time Measurement

Speech acoustics is concerned with the physical nature of the sounds that travel through the air from speaker to hearer. A sequence of such sounds (the speech signal) forms both the output of the speaking process and the input to the listening process. Therefore speech acoustics can yield interesting evidence about both the production and the perception of speech. The account given here is selective, in that it concentrates on those aspects of the acoustics of speech that are of most relevance for explaining the process of spoken communication. The acoustic phenomena themselves are described with reference to their articulatory production and to their functions in language.

This chapter is concerned with information that can be gained from waveforms of speech. It deals with the different types of speech waveforms and with the measurement of duration and speech rate from speech waveforms.

SOUND WAVES

In the production of a normal utterance, a speaker makes a sequence of movements of the speech organs. These movements create disturbances in the surrounding air, which can be detected by the ears of a listener. Disturbances in the air that are detectable by the human ear are called *sound waves*. They consist of the backward and forward movements of air particles. These backward and forward movements create alternations of positive and negative pressure and they are transmitted through the air in an ever-expanding sphere from the mouth of the speaker, weakening all the time until they die away.

The transitory and invisible nature of sound waves makes them relatively inaccessible to inspection and analysis for scientific purposes. It is therefore desirable to make a permanent recording of any speech signal that is the object of analysis. The invention of magnetic tape allowed the convenient recording of vast amounts of speech data. Nowadays, even more conveniently, recordings are usually made, in digital form, onto a computer. Scientific analysis relies heavily on the visual mode, so the recording must then be transformed into a visual display, in order that patterns can be identified and measurements can be made. This chapter is concerned with one sort of visual representation of sound waves, namely waveforms.

WAVEFORMS

A sound wave can be represented by a graph that shows how the amplitude of some dimension of the sound changes over time. Such a graph is called a *waveform*. Figure 8.1 is the sound pressure waveform of an utterance of the vowel [ɑ], recorded from a microphone held about 20 cm in front of the mouth of the speaker. It shows how amplitude of pressure (represented on the vertical axis) varies over time (represented on the horizontal axis). The zero point on the vertical axis represents the ambient, atmospheric pressure and so the excursions of the trace above and below the line represent alternations of pressure above and below atmospheric pressure. No scale of pressure amplitude is shown; measurement of sound pressure amplitude is discussed in more detail in chapter 10. A sound pressure waveform is sometimes called an audio waveform or a "raw waveform." As the latter term implies, the sound pressure waveform is the most basic and least processed representation of a speech signal, and where the term waveform is used by itself, it should be taken to mean sound pressure waveform. (Chap. 9 contains an example of a different type of waveform, a fundamental frequency waveform.)

Figure 8.2 shows the (sound pressure) waveform of a whole utterance, "Don't miss the party." Notice that the time scale of Fig. 8.2 is not as large as that of Fig. 8.1 so that the waveform, in addition to being more variegated (because it is of a succession of sounds rather than just one), is also more compressed along the horizontal dimension.

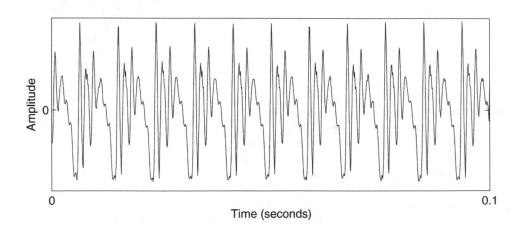

FIG. 8.1.   Waveform of [ɑ], over a time-span of one tenth of a second.

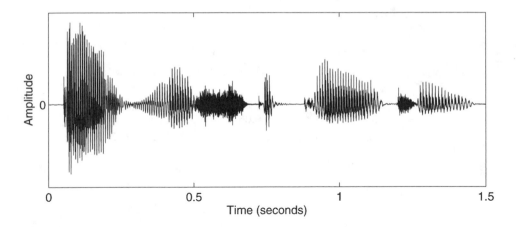

FIG. 8.2.   Waveform of "Don't miss the party."

WAVEFORM TYPES

Waveforms of speech sounds can be classified into four basic types. These are: periodic, random, quiescent, and transient. They are illustrated in Figs. 8.3 to 8.5. The differences among these waveform types are the result of the different ways in which the source of energy for the sound is generated in the speaker's vocal tract.

Periodic

The waveforms in Fig. 8.3 all have a cycle that repeats. Waveforms of this sort are called *periodic*. Each of the waveforms of Fig. 8.3 displays about 10 cycles. All nasals, vowels, and approximants (i.e., all the so-called sonorant sounds) have periodic waveforms. The reason is that the source of all these sounds is the periodic vibration of the vocal folds.

Random

The waveforms of Fig. 8.4 and Fig. 8.5 do not have a repeating cycle and can therefore be described as *aperiodic*. Those of Fig. 8.4 dart chaotically up and down from the zero line and are called *random*. Fricative consonants have random waveforms because the source for these sounds is the noisy turbulence created by forcing a stream of air through a narrow gap between two articulators. As the relative amplitudes of these waveforms suggest, the sibilant fricatives, /s/ and /ʃ/, tend to achieve greater amplitude than other fricatives. The aspiration phase of a voiceless plosive (created by noisy turbulence at the glottis), transcribed by a raised [ʰ], also has a random waveform.

Quiescent

In interactions involving spoken language, a silent pause in the conversation can convey a lot of meaning. Silence can also be significant at the

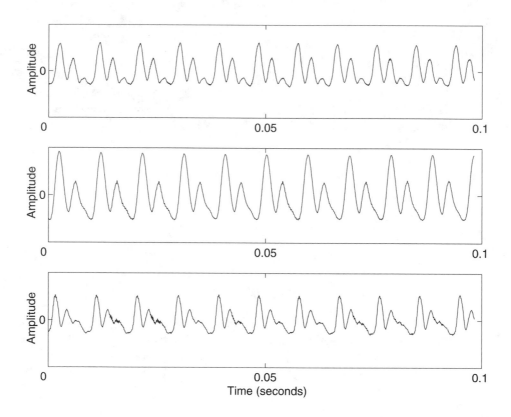

FIG. 8.3.   Periodic waveforms. The vowel [u] (top), the nasal consonant [n] (middle), and the approximant [l] (bottom).

microlevel in phonetics. During the closure phase of voiceless plosives like [p], [t], and [k], when the articulators close off the airway and the vocal folds are not vibrating, no sound issues forth and the waveform is therefore simply a straight line. Following the example of Shoup and Pfeifer (1976), we call this waveform type *quiescent*. It is illustrated, for the sake of completeness, in Fig. 8.5 (left). (Actually, most speakers of English also produce voiced stops without vibration during the closure, at least in initial position. The distinction between an initial /t/ and a /d/, for example, rests largely on the property of voice onset time, which is described later in this chapter.)

Transient

Transients are associated with the second phase of a plosive, in which the air pressure that builds up behind an articulatory closure is released with an explosion. This creates a sound that has an aperiodic waveform but that is distinguished from the random waveform in that it decays very quickly. Transients are not transcribed by any separate symbol, on a normal phonetic transcription. The spike in the waveform of Fig. 8.5 (right) is a transient.

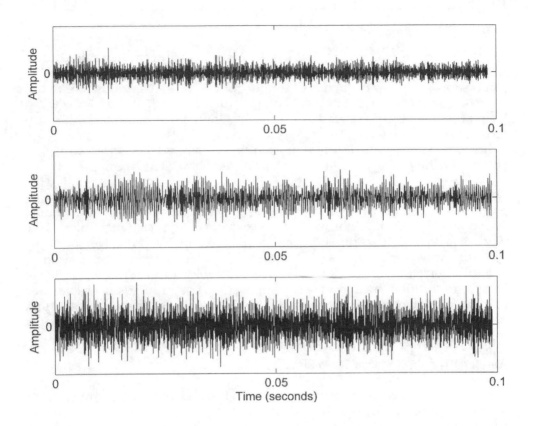

FIG. 8.4.   Random waveforms. The fricative [s] (top), [ʃ] (middle), and [f] (bottom).

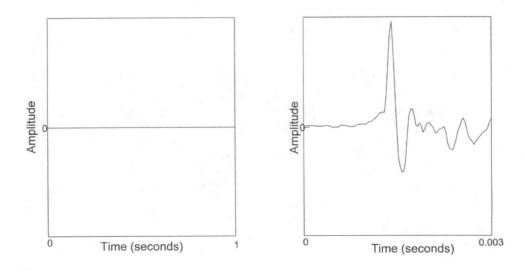

FIG. 8.5.   Quiescent waveform (left) and transient waveform (right).

The Four Types Illustrated in a Single Word

The occurrence of all four types of waveform as they occur in a single word, "sky," is illustrated in the waveform of Fig. 8.6. Note that the term waveform can be applied to any sequence of sounds, not just a single sound, so we can refer to "the waveform of 'the sky is blue'," "the waveform of 'sky'," "the waveform of '/s/'," and so on. Strictly speaking, it should be "the waveform of *an utterance of* ..." because all utterances of, for example, "the sky is blue" are liable to be at least slightly different from each other and therefore have different waveforms—but this can make for cumbersome sentences.

A Note on Voiced Fricatives.   Voiced fricatives, like /z/ and /v/, are (somewhat paradoxically) both random and periodic. They are produced with a dual sound source: periodic vibration of the vocal folds and frictional noise at the place of articulation. As the end result is a sound that does not have a perfectly repeating waveform, it could be classified as random. However, the waveform of a fully voiced fricative, like that of Fig. 8.7, looks like a periodic waveform with some random waveform superimposed on it and the listener can hear and distinguish both these elements. (In running speech, little or no vocal fold vibration may occur during a "voiced" fricative, in English. It may be just weaker and shorter than its voiceless counterpart.)

Waveform Types and Speech Sound Classes

Table 8.1 summarizes the correspondences between the waveform types and the major classes of speech sounds. Note that plosives are complex sounds. From the acoustic point of view a plosive is a sequence of at least two sounds: the quiescent portion followed by the transient. A voiceless aspirated plosive contains a third phase, the aspiration, which has a random waveform. In fact,

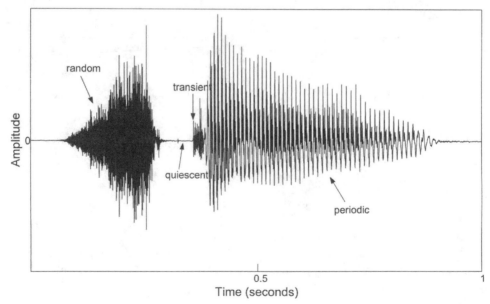

FIG. 8.6.   Waveform of "sky."

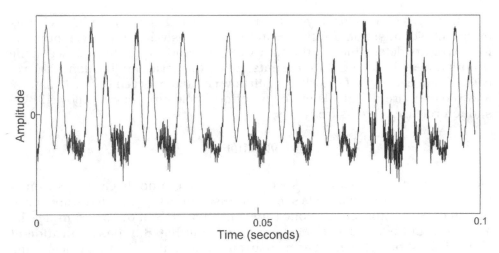

FIG. 8.7. Waveform of [z].

TABLE 8.1 **Correspondences Between Waveform Types and Classes of Speech Sounds**

Waveform Type	*Speech Sound Class*
Periodic	Sonorants (vowels, nasals, approximants)
Random	Fricatives, voiceless plosives (aspiration phase)
Quiescent	Plosives (closure phase)
Transient	Plosives (release phase)

Practice 8.1

1. What dimension is represented on the horizontal axis of a wave-form?
2. What does zero signify on the vertical axis of a sound pressure waveform?
3. What is the waveform type of [θ]?
4. What is the waveform type of [l]?
5. What is the waveform type of [tʰ]?
6. What is the waveform type of [u]?

Answers. 1. Time 2. Atmospheric pressure 3. Random 4. Periodic 5. Quiescent then transient then random 6. Periodic

---

in between the transient and the aspiration, there is likely to be a brief interval of frication created in the mouth or at the lips, as the lower articulator (the tongue, e.g.) drags away from the upper. This too, of course, is random, so these two phases are not distinguished by waveform type. (In most contexts, the term aspiration is used informally to cover the entire nonquiescent phase of a voiceless plosive.)

Differences of waveform type, then, serve to distinguish the major classes of speech sounds: sonorants, fricatives, and plosives. Differences of waveform type are determined by the nature of the sound source that is used in the production of the sound: In sonorants, this is the periodic vibration of the vocal folds; in fricatives it is turbulent airflow created between two articulators; and plosives are distinguished by a period of closure that is followed by a sudden release of pressure.

DURATION

Measurements of duration in speech are most commonly given in seconds (for which the abbreviation is s) or in milliseconds (for which the abbreviation is ms). A millisecond is one thousandth of a second. For example, the waveform of the utterance "My parrot died," in Fig. 8.8, has a duration of about 1.53 s, or 1530 ms. The measurement was made from the beginning of the /m/ of "my" to the point of release of the final /d/ in "died." When measurements are made directly from the computer screen, it is often possible to position time-labeled cursors for making convenient and accurate temporal measurements. To assist with measurements on a printed waveform,

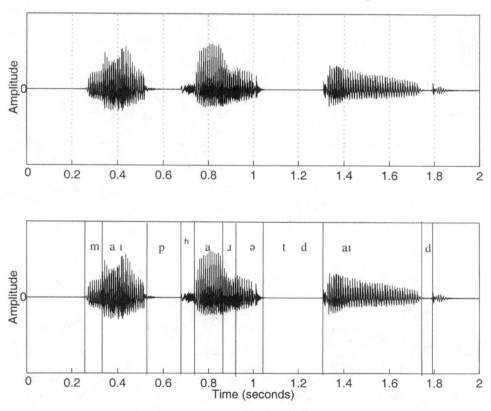

FIG. 8.8.   Top: waveform of the utterance "My parrot died." Calibration lines are at intervals of 200 ms. Bottom: the same waveform, segmented, with transcription symbols added.

vertical calibration lines can be added; on the waveform of Fig. 8.8 (top) these are at 200 ms intervals.

Temporal measurements of the waveforms of utterances reveal striking differences in duration among different speech sounds. Vowels tend to have greater duration than consonants, stressed vowels have greater duration than unstressed vowels, and so on. Such differences are not easily represented on a phonetic transcription.

Measuring individual speech sounds entails segmenting the waveform, that is, drawing boundaries between adjacent sounds. For these purposes "sound" usually means a stretch of waveform taken to coincide with a transcription symbol; however, the two elements of a diphthong are usually counted as one, whereas the closure and aspiration phases of a voiceless plosive are usually segmented into two. Segmentation is a common preliminary for many types of phonetic analysis but it is necessary to be aware of the uncertainties involved. Figure 8.8 (bottom) shows a segmentation of the same waveform of "My parrot died." Where there is a change of waveform type from one sound to the next the waveform usually exhibits an abrupt discontinuity, which provides a useful criterion for positioning a segment boundary. For example, the boundary between [pʰ] and [a] in "parrot" is placed where the waveform changes from random to periodic. If two adjacent sounds share the same waveform type, however, it is often difficult to decide where to draw the boundary between them. The boundary that has been drawn between the [m] of "my" and the following vowel is a guess, guided by the way the amplitude changes, and the same is true of the boundaries within the [aɹə] sequence in "parrot." For segmenting sequences like these, a spectrogram (see chap. 12) is more helpful. However, there is no phonetic basis for determining a boundary within the [td] sequence in "parro**t** **d**ied." It is impossible to determine the boundary between the two sounds because they have the same place of articulation, the [**t**] was unreleased, and the [**d**] was not voiced. The result is simply a continuous quiescent waveform.

Durational Differences Among Speech Sounds

Phonological Function of Duration.   Many languages of the world use duration for some of their phonological contrasts. A contrast between a short and a long vowel is most common but some languages have contrasts between

---

Practice 8.2

All these questions refer to Fig. 8.8.

1. What was the approximate duration, in ms, of the nonquiescent waveform of the word "parrot"; that is, from the release of the /p/ to the end of the vowel?
2. What was the approximate duration, in ms, of the word "my?"
3. What was the approximate duration, in ms, of the [td] sequence in "parrot died?"
4. What was the approximate duration, in ms, of the diphthong in "died?"

Answers. 1. 360 ms 2. 270 ms 3. 270 ms 4. 410 ms

short and long consonants. Finnish has both, as in /mutɑ/ "mud," /muuta/ "other," /mutta/ "but" (Engstrand & Krull, 1994; a doubled symbol here means a lengthened sound). It is difficult to find examples from English in which a phonological distinction is conveyed just by a difference in duration. The best example we know of is the distinction in Scottish English between "brood" and "brewed" (and a few other pairs of words; Scobbie, Hewlett, & Turk, 1999), in which the vowel of "brood" is short and that of "brewed" is reliably longer. However, duration may play a secondary role in some vowel contrasts, in many accents of English. For example, /i/ is sometimes said to be longer than /ɪ/ in RP, although admittedly in the waveforms of "sick" and "seek," in Fig. 8.9 (top), spoken by an RP speaker, the difference is small.

Variation According to Context. Durations of sounds and syllables can vary according to where they occur in an utterance. The phenomenon of phrase-final lengthening, for example, is a tendency for the syllables at the ends of utterances to be longer than similar syllables mid-utterance. Vowel duration, in particular, may also be influenced by the nature of an adjacent sound. The most well-known example is the near-universal tendency among the languages of the world for a vowel to be longer before a voiced than a

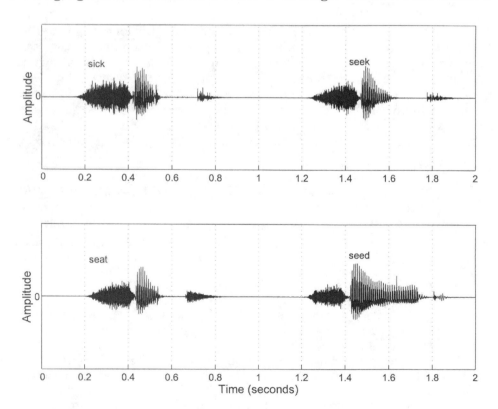

FIG. 8.9.   Waveforms illustrating vowel durations. Top: Utterances of "sick" and "seek," by an RP speaker. Bottom: Utterances of "seat" and "seed," by an RP speaker. Calibration lines are at intervals of 200 ms.

Practice 8.3

1. What were the durations of the vowels in "seat" and "seed," in Fig. 8.9?
2. Were the plosives at the end of "sick" and "seek" audibly released?
3. How do we know?
4. What was the duration of the /k/ closure of "sick?"

Answers. 1. "seat": 100 ms, "seed": 320 ms 2. Yes 3. The random waveforms, centered around 0.75 seconds in the case of "sick" and 1.8 seconds in the case of "seek," which follow the closure at the end of each word (the same is true of "seat" and "seed") 4. 180 ms

---

voiceless consonant. In many accents of English this tendency is exaggerated to the point where the durational difference in the vowel becomes a major cue in distinguishing pairs of words like "leak" versus "league," "seat" versus "seed," and "safe" versus "save," which we usually think of as being distinguished only by the voicing status of the final consonant. Figure 8.9 (bottom) shows waveforms of "seat" and "seed" by an RP speaker, which illustrates the longer vowel before the voiced consonant. This length difference does not occur (or is minimal) in Scottish English, at least in syllables with close vowels like "seat" and "seed."

Voice Onset Time. The most extensively investigated, and most voluminously reported, durational feature of speech must be that of voice onset time, commonly abbreviated to VOT. It is a measure that applies to plosive consonants that are followed by a vowel or other sonorant sound, as in "pay," "bay," "play," "true," "okay," "potato." *Voice onset time (VOT)* is the time that elapses between the release of the consonant closure and the onset of vocal fold vibration. In the case of voiceless plosives in most varieties of English, this comprises the transient and the aspiration (in other words, the portion transcribed by a raised "h" in a phonetic transcription). In the case of a voiced plosive, it comprises the transient and whatever short stretch of aspiration there may be. Therefore, voiceless plosives have longer VOTs. When measuring VOT from a speech waveform, the starting point (release of closure) is determined from where the waveform changes from quiescent to transient; the end point (the onset of vocal fold vibration) is determined from where the waveform becomes periodic. Figure 8.10 shows waveforms of the words "bit" and "pit" (top; with VOT arrowed) and "tie" and "die" (bottom). The [pʰ] of "pit" has a VOT of 57 ms and the [b] of "bit" has a VOT of 12 ms.

VOT is the most important feature distinguishing voiced from voiceless plosives in syllable initial position in English. Voiceless plosives have longer VOTs than their voiced counterparts. Numerous experimental studies have made use of this measure, for example in investigating speech production differences among different languages, in studies of the development of speech in children and in attempts to discover different types of speech difficulties experienced in different types of aphasia. Table 8.2 shows mean voice onset times for the plosives /p t k b d g/ reported in a study by Docherty (1992). The words were spoken in the carrier sentence

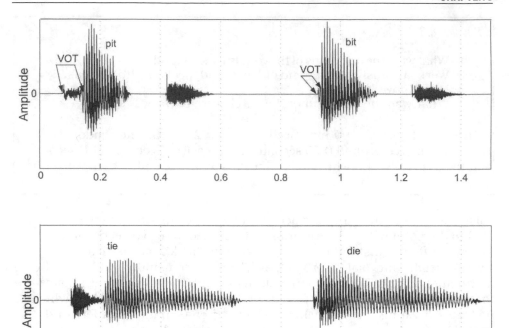

FIG. 8.10. Voice onset time (VOT). Waveforms of "pit" and "bit" (top) and "tie" and "die" (bottom). The VOT interval is arrowed on the waveforms of "pit" and "bit."

Practice 8.4

1. To which sounds could a measure of VOT be applied, in each of the following words?

   (a) tame (b) doll (c) cup (d) lit (e) impossible (f) wallflower

2. What were the VOTs of the /t/ of "tie" and the /d/ of "die" in Fig. 8.10?
3. What was the VOT of the /p/ of "parrot" in Fig. 8.8?

Answers. 1. (a) /t/ (b) /d/ (c) /k/ (d) None (e) /p/, /b/ (f) None 2. /t/: 115 ms, /d/: 15 ms 3. 55 ms

---

"Say _____ instead," by subjects with an RP accent. Notice that VOTs of bilabial consonants tend to be shorter than those of alveolars and velars, in both the voiceless and voiced categories. (The results of some other studies have suggested, in addition, a tendency for velar VOTs to be longer than alveolar.) Voice onset times of voiced plosives may in fact be negative, that is, the voicing may start *before* the articulatory closure is released. This is the way that voiced plosives are routinely produced in Spanish, for example.

TABLE 8.2   Mean VOTs, in Milliseconds, for Word Initial English Plosives

Bilabial		Alveolar		Velar	
/p/	/b/	/t/	/d/	/k/	/g/
42	15	65	21	62	27

Note. Values are from Docherty (1992, p. 116, Table 3.5).

For most speakers of English, however, this is not a usual pattern. The few cases of such pre-voicing found by Docherty were excluded from the calculation of the means reported in Table 8.2.

Speech Rate

Speech rate is most commonly measured in syllables per second. It may also be measured (rather less accurately) in words per second or (more accurately) in phonemes per second. Following Laver (1994), the term *speaking rate* is used where pauses are included, whereas the term *articulation rate* is used where pauses have been excluded from the calculation. Speaking rate is the easier one to measure. Having identified a stretch of speech, the number of units (words, syllables, or phonemes) is counted. Compound words can cause difficulty: for example, is air stream (airstream) one word or two? In the case of syllables and phonemes, the difficulties tend to be more phonetic. For example, unstressed syllables are sometimes elided in running speech. So, for example, the word "career," pronounced carefully, has two syllables but if pronounced fast/casually it is sometimes pronounced with one ("creer"); and sometimes it is difficult to decide whether it was pronounced with one or two.

The second measure that is needed is the total duration of the stretch of speech to be measured. Computer-based measurement, using cursors on a screen display of the waveform, makes this quick and simple. If the speech sample begins with a stop consonant then the stop closure cannot be included, because it cannot be distinguished from a preceding pause (Fig. 8.2 is an illustration), but this is not a serious inaccuracy if the sample is long enough. The calculation is made by dividing the number of units by the total duration of the speech, in seconds. For example, for speaking rate in syllables/second:

$$\textbf{\textit{Speaking Rate}} = \frac{\textbf{\textit{Number of syllables}}}{\textbf{\textit{Total duration}}} \qquad \textbf{(8.1)}$$

The formula for calculation of articulation rate is:

$$\textbf{\textit{Articulation Rate}} = \frac{\textbf{\textit{Number of syllables}}}{\textbf{\textit{Total duration}} - \textbf{\textit{Pauses}}} \qquad \textbf{(8.2)}$$

The problem with subtracting the pauses is that both pauses and stop closures have quiescent waveforms and we don't want to eliminate the latter. A common convention is to count only quiescent waveforms lasting more than 250 ms as pauses. (Admittedly, the [td] sequence in "parro*t d*ied," in Fig. 8.9, lasts approximately 270 ms. The 250 ms limit may have to be increased for slow, careful speech.) There is also the problem of filled pauses (hesitation sounds, coughs, laughs, and so on), which should probably also be subtracted from the total duration measure when calculating articulation rate.

The research literature suggests that a normal Speaking Rate is something like 3 to 5.5 syllables/second. There is less information on Articulation Rate. Goldman-Eisler (1956) reported Articulation Rate values for eight speakers, ranging from 4.4 to 5.9 syllables/second and Laver (1994, p. 158) quoted 5.3 syllables/second as a "medium articulation rate." A study of the conversational speech rates of 12 young adult subjects from Edinburgh (Hewlett & Rendall, 1998) found an average Speaking Rate of 4.3 syllables/second and an average Articulation Rate of 5.5 syllables/ second.

Some speakers, characteristically, speak faster than others. It has yet to be established whether different languages, or different dialects of the same language, have characteristically different speech rates. Rural accents are often said to have slower speech rates than urban accents. There may be such a tendency but it is probably not universal. The study just mentioned (Hewlett & Rendall, 1998) compared the Edinburgh speakers' rates with those of subjects from the island of Orkney, in the north of Scotland. In the conversation of the rural (Orkney) subjects, mean Articulation Rates and Speaking Rates were, if anything, slightly faster than those of the urban subjects.

EXERCISES

1. Make sketches to illustrate the four different waveform types: periodic, random, transient, and quiescent.
2. Measure and state the durations of the vowels in the words "tie" and "die" in Fig. 8.10 (bottom).
3. Measure and state the VOT of the /k/ in "sky" in Fig. 8.6.
4. Measure and state the VOT of the initial /d/ of "died" in Fig. 8.8.
5. Figure 8.11 shows the waveform of the sentence "We saw the wide car," spoken by an RP speaker. Do the following:

   a. State the waveform type of each of the sounds /w/, /i/, /s/ and /kʰ/.
   b. Measure and state the duration of the /s/ of "saw."
   c. Measure and state the VOT of /k/ in "car."
   d. Measure and state the duration of /ð/ in "the."
   e. Measure and state the Articulation Rate with which the sentence was uttered, in (i) words/second, (ii) syllables/second, and (iii) phonemes/second, counting the diphthong in "wide" as a single phoneme and likewise the plosive /k/. (Note that in this utterance the Articulation Rate and the Speaking Rate were the same, because there were no pauses.)

6. Is this Articulation Rate (the one in the answer to 5e) slower than average?

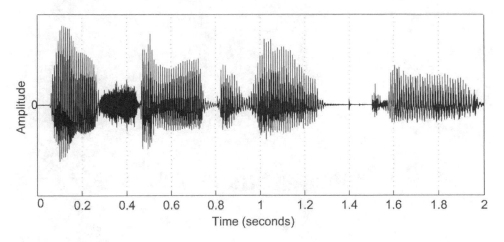

FIG. 8.11.   Waveform of "We saw the wide car" by an RP speaker. Calibration lines are at intervals of 200 ms.

9

Fundamental Frequency

The fundamental frequency of a sound is responsible for the pitch that we hear. The range of fundamental frequencies in a person's voice is part of what characterizes them as a speaker, leading to descriptions like "high-pitched voice," "low-pitched voice," and "monotonous voice." During an utterance, changes of fundamental frequency help to signal the relationships among the words and it is also involved in conveying less tangible things, like the speaker's attitude and emotional state. This chapter first explains fundamental frequency and describes how it is measured. It goes on to describe typical and extreme values of the fundamental frequency of human voices. It also illustrates the role of fundamental frequency in signaling meaning, in words and sentences.

DEFINITION AND MEASUREMENT

The *fundamental frequency* of a sound is the frequency with which its wave cycle repeats in time. Fundamental frequency is an attribute only of periodic sounds, as only periodic sounds consist of repeated cycles. In speech this means the sonorant sounds: vowels, nasals, and approximants. Marginally, it applies to other sounds with voicing, like voiced fricatives (the status of voiced fricatives was discussed briefly in chap. 8). The fundamental frequency of a speech sound is determined by the fundamental frequency of vibration of the vocal folds, and the relationship between the two (fundamental frequency and vocal fold vibration) is quite straightforward: One complete cycle on a periodic waveform corresponds to one complete cycle of opening and closure of the vocal folds.

Measurement of Fundamental Frequency from the Waveform

Frequency is measured in cycles per second, the term for which is hertz, abbreviated to Hz. So a fundamental frequency (f_0 from now on) of 110 Hz (which would be a comfortable rate of vibration for typical adult male vocal folds) means 110

120

cycles per second. Likewise a f_0 of 220 Hz (which would be a comfortable rate of vibration for typical adult female vocal folds) means 220 cycles per second.

f_0 may be calculated from a waveform by measuring the duration of a single cycle. The duration of a single cycle can be measured from any point on the waveform to the subsequent point at which the pattern starts repeating. This is illustrated on the waveform of Fig. 9.1. The duration of the cycle is called the *period* of the waveform. The period is symbolized by T (not our idea!). The period of the waveform of Fig. 9.1 is 4 ms. The vertical calibration lines of Fig. 9.1 are at 5 ms intervals and it is easy to see that the period is a bit less than this. With the aid of a ruler a more accurate estimate can be made but the measurement of 4 ms was made on a computer screen using time-labeled cursors.

In order to arrive at the f_0, in hertz, of the waveform of Fig. 9.1 we must calculate how many such periods would occur in one second. Because the period is 4 ms and there are 1000 ms in a second, the answer is 1000/4 = 250. Therefore the waveform of Fig. 9.1 has a f_0 of 250 Hz. Obviously, the longer the period the fewer the number of cycles that will occur in one second.

Sometimes it is convenient to begin by measuring the total duration of a number of cycles. For example, if three cycles of a waveform have a total duration of 26.1 ms, then:

$$T = 26.1/3 = 8.7 \text{ ms}$$

and therefore:

$$f_0 = 1000/8.7 = 115 \text{ Hz}$$

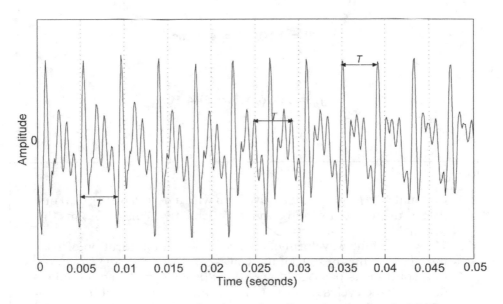

FIG. 9.1.   Waveform of [ɑ], by a female speaker, illustrating the period of the waveform, symbolized by T, measured at three different points. Calibration lines are at 5 ms intervals.

(We give measurements of periods, in milliseconds, to one decimal place, and measurements of f_0, in Hz, to the nearest whole number.) In an ideal case these alternatives will, of course, give the same result. However, where the time scale is somewhat compressed, as it is in Fig. 9.2, a single cycle is more difficult to measure accurately. Figure 9.2 is the waveform of the entire vowel in "top." Conveniently, almost exactly five periods reside between the calibration lines at 0.08 s and 0.1 s, from which we can estimate:

$$T = 20/5 = 4 \text{ ms}$$

and

$$f_0 = 1000/4 = 250 \text{ Hz}$$

Because speech sounds are produced by humans, they are rarely exactly periodic even when the speaker aims to produce a perfect monotone. There are liable to be small, cycle-to-cycle differences in the period. So it is often just as well to take the mean of several cycles. Furthermore, the production of an utterance with a normal intonation contour requires that f_0 is continually changing. In practice, we are usually interested in measuring the f_0 averaged over some amount of time: the duration of a vowel, say, or of a whole phrase, or even of all the periodic sounds in a long passage of continuous speech. The average (mean) f_0 of the vowel in "top," in the waveform of Fig. 9.2, was estimated to be 244 Hz. Ignoring the first and the last few cycles (these cycles often lack definition, due to starting and ending characteristics of vocal fold vibration), a total of 27 cycles were found to have a total duration of 110 ms.

So:

$$T = 110/27 = 4.1 \text{ ms}$$

and

$$f_0 = 1000/4.1 = 244 \text{ Hz}$$

Practice 9.1

1. Calculate the f_0, in Hz, for a waveform with a period of: (a) 11.0 ms (b) 9.2 ms (c) 8.0 ms (d) 6.3 ms (e) 5.5 ms (f) 4.0 ms (g) 3.6 ms (h) 2.7 ms
2. 15 cycles of the waveform of a vowel have a total duration of 105 ms. What is the mean f_0 of the vowel?
3. In a continuous passage of speech a speaker produced a total of 988 periodic cycles and the total duration of these added up to 8872 ms. What was the mean f_0?
4. The period of a waveform is 0.004 s. What is its f_0?

Answers. 1. (a) 1000/11 = 91 Hz (b) 109 Hz (c) 125 Hz (d) 159 Hz (e) 182 Hz (f) 250 Hz (g) 278 Hz (h) 370 Hz 2. Mean period = 105/15 = 7 ms so mean f_0 = 1000/7 = 143 Hz 3. Mean period = 8872/988 = 9 ms so mean f_0 = 1000/9 = 111 Hz 4. 1/0.004 = 250 Hz

In question 4, in Practice 9.1, the same time unit (seconds) is used for both the period and the f_0, so it illustrates the basic relationship between the two:

$$f_0 = \frac{1}{T} \tag{9.1}$$

from which it follows that:

$$T = \frac{1}{f_0} \tag{9.2}$$

(Check that for yourself by making up some examples.)

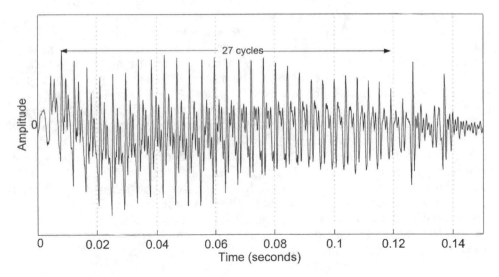

FIG. 9.2. Waveform of the vowel of "top," by a female speaker. Calibration lines are at intervals of 20 ms.

Practice 9.2

State the period of each f_0, in seconds (to four decimal places) and in milliseconds.

(a) 100 Hz (b) 200 Hz (c) 250 Hz (d) 380 Hz (e) 95 Hz (f) 116 Hz

Answers. (a) 0.01 s, 10 ms (b) 0.005 s, 5 ms (c) 0.004 s, 4 ms (d) 0.0026 s, 2.6 ms (e) 0.0105 s, 10.5 ms (f) 0.0086 s, 8.6 ms

   Notice that the first step is always to measure the period of the waveform. The second step is to work out the number of periods in a second, to give a measure of f_0. It could be argued that this second step is superfluous because specifying the period is sufficient. After all, once you have specified that the period of a waveform is n seconds long, then obviously there must be $1/n$ periods in one second. So we could have called this chapter "Period" and just pointed out the relationship described in the previous sentence. However, this would not have been helpful because, for some reason, there is an almost universal preference for taking the second step and describing this property in terms of frequency.

The Semitone Scale

Fundamental frequencies of individual sounds, and long term average f_0, are invariably quoted in hertz in phonetics. However, when a comparison is being made between two frequencies, or where a frequency *range* is being quoted, it is quite usual to use semitones. Octaves and semitones may be familiar from music theory. An *octave* is a doubling of frequency. Thus the interval between 100 Hz and 200 Hz is an octave, as is the interval between 450 Hz and 900 Hz. An octave is subdivided into 12 *semitones*. So the interval between 450 Hz and 900 Hz has the same value as the interval between 100 Hz and 200 Hz on the semitone scale, namely 12 semitones (or one octave). The semitone scale is well established in music (for a more extensive account, see the chapter on musical measures of frequency, in Hartmann, 1997). Its applicability to speech is less certain (see chap. 15 for further discussion of this issue). However, it is common to quote maximum f_0 ranges of the human voice in semitones (as illustrated in the following section), and sometimes the f_0 range of speech is quoted in semitones as well. Traunmüller and Eriksson (1995) asked listeners to give a "liveliness rating" to specially constructed speech samples, which differed according to amount of excursion of f_0 above and below the mean. They found, as expected, that greater variation in f_0 produced a higher liveliness rating. On a normal (linear) hertz scale, the lower, male voices required a relatively small increase in f_0 excursion in order to transform a low liveliness rating into a high rating; the higher, female voices required a much greater increase. However, when they were computed on a semitone scale, the increases in f_0 excursion required by the female voices were almost exactly the same as those required by the male voices. Equation 3, following, can be used to convert a range in hertz into a number of semitones.

$$\textbf{number of semitones} = \textbf{39.863 x log} \left(\frac{\boldsymbol{f_{02}}}{\boldsymbol{f_{01}}} \right) \qquad \textbf{(9.3)}$$

where f_{01} is the lower fundamental frequency, in hertz, and f_{02} is the higher.

   Example.   The range of a person's voice was found to be 180 Hz to 840 Hz. What is this range in semitones?

$$\text{Number of semitones} = 39.863 \times \log (840/180)$$

$$= 39.863 \times \log 4.67$$

$$= 39.863 \times 0.669$$

$$= 27 \text{ semitones (or 2 octaves and 3 semitones)}$$

"Log" stands for "logarithm." The logarithm of a number can be obtained from a scientific calculator by pressing the "log" key either before or after (depending on your calculator) entering the number. Logarithms are explained in chapter 10. Meanwhile, here is some practice in their use, through applying the foregoing formula.

Practice 9.3

Convert these frequency ranges into semitones (rounded to the nearest whole number).

1. 200 Hz to 400 Hz
2. 500 Hz to 1000 Hz
3. 72 Hz to 144 Hz
4. 92 Hz to 532 Hz
5. 214 Hz to 935 Hz

Answers. 1. 12 semitones   2. 12 semitones   3. 12 semitones 4. 30 semitones 5. 26 semitones

---

Notice that although conversion to semitones creates a useful alternative portrayal of f_0 *ranges*, the underlying f_0 values themselves are lost in the process; so it is often best to give both the range in semitones and the upper and lower values in hertz. For example, the ranges in questions 1 to 3, in Practice 9.3, are all 12 semitones (one octave) but the least and greatest frequencies would probably be of interest as well. The lower value of 72 Hz, in question 3, would be particularly interesting because it is very low in the human voice range.

THE FUNDAMENTAL FREQUENCY OF THE HUMAN VOICE

As described earlier, the f_0 of a sound (of speech, singing, etc.) produced by the human vocal apparatus is directly determined by the rate of vibration of the vocal folds. If the vocal folds are opening and closing 150 times every second (150 Hz), then the sound that issues forth from the mouth will have a f_0 of 150 Hz. So the f_0 range of a person's voice is limited by how slowly and how fast the vocal folds can be set into vibration (on the mechanism of vocal fold vibration, see chap. 18). The ordinary range of f_0 of the human voice in general could be put at approximately 90 Hz to 1000 Hz, but this range would not be available to a single individual. Male voices tend to occupy the lower part of the range and women the upper part. The difference is due to the enlargement of the male vocal folds, which occurs at puberty. If outstanding singing performances are included, then minimum f_0

goes down at least as far as 65 Hz. Lee Marvin, who is famously deep in his rendering of the song *Wanderin' Star*, achieves 65 Hz (two octaves below middle C) on the vowel of "mud" in the line "Mud can make you prisoner ...," for example. Even lower f_0s can occur, however, when the vocal folds go into a distinctive mode of vibration known as creak (see chap. 18), which makes a strained, rattling sound. At the other end of the range, a soprano singer might be capable of reaching above 1500 Hz. Mozart's *Popoli di Tessaglia* includes the note G6 (two octaves and seven semitones above middle C), which, at around 1570 Hz, would be an exceptional achievement even for a trained soprano. Frequencies at the very top of a person's range are usually achieved using a falsetto mode of vibration, in which the vocal folds are stretched and thin (see chap. 18). This is more distinctive in male voices than in female. Counter-tenors are male singers who sing entirely in falsetto. The counter-tenor Alex Potter, for example, singing the lament in *Orpheus and Eurydice*, by Gluck, (which is traditionally sung by a counter-tenor), uses a range of approximately 200 Hz to 730 Hz.

When reporting f_0 ranges it is necessary to distinguish between measures of the highest and lowest *possible* frequencies that an individual can produce and measures of the range of f_0 the individual uses during normal speech. Neither is entirely fixed. Maximum performance changes with age (and can even vary to some extent from one day to the next) and f_0 range during speaking varies according to mood, topic, and other factors. Nevertheless, group data from a number of studies are useful in giving an indication of typical f_0 ranges.

Maximum Fundamental Frequency Range of Individual Voices

The focus of interest here is on discovering a person's maximum f_0 range (i.e., the highest and the lowest f_0s that that person can possibly produce). Once the approximate maximum f_0 range that can be expected of a normal, healthy adult has been established, it can be used as a basis for comparison with other groups and individuals, such as children at various stages of development, specialist voice users, or people with voice problems.

Different methods of investigation can produce rather different results. Notably, there is the problem of which vocalizations are included or excluded: Are ghastly groans included at the lower end and mouselike squeaks at the upper, or are only reasonably melodious sounds included in the analysis? Kent, Kent, and Rosenbeck (1987, p. 373) addressed this question by distinguishing "physiological frequency range" from "musical frequency range." Most recent studies appear to have inclined toward the latter, as being safer for the participants and giving more consistent results. There is also the question of how the productions are elicited from the participants in the experiment. Reich, Frederickson, Mason, and Schlauch (1990) used several different elicitation methods in measuring the musical f_0 range of a group of male adults and a group of female adults. Table 9.1 summarizes their results, averaged across all elicitation methods. Notice that the women's range, in hertz, was considerably greater than the men's, but both sexes had a range of 34 semitones, which is a bit under three octaves. In a more recent study, Zraick, Nelson, Montague, and Monoson (2000) also found a mean range of 34 semitones, in a group of female subjects. (The two studies appear to have used different criteria with respect to the inclusion of falsetto vocalizations but this may not have made much difference, so far as the female participants were concerned, as falsetto voice is not very distinctive in women.)

TABLE 9.1 **Mean Values of the Results of a Test of Maximum f_0 Range in a Group of Men and a Group of Women**

	Lowest Possible f_0 in Hertz	Highest Possible f_0 in Hertz	Range in Hertz	Range in Semitones
Males	83	588	505	34
Females	154	1097	943	34

Note. Based on data reported in Reich, Frederickson, Mason, and Schlauch (1990).

Speaking Fundamental Frequency

A compilation by Baken and Orlikoff (2000, p. 175; see their Table 6-2) of results of a number of studies suggests an average speaking f_0 for male voices of something over 100 Hz and an average for female voices of around 200 Hz. Average and range of f_0 can of course vary considerably within the same speaker, according to all sorts of aspects of the content and context of the speech and this could explain some of the variability that is found among the results of published studies of speaking f_0. There are other factors beside the obvious one of gender that can promote differences between speakers, like age, for example. Krook (1988) measured the average speaking f_0 and range of speaking f_0 of a large number of adult Swedish speakers of different ages, while they were reading aloud a passage of text. The average speaking f_0 of the male participants (age range 20–79 years) was 116 Hz and that of the female participants (age range 20–89 years) was 188 Hz. Both groups used a range of just over five semitones. The results for the different age groups suggested a tendency for average speaking f_0 to decrease with age in women and also for a rise in f_0 among men in old age. The average speaking f_0s for just the 20 to 29 year old age group were 112 Hz for the males and 196 Hz for the females.

Speaking f_0 is constrained by physiology, of course, but not entirely so. There is scope for a speaker to exercise choice over their habitual f_0, which raises the possibility that speaking f_0 could be open to cultural influences. Pemberton, McCormack, and Russell (1998) analyzed high quality recordings made in 1945 of a group of 18 to 25 year old Australian women with further recordings, using the same speech material, of a similar age group in 1993. They found a significant drop in mean f_0, from 229 Hz in 1945 to 206 Hz in 1993, a drop that they ascribe to social influence, suggesting that high-profile female role models had recently been adopting a deeper style of voice production.

LINGUISTIC ROLE OF f_0

Intonation

Intonation is the meaningful variation in f_0 over the course of an utterance (although it is often used in a wider sense, as explained later). A f_0 waveform is a graph that plots changes in f_0 over the time course of an utterance. Such a graph is often called a pitch contour (cf. the remarks about the term pitch in the opening paragraph of the section "Definition and Measurement," earlier). Figure 9.3 shows f_0 waveforms of different utterances of the sentence "Here are my answers" (RP accent). Notice first that there is a break in each of the contours. This coincides with the [s] in the middle of "answers," which, being a sound with a random waveform, has no f_0. Another, though not so immediately obvious, feature common to all four waveforms is a tendency for a general downward trend in f_0 over the course of the utterance. This is typical and is known as *declination*. *Declination* is the term for the downward trend in f_0 that tends to occur over the time course of an utterance. It is a tendency that is easily enough reversed of course, by an effort on the part of the speaker and it often *is* reversed for a particular meaningful effect, notably in conveying a question, or a questioning attitude on the part of the speaker.

The differences among the waveforms of Fig. 9.3 arise from the fact that the main stress falls on a different word, in each different version of the sentence. In the top left waveform, there is a rise in the contour about two thirds of the way along. This occurred on the first syllable of the word "answers," and has the effect of giving the main stress to this word: "Here are my ANswers" [hɪəɹ ə maɪ ˈɑnsəz]. The main stress is on a different word in each of the other waveforms. In the top right waveform, the main stress was on "my": "Here are MY answers" [hɪəɹ ə ˈmaɪ ɑnsəz]. Notice that this pronunciation almost inevitably invites the listener to focus particularly on the fact that the answers are mine,

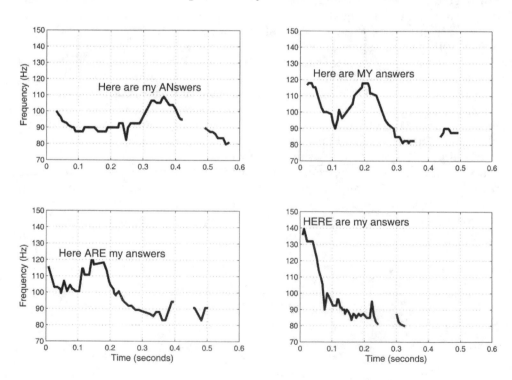

FIG. 9.3. f_0 waveforms of four utternaces of the sentence "Here are my answers," with the main stress placed on a different word in each use. (The stressed word is capitalized.) Calibration lines are at intervals of 10 ms.

as opposed to yours or anybody else's. In the bottom left waveform, the stress was on "are": "Here ARE my answers" [hɪəɹ 'ɑ maɪ ɑnsəz]. And in the bottom right waveform, it was on "here": "HERE are my answers" ['hɪəɹ ə maɪ ɑnsəz]. In each case the stressed syllable is signaled by a rise in f_0.

Variations of f_0 in signaling different meanings are often closely combined with variations of duration (see the previous chapter) and, to a lesser extent, variations in amplitude (see the following chapter). Factors associated with the f_0, duration, and amplitude of speech are collectively called *prosody*. However, the term intonation is often used more or less interchangeably with prosody, presumably because f_0 variation is the most important parameter. Prosody provides a great challenge to phonetic theory. It is an aspect of speech that is difficult to transcribe. Indeed, it is routinely omitted from phonetic transcriptions, unless the focus of the analysis is specifically on prosody. This difficulty is compounded by the fact that the differences of meaning signaled by prosody are very often continuous rather than discrete in nature, which makes prosody-meaning associations difficult to define. Also, the meanings conveyed encompass nonlinguistic meanings as well as linguistic meanings: For example, the sentence "Here are my answers" could be uttered with varying degrees of pleasure, and the degree of pleasure would be conveyed partly by the intonation pattern. Here, we give just a few, relatively clear, examples of the way in which intonation can modify the linguistic meaning of an utterance. In each case, prosody/intonation affects the linguistic meaning of the utterance, in an all-or-none fashion.

Signaling a question by means of a rise in f_0 has already been mentioned. A sentence with the syntax of a statement, like "He's late," can be turned into a question by a rise in f_0 on the final word. This is conveyed in writing by a question mark: "He's late?" Punctuation, often aided by other devices like the use of italics and so forth, is an attempt to convey some of what is conveyed in speaking by intonation. Variations of the intonation contour of "He's late?" could convey further, emotional meaning, such as surprise or disgust. The second example concerns restrictive versus nonrestrictive relative clauses. In writing, the distinction can be conveyed by commas:

(a) The boys, who traveled by car, were sick.
(b) The boys who traveled by car were sick.

Sentence (a) implies that all the boys were sick; sentence (b) that only some were sick. Sentence (a) would be pronounced with a complex f_0 movement over the word "boys," ending with a rise, and with a potential pause occurring after this word as well. These devices serve to isolate the relative clause, "who traveled by car," and give it a separate intonation contour. In (b), the word "boys" fits smoothly into the single intonation contour with which "The boys who traveled by car" is spoken. Similar devices can be used to distinguish, for example:

(c) They walked, naturally.
(d) They walked naturally.

The examples discussed so far are cases in which intonation disambiguates a syntactically ambiguous sentence. More commonly, intonation helps signal relationships that are conveyed by other means as well. Consider, for example:

(e) The concrete mixers blocked the view.
(f) The concrete pillars blocked the view.

In (e), "concrete mixers" is a compound ("concrete" is a noun) but in (f) "concrete pillars" is an adjective–noun sequence (the pillars are concrete). The reader is invited to ponder whether, and if so how, their intonation patterns for "concrete pillars" and "concrete mixers" would differ in these sentences.

Several chapters in Brown (1990) deal, in an accessible way, with English prosody. Cruttenden (1997) provided a clear and comprehensive introduction to the topic. Ladd (1994) is also a useful text, from a more theoretical perspective.

Phonemic Use of f_0

In the majority of languages (although not in English), f_0 plays a role in lexical identity, that is, in distinguishing one word from another. Such languages are called tone languages. In Cantonese, for example, as described by Yip (1994), the syllable /si/ forms seven different words, according to the f_0 contour with which the syllable is spoken. Three of them are illustrated in Fig. 9.4. An f_0

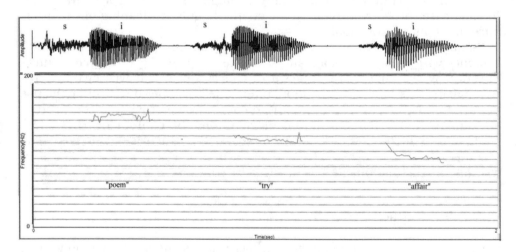

FIG. 9.4.   Three words spoken by a Cantonese speaker. They all consist of the syllable /si/ but they are distinguished by f_0. Calibration lines are at intervals of 10 Hz.

Practice 9.4

1. What was the f_0, to the nearest 10 Hz, of each of the words in Fig. 9.4, at the midpoint of the vowel?
2. Why is there no f_0 contour corresponding to the /s/ in /si/ in any of the waveforms?

Answers. 1. 150 Hz (/si/ meaning "poem"), 110 Hz (/si/ meaning "try"), 90 Hz (/si/ meaning "affair") 2. /s/ is voiceless and therefore has no f_0

contour that forms part of a word's identity is a *tone*. Tones could be described as "f_0 phonemes." There are eight different tones in Cantonese. Speakers of languages like English, which do not have tones, often have difficulty with the tones if they try to learn a tone language as a second language in adulthood. However, in the natural course of language acquisition in childhood, tones are typically acquired early and easily; also, problems with tones rarely form part of the speech problems of children with developmental speech disorders (Li Wei, Zhu Hua, & Dodd, 2002).

A NOTE ON TRILLS

For the sake of completeness, we should mention trills, which also have fundamental frequency. Trills are created by vibration of structures in the supralaryngeal vocal tract and descriptions of trilled consonants can be found in chapters 4 and 6. As the structures involved are bulky compared to the vocal folds, trills tend to have comparatively low fundamental frequencies. Trills are most usually voiced, that is, they are produced with simultaneous vocal fold vibration. The most common trilled speech sound is the alveolar trill, [r], in which the tip of the tongue vibrates against the alveolar ridge. Figure 9.5 is the waveform of a sustained alveolar trill. The period of the trill is 0.04 seconds and therefore the f_0 is 25 Hz.

EXERCISES

1. The periods of a number of periodic sounds are given in the following list. Calculate the f_0 of each (to the nearest whole number).

   a. 10 ms   e. 13 ms   i. 1 ms

   b. 2 ms   f. 8 ms   j. 6.5 ms

   c. 9 ms   g. 4 ms

   d. 15 ms   h. 9.5 ms

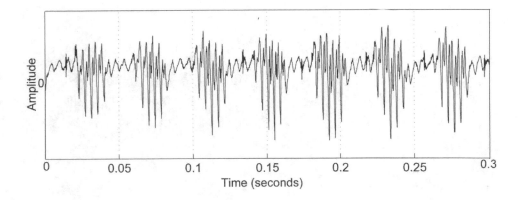

FIG. 9.5.   Waveform of an alveolar trill.

2. Judging from the f_0 s of the waveforms of Fig. 9.3, was the speaker most likely to be female or male?
3. Figure 9.6 is the waveform of an utterance of the word "see-saw."

  a. Without doing any actual measurement, say which syllable you think was uttered with the higher f_0 and give the reason for your conclusion.
  b. Estimate and state the f_0 of the vowel of "saw" /sɔ/, between 0.5 and 0.6 s. Explain the method you used.
  c. Judging from the f_0 of this word, was the speaker most likely to be female or male?

4. The fundamental frequencies of a number of sounds are given in the following list. Calculate the period of each in seconds (to four decimal places).

a. 180 Hz	e. 510 Hz	i. 536 Hz
b. 90 Hz	f. 80 Hz	j. 960 Hz
c. 210 Hz	g. 375 Hz	k. 470 Hz
d. 150 Hz	h. 123 Hz	l. 85 Hz

5. The periods of a number of different sounds are given in the following list, in seconds. In each case, state the f_0, in Hz, and also state whether it would be possible (P) or impossible (I) for normal human vocal folds (male or female, including professional singers) to vibrate at this frequency.

a. 0.005 s	e. 0.0026 s	i. 0.0001 s
b. 1 s	f. 0.009 s	j. 5 s
c. 2 s	g. 0.001 s	k. 0.00005 s
d. 0.5 s	h. 0.0008 s	l. 0.015 s

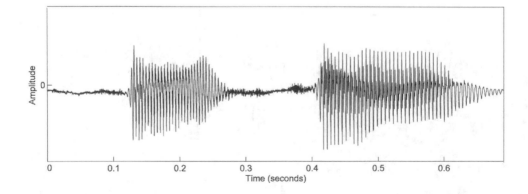

FIG. 9.6.   Waveform of "see-saw." The vertical calibration lines are at 100 ms intervals.

6. This chapter described how the f_o of the adult human voice, including both male and female, and extreme perfomance, ranges from approximately 65 Hz to 1400 Hz. What is this range in semitones?

7. Verify the semitone ranges given in Table 9.1, for the male and female subjects, by using the formula given in this chapter for converting a range in hertz into a range in semitones. If the semitone ranges are calculated to two decimal places, which subject group had the greater semitone range?

10

Sound Magnitude

Magnitude is a general term that we use for the property of a sound wave that determines the loudness that a listener experiences: Other things being equal, the greater the magnitude the greater the loudness. A measure of sound magnitude is the sound pressure amplitude of a sound wave (an alternative measure, intensity, is described briefly later). On a sound pressure waveform, amplitude of pressure corresponds to the height of the line above or below zero. Figure 10.1 (top) is a waveform of [ɑ] (like that of Fig. 8.1). Figure 10.1 (bottom) represents the waveform of a sound similar in all respects to that of the waveform above it, except that it has less amplitude. The sound represented in Fig. 10.1 (top) would be heard as louder than that represented in Fig. 10.1 (bottom). An increase in amplitude (other things being equal) produces an increase in the loudness of a sound. The term loudness is reserved for the sensation experienced by the listener, rather than sound magnitude itself, and this usage is consistent throughout the speech and hearing science literature. The relationship between loudness and sound pressure amplitude is described in Chapter 14.

Apart from the fact that in any conversation a certain magnitude is a *sine qua non* ("without which nothing") for successful communication, sound magnitude does not play much of a role in signaling meanings in language, although it can help to convey a speaker's attitude and emotion. There is no language (we confidently assert!) in which two words are distinguished solely by one being pronounced more loudly than the other. Variation in magnitude does make a contribution toward signaling relationships among the words in a sentence but its role in this respect is less than those of f_0 variation and comparative duration. To those whose primary interest is the way in which linguistic meanings are realized phonetically, a precise understanding of sound magnitude may seem comparatively unimportant. It is, however, very important in the fields of hearing science and clinical speech science and for experimental work in speech perception.

MEASUREMENT OF SOUND MAGNITUDE

A commonly used unit of sound pressure is the Pascal, abbreviated to Pa. The vertical scales of the waveforms of Fig. 10.1 show by how much the sound pressure amplitude, in Pascals, deviates from atmospheric pressure. Atmospheric pressure is represented by zero on these scales (normal atmospheric pressure is actually in the region of 100000 Pa). It is not usual to show an amplitude scale in Pascals on speech waveforms. In the usual process of sound recording, changes in amplitude are converted to changes in electrical voltage, and on most computer-based waveform displays, the amplitude scale is shown in units that are arbitrary from the acoustic point of view. The pressure values for the waveform of Fig. 10.1 are estimates only.

A measurement of sound pressure amplitude taken at one instant on the time scale of a sound pressure waveform is not very informative because the sound pressure changes from one instant to the next. An average amplitude, in which successive sound pressure values are collected together and averaged, is of more interest. A special kind of average is used for this purpose, called the root mean square (RMS) amplitude, which ensures that positive and negative sound pressure values do not cancel each other out. (For an explanation of the root mean square calculation see, e.g., Speaks, 1996.) Hence-

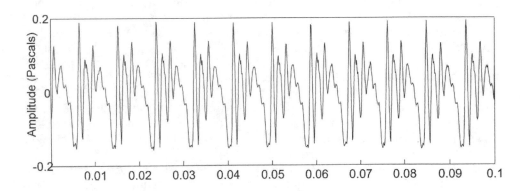

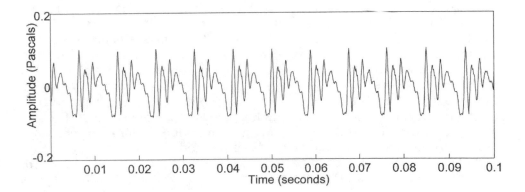

FIG. 10.1. Waveforms of [ɑ], identical except that the top waveform has greater sound pressure amplitude than the one beneath.

forth, unless the context suggests otherwise, "sound pressure amplitude" can be taken to mean "RMS sound pressure amplitude."

Another measure of sound magnitude is intensity. *Intensity* is defined as the acoustic power delivered to a unit area ("window") in the path of the sound wave. Intensity and amplitude are related in that intensity is proportional to the square of the amplitude. Intensity is recorded in watts per square meter. However, sound magnitude is most often quoted neither in Pascals nor watts per square meter but in terms of a scale called the decibel scale. A sound level meter, for example, gives readings of sound magnitude in decibels. We devote a considerable proportion of this chapter to an explanation of the decibel scale.

THE DECIBEL SCALE

The decibel is a familiar unit because levels of environmental noise are quoted in decibels. The abbreviation for decibel is dB. Decibel values can be derived from measurements either of the sound pressure amplitude or of the intensity of a sound. The decibel value is the same regardless of whether it is derived from the one or the other. The account that follows describes how decibel values are calculated from sound pressure amplitude values.

The decibel scale solves two problems in the measurement of sound magnitude. One is that the focus of interest is often on the *relative* amplitude of a number of sounds, or sound components, rather than their absolute magnitude. Another is that the range of amplitudes that are within the scope of human hearing is enormous.

Important Characteristics of the Decibel Scale

The decibel scale has two notable characteristics: (a) A decibel value denotes a *ratio* of two sound pressure amplitudes, and (b) It is a *logarithmic* scale. These characteristics are explained and illustrated in turn.

A Decibel Value Denotes a Ratio of Two Sound Pressure Amplitudes. A decibel is not a unit of sound magnitude. Rather, a decibel value tells us how many times greater (or less) one sound is than another sound. For example, if a sound is described as having a magnitude of 40 dB this means that it has a sound pressure amplitude 100 times greater than the sound to which it is being compared. (The reason why it is 100 times and not 40 times is explained later.) The sound that is recorded as 40 dB in this example would be dubbed "the sound of interest" and the sound to which it was compared would be known as "the reference sound."

Obviously, if 40 dB is to be used to report the actual magnitude of a particular sound then we must know what the amplitude of the reference sound is. In other words, "40 dB" means "100 times greater in amplitude"; but for many purposes we need to know the magnitude of the reference sound. A commonly agreed standard reference, known as Sound Pressure Level (SPL), is an amplitude of 0.00002 Pascals, that is, 20 millionths of a Pascal or 20 microPascals, which is written 20 μPa. It was chosen because it was estimated that a sound of this size was at the threshold of normal human hearing (see chap. 14 for more on this). Any decibel value that is calculated according to this reference is (or should be) labeled dB SPL. So 40 dB SPL means "a sound pressure amplitude 100 times greater than 20 μPa." Table 10.1 shows dB SPL values for some sounds commonly encountered in an industrialized society. They are only very approximate of course, designed to give a rough idea of the sorts of values involved, but they illustrate that we live in the context of constant sound; and because there is no auditory equivalent to the visual exclusion we can achieve by closing our eyes, there is no escaping this sound. The sound level of the human environment rarely goes below about 30 dB SPL. At the other end, consistent exposure to sound above about 85 dB SPL can result in hearing loss. The European Union's Council Directive 86/188/EEC (Official Journal of the European Communities, 1986) stipulates that a worker should not be exposed, long term, to levels greater than this in the workplace. (Actually, the regulation is stated in terms of a specially weighted version of the decibel scale, called the dBA scale, which is designed to reflect more precisely the response of the human ear.)

Although 140 dB SPL is the greatest sound magnitude illustrated on Table 10.1, it is not the maximum possible. An often-quoted maximum possible sound pressure level, for a sound wave produced in air at normal atmospheric pressure, is 194 dB SPL, corresponding to a sound pressure amplitude of about 100000 Pa. The reasoning is that if a sound wave had negative peaks lower than about –100000 Pa then these negative peaks would have to go below a vacuum, which is not physically possible (Turner & Pretlove, 1991, p. 15). The effects of a sound level of 194 dB SPL on the human ears (indeed on the human body) are too awful to contemplate.

TABLE 10.1   **Typical Amplitudes, in Decibels, of Various Sounds From Everyday Life**

dB SPL	Example
0	A just-audible sound
10	Rustle of leaves
20	Broadcasting studio
30	Quiet garden
40	Library
50	Quiet office
60	Conversational speech
70	Average radio
80	Noisy factory
90	Pneumatic drill
100	Symphony orchestra (fortissimo)
110	Rock band
120	Jet aircraft taking off
130	Threshold of pain
140	Gunfire at gunner's ear

Note. Adapted from similar tables in, for example, Bruel and Kjaer, 1984; Fry, 1979; Turner and Pretlove, 1991; and White, 1975.

SPL in sound measurement may be compared to sea level in geography, the reference level from which the heights of mountains are measured. However, in reporting heights we do not always use the sea level reference. For example "The height of the Scott Monument is 61 meters" would be interpreted to mean 61 meters above the ground beneath, not 61 meters above sea level. Similarly in phonetics it is sometimes more relevant to report the magnitude of a sound relative to, for example, the ambient noise. In this case 40 dB would mean "40 dB (100 times) greater in amplitude than the surrounding noise." This is in fact a common measurement, called the *signal-to-noise ratio* (S/N ratio).

The Decibel Scale is a Logarithmic Scale.   Assuming that it is desirable to express sound magnitudes relatively (as ratios), why couldn't we just say "This sound is 100 times the reference level," "This sound is 100,000 times the reference level," and so on? Well, we could, of course. However, the numbers involved encompass an enormous range. The sound of a jet aircraft taking off is some 1,000,000 times greater in amplitude than a sound at the threshold of hearing. A logarithmic scale was therefore adopted. A logarithmic scale compresses the range and at the same time it fits better with the response of the human ear.

1,000,000 is 10^6 (10 to the power of 6). Six (6) is therefore the *logarithm* of 1,000,000. Similarly, two (2) is the logarithm of 100 because $100 = 10^2$; 2.6 is the logarithm of 398 because $398 = 10^{2.6}$, and so on. In other words the logarithm (to base 10) of a number is the power by which 10 must be raised in order to obtain that number. The word logarithm is usually reduced to log, thus: log 1,000,000 = 6, log 100 = 2, log 398 = 2.6, and so on. Logarithms are available on any scientific calculator.

Notice that the logarithm of 1 is 0 (that is, $10^0 = 1$) and that the logarithms of fractions below 1 are negative. For example, the logarithm of 0.01 is –2, because $10^{-2} = 0.01$. A more detailed account of logarithms can be found in Speaks (1996). Tutorial help with such things can also be got by searching the Internet.

A Bel, named after Alexander Graham Bell, a pioneer of speech and hearing research, is the logarithm of the ratio of two sound intensities. However, the Bel scale was found to be too small because it compresses the range *too*

Practice 10.1

(You will need a scientific calculator for some of these questions.)
Find the logarithm of:

1.	100	6.	1
2.	10	7.	500/5
3.	1000	8.	34
4.	100000000	9.	2
5.	10000	10.	0.005

Answers.

(1) 2   (2) 1   (3) 3   (4) 8   (5) 4
(6) 0   (7) 2   (8) 1.53   (9) 0.3   (10) –2.3

much. This was remedied by the simple expedient of multiplying Bel values by 10: thus the decibel. Because, in the present account, decibel values are derived from measurements of sound pressure amplitude, rather than intensity, the formula for calculating a decibel value involves (for reasons it is not necessary to go into) multiplying by 20 instead of 10. The formula, then, for deriving a decibel value from the ratio of two sound pressure amplitudes is:

$$\textbf{dB value} = \textbf{20 x log}\left(\frac{\textbf{\textit{P}}}{\textbf{\textit{P}}_0}\right) \tag{10.1}$$

where P is the pressure of the sound of interest and P_0 is the reference.

Here are three examples of the calculation of decibel values from two sound pressure amplitudes.

Example 1

P = 3994 μPa and P_0 = 252 μPa.
P/P_0 = 15.85
log P/P_0 = 1.2
20 x log P/P_0 = 24 dB

Example 2

P = 116 μPa and P_0 = 750 μPa.

P/P_0 = 0.155
log P/P_0 = –0.81
20 x log P/P_0 = –16 dB

Example 3

P = 982 μPa and P_0 = 982 μPa
P/P_0 = 1
log P/P_0 = 0
20 x log P/P_0 = 0 dB

Because of the properties of logarithms, described earlier, where the sound of interest is smaller than the reference, as in Example 2, their ratio is less than 1 and the decibel value is negative. And Example 3 demonstrates that a sound of 0 dB does not denote silence; rather, it means that the sound of interest has the same amplitude as the reference.

When the magnitude of a sound is expressed in decibels, it is more usual to speak of its "level," instead of its "amplitude" (or "intensity"): thus "a level of 50 dB" instead of "an amplitude of 50 dB," for example. In this book however, the word amplitude is often used for dB values. When the expression "sound pressure level" is used, the implication is that the decibel value is referenced to SPL: thus "a sound pressure level of 50 dB" implies 50 dB SPL. Therefore the phrase "a sound pressure level of 50 dB SPL," for example, contains some harmless repetition.

Practice 10.2

These are sound pressure amplitudes, in Pascals. Express each in dB SPL, rounded to the nearest whole number. (Remember: SPL = 0.00002 Pa.)

1. 0.00004 Pa
2. 0.009 Pa
3. 0.1 Pa
4. 2.8 Pa
5. 25.4 Pa
6. 0.00002 Pa

Answers. 1. $20 \times \log(0.00004/0.00002) = 6$ dB SPL 2. 53 dB SPL 3. 74 dB SPL 4. 103 dB SPL 5. 122 dB SPL 6. 0 dB SPL

AMPLITUDE OF THE HUMAN VOICE

Here, "voice" must be interpreted in its looser sense: whereas vocal fold vibration is a major influence on the amplitude of human vocal output, the shape and size of the vocal tract above the larynx are also involved. Notably, in the case of vowel sounds, the more open the vowel the greater is its sound pressure amplitude, other things being equal. Thus a speaker will be able to achieve greater amplitude on an /ɑ/ sound than on an /i/ sound.

As with f_0, it is important to distinguish between maximum performance measures and typical values for everyday speech. Maximum performance measures are useful in assessments of vocal health and also for professional singers, who need to be able to produce high amplitude sound over long periods without damage to their vocal folds. The phonetogram is a useful technique for measuring the *dynamic range*, that is maximum and minimum amplitudes, of a person's voice.

Phonetograms

The maximum and minimum sound pressure amplitudes that a person can achieve vary, for voiced sounds, with the f_0 of the sound. Maximum amplitude will probably be achieved at a frequency somewhat above the middle of the person's range and minimum amplitude at a frequency near the lower end of the range.

A *phonetogram* is a graph showing the pattern of maximum and minimum sound pressure levels attained across a person's f_0 range. At each note in the range, the subject is asked to produce the loudest /ɑ/ sound they can and then the quietest /ɑ/ sound (keeping the sound fully voiced). The sound level is read from a sound level meter and recorded on the dB scale (the weighted scale called the dBA scale is usually used, as in this case) on the vertical axis of the graph. When measuring and comparing vocal amplitudes it is very important to hold constant the distance from mouth to microphone, otherwise spurious differences will be recorded. A commonly used mouth-to-microphone distance is 30 cm. Figure 10.2 is the phonetogram of a male subject, an amateur singer who has an impressive frequency range of 43 semitones. This phonetogram has the "lemon" shape typical of phonetograms of normal speakers: Maximum and minimum levels begin to approach each other at the bottom of the frequency range and going up the scale the minimum level achievable rises ever more steeply. Notice that the downward trend after 330 Hz on Fig. 10.2 is reversed as the voice goes from modal voice (which can be thought of as normal vibration for present purposes) into falsetto, which is marked by a square instead of a cross (see chap. 18, Phonation Types, for more on modes of vocal fold vibration).

Awan (1991) compared phonetograms of trained singers with those of untrained voices. The singers achieved a level 14 dB greater than that of the nonsingers on the maximum loudness phonations as well as having greater f_0 ranges. (Curiously enough though, the nonsingers achieved lower mean amplitude on the minimum loudness phonations.) Phonetograms have been found a useful tool in voice clinics, especially for assessing voice problems in professional singers, although the reliability of the technique (in the sense of the consistency of the picture it gives of the same person's voice from one occasion to the next) is a bit uncertain. Sihvo, Laippala, and Sala (2000) found that maximum levels were more consistent, from one occasion to the next, than minimum levels. Also, comparability among the results of different studies is reduced by differences in method. Coleman (1993) provided a useful and comprehensive review of sources of variation, which covers both variation in the way vocalizations have been elicited from participants and variation in the instrumentation and instrumental settings.

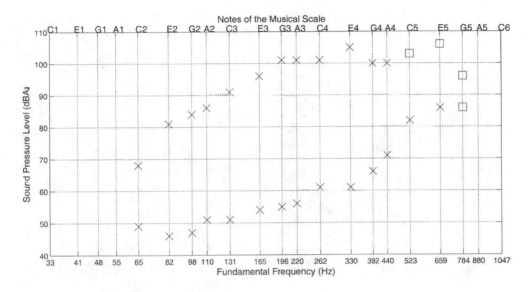

FIG. 10.2. Phonetogram of the voice of an amateur male singer.

Practice 10.3

Verify that the person whose phonetogram is shown in Fig. 10.2 has a range of 43 semitones by using the equation in chapter 9 (Equation 3) to convert his range in Hertz into the corresponding range in semitones.

Amplitude During Speaking

This varies considerably, of course, according to the circumstances. Figure 10.3, adapted from Fox and Ramig (1997, p. 89), shows (filled bars) the mean sound pressure levels of the speech of 14 normal adults during four different speaking tasks. They are in the region 72 dB SPL to 74 dB SPL, which is probably typical of clear, formal speech, measured at a mouth-to-microphone distance of 30 cm. Achievement of appropriate speech amplitude can be a problem for some people, for example, for some people with Parkinson disease. The unfilled bars on Fig. 10.3 show the mean sound pressure levels of 30 subjects with Parkinson disease, on the same tasks. They were in the region 69 dB SPL to 71 dB SPL, significantly lower than those of the healthy subjects.

Relative Amplitudes of Speech Sounds

Vowels generally have the greatest amplitude in any stretch of speech, just as they are the class of sounds that can be produced with greatest amplitude at maximum performance. Some aspects of phonological theory appeal to a "sonority hierarchy" (sonority in this usage means "amplitude") in which the different classes of speech sounds are ordered as follows:

vowels > approximants > nasals > fricatives > plosives

Syllable structure has been claimed to be governed by the sonority hierarchy. The peak of the syllable, its most sonorant portion, is usually a vowel. Conso-

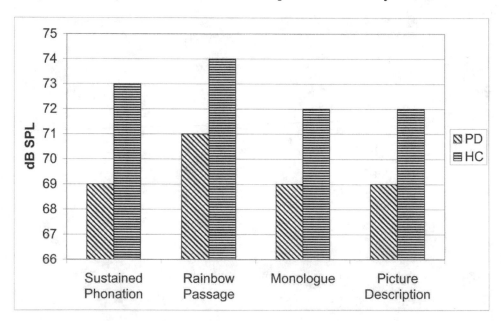

FIG. 10.3.   Mean sound pressure levels of speech, in dB SPL, of 30 subjects with Parkinson Disease (PD) and 14 normal ("Healthy Comparison," HC) subjects, during performance of four speaking tasks. After Fox and Ramig (1997, p. 89, Fig. 10.1). The Rainbow Passage (Fairbanks, 1960) is a passage of text, containing a representative balance of the speech sounds of English, which is often used in speech research.

nants preceding the peak become successively more sonorant toward the peak and consonants following the peak become successively less sonorant. The English word "print" /prɪnt/ would be an example. Sonority increases, from the /p/ to the /r/ to the /ɪ/ and then decreases, from the /ɪ/ to the /n/ to the /t/. Notice that the rule is broken by English consonant clusters beginning with /s/, like "sprint" /sprɪnt/, because the initial /s/ is *more* sonorant than the plosive that follows it. This is one reason why some phonologists describe /s/ as being "extra-syllabic," in such circumstances (see Harris, 1994, pp. 56–63).

EXERCISES

1. Copy and complete Table 10.2 below, in which the left-hand column gives sound pressure amplitude ratios and the right-hand column gives corresponding decibel values. In order to fill in the gaps in the left-hand column, you will need to apply the formula for decibel values in reverse, so you will need the inverse log function on your calculator.
2. Besides stipulating a maximum average level for exposure to noise, the European Union's directive on noise in the workplace, mentioned in this chapter, also states that a worker must not be exposed to an instantaneous noise that is greater than 200 Pa. What would this be in dB SPL?
3. Table 10.3 shows the result of a "Speech-In-Noise" test, carried out as part of an assessment of a 7-year-old child with a cleft palate (people with cleft palate often also have hearing problems). The test involves asking the child to identify spoken words, while the ambient noise is systematically varied. The Signal-to-Noise Ratio (S/N ratio) specifies how many times greater (or less, as the case may be) in amplitude the speech was than the noise, for each series of words.

    a. The tester's comment is "These results indicate poor auditory figure/ground skills." In the light of this comment, what difference would you expect to see in the pattern of results for a child with normal hearing?
    b. Which is the correct completion of the sentence?
       A S/N ratio of 0 dB implies …

       A. the words were spoken in noise-free conditions.
       B. the noise had the same sound pressure amplitude as the speech.
       C. the sound pressure amplitude of the speech was 10 times greater than that of the noise.
       D. the sound pressure amplitude of the noise was 10 times greater than that of the speech.

    c. On Table 10.3, the decibel values are labeled merely dB rather than dB SPL. Was this carelessness on the part of the tester or was it appropriate? Explain.
    d. Explain, in words, what is meant by a S/N ratio of –5 dB.

TABLE 10.2   **Sound Pressure Amplitude Ratios and Corresponding Decibel Values**

P/PO	dB
1	
	6
10	
20	
	40
50000	
178000	
14200000	
	–6
0.00023	

TABLE 10.3   **The Results of a "Speech-In-Noise" Test**

S/N ratio	% correct
+30 dB	87
+10 dB	80
+ 5 dB	67
0 dB	47

Note. Four series of words were spoken to the subject. The left column shows the signal-to-noise ratio, in decibels, for each series; the right column shows the percentage correct identification of the words by the subject.

11 Spectra of Speech Sounds

Chapter 8 described the different types of waveform distinguishing the different major sound classes. However, it did not deal with qualitative differences among sounds that are of the same type. Take, for example, the two vowel sounds [ɑ] and [i]. None of the acoustic properties described so far would account for the perceptual difference between these two sounds. They both have periodic waveforms and even when they are uttered with identical fundamental frequency, amplitude, and duration they remain perfectly distinct. A perceptual difference that does not rely on pitch, loudness, or length is a difference of *quality* (an alternative term is timbre). Quality itself is discussed in chapter 15; the present chapter is concerned with the main acoustic properties associated with it. Chapter 8 described how gross differences of quality between vowels and fricatives and plosives were associated with differences in waveform type. The finer differences in perceptual quality that exist among, for example, the different vowel sounds are related to finer differences in waveform shape. As Fig. 11.1 illustrates, the waveforms of [ɑ] and [i] have quite different shapes, although they are both periodic.

An explanation of the acoustic basis for these finer differences in quality cannot be achieved merely by a close examination of waveform shapes. It is necessary to delve more deeply into the properties of the sound. Speech sounds are made up of components at different frequencies. That is why we were careful to call the frequency of repetition of the whole cycle of a periodic wave the *fundamental* frequency. There are other frequencies above it. The quality of a sound is determined by the relative amplitudes among these higher frequency components. The analysis of the frequency components that make up a sound is called frequency analysis or frequency domain analysis in acoustic phonetics, as distinct from the time domain analysis that previous chapters have been concerned with. The results of a frequency analysis are typically displayed on a graph called a spectrum, thus the term spectral analysis. Spectral analysis has been most extensively and successfully applied in the phonetic description of vowels (of monophthongal vowels, in fact), to which the bulk of this chapter is devoted. Spectra of consonants are dealt with more briefly at the end.

SINE WAVES

A *sine wave* represents a kind of movement called simple harmonic motion. A nonacoustic example would be the motion of a swinging pendulum. A graph of displacement over time during the swinging of a pendulum would be a sine wave. An acoustic example would be the sound made by a tuning fork. When a tuning fork is struck it sets the surrounding air particles moving backward and forward in simple harmonic motion. Figure 11.2 illustrates some sine waves of different amplitudes and frequencies. Sine waves, whatever their frequency or amplitude, all have the same recognizably sinusoidal shape, in which the amplitude increases and diminishes in a smooth fashion.

Simple harmonic motion is "simple" because the relationships among the various physical factors that govern how the air particles move, namely velocity, acceleration, and displacement amplitude, are at their simplest. Periodic motion takes place in an elastic medium, air being the relevant medium in speech. An elastic medium is such that if an element is displaced from its rest position

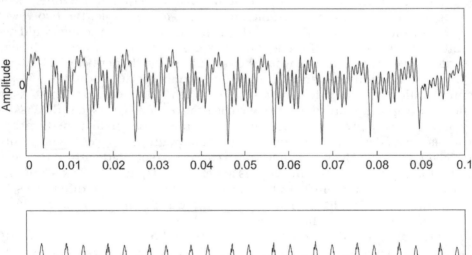

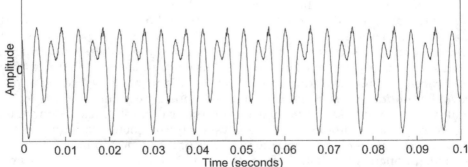

FIG. 11.1.   Waveforms of /ɑ/ (top) and /i/ (bottom).

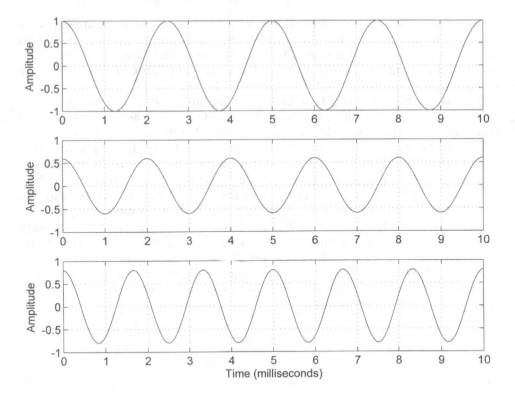

FIG. 11.2.   Examples of sine waves, of differing amplitudes and frequencies.

it becomes subject to a restoring force impelling it back toward that rest position, which it then overshoots. The result is a "to and fro" movement, something like the motion of a child's swing, in which the swing achieves its greatest speed as it passes through the rest position and gradually slows toward the apex of its travel. Armed with this information, we may define simple harmonic (sine wave) motion in air as follows: An air particle moves in simple harmonic motion if, and only if, the magnitude of the restoring force acting on it remains proportional to its amplitude of displacement at every instant. In other words, at all times, the further away the particle is from its rest position, the correspondingly greater is the force acting to bring it back to that rest position.

COMPLEX WAVES

A *complex wave* is most easily defined in a negative fashion: It is any wave which is not a sine wave. The sounds produced in human speech have complex waveforms. However, the sine wave is a vital feature of the analysis of speech because of a very important relationship that exists between complex waves and sine waves. It is this: A complex wave is made up of a number of sine waves added together. This relationship was described by a French mathematician, Jean-Baptiste-Joseph Fourier, in the early 19th century, and so the analysis of a complex periodic wave as the sum of a series of sine waves is called Fourier analysis. The relationship is illustrated in Fig. 11.3, which shows a complex wave, labeled A + B, which is the result of adding together the two sine waves, A and B. This can be verified by taking any time point (the waveforms share the same timescale), noting the amplitudes of A and B at that point and adding the values together. The resultant value should be that of waveform A + B.

The sine waves that together make up a complex wave are called its sine wave components. In the case of complex periodic waves, these sine wave components can be called harmonics. Figure 11.3 illustrates two important facts about the harmonics of periodic waveforms of speech: (a) The first harmonic (that is the harmonic of lowest frequency) has a frequency identical to the fundamental frequency of the complex wave itself, and (b) all higher harmonics are whole-number multiples of the first. Thus sine wave A in Fig. 11.3 is the first harmonic of the complex wave A + B. It has a frequency of 200 Hz, which is the same as the fundamental frequency of the complex wave A + B. Sine wave B, the second harmonic, has a frequency of $2 \times 200 = 400$ Hz. Harmonics represent the presence of sound energy so a complex periodic wave has energy at other frequencies besides the fundamental. The sound emitted by a tuning fork consists of a single sine wave and thus has energy at only one frequency.

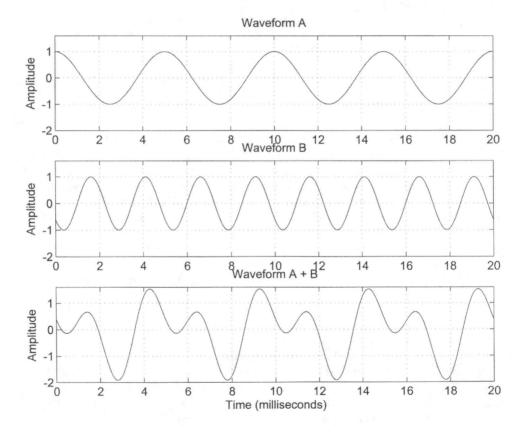

FIG. 11.3.   Sine wave components of a complex wave. The complex waveform at the bottom, labeled A + B, is the sum of the two sine waves, A and B, above it.

Practice 11.1

(These questions relate to Fig. 11.3.)

1. What is the amplitude of waveform A at 5 ms?
2. What is the amplitude of waveform B at 5 ms?
3. What is the amplitude of waveform A + B at 5 ms?
4. Is the amplitude of waveform A + B at 5 ms the sum of the amplitudes of A and B, at 5 ms?

Answers. 1. 1 2. –0.6 3. 0.4 4. Yes, because 1 + (–0.6) = 0.4

Practice 11.2

A vowel sound was spoken with a f_0 of 162 Hz. Give the frequency of its

1. first harmonic
2. second harmonic
3. third harmonic
4. fourth harmonic
5. 20th harmonic

Answers. 1. 162 Hz 2. 324 Hz 3. 486 Hz 4. 648 Hz 5. 3240 Hz

SPECTRA

A *spectrum* (plural "spectra") is a graph of amplitude over frequency. A line spectrum is a graph that provides a means of representing all the vital information about the component structure of a complex periodic wave. What information needs to be given? The waveform *shape* of each of the harmonics is the same (sinusoidal) so this need not be included. Their amplitudes and frequencies are all that need be specified. Figure 11.4 is an example of a line spectrum. In fact, it is a line spectrum of the complex wave in Fig. 11.3. Each line of a line spectrum represents a harmonic. The line's position along the horizontal (frequency) axis represents the frequency of the harmonic and its height represents the amplitude of the harmonic. Amplitude is usually given in dB. However, because it is the *relative* amplitudes of the harmonics that determines the quality of a sound, it is not, for most purposes, necessary to specify amplitude in dB SPL. Some other convenient amplitude may be used as the reference, such as the amplitude of the greatest (or least) harmonic present in the sound.

A Note on Phase

A line spectrum would not provide quite enough information from which to reconstruct the original waveform. From an examination of Fig. 11.3, it can be appreciated that not only the amplitude but also the *phase* of each sine wave component could affect the shape of the resultant waveform. That is, if one of the sine waves of Fig. 11.3 was shifted a bit leftward or rightward relative to the other, this would produce some change in the shape of the resultant waveform. A spectrum like that of Fig. 11.4 is more accurately called an "amplitude spectrum," to distinguish it from the "phase spectrum," which would supply the remaining information needed to make an exact reconstruction of the waveform. However, the human ear is not very sensitive to phase and for most purposes it can be ignored in the analysis of speech sounds (for which we must be grateful, as speech spares us few of the available complications of acoustic analysis.)

Line Spectra of [ɑ], [i], and [u]

Figure 11.5 shows line spectra of the vowels [i], [u] and [ɑ]. There are harmonics on these spectra up to 4000 Hz, the limit of the frequency scale of the graphs, but in fact they would continue, with appreciable amplitude, well beyond this. The vowels were uttered at different fundamental frequencies and so their first harmonics were at different frequencies and the higher harmonics occurred at different frequency intervals. This has nothing to do with vowel identity, it is just a consequence of the fact that any vowel can be uttered on any f_0, within the range of a given speaker.

Unlike the spectrum of Fig. 11.4, the spectra of Fig. 11.5 have harmonics of differing amplitudes. The relative amplitudes among the harmonics give the spectrum its distinctive overall shape. The shape of the spectrum determines the auditory quality of a sound. Notice that each of the spectra of the vowels of Fig. 11.5 contains a number of peaks. It is the frequencies at which these peaks occur that is most important for distinguishing the identity of a vowel sound, that is, in distinguishing [i], for example, from [ɑ] and from [u] and from all other vowels. In the spectrum of [i], there is a peak around 250 Hz,

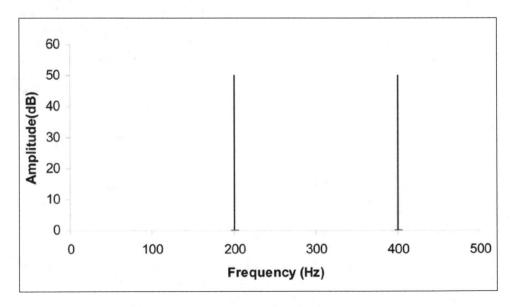

FIG. 11.4.   Line spectrum of the complex wave of Fig. 11.3.

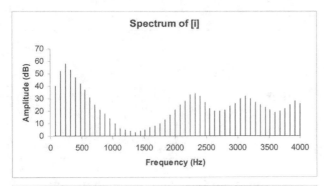

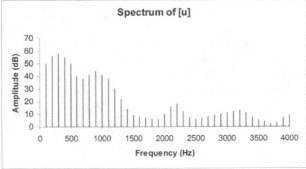

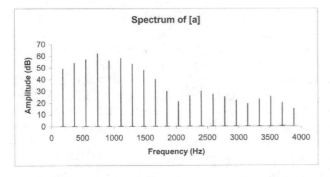

FIG. 11.5. Line spectra of the vowels [i] (top), [u] (middle), and [ɑ] (bottom).

Practice 11.3

(All these questions relate to the spectra of Fig. 11.5.)

1. With what f_0 was the vowel [i] uttered? (*Hint:* Instead of trying to estimate directly the position of the first harmonic on the frequency axis, it is easier to find the frequency of a convenient higher harmonic and calculate from that.)
2. With what f_0 was the vowel [u] uttered?
3. Is it true a vowel uttered with a higher fundamental frequency will have harmonics at wider frequency intervals?
4. State the frequency of the 12th harmonic of [i].
5. State the amplitude of the 8th harmonic of [u], to the nearest 10 dB.
6. State the amplitude of the 6th harmonic of [ɑ], to the nearest 10 dB.

Answers. 1. 80 Hz (Notice that the 25th harmonic is at exactly 2000 Hz; so the f_0 must be 2000/25 = 80 Hz) 2. 100 Hz 3. Yes 4. 960 Hz 5. 40 dB 6. 60 dB

Practice 11.4

In the spectra of Fig. 11.5:

1. What are the approximate frequencies of F1, F2, and F3 of [u]?
2. What are the approximate frequencies of F1, F2, and F3 of [ɑ]?

Answers. 1. 300 Hz, 900 Hz, 2200 Hz 2. 700 Hz, 1050 Hz, 2275 Hz

another around 2300 Hz, a third around 3100 Hz, and a fourth around 3900 Hz The fatness or thinness of a peak (bandwidth being the technical term) is not so important, nor is its amplitude or the depth of the trough between one peak and the next. The peaks are called formants. The peak of lowest frequency is called the first formant, or F1, the next is the second formant (F2), and so on. In an acoustic description of the vowels of a language, the frequencies of F1 and F2 are routinely given and usually that of F3 as well. The frequencies of higher formants (F4 upward) are rarely quoted because they have been found to make comparatively little contribution to vowel identity.

Formant Frequency and Vocal Tract Shape

Formants are resonances of the vocal tract. At resonant frequencies, the sound energy is transmitted most efficiently through the vocal tract out into the open air. Thus the peaks in amplitude on a line spectrum, where one line rises above its neighbors, occur at or near resonant frequencies. The frequencies of the resonances are determined by the shape of the vocal tract. The process of speech production involves changing the shape of the vocal tract, mainly by adjusting the shape and position of the tongue and the lips, in order to create different formant frequencies that in turn create different auditory qualities for the listener. Resonance and articulatory–acoustic relationships are discussed in more detail in chapter 17. Meanwhile, here are two generalizations about how tongue position (as described in terms of the dimensions of the vowel quadrilateral; see chap. 5) affects the frequencies of F1 and F2:

F1 frequency rises with increasing openness of the vowel

and

F2 frequency rises with increasing frontness of the vowel

These rules apply in the spectra of Fig. 11.5. They are reliable, for the most part, although they should not be interpreted as expressing a direct cause and effect relationship.

The vowels [i], [ɑ], and [u] are the so-called corner vowels and represent extremes of tongue placement. Using [i], [ɑ], and [u] for reference, approximate positions of F1 and F2 can be estimated for other vowels.

FFT Spectra

The line spectrum is an idealization (a perfect line spectrum is a spectrum of an exactly periodic wave of infinite duration). Nevertheless, most speech anal-

ysis software provides a spectral display that distinguishes individual harmonics and thus approximates a line spectrum. The Fast Fourier Transform
(FFT), with suitable settings, can be used to produce a spectrum on which the
individual harmonics are resolved as a sequence of narrow pinnacles, equivalent to the lines of a line spectrum. An example is shown in Fig. 11.6, which is
an FFT spectrum of the vowel [ɑ].

Practice 11.5

Insert the word "high" or "low":

  1. [ɑ] is an open vowel so it has a _____ F1
  2. [ɑ] is a back vowel so it has a _____ F2
  3. [i] is a close vowel so it has a _____ F1
  4. [i] is a front vowel so it has a _____ F2
  5. [u] is a close vowel so it has a _____ F1

Answers. 1. high 2. low 3. low 4. high 5. low

Practice 11.6

Insert the word "higher" or "lower":

  1. [ɛ] is more open than [i] therefore it has a _____ F1
  2. [ɛ] is less open than [ɑ] therefore it has a _____ F1
  3. [a] is less front than [i] therefore it has a _____ F2
  4. [ɒ] is more open than [u] therefore it has a _____ F1
  5. [a] is more front than [ɑ] and therefore it has a _____ F2

Answers. 1. higher 2. lower 3. lower 4. higher 5. higher

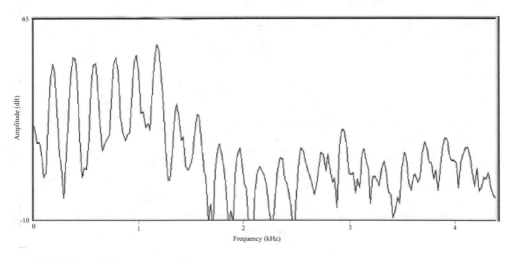

FIG. 11.6.   FFT spectrum of [ɑ].

LPC Spectra

It is the shape of the vocal tract (and not f_0) that determines the frequency at which a formant occurs. It is true that on a line spectrum the peaks are better defined if the f_0 is low, because at a lower f_0 the harmonics are more closely spaced. However, in principle, the spectrum retains the same shape regardless of the f_0. A spectrum that displayed just the formant peaks, without the superfluous information about the precise frequencies of individual harmonics, would be best for capturing the acoustic differences that are responsible for the differences in vowel quality. A technique called Linear Prediction Coding (LPC) is useful for achieving this and the LPC spectrum is another tool that is available in many speech analysis software packages. Figure 11.7 shows LPC spectra of [ɑ], [i], and [u] in which the formant peaks show up clearly but the individual harmonics are not resolved. (For a relatively nontechnical account of both the Fast Fourier Transform and Linear Prediction Coding, see Johnson, 2003.)

Choosing a Time Point to Take a Spectrum

A spectrum provides an analysis for a single point in time. When analyzing the frequency structure of a monophthong it is usual to choose a point somewhere near the middle of the vowel, when it is most likely to have settled down to its "steady state" and least likely to be showing the influence of a preceding or upcoming adjacent sound (although the absence of such influences cannot be guaranteed). Figure 11.8 illustrates the usual procedure, whereby the time point is selected on the waveform of the sound, by means of cursor placement, and the spectrum of the sound at this time point is displayed.

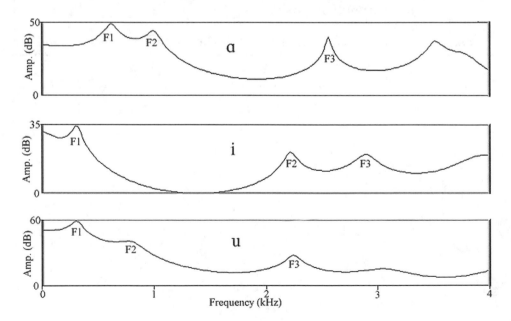

FIG. 11.7.   LPC spectra of [ɑ] (top), [i] (middle), and [u] (bottom).

Practice 11.7

In the case of each term, A to D, say which statement, or statements, from among Z to U, accurately describes it.

A. harmonic   Z. a graph of amplitude over frequency

B. formant   Y. a resonance of the vocal tract

C. spectrum   X. all waves except sine waves

D. complex wave   W. a sine wave component of a complex periodic wave

                              V. a peak in the spectrum of a vowel sound

                              U. a sine wave component, the frequency of which is a whole number multiple of the f_0.

Answers. A→W, A→U, B→V, B→Y, C→Z, D→X

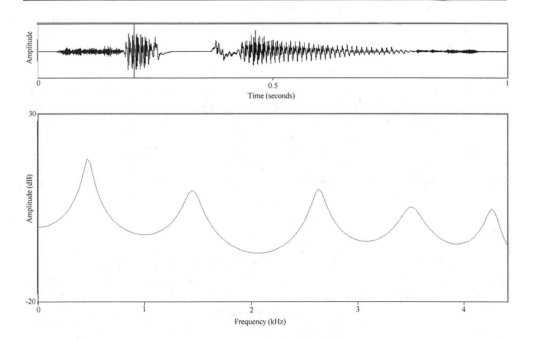

FIG. 11.8.   Waveform and spectrum. The waveform is of the word "suppose." The spectrum is of the first vowel, [ə], at the point marked on the waveform by the cursor.

A diphthong cannot be adequately analyzed by a single spectrum because the essence of a diphthong is the way it changes in quality over time. A three-dimensional display of successive spectra, known as a waterfall spectrum, is available in some speech analysis software packages, although it has not been extensively used in phonetic research. Analysis of spectral change over time is more usually done using spectrograms, which are described in chapter 12.

VOWEL FORMANTS OF ENGLISH

The formant frequencies of a person's vowels are conditioned by linguistic factors and physical factors. Vowels form part of language, so the vowel quality targets for a person's language must be represented in some way in the brain; but they are produced by means of a physical system, the vocal tract, the dimensions of which constrain the range of possible formant frequencies. When gathering and reporting information on vowel formant frequencies from a group of subjects, it is therefore usual to control for language and also to control at least for sex and for age (child vs. adult). In the case of a comparatively well-researched language like English, for which many different accents have been identified and named, it is usual to narrow the focus to a particular accent or accents. Obviously, the more tightly defined the language variety, and the more uniform the physical characteristics of the speakers, the more consistent the formant frequencies are likely to be across speakers. We report here some results from the literature on three accents of English, namely American English, RP, and Scottish English.

American English

A classic early study was that of Peterson and Barney (1952), who measured spectral properties of the vowels of a large number of men, women, and children who were all speakers of American English. Table 11.1 shows the average frequencies of F1 and F2 for six vowels, by men and women, taken from Peterson and Barney's study. As the values in Table 11.1 demonstrate, men tend to have lower formant frequencies than women. This is because they tend to have longer vocal tracts (note that it is *not* due to men's lower f_0; formant frequencies are independent of f_0). Children, with the shortest vocal tracts, have the highest formant frequencies.

RP

Table 11.2 shows average F1 and F2 values for a similar set of vowels of a group of 10 adult male RP speakers, taken from a study by Henton (1983). Of course, where the same transcription symbol is used, one would not expect large differences to be found between two vowels in different accents (or languages for that matter), and most of the values for the RP vowels are quite close to those of their American counterparts in Table 11.1. [æ] in Amercian English has a somewhat lower F1 and higher F2 than its RP counterpart (for which we have adopted the symbol [a], following Laver, 1994), suggesting that it is closer and more fronted. Also, the F2 of /u/ is much higher in RP than in American English, suggesting a more fronted tongue position.

    The American English data of Table 11.1 date from the early 1950s whereas the data from Henton, reproduced in Table 11.2, date from 1982, so we are not quite comparing like with like. However, Henton's study included a comparison with RP data reported from 1962. This demonstrated that /u/ in RP had moved forward over the intervening years (although even in 1962 it was more fronted than its American counterpart). Another study,

Table 11.1   **Average Formant Frequencies (F1 and F2) of Six Vowels Produced by a Group of American English-Speaking Men and Women**

Vowel	Formant	Frequency (Men)	Frequency (Women)
i	1	270	310
	2	2290	2790
ɛ	1	530	610
	2	1840	2330
æ	1	660	860
	2	1720	2050
ɑ	1	730	850
	2	1090	1220
ɔ	1	570	590
	2	840	920
u	1	300	370
	2	870	950

Note. The values are taken from an extensive set of data reported in Peterson and Barney (1952).

by Bauer (1985), analyzed vowels of RP from data recorded between 1949 and 1966 and from further recordings in 1982, which confirmed the fronting of /u/ in RP over the intervening years.

Scottish English

Table 11.3 shows the average frequencies of the first two formants of all nine monophthongs of Scottish Standard English, as spoken by four men and four women. Notice that /ɪ/ has a higher F1 and lower F2 than its closer and more peripheral counterpart /i/ and a similar relationship holds between /ɛ/ and /e/. If /u/ in RP English continues to move forward it will come to sound more like the corresponding vowel in Scottish English, which is actually transcribed using the symbol /ʉ/, which denotes a close central rounded vowel. The appropriateness of this can be appreciated from examining the frequency of its F2 in Table 11.3, which is considerably higher even than that of RP. Interestingly enough, the F2 of /ʉ/ as spoken by the female Scottish speakers had a *lower* mean frequency than in the male speakers. This suggests that in the case of the female speakers the vowel was not articulated quite so far forward.

Variability of Vowel Formant Frequencies

Vowel formant frequencies not only vary from one accent to another and from one speaker to another, they also vary within the speech of the same speaker. Variability is likely to be at a minimum where vowels are elicited in the same words repeated in the same circumstances, a situation that is usually striven for in an investigation of typical formant values of a particular (accent of a) language. Figure 11.9 shows a F1–F2 plot of five repetitions each of five vowels by a single speaker of Ulster English, in which the productions for each vowel are tightly bunched together. It illustrates a commonly used method of plotting the formant frequencies of a number of vowels on the same graph. Having the origin of the graph at top right instead of bottom left means that the distribution of vowels on the graph is closer to that of the conventional vowel quadrilateral (see chap. 5), with close front vowels inclining to the upper left area of the graph and open back vowels toward the bottom right. (Greater congruence still can be achieved by introducing modifications to the frequency scales or alternatively by plotting F1 against the difference between F2 and F1; see Ladefoged & Maddieson, 1996).

   The precise quality of a vowel may be influenced by such factors as immediate phonetic context, the degree of stress of the syllable in which it occurs, or

Table 11.2   **Average Formant Frequencies of Six Vowels Spoken by Male RP Speakers**

Vowel	Formant	Frequency (Hz)
i	1	272
	2	2361
ɛ	1	525
	2	1943
a	1	713
	2	1615
ɑ	1	636
	2	1050
ɔ	1	429
	2	697
u	1	347
	2	1149

Note. We have used the symbol "a" instead of the original "æ." Data from Henton (1983).

Table 11.3	**Formant Frequencies of the Nine Vowels of Scottish English**		
Vowel	*Formant*	*Frequency (Men)*	*Frequency (Women)*
i	1	295	343
	2	2329	2689
ɪ	1	436	531
	2	1936	2255
e	1	361	473
	2	2334	2590
ɛ	1	508	677
	2	2039	2317
a	1	807	874
	2	1451	1621
ʌ	1	674	865
	2	1340	1603
ɔ	1	539	734
	2	945	1080
o	1	409	489
	2	821	892
ʉ	1	355	411
	2	1587	1576

Note. We are grateful to Vivien Walker for supplying the data.

speech style (casual vs. formal). The freedom that a vowel has to vary in quality from one occasion to another is constrained by the requirement to keep it reasonably well distinguished from all other vowels. This implies that speakers of a language with a small number of vowels in its system would have more scope for variability because in these circumstances a vowel could, so to speak, wander more freely within the vowel space without trespassing on the territory of another vowel. There is some evidence that this is what actually happens. For

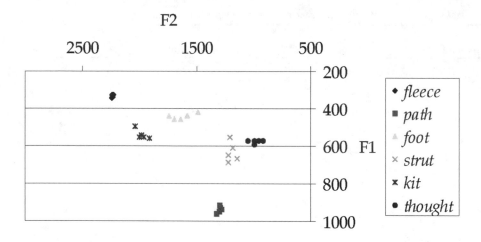

FIG. 11.9. Frequencies (in Hertz) of F2 plotted against F1, for five tokens each of six vowels of Ulster English (/i a u ʌ ɪ ɔ/), spoken by the same speaker. (We are grateful to Corrie Moore for supplying this figure.)

example, Ladefoged and Maddieson (1996, pp. 286–287), show that the F1 and F2 values for multiple tokens of a single vowel by a speaker of Arrernte, an Australian language that has only three vowels, are highly variable.

SPECTRA OF CONSONANTS

Sonorant consonants (nasals, liquids, and glides), being periodic, are similar to vowels in having a spectral structure of harmonics and formants. However, liquids and (especially) glides have little steady state and so in their case spectral analysis at a single time point is less revealing. Fricative consonants and the burst phase of plosives, being aperiodic, do not have a harmonic structure; rather, their energy is spread continuously across the spectrum.

Spectrum of a Nasal Consonant

Figure 11.10 shows the spectrum of a nasal consonant, [n]. This figure illustrates that sonorant consonants have a spectral structure comparable to vowels. The spectrum of Fig. 11.10 shows so-called nasal formants at around 200 Hz and 2800 Hz. These formants are not always clearly discernible because spectra of nasal consonants are characterized by a sharp drop in amplitude above about 1 kHz. Nasal consonants are also distinguished by frequency regions of very low energy (anti-resonances), which show as deep troughs in the spectrum.

Spectra of Fricatives

Sounds with random waveforms can be analyzed as containing sine wave components at all frequencies; that is, as having an infinite number of sine wave components within a given frequency range, rather like the infinite number of points theoretically contained by a circle. They are not, of course, harmonics, as harmonics occur at regular intervals of frequency. Differences in quality among fricatives depend on the way the energy is distributed across the spectrum.

Figure 11.11 shows spectra of [s] and [ʃ]. In these spectra, the frequency scale goes higher than the frequency scale used for the vowel spectra in this chapter, because the sound energy at higher frequencies plays a more significant role when it comes to distinguishing one fricative from another. [s] has a significant peak of energy at a particularly high frequency (about 7500 Hz in the spectrum of Fig. 11.12, top). The main peak of [ʃ] is considerably lower in frequency, at about 3500 Hz.

Spectra of Plosives

Spectra of the burst phase of plosives vary according to the place of articulation. This is particularly apparent with strongly released and aspirated voiceless plosives. Figure 11.12 shows spectra of [pʰ], [tʰ] and [kʰ] taken at a time point early on in the aspiration. A classic /p/ spectrum is one that shows a fall in amplitude with rising frequency, in contrast with /t/, which shows the opposite, namely a rise in amplitude with rising frequency. A classic /k/, on the other hand, is characterized by a mid-spectral peak. These patterns have been described as, respectively, diffuse falling, diffuse rising, and compact (Stevens, 1998).

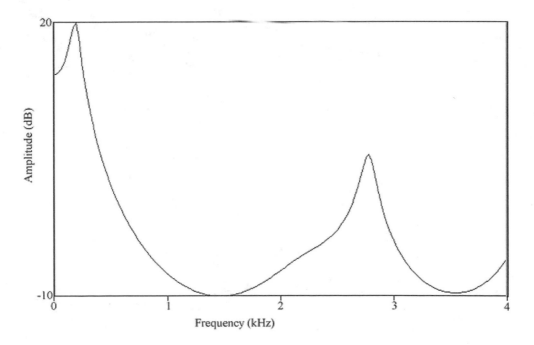

FIG. 11.10.   Spectrum of the consonant [n].

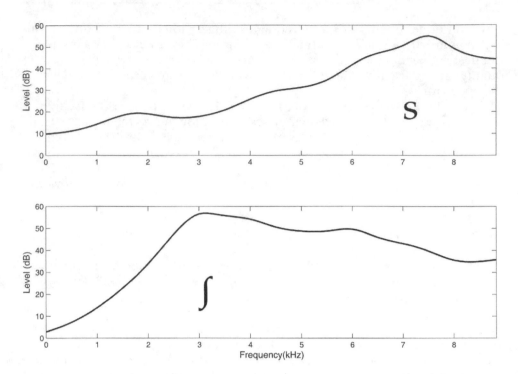

FIG. 11.11.   Spectra of [s] (top) and [ʃ] (bottom).

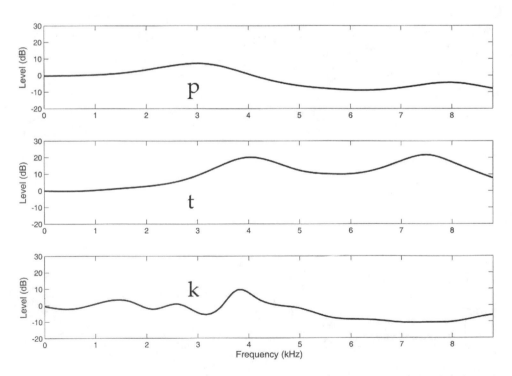

FIG. 11.12.   Spectra of the burst phase of [pʰ] (top), [tʰ] (middle), and [kʰ] (bottom).

EXERCISES

1. Label each of the statements below either T(rue) or F(alse).

    a. All periodic sounds have complex waveforms.
    b. When describing the spectrum of a normal, voiced vowel sound, the terms "harmonic" and "sine wave component" can be used interchangeably.
    c. "Formant" is another word for "harmonic."
    d. In periodic speech sounds, the frequency of a harmonic is always a whole number multiple of the fundamental frequency of the complex wave.
    e. On a spectrum, a formant appears as a region in which the harmonics have comparatively greater amplitude.
    f. The different vowel sounds are distinguished by their differing formant frequencies.
    g. The formant frequencies of a sound are determined by the shape of the vocal tract.
    h. An increase in fundamental frequency must produce an increase in formant frequencies.
    i. The lines of a line spectrum will be closer together in the spectrum of a sound with a fundamental frequency of 195 Hz than in the spectrum of a sound with a fundamental frequency of 90 Hz.
    j. A spectrum is a graph of time over frequency.
    k. It is impossible to make a spectrum of a fricative sound.
    l. Nasal sounds have harmonics and formants.
    m. Sine waves cannot be detected by the human ear.
    n. The vowel [ɑ] has a comparatively high first formant.
    o. When we are talking about speech sounds, "energy at lower frequencies" would usually refer to energy below about 12 kHz.

2. A periodic sound has a f_0 of 118 Hz. What is the frequency of its fifth harmonic?
3. Suppose the three sine waves of Fig. 11.2 were successive harmonics forming part of the same complex wave. What would be the frequency of the first harmonic of this complex wave?
4. A periodic sound has a f_0 of 279 Hz. What is the frequency of its first harmonic?
5. Sketch a line spectrum of a sine wave with a frequency of 500 Hz and an amplitude of 50 dB SPL.
6. State which of the following is the best estimate of the f_0 of the vowel [ɑ] in Fig. 11.5:

    a. 175 Hz
    b. 185 Hz
    c. 195 Hz
    d. 205 Hz

7. Sketch a line spectrum (range: 0–4 kHz) of a complex wave that has a fundamental frequency of 130 Hz and formants around 600 Hz, 1350 Hz, and 3800 Hz. Label the amplitude axis in dB and use your discretion over the precise amplitudes of the harmonics.

12

Spectrograms

We have so far considered two types of graph: waveforms and spectra. Each has its advantages and disadvantages for analysis of the speech signal. The waveform displays changes over time; however, it does not display the frequency composition of the signal. The spectrum shows the frequency composition but only at one moment in time. Continuously changing sound quality is an essential characteristic of speech, thus the most useful sort of graph would be one that showed how the frequency composition changed over time. The spectrogram is just such a graph, which was designed especially with speech in mind. This chapter provides an introduction to spectrographic analysis with illustrative examples of the spectrographic characteristics of different types of speech sounds. It also explains how spectrography can facilitate the study of speech as a dynamic process.

DEFINITION AND EXAMPLE OF A SPECTROGRAM

The *spectrogram* is a three-dimensional graph of time, frequency, and amplitude. Figure 12.1 is a spectrogram of an utterance of the word "sailing," with the corresponding waveform displayed above it, on the same time scale. Frequency is represented on the vertical axis, on a scale 0 to 5.5 kHz. Time is represented on the horizontal axis. Amplitude is represented by degree of darkening on the paper (thus the term grayscale, for this type of spectrogram). A darkened region represents a relatively large amplitude. A blank region, on the other hand, indicates that the amplitude level was too low to register. The beginning of the spectrogram shows considerable energy in the upper frequencies whereas toward the end of the spectrogram no energy is registered in the upper frequencies. The spectrograms in this book were all prepared using a commercially available software system, Multispeech™ (this software was also used for the spectra shown in chap. 11). There are nowadays a comparatively large number of alternative software systems for the acoustic analysis of speech, some of which are available free on the Internet. A well-established and well-supported system is PRAAT, which is available free at http://www.fon.hum.uva.nl/praat/

The initial [s] sound on Fig. 12.1, which has a random waveform, shows up as a region of gray drizzle. The spectrographic representation allows us to observe that this [s] lasts for about 200 ms and that although it has little energy at lower frequencies (below about 3 kHz) it has much greater energy at higher frequencies. The rest of the word, /eɪlɪŋ/, consists of a sequence of periodic sounds. Here the energy is greater in the lower half of the spectrogram. This portion is also distinguished by a sequence of vertical parallel striations that run all the way through it. Each striation reflects the energy peak of a cycle of vocal fold vibration; so the interval between adjacent striations is the period of the waveform.

There are dark, horizontally running bands in the /eɪlɪ/ portion of the spectrogram. They can be traced on into the final nasal consonant, where they are fainter. These are the formants and the spectrogram allows us to observe how the formant frequencies change over time. The second formant (F2) rises through the /eɪ/ diphthong before sinking a little toward the onset of the /l/. A sequence like /eɪlɪŋ/ is easier to segment on a spectrogram than on a waveform, because of its combination of temporal and frequency information. /l/ coincides with the interval during which F2 sinks. Its onset can be marked where there is what looks like an extra voicing striation squeezed between two others—but notice that this one does not go all the way down to the base of the spectrogram. It is probably a transient, resulting from the lateral edges of the tongue being pulled down while the tongue tip is braced against the alveolar ridge. There is no such convenient discontinuity to mark the precise offset of /l/ though. Notice

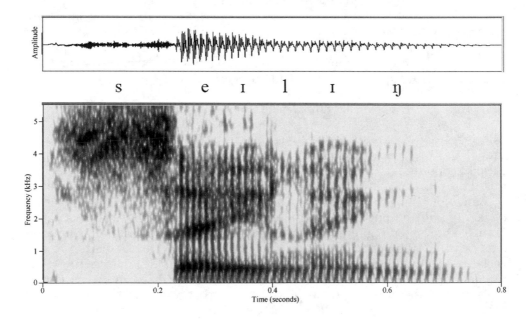

FIG. 12.1.   Spectrogram of "sailing."

Practice 12.1

These questions all relate to the spectrogram of Figure 12.1.

1. Which syllable of "sailing" was spoken with the higher f_0, the first or the second?

2. Estimate the average f_0 between 0.2 and 0.4 seconds, by counting the number of periods that occurred (use the voicing striations).

3. State in each case which formant (F1, F2, etc.) is being described.

   a. It runs more or less straight during /eɪ/, at just below 3 kHz, becomes indistinct during /l/, then continues at the same frequency during /ɪ/.

   b. It is only visible during /ɪ/, in which it lies a bit above 4 kHz.

   c. It is at about 400 Hz during the first element of the diphthong. Its frequency changes little thereafter. It tends to sink a bit over the course of the spectrogram, apart from a slight recovery during /ɪ/.

   d. It begins at about 1.5 kHz, rises to about 2 kHz, then sinks toward and during the /l/, following which it has a rising trajectory for the rest of the spectrogram.

Answers. 1. The first 2. 70 Hz (14 cycles in 0.2 seconds) 3. a. F3 b. F5 c. F1 d. F2

---

that F2 changes just as much during the monophthong /ɪ/ as during the diphthong /eɪ/. A spectrogram reminds us that during connected speech the articulators do not lurch precipitately from one sound to the next. They are in more or less continuous movement. Quality is likely to be changing over the time course of any given sound, reflecting the influence of a previous sound and/or the influence of a following sound. There are also, of course, very obvious discontinuities, like that between the /s/ and the following vowel; even here, though, some anticipation of the formant structure of the vowel can be discerned in the latter part of the /s/. Examining a spectrographic record makes clear how *unlike* writing (especially print) speech is, in this respect, and suggests that the dynamic properties of speech are at least as deserving of analysis as the static ones. The voicing striations continue during the nasal, /ŋ/, but here the formant-like activity is quite faint, at least above about 1000 Hz.

The speaker whose spectrogram appears in Fig. 12.1 had a throat infection at the time of the recording, which accounts for the low f_0 in this case (swollen vocal folds produce a slower rate of vibration). The effect on spectrograms can be quite beneficial. Similar remarks apply to spectrograms as to spectra: A lower f_0 results in closely packed harmonics, which means that the formants are better defined. Different styles of spectrograms are available and modern spectrographic software allows fine adjustments to the various settings in order to optimize the display. Most usually, the settings are adjusted with a view to displaying the vowel formants as broad, dark bands, without resolving the individual harmonics. Color spectrograms are available, however, they are not, for most purposes, significantly clearer than the grayscale continuum. Figure 12.1 could be described as a broadband, grayscale spectrogram, which is the most common variety found in textbooks and research papers. The spectrograms in this chapter are all of this sort.

A SPECTROGRAM OF A SENTENCE

Figure 12.2 is a spectrogram of the sentence "Larry might try sailing." The first portion [laɹimaɪ] is all periodic and so is characterized by the presence of vertical striations and horizontally running formant bands.

The paths of the formants can be traced more or less continuously through the whole of the first word, "Larry," from the onset of the [l] to the end of the [i]. The position of the [ɹ] can be located where F3 lowers down onto F2. At the [m] of "might," the opening of the velum produces a more abrupt change in formant structure (as well as a reduction in amplitude at higher frequencies), a change that is mirrored at the offset of the sound. (The [ŋ] of "sailing," at the end of the utterance, is similar although not quite so distinctive.)

The closure of the [tt] sequence in "might try" produces a longish gap. This is followed by the aspiration of the second [t], which shows up as a region of drizzle. It is followed by the [ɹ] of "try," which is difficult to segment from the following diphthong. The downward trajectory of the dark band at the bottom of the aspiration may reflect a rhotic gesture of the tongue, so the signaling of the /ɹ/ may well be shared between the end of the aspiration and the beginning of the vowel. The [aɪ] diphthong of "try" is a little longer than that of "might," probably because "try" is an open syllable. It is followed by the word "sailing," which, allowing for differences of speaker and scale, has a similar pattern to that of Fig. 12.1.

The following sections review the spectrographic patterns associated with different speech sounds, mostly in sentence contexts, which allows the illustration of dynamic features.

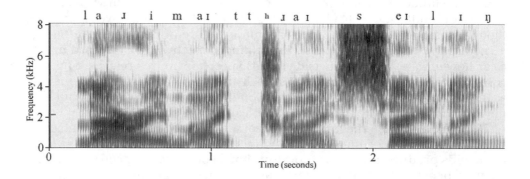

FIG. 12.2.   Spectrogram of "Larry might try sailing."

Practice 12.2

Which of the following statements are *true*?
On a spectrogram:

1. frequency is on the vertical axis.

2. frequency is on the horizontal axis.

3. time is on the vertical axis.

4. time is on the horizontal axis.

5. amplitude is on the vertical axis.

6. amplitude is on the horizontal axis.

Answer. 1, 4

SPECTROGRAPHIC CHARACTERISTICS OF MONOPHTHONGS

Chapter 11 described the formant frequencies of monophthong vowels in English. Instead of going over the same ground here, we illustrate the nature of the correspondence between spectrum and spectrogram and also some advantages of the spectrographic format for comparing vowel formant frequencies graphically.

Figure 12.3 shows a spectrogram of the vowel [ɑ] pronounced in isolation and beneath it a spectrum of the same vowel. The cursor on the spectrogram indicates the time point at which the spectrum was taken. On the spectrum, the formants show as peaks whereas on a spectrogram they show as dark horizontal bands. The center of the lowest peak of the spectrum should correspond in frequency with the middle of the lowest dark band on the spectrogram, and similarly the next peak with the next dark band and so on. Of course, the spectrum allows more accurate measurement of formant frequencies then the spectrogram. On the spectrogram, the amplitude peaks are not so well defined and where two formants are close together in frequency, as is the case with /ɑ/, they can be difficult to distinguish. Also, since the lower harmonics of a vowel have relatively large amplitude, there is often considerable darkening at the base of the spectrogram, which can be confusing. Therefore, for precise measurement of formant frequencies, at a single time point, a spectrum is preferable. However, the spectrographic format can be used to provide a convenient visual comparison of formant frequencies among a set of monophthongs. Figure 12.4 is an example. It shows the average frequencies of F1, F2, and F3 for six vowels by a group of female adult American English speakers (the values for F1 and F2 have already appeared, in Table 11.1), in a spectrogram-style format, which allows the formant frequencies to be readily compared with one another. For example, the relationships described in chapter 11, between the frequencies of F1 and F2 and tongue position can easily be appreciated from looking at Fig. 12.4.

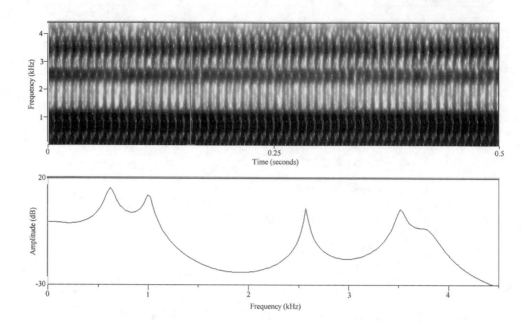

FIG. 12.3.   Spectrogram of the vowel [ɑ] (top), with a cursor placed at the time point at which the spectrum (bottom) was made.

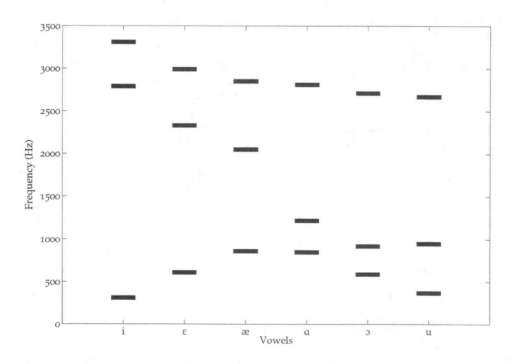

FIG. 12.4.   Spectrographic representation of vowel formants of American English-speaking women. (Values taken from Peterson & Barney, 1952).

SPECTROGRAM OF A SENTENCE WITH DIPHTHONGS

With its combination of time domain and frequency domain, spectrography is useful for examining the acoustic structure of diphthongs. The spectrogram of Fig. 12.5, of the sentence "The boys say 'go' quite loud" /ðə bɔɪz seɪ goʊ kwaɪt laʊd/, includes five diphthongs found in many varieties of English. F2 has an upward trajectory in the three vowels that end in /ɪ/, namely /ɔɪ, eɪ, aɪ/, and a downward trajectory in those ending in /ʊ/ (/oʊ, aʊ/). The movements of F2 are often the most extensive and measurements of F2 are frequently used as indicators of tongue travel. F2 of /ɔɪ/ has a brief period of steady state during the /ɔ/ phase before a rapid rise, which coincides with a downward trend in F1. During /eɪ/ (this vowel is a monophthong in some accents of English), there is no steady state in F1 or F2. Notice, however, the short voiceless portion at the beginning, which occurred during the transition from fricative to vowel, in which the first three vowel formants are clearly anticipated. The vowel of "go," on the other hand, contains far less dramatic transitions (this too is a monophthong in some accents). The brief, steep transitions at the very beginning of this vowel are not a feature of the vowel itself but rather they reflect the influence of the preceding /g/. F2 rises steeply during /aɪ/, from a low position characteristic of /a/ to a high position characteristic of /ɪ/. The F2 movement in "loud" is a little more complex. The first part of this word is taken up by the /l/ sound, which has a low second formant. From here, F2 rises surprisingly high in the first element of the diphthong, before descending again to a quite well defined /u/ phase. The explanation is that in this speaker's accent, the first element of the diphthong in /aʊ/ is quite fronted and that of /aɪ/ quite backed. In fact a better transcription might be /kwɑɪt læʊd/. /æ/ has a notably higher F2 than /ɑ/, as can be seen on Fig. 12.4.

There are other features of the spectrogram of Fig. 12.5 that are worth pointing out. At the beginning, /ð/ shows weak frication without voicing. In the /ə/ that follows, there is no evidence of any formants, just some strong voicing striations at the base of the spectrogram. This doesn't necessarily mean that formants were absent, or even inaudible. With some adjustment to the gray scale continuum of this spectrogram it should have been possible to make

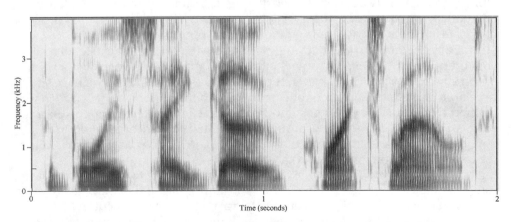

FIG. 12.5.   Spectrogram of the sentence "The boys say 'go' quite loud" [ðə bɔɪz seɪ goʊ kʰwaɪt laʊd].

formants visible, but only at the price of blackening much of the rest of the spectrogram. However, the last couple of these voicing striations may well have occurred after the beginning of the /b/ closure. A strong transient is evident (the long vertical spike) at the release of the /b/. The spectrogram gives no clues as to where to segment the final /z/ of "boys" from the word-initial /s/ that follows. There is no voice bar during any of the fricative interval. The vowel before the /g/ ends with a coming together of F2 and F3, a pattern that frequently announces a velar place of articulation (it is known as the *velar pinch*). Less clearly, but still discernible, there is another velar pinch, a mirror image of the previous one, after the release of the /g/. There was voicing all through the closure of the /g/, with vibration only failing, briefly, at the release. The pattern that reveals the voicing, a row of voicing striations confined to the base of the spectrogram, is known as a *voice bar*. The blank interval a bit after one second is the closure of the /k/ of "quite." No velar pinch is evident either at the onset or the offset of this velar sound and also it looks as though it was weakly released because no transient is evident and the aspiration is also not strong. Probably, at the release of the /k/ closure the lips were already rounded for the /w/. This would concentrate the aspiration at lower frequencies. This interval of aspiration and the onset frequencies of the vowel formants probably had a joint role in signaling the presence of a /w/. It is not possible to mark off a distinct phase corresponding to a /w/ segment, anyway. The /t/ of "quite" (the closure is the blank interval) was in this case strongly released and aspirated (shown by the interval of drizzle extending from high to low frequencies). A phase corresponding to the /l/ of "loud" can (in contrast to /w/) be made out on this spectrogram. The /l/ formants are fainter than those of the following vowel and there is not so much a smooth transition as a sudden break between the /l/ and the vowel. Finally, there is a faint voice bar extending into the closure of the /d/, which is strongly released. Figure 12.6 is an annotated version of Fig. 12.5, with lines drawn through the middle of F1, F2, and F3.

SPECTROGRAM OF A SENTENCE WITH LIQUIDS AND GLIDES

Figure 12.7 is a spectrogram of the sentence "We love your rye" /wi lʌv jɔ ɹaɪ/, which contains the two glides of English, /j/ and /w/, and the two liquids, /l/ and /ɹ/, all in word- initial position. /w/ is very similar spectrally to the vowel /u/. The /w/ of Fig. 12.7 has little steady state and its presence is probably signaled more by its steep F2 trajectory into the following /i/. This is what one might expect in a glide, which implies a fleeting, dynamic sound on the margin of a vowel. /j/ is similar spectrally to the vowel /i/. However, the /j/ of "your," on Fig. 12.7, does have an appreciable steady state, a longer one, ironically, than the /i/ of "we." The /l/ is well defined by an interval of voicing and formant structure that is fainter than the vowels either side. The onset and offset of this reduced amplitude are both abrupt. Of all these sounds, /l/ is most easy to mistake for a nasal consonant (see the following section) on a spectrogram. It tends to have a low first formant, with higher formants being somewhat dependent on the position of the body of the tongue behind the tongue tip closure. The beginning and end of the /ɹ/ is not quite so well demarcated, but its presence is betrayed by the movement of F3, which swoops down toward F2, which is also low. Where /ɹ/ occurs between two vowels, a mirror image usually occurs at offset, where F3 rises.

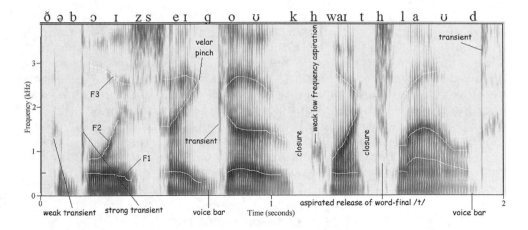

FIG. 12.6.   The same spectrogram as that of Fig. 12.5, annotated. Lines have been drawn through the centers of F1, F2, and F3.

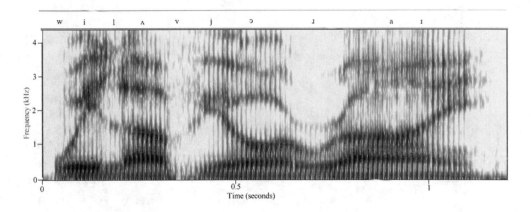

FIG. 12.7.   Spectrogram of "We love your rye."

SPECTROGRAM OF A SENTENCE WITH NASALS

Figure 12.8 is a spectrogram of "The name of the singer is Hannah," illustrating the spectrographic patterns of [m], [n], and [ŋ]. When it occurs between two vowels, as all the nasals in this sentence do, the onset of the nasal is signaled by an abrupt drop in amplitude and its offset by an abrupt gain in amplitude. In between (i.e., during the nasal consonant itself), formant activity continues and there is an appreciable steady state. However, the amplitude drop during a nasal is especially great at higher frequencies and very often there is not much to be seen on the spectrogram above about 1000 Hz. In preparing the spectrogram of Fig. 12.8, the darkening threshold was lowered. The result is that, although some of the other sounds are somewhat blackened, the formant structure of the nasals shows up quite well. Nasals share a low frequency formant at around 250 Hz to 300 Hz,

which shows up quite well on Fig. 12.8, especially in the /n/ of "Hannah."
Above this, formant structure can be quite variable. Compare, for example,
the /n/ of "name" with the "n" of "Hannah." However, having established that
something is probably a nasal, clues to place of articulation can frequently
be found by examining the formant transitions from and into adjacent vowels. The velar pinch, associated with the velar place of articulation, was
mentioned earlier and a (not quite complete) velar pinch can be seen just
before the /ŋ/ of "singer" (there is actually a more complete and convincing
pinch made by F4 and F5, in this case). F2 of the /ə/ before "name," has a
rising trajectory and F2 before the /n/ of "Hannah" has a slightly falling trajectory but they both appear to be aiming toward approximately the same
frequency.

A SPECTROGRAM WITH FRICATIVES

Figure 12.9 includes the fricatives /h, f, v, θ, ð, s, z, ʃ/ in the sentence "He
found Thora the seven shawls" /hi faʊnd θɔɹə ðə sɛvən ʃɔlz/. The frequency

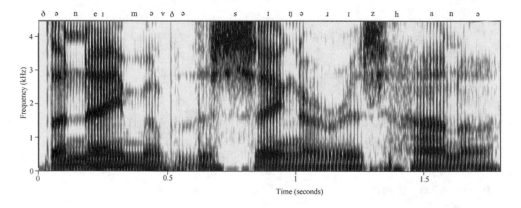

FIG. 12.8.   Spectrogram of "The name of the singer is Hannah."

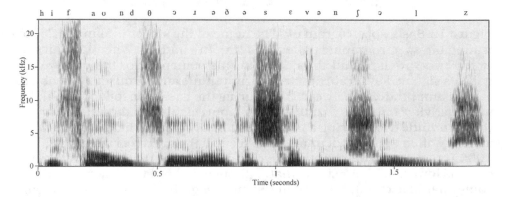

FIG. 12.9.   Spectrogram of "He found Thora the seven shawls."

range of this spectrogram extends to just above 22 kHz, far higher than any others in this chapter. The range was chosen in order to illustrate that fricative energy can be maintained into remarkably high frequencies. The /h/ of "he" is unfortunately hardly evident on this spectrogram. A better example is the /h/ of "Hannah" in Fig. 12.7. The energy distribution in an /h/ tends to replicate that of the following vowel, of which it is more or less a voiceless version. /f/ and /θ/ show the drizzle effect, which is characteristic of fricative sounds, extending to higher frequencies than any of the others, above 20 kHz. However, only young people with acute hearing would be able to make use of the higher frequency information displayed on this spectrogram in distinguishing auditorily among the different fricative sounds (see chap. 13). Others manage to distinguish among fricatives fairly successfully most of the time, although, for easy identification, it is helpful to be able to hear well above 5 kHz, probably to 8 kHz or more. Telephone lines do not transmit frequencies above 5 kHz and fricative sounds are sometimes hard to distinguish from each other on the telephone. /θ/ tends to be confined to higher frequencies than /f/. /s/ and /ʃ/ are high amplitude fricatives, with the amplitude of /s/ being concentrated at higher frequencies than /ʃ/. (This can be appreciated just by listening to extended versions of each sound.) The /v/ of "seven" was short and weak, but with voicing (doubtless helped by the occurrence of voiced sounds either side). /z/, on the other hand, shows little evidence of voicing. Its drizzle, however, contains some formant-like bands of energy.

Both the voicing and frication of voiced fricatives are vulnerable, according to the phonetic context in which they occur. This is especially true of /ð/, in English. This sound most often occurs at the beginning of unstressed grammatical words, and in many cases it is more stop-like than fricative. The /ð/ of Fig. 12.9 was voiced but there was apparently no frication and it had a transient release.

Practice 12.3

In the last sentence, the following claims were made about /ð/, in Fig. 12.9:

1. It was voiced.

2. There was no frication.

3. A transient was produced at its release.

Describe the spectrographic features that provide the evidence for each of these claims.
Answers. 1. There is a voice bar 2. There is no drizzle 3. There is a vertical spike

---

STOPS: FORMANT TRANSITIONS AND ACOUSTIC LOCI

Vowel transitions contribute to the identification of the place of articulation of plosive and nasal consonants. The importance of vowel formant trajectories to the identity of consonants in CV syllables was appreciated very early on in the history of spectrography. A discussion can be found in Potter, Kopp, and Green (1947). A series of classic experiments in the 1950s carried the implication that the place of articulation of a consonant may reside not so much in some feature of the spectrum at a particular point in time but rather in the transition of the second formant at the beginning of the vowel. The phenomenon is illustrated in the spectrograms of /di/ and /du/ in Fig. 12.10. In /di/, F2 is ascending, whereas in /du/ it is descending. Delattre, Liberman, and Cooper (1955) proposed that the initial consonant is perceived as a /d/ because in all cases F2 is pointing back (so to speak) toward a common origin. Their evidence came from perceptual judgements of artificially synthesized CV syllables involving F2 transitions into seven different vowels:

> … the various transitions that produce the best /d/ with each of the seven vowels do, in fact, appear to be coming from the same general region, and on the assumption that the first part of the acoustic transition is somehow missing, one may suppose that the transitions originate from precisely the same point. (Delattre et al., 1955, p. 770)

They termed the apparent point of origin of F2 the *locus* of F2. They identified an F2 locus of around 1800 Hz for alveolar consonants, one of around 720 Hz for bilabials, and one of around 3000 Hz for velars.

SPECTROGRAM READING

Spectrography was originally devised with deaf people in mind. The hope was that deaf people would be able to learn to interpret spectrographic displays accurately and rapidly so that they could have access to spoken language through visual means. This would have been an enormous benefit had it proved possible, especially now that on-screen, real-time continuous spectrography is available. Unfortunately, it turns out that spectrographic patterns simply cannot be interpreted fast or reliably enough to be of use for this purpose, even after much practice. Identifying an utterance from a spectrogram, with all possibilities open, can be a difficult and time-consuming task. It is, of course, much easier to interpret a spectrogram correctly when a restricted set of possibilities is offered.

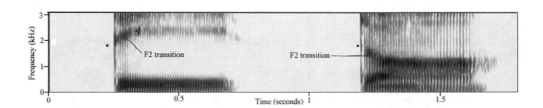

FIG. 12.10. Spectrogram of /di/ and /du/. The estimated F2 locus (see text) of each initial /d/ is indicated by the filled square.

EXERCISES

1. The five spectrograms of Figures 12.11 to 12.15 are of the titles of five of Shakespeare's plays, spoken in a RP accent. Identify and state each one and write a phonetic transcription of how you think it was pronounced. (All the plays are famous—there are no obscure ones. If you are superstitious about these things, for one of them you can just write *The Scottish Play*.)
2. Estimate and state the VOT of the medial, syllable-initial plosive in the spectrogram of Fig. 12.11.
3. Estimate and state the f_0 of the first vowel in the spectrogram of Fig. 12.12.
4. Estimate and state the highest and lowest frequencies reached by F2 during the vocalic portion of the second syllable in the spectrogram of Fig. 12.13.
5. What is the evidence that the "r" at the end of the last word in the spectrogram of Fig. 12.14 was not pronounced by this speaker?
6. The spectrogram of Fig. 12.15 contains a succession of two voiced, labiodental fricatives. What is the evidence that these two fricatives were indeed voiced?

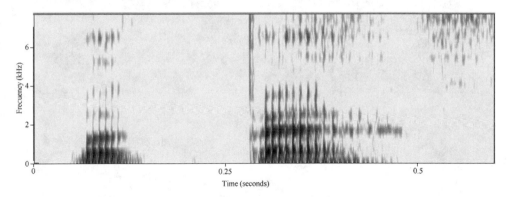

FIG. 12.11.   Spectrogram of the title of a Shakespeare play (see Exercise 1).

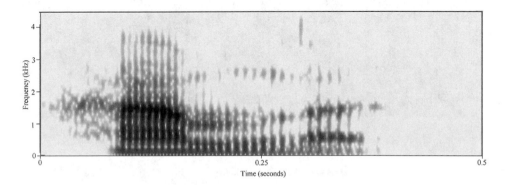

FIG. 12.12.   Spectrogram of the title of a Shakespeare play (see Exercise 1).

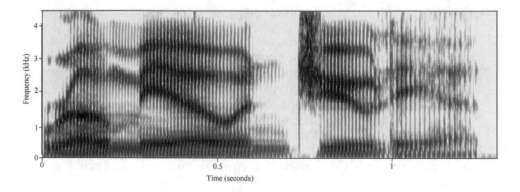

FIG. 12.13.   Spectrogram of the title of a Shakespeare play (see Exercise 1).

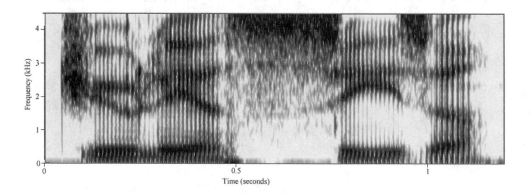

FIG. 12.14.   Spectrogram of the title of a Shakespeare play (see Exercise 1).

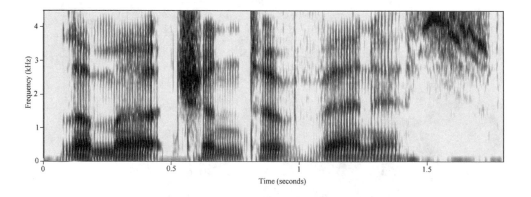

FIG. 12.15.   Spectrogram of the title of a Shakespeare play (see Exercise 1).

178

Auditory Phonetics

13

The Mechanism of Hearing

Hearing is the sensation caused by sound. The organs of hearing are the ears, from which signals travel to the auditory centers of the brain. We have two ears but it is usual to talk about "the ear," except where *binaural hearing* (the use of both ears) is the subject of discussion—as it will be, for example, in a discussion of the detection of sound direction.

Evolution has ensured that human hearing and human speech are well matched. So human hearing is sensitive to the amplitudes, frequencies, and durations that are important for distinguishing one speech sound from another. Of course, humans respond to many other acoustic signals besides speech, and the process of hearing (in its initial stages at least) is the same, regardless of the status of the sound. Much of the research into hearing has been conducted using specially controlled, nonspeech sounds, and without particular reference to the hearing of speech.

The present chapter describes the mechanism of the ear (peripheral auditory processing); transmission of auditory signals from ear to brain (central auditory processing) is not included in this book. The study of the sensations caused by acoustic signals goes by the name of *psychoacoustics*. The sensation of loudness is dealt with in chapter 14 and the sensations of pitch and quality are dealt with in chapter 15. Chapter 16, the final chapter in this section, addresses *speech perception*, that is, distinguishing speech units in the acoustic signal of speech. Moore (2003) is the most comprehensive and definitive text currently available on the process of hearing.

THE EAR AND HEARING: A BRIEF OVERVIEW

In the process of hearing, the auditory nerve detects sound waves and transmits corresponding neural impulses to the brain. However, the auditory nerve is not directly connected to the outside air where the sound waves occur. It is connected instead to a fluid-filled compartment deep inside the ear. So the ear must convert sound waves in air into waves in this fluid. Direct transmission of airborne waves into a fluid is inefficient. When airborne sound waves encounter a fluid medium much of the signal is reflected back. This is because the impedance of the two media is different (impedance being the combination of factors that oppose the flow of energy through the medium). The mechanism of the ear overcomes this problem to a significant extent. It does it by first converting the airborne sound waves into the mechanical oscillations of a chain of bones. The chain of bones is constructed so that it has the effect of matching the impedance of the air to the impedance of the fluid (at least over a certain frequency range). Airborne sound waves enter the ear and drive a back-and-forth movement in the chain of bones; the movement of the bones creates waves in the fluid and these waves are detected by the auditory nerve. Thus:

waves in air $\rightarrow$ oscillation of bones $\rightarrow$ waves in fluid $\rightarrow$ neural impulses to the brain

Each stage of the process outlined corresponds with an anatomical part of the auditory system.

The Human Ear

Figure 13.1 shows the anatomy of the ear. The ear divides naturally into three parts: the outer ear, the middle ear, and the inner ear. The inner ear contains the semicircular canals and the cochlea. The semicircular canals are involved with balance rather than hearing. The cochlea is a curled, fluid-filled cavity encased by bone, in which there are connections to fibers of the auditory nerve. The middle ear contains air rather than fluid, at least in its healthy state. The Eustachian tube runs from the middle ear into the nasopharynx (the region of the throat behind the nasal cavity) and this connection between middle ear and throat provides the means for achieving an air pressure within the middle ear that is approximately equal to the outside ambient air pressure. The middle ear houses a chain of three tiny bones, the malleus, incus and stapes (these are the Latin words for "hammer," "anvil," and "stirrup," respectively). At the inner end of the chain, the stapes connects with the cochlea at the oval window; at the outer end the malleus is fastened to the tympanic membrane. The tympanic membrane (eardrum) is an elastic sheet of tissue between the middle ear and the outer ear. The outer ear consists of the external auditory canal (meatus), which is a passage between the tympanic membrane and the open air, and the pinna (also called the auricle), which is the external structure of cartilage and skin.

The Process of Hearing

A sound wave travels down the external auditory canal. The tympanic membrane deforms inward and outward in response to the alternating pressure of the sound wave. The movements of the tympanic membrane create movements of the malleus, incus, and stapes. The back-and-forth motion of the sta-

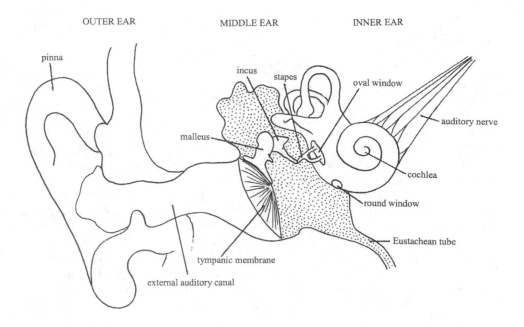

OUTER EAR   MIDDLE EAR   INNER EAR

FIG. 13.1.   Diagram of the ear. After Truax (1999).

Practice 13.1

Bryson (2003) described experiments carried out by J. B. S. Haldane, on himself and others, using a pressure chamber: "Collapsed lungs were a routine hazard. Perforated eardrums were quite common, too; but, as Haldane reassuringly noted in one of his essays, 'the drum generally heals up; and if a hole remains in it, although one is somewhat deaf, one can blow tobacco smoke out of the ear in question, which is a social accomplishment'" (p. 301). How could tobacco smoke taken into Haldane's mouth have emerged from his ear?

Answer. The smoke must have been forced up the Eustachean tube into the middle ear and from there it must have leaked into the external auditory canal, via the hole in the eardrum, and so into the outside air.

---

pes results in the oval window being deformed inward and outward. The motion of the oval window sets up waves traveling through the fluid of the cochlea. Highest frequencies cause greatest agitation near the oval window end (the base) whereas the lowest frequencies cause greatest agitation near the apex, with a continuum in between. The different regions along the length of the cochlea are connected with different fibers of the auditory nerve. Thus different frequencies give rise to distinct neural impulses. The auditory nerve transmits the impulses to the auditory brainstem, which in turn transmits information to the auditory cortex in the brain.

Each stage of the process of hearing is closely associated with an anatomical structure. The subsequent sections of this chapter review each stage, with its associated structure, in more detail.

THE OUTER EAR

The pinna is the familiar, visible part of the outer ear. The bowl-shaped part of the pinna, around the entrance to the external auditory canal, is called the concha. The entrance to the external auditory canal, when viewed from the side, is partly obscured by the tragus, a roughly triangular protruberance of cartilage.

The external auditory canal (tunnel or passage would be a better description) is about 27 mm long, with a diameter of about 7 mm (the dimensions vary somewhat from one person to another). It ends at the tympanic membrane (eardrum). This membrane is circular in outline, and slightly conical in shape (it presents a concave surface to the external auditory canal). The tympanic membrane is the first moving part in the mechanism of hearing: It bends inward and outward in sympathy with the pressure alternations of an incoming sound wave. Its outer surface is continuous with the skin lining the external auditory canal; its inner surface is covered by the mucous membrane lining the middle ear cavity; sandwiched between them is a layer of tough, fibrous tissue.

Transfer Function of the Outer Ear

When a wave encounters an obstacle, or when it passes through a narrow passage, it undergoes change. The spectrum of a complex sound wave is changed by encountering the head and pinna and changed further by passing through the external auditory canal. Some energy may be absorbed, some components may be reflected back to interact with cycles yet to arrive at the obstacle, some may wrap around the obstacle and continue on their way. When a wave enters a cavity or passage, some components may gain in amplitude, others may lose amplitude or remain at approximately the same amplitude. By components we mean sine wave components. As explained in chapter 11, any complex wave is composed of sine waves of different frequencies. A sine wave is not changed in frequency by encountering an obstacle or passing through a cavity or tube but it may be changed in amplitude. The factor by which a component changes in amplitude is known as the *gain* and gain may be positive or negative (a negative gain being a loss, of course).

The change that a structure, like the outer ear, will make to the spectrum of an incoming sound wave is defined by its transfer function. The *transfer function* of a structure is an input–output function. It specifies the gain that an input will acquire as a result of encountering the structure. A transfer function could be as simple as "x 3"—that is, every input emerges with three times the amplitude. More usually, however, the gain varies according to the frequency of the input. So the transfer function must specify the gain according to frequency, across the relevant range of frequencies. A transfer function is usually given as a graph that plots gain, in decibels, against frequency.

Figure 13.2 shows the transfer function of the outer ear (actually, of the outer ear plus all other relevant parts of the human body that a sound wave encounters on its way to the tympanic membrane; some contribution is made also by the head, shoulder, neck, and torso). The transfer function of Fig. 13.2 specifies the gain in amplitude, over a frequency range of 200 Hz to 12000 Hz, that occurs when a sound wave travels from the free air outside to a point next to the tympanic membrane. Gain is shown in decibels on the vertical axis; in this case, the reference is the level of the input, so, for example, 21 dB on the vertical scale means that the output is 21 dB greater than the input. Frequency, in hertz, is shown along the horizontal axis. The graph therefore has the same character as a spectrum. Notice, however, that the frequency scale of Fig. 13.2 is logarithmic. This is usual practice in texts on hearing (in contrast to texts on speech acoustics and speech production, where it is less prevalent) and we follow the practice, for the most part, in this section of the book. On a logarithmic scale, equal intervals of powers of 10 (10^1, 10^2, 10^3, and so on) are equally spaced. On a logarithmic scale, for example, the distance between 100 Hz and 1000 Hz is the same as that between 1000 Hz and 10000 Hz; the distance between 2 kHz and 4 kHz is the same as that between 4 kHz and 8 kHz; in general, any doubling (tripling, etc.) of frequency takes up the same distance along the frequency scale. In effect, the scale is relatively expansive at lower frequencies and becomes increasingly squeezed at higher frequencies. As on Fig.

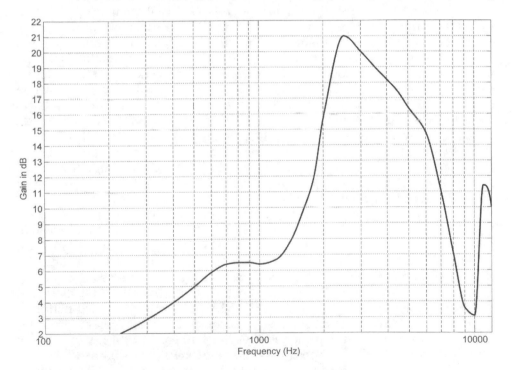

FIG. 13.2. The transfer function of the outer ear (plus other structures, e.g., the shoulder). This graph shows the transfer function of the outer ear for sounds approaching the ear at an angle of 45^0 (straight ahead being 0^0). The frequency range shown is 200 Hz to 12000 Hz. Vertical calibration lines are every 100 Hz, from 200 Hz to 1000 Hz; every 1000 Hz from 1000 Hz to 10000 Hz; the final interval is 2000 Hz. Data from Shaw (1974).

13.2, it is usual to supply calibration lines at 100 Hz intervals from 100 Hz to 1000 Hz; at 1000 Hz intervals from 1000 Hz to 10000 Hz; and at 10000 Hz intervals from 10000 Hz to 100000 Hz (although the scale of Fig. 13.2 finishes at 12000 Hz).

The transfer function of Fig. 13.2 shows that the outer ear effects at least a modest gain over the whole range from just over 200 Hz to 9 kHz, with a notable gain of 16 dB or more in the range 2 kHz to 5 kHz, within which there is a peak at around 2.6 kHz.

How Was the Transfer Function of the Outer Ear Discovered?

It would be very difficult to work out all the details of the transfer function of the outer ear (plus surrounding structures) purely from the dimensions of the structures involved, because the factors are many and complex. Determining it experimentally, however, is relatively straightforward, given the appropriate facilities. The procedure is something like this. A microphone is placed in an *anechoic chamber* (an anechoic chamber is an echo-less and very well-insulated room for sound recording). A sine wave signal of (say) 500 Hz is played at (say) one meter away from the microphone. The amplitude of the signal at the microphone is recorded. Then a person is brought into the chamber and they are positioned so that their head is in the place that the microphone had been. The microphone is then inserted down their external auditory canal and placed next to the tympanic membrane (it is a very small microphone). The same signal is played again, from one meter away, and again the signal picked up by the microphone is recorded. Any difference in amplitude between the two signals must be because the second signal has passed through the outer ear. Therefore comparison of the amplitude of the two signals recorded by the microphone yields a measure of the gain at 500 Hz. Inspection of Fig. 13.2 shows that at 500 Hz the gain is approximately 5 dB. So a 500 Hz sine wave that has a level of 50 dB at the tympanic membrane would (in "free field," i.e., in the absence of any structures in the path of the sound wave) otherwise have had a level of only 45 dB. The procedure is repeated for signals of many different frequencies.

Even recent textbooks on hearing, like Moore (2003), Pickles (1988), and Yost (2000), rely on the work of Shaw (1974), who collated the results from a number of previous studies dating as far back as 1933. Given that the method for determining the outer ear transfer function is comparatively straightforward, there are surprising differences among different sources as to the frequency of its main peak. Several authorities (e.g., Moore, 2003; Stevens, 1998) describe it as being around 3 kHz, which is a broad approximation of Shaw's findings (Fig. 13.2 suggests a peak around 2.6 kHz). Others quote 3.4 kHz as the frequency of the peak and Zwicker and Fastl (1999) even put it as high as 4 kHz. These differences may to some extent be explained by a discrepancy between the theoretically predicted frequency of the peak and the experimentally determined frequency. The peak is assumed to arise from a resonance of the external auditory canal. The frequency of a resonance in a narrow tube is determined by the length of the tube. The external auditory canal is around 25 mm to 28 mm long, which would give a resonance peak well above 3 kHz. (A description of the principles of tube resonance is given in chap. 17; and see in particular Exercise 3 at the end of chap. 17.) Durrant and Lovrinic (1995) pointed out the inaccuracy of the theoretical prediction and ascribed the discrepancy to the influence of other structures; the pinna (particularly the concha), and also the shoulder and head, contribute to the lowering of the resonance peak.

As the frequency of the main peak is at least substantially influenced by the length of the external auditory canal, it varies somewhat with head size, from one person to another.

Effects of the Outer Ear Transfer Function on Speech Sounds

In Fig. 13.2, the gain is shown for frequency components up to 12 kHz, which is somewhat higher than is usually considered relevant in the analysis of speech sounds (with the possible exception of voiceless fricatives). No pub-

---

Practice 13.2

Examine Fig. 13.2 in order to answer these questions. (In the case of questions 1–5, assume that the transfer function of Fig. 13.2 is the only factor involved.)

1. A sine wave of 500 Hz, with an amplitude of 40 dB SPL, enters a person's ear. What amplitude will it have when it reaches the tympanic membrane?
2. A sine wave of 1000 Hz, with an amplitude of 40 dB SPL, enters a person's ear. What amplitude will it have when it reaches the tympanic membrane?
3. A sine wave of 3000 Hz, with an amplitude of 40 dB SPL, enters a person's ear. What amplitude will it have when it reaches the tympanic membrane?
4. A sine wave of 7 kHz, with an amplitude of 40 dB SPL, enters a person's ear. What amplitude will it have when it reaches the tympanic membrane?
5. A sine wave of 0.4 kHz, with an amplitude of 40 dB SPL, enters a person's ear. What amplitude will it have when it reaches the tympanic membrane?
6. If the frequency scale of the graph of Fig. 13.2 was extended down to 10 Hz, at what interval, in hertz, would the calibration lines most likely be placed, from 10 Hz to 100 Hz?
7. If an accurate estimate of the gain at 1500 Hz was needed, would it be legitimate to estimate it from a point on the frequency scale halfway in distance between the 1000 Hz and 2000 Hz calibration lines?
8. Use a ruler to measure the distance between the 100 Hz and 200 Hz calibration lines and between the 3000 Hz and 6000 Hz calibration lines. Are they the same?

Answers. 1. 45 dB   2. 46.5 dB   3. 60 dB   4. 51 dB   5. 44 dB   6. 10 Hz
7. No   8. They should be!

lished information has been found concerning the transfer function at frequencies below 200 Hz. The frequencies most important for distinguishing among vowels and other sonorant sounds of speech lie in the range approximately 250 Hz to 4 kHz (see chap. 11). This is the region that contains the first three formants in most of the speech that we hear, whether from men, women, or children. Figure 13.2 suggests that the upper part of this range is well served by the outer ear transfer function, whereas in the lower part of the range the gain is much less. However, recall (from chap. 11) that in the spectra of periodic speech sounds the amplitude is already comparatively large at lower frequencies and there is a tendency for amplitude to diminish with increasing frequency.

In the case of fricatives, it is the frequencies above 3 kHz that are most important. From 3 kHz, the gain at the tympanic membrane remains substantial for several kilohertz. It decreases to a low at around 10 kHz, where it begins rising again.

Effects on the Transfer Function of Sounds From Different Angles

The influence of external structures (pinna, head, shoulder) on the shape of the outer ear transfer function has already been mentioned (in fact, the transfer function is also known as the head-related transfer function). The influences from these structures, however, vary according to the direction of the sound source with respect to the listener's ear. Only differences in the horizontal plane are described here. If we consider just the right ear (for the sake of the exposition) then the highest overall gain is achieved when the sound comes from in front and a bit to the right. The transfer function of Fig. 13.2 is that for a sound striking the right ear of the listener at an angle of 45°. The transfer function for a sound coming from directly in front (an angle of 0°) has a similar shape but with reduced gain (except at the very highest and very lowest frequencies, where the reduction is trivial).

As the sound source moves round from an angle of about 45° through to an angle of about 150°, a resonance of the concha emerges as a distinct second peak in the 5 kHz to 7 kHz region (although it should be borne in mind that above 5 kHz the details of the transfer function vary more substantially from one individual to another). This peak can be seen on Fig. 13.3 (upper line), which shows the transfer function when the sound comes directly from the right side (an angle of 90°). As the sound source moves further around to behind the listener's head, this peak reduces and then disappears. The lower line of Fig. 13.3 shows the transfer function when the sound comes from directly behind the listener (an angle of 180°). You might expect that the transfer function for a sound at 0° (directly in front) would be the same as that for one of 180° (directly behind). However, scattering of higher frequency components against the edges of the pinna is responsible for a reduction in gain at higher frequencies for sound sources from behind, compared with sound sources from in front. As the sound source moves further around, to the opposite side of the head, the function retains its same basic shape, but with some loss of gain. The trough just below 10 kHz, which also derives from the concha, remains a feature of the transfer function at all angles of a sound source.

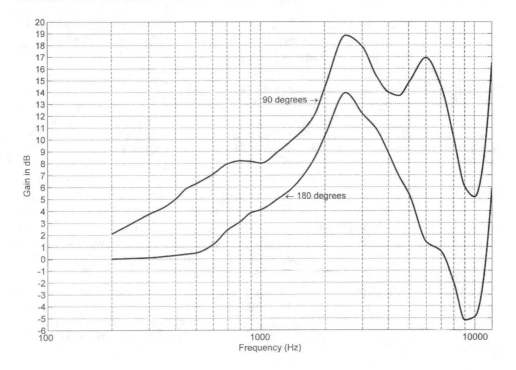

FIG. 13.3. Transfer functions of the outer ear when the sound source is directly to one side of the listener (90°) and from directly behind (180°). Data from Shaw (1974).

In summary, the outer ear produces a gain in the magnitude of an incoming sound wave. The gain is frequency dependent. There is a peak at around 2.6 kHz, due to the external auditory canal. According to the findings represented in Fig. 13.2, this peak typically rises above 20 dB when the sound is coming from in front and slightly to one side of the listener's ear. There is a trough, due to the concha, just below 10 kHz. A second peak, in the 5 kHz to 7 kHz region, due to the concha, becomes apparent when the sound arrives from sideways-on to the listener's ear.

Using Two Ears to Locate the Direction a Sound is Coming From

Effects due to the angle of the sound source have been mentioned, making this is a convenient point to take a brief look at binaural hearing. *Binaural hearing* (i.e., hearing with two ears) is an important feature of the human sense of hearing. The second ear is not just a spare. Listeners use the difference between the signals to the two ears to estimate the direction a sound is coming from, a process known as localization.

A sound coming from a listener's right will reach their right ear before it reaches their left ear. The wave front, as it is called, will first encounter the right ear, then travel on and flow around the head to reach the left. The time that lapses between arrival at one ear and arrival at the other is called the *interaural time difference.* There will also be some loss in sound pressure amplitude; a measure of this difference is called the *interaural level differ-ence.* Both provide cues to the listener. Here we explore only the interaural time difference, by considering one example in some detail. (This is not to im-ply that the interaural time difference is necessarily more important than the interaural level difference—in some circumstances the latter is more impor-tant. For more on this, see Moore, 2003, pp. 235–240, and Bronkhurst & Plomp, 1988.)

In this example, a sound wave approaches directly from the right of the lis-tener. We call this an angle of 90°, with 0° being the direction the listener is fac-ing. Figure 13.4 (top) shows the wave front arriving at the right ear (in reality, of course, the wave front will be somewhat curved because the wave fronts of sound waves are spherical; however, assuming the sound source is some dis-tance away, a straight wave front is a good enough approximation). It may be easier to appreciate what will happen next if the wave is imagined as a water wave—the same principles apply. The wave front will continue on, reaching ei-ther end of the head and then flowing on around to encounter the left ear. The path is shown by the thick arrow on Fig. 13.4 (bottom). How long does the wave take to travel this path? To answer the question, we need to know the speed of sound and the length of the path. The speed of sound through air is approximately 340 meters/second (it varies slightly according to the density of the air). The circumference of an adult human head is something like 540 mm. So:

- the speed of sound is 340 meters/second
- the circumference of the head is 540 mm (0.54 meters)
- the radius of the head is therefore 86 mm (0.086 meters)

Inspection of Fig. 13.4 (bottom) shows that the straight bit of the path is equivalent to the radius of the head, that is 0.086 meters, and the curved bit is equivalent to one quarter of the circumference, that is 0.54/4 meters, or 0.135 meters. So the total distance is 0.086 + 0.135 = 0.221 meters. Sound travels at 340 meters/second, thus the interaural time difference is:

$$0.221/340 = 0.00065 \text{ seconds}$$

$$= 0.65 \text{ ms}$$

Experiments have shown that listeners can distinguish the direction of sound sources to an accuracy as good as 2° (see Exercise 6, at the end of this chapter). Notice, however, that the interaural time difference gives ambiguous information except for sound sources coming at 90° and at 270°. A right-to-left interaural time difference of 0.65 ms can only mean a sound coming at an angle of 90°, and a left-to-right interaural time difference of 0.65 ms can only mean a sound com-ing at an angle of 270°. At all other angles there are two possibilities: If the sound comes at an angle forward of the nearest ear there will be a corresponding angle back from the nearest ear that would give the same interaural time differ-ence—and vice-versa. (Actually, if this account were not restricted to the horizon-tal plane, there would be many possibilities.) However, spectral cues from the effects of the pinna, mentioned in the previous section, might help to resolve such ambiguities. A slight turn of the head, which will either increase or decrease the interaural time difference, can also resolve it.

THE MIDDLE EAR

The tympanic membrane provides the means for converting the airborne vibrations in the external auditory canal into mechanical oscillations along the chain of bones in the middle ear. The handle of the malleus, fastened securely into the fibrous middle layer of the tympanic membrane, is rocked back and forth by the motion of the membrane and the other two bones in the chain, the

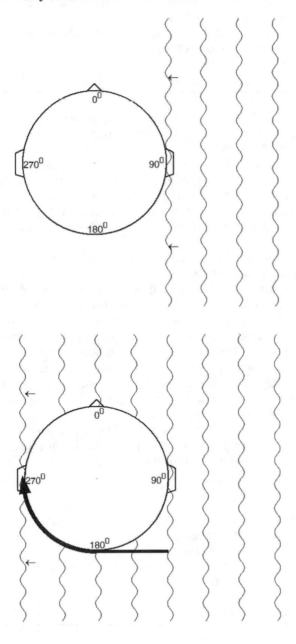

FIG. 13.4. Sound location. The circles represent a head, viewed from above, with ears and nose. Top: A wave front arrives at the right ear. This sound wave comes directly from the right of the listener (an angle of 90°); the rippled lines are intended to convey the idea of an advancing wave front. Bottom: The wave front arrives at the left ear. The distance the wave front has traveled, between reaching the right ear and reaching the left ear, is shown by the thick arrow.

Practice 13.3

1. At 90° the right-to-left interaural time difference is 0.65 ms. At what angle of sound source is the left-to-right interaural time difference 0.65 ms?
2. At what two angles of source is the interaural time difference zero?
3. A sound wave approaches a listener at an angle of 30°. After arriving at the right ear, the wave front must travel a further 0.088 meters before reaching the left ear. What is the interaural time difference?
4. At what other angle of source will the right-to-left interaural time difference be the same as that in question 3?
5. At what other angles of source will the interaural time difference be the same as that in question 3, but left-to-right?

Answers. 1. 270° 2. 0° and 180°   3. 0.26 ms   4. 150° 5. 210° and 330°

---

incus and the stapes, are rocked with it. The stapes is the smallest bone in the human body. Through its attachment to the membrane of the oval window it drives waves into the fluid of the cochlea.

The role of the middle ear is one of "impedance matching." The impedance of air is less than the impedance of fluid—"impedance" being the combination of properties that oppose the flow of energy through a medium. So the middle ear increases the amplitude of the pressure variations coming from the air in order to ensure that the signal is transmitted into the fluid of the cochlea with comparatively little loss.

The tympanic membrane has an effective area of about 50 mm² whereas the base of the stapes (and also the oval window itself) has an area of about 3 mm². The tympanic membrane is therefore about 17 times bigger than the base of the stapes. This size factor plays the main role in overcoming the mismatch between air and fluid in the transmission of sound waves from outer to inner ear. The pressure alternations are transmitted from a relatively large area to a relatively small area. *Pressure* is force per unit area. Therefore when a pressure is transmitted to an area 17 times smaller, the pressure is increased by a factor of 17. Two subsidiary factors (leverage of the bones and buckling of the tympanic membrane) have been estimated to multiply this by a further 2.6, giving a total pressure gain of $17 \times 2.6 = 44.2$. A gain of 44.2 is equivalent to 33 dB. However, the middle ear does not achieve this gain at all frequencies. The gain varies with frequency. Therefore, we need to specify the transfer function of the middle ear as a graph of gain over frequency, as in the case of the outer ear.

Practice 13.4

In the previous paragraph, it was stated that "A gain of 44.2 is equivalent to 33 dB." Show that this is indeed the case and give the decibel value to three decimal places. (*Hint.* A gain of 44.2 means a ratio of 44.2/1. You may want to refresh your memory of the method for calculating decibel values by looking again at Equation 1 in chap. 10).

Answer. $20 \times \log 44.2/1 = 32.908$ dB

Transfer Function of the Middle Ear

The transfer function of the middle ear specifies the gain in pressure at the oval window compared to the pressure at the tympanic membrane, for a range of frequencies. It is not at all easy to determine. Getting access to the middle ear with instrumentation for measurement is destructive, which rules out measuring the transfer function experimentally on live, human subjects. Two alternative approaches have been tried: measurement using human cadavers (e.g., Aibara, Welsh, Puria, & Goode, 2001) and measurements on live animals, most often guinea pigs or cats (e.g., Magnan, Dancer, Probst, Smurzynski, & Avan, 1999). Figure 13.5 shows the transfer function found by Aibara et al., who used special instrumentation to measure sound pressures at the tympanic membrane and at the oval window in 11 human cadavers, over a number of frequencies ranging from 50 Hz to 10 kHz. The gain increases fairly smoothly, from around 2 dB at 50 Hz, to reach a maximum of 23.5 dB at 1.2 kHz. Above this, it decreases fairly smoothly down to around 4 dB at 10 kHz.

Middle Ear Reflex. The transfer function of a normal, healthy middle ear remains more or less constant. It almost certainly remains unaffected by,

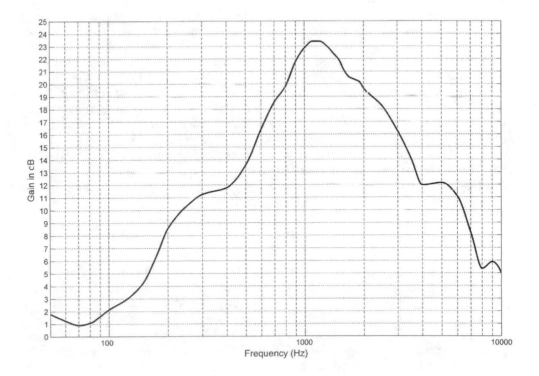

FIG. 13.5. Transfer function of the middle ear. Mean of the response of 11 cadaver ears. Values taken from Aibara et al. (2001, p. 104, Fig. 2).

Practice 13.5

Use Fig. 13.5 to answer these questions.

1. A sine wave of 100 Hz has a sound pressure amplitude of 50 dB at the tympanic membrane. What amplitude will it have at the oval window?
2. A sine wave of 2 kHz has a sound pressure amplitude of 50 dB at the tympanic membrane. What amplitude will it have at the oval window?
3. A sine wave of 200 Hz has a sound pressure amplitude of 30 dB at the tympanic membrane. What amplitude will it have at the oval window?

Answers. 1. 52.1 dB   2. 69.5 dB   3. 38.5 dB

for example, the orientation of the head in space, because ligaments attached to the middle ear bones hold them securely in the same position despite changing gravitational forces. The only routine modification to the transfer function comes from the contraction of two muscles, the tensor tympani muscle and the stapedius muscle. The tensor tympani is attached to the handle of the malleus and the stapedius is attached to the neck of the stapes. The contraction of these muscles is known as the *middle ear reflex*. The middle ear reflex has the effect of stiffening the chain and thereby significantly reducing the gain at frequencies below about 1 kHz. The reflex operates in response to loud sounds (of any audible frequency) and also when the person (i.e., the owner of the ear) starts speaking. Modern authorities tend to express caution concerning the uses of the reflex, emphasizing that the response time is too slow to protect the ear from damage by noises that are shorter than 50 ms to 150 ms and that it protects mainly from lower frequency sounds. However, this protection after 150 ms is still valuable and the findings quoted previously lead to the reasonable conclusion that the functions of the reflex include reduced sensitivity to the sound created by one's own voice and some protection from damage or discomfort from loud sounds in the environment.

THE INNER EAR

Within the inner ear, the organ for hearing is the cochlea. Figure 13.6 shows a three dimensional view of it and Fig. 13.7 shows a schematic, longitudinal section of it as if uncurled (it is not physically possible to uncurl the cochlea because it is a cavity in bone). The fluid with which the cochlea is filled has a consistency similar to sea water. It is divided longitudinally, by membranes, into three passages, called scalae: the scala vestibuli, the scala tympani, and the scala media (also called the cochlear duct). The scala vestibuli runs from the oval window and meets the scala tympani in a narrow opening, the helicotrema, at the end. The scala tympani ends at the round window, another membranous window between cochlea and middle ear.

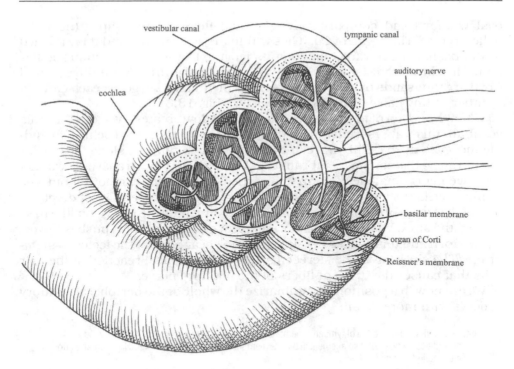

FIG. 13.6.   Three dimensional view of part of the cochlea. After Truax (1999).

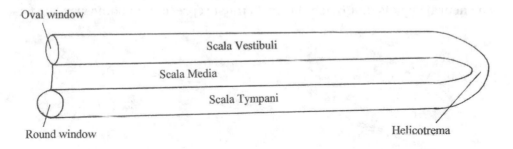

FIG. 13.7.   Schematic view of the cochlea, as if uncurled.

The role of the cochlea is to produce neural (bioelectrical) signals in response to the waves traveling through the fluids of its scalae. Due to its location and the fragility of its structures, the cochlea is even more difficult to investigate than the middle ear. Information about its function derives from experiments on human cadavers and experiments on other mammals, relying on the basic similarity of the hearing mechanism among mammals.

Two structures, attached to each other, are crucial to the process of deriving neural signals from cochlear waves and the rest of this account is almost wholly concerned with them. They are the basilar membrane and the organ of Corti. The basilar membrane lies between the scala media and the scala tympani. It is comparatively narrow and stiff at its basal end (i.e., near the oval window) and comparatively wide and flexible at the apex (near the helicotrema). The organ of Corti lies within the scala media and it is attached to the basilar membrane, all along its length. The tectorial membrane lies above it (above, that is, in the way it is usually drawn). Within the organ of Corti are thousands of hair cells, which, as their name suggests, each end in a number of tiny hairs, called stereocilia (see Fig. 13.8).

When the action of the stapes on the oval window creates a wave in the scala vestibuli, this wave is transmitted though all the fluids of the cochlea, including the scala media. This wave in turn sets a wave running along the basilar membrane—that is, the membrane itself is subjected to a transverse wave of displacement. (Imagine a hump in a carpet. As you try to smooth it out, the hump travels the length of the carpet. This is a transverse wave of displacement.) The wave of displacement of the basilar membrane runs from the base toward the apex. Where the basilar membrane is displaced, it pushes the organ of Corti and this causes the stereocilia to shear against the tectorial membrane. The shearing of the stereocilia sets up a chemical reaction in the hair cells that causes the firing of fibers of the auditory nerve.

We are now in a position to summarize the whole of the peripheral auditory process with more detail:

airborne sound wave → motion of tympanic membrane → motion of bones → motion of oval window → wave in cochlear fluids → wave of displacement in basilar membrane → shearing of stereocilia in organ of Corti → chemical reaction → firing of fibers of auditory nerve

This summary leaves out of account any indication of how *different* sounds give rise to *different* activities in the cochlea and thus different neural signals. The neural signals that reach the brain must represent, in some way, the fre-

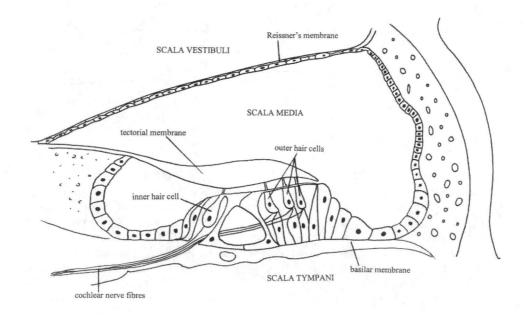

FIG. 13.8.   Cross-section of the scala media, including the basilar membrane and the organ of Corti.

quencies and amplitudes in the original sound wave, in order for the brain to be able to distinguish one sound from another. A precise description of the wave motion in the basilar membrane, pioneered by von Békésy in the 1940s and 1950s, suggests the principles by which the physical characteristics of a sound might be encoded in the cochlea.

How the Basilar Membrane Responds to Different Frequencies

A wave along the basilar membrane grows to a maximum amplitude of displacement and then dies quickly away. The point along the membrane at which this maximum occurs depends on the frequency of the wave. The construction of the basilar membrane is such that a wave of very high frequency (20 kHz, say) will grow to its largest displacement immediately (i.e., very near to the oval window) and disappear. A wave of very low frequency (50 Hz, say) will travel all the way to the opposite end (near the helicotrema) before reaching its maximum. Waves of intermediate frequencies will have their maxima at intermediate points along the basilar membrane. Figure 13.9 illustrates this for some low frequencies.

The point of maximum displacement, then, provides one means for distinguishing one frequency from another. The point of maximum displacement will be the point where the stereocilia of the organ of Corti bend most against the tectorial membrane and so the strongest signal will come from the fibers of the auditory nerve connected to this region.

Place Theory and Temporal Theory

Speech sounds are complex sounds and so contain energy at different frequencies (see chap. 11). They therefore create a series of peaks along the basilar membrane. A vowel sound with an f_0 of 120 Hz, for example, will create peaks on the basilar membrane at points corresponding to 120 Hz, 240 Hz, 360 Hz, and so on. In this way, the basilar membrane performs the equivalent of a Fourier analysis on the sound wave, yielding a spectrum of the sound. The precision of this spectrum (the limitations on its frequency resolution) is the subject of chapter 15.

The *inner hair cells*, which are arranged in a single row all the way along the organ of Corti, transmit the information about the location of the peaks. The hair cells that are located where a peak occurs in the traveling wave are the ones that are stimulated, through the shearing action against the tectorial

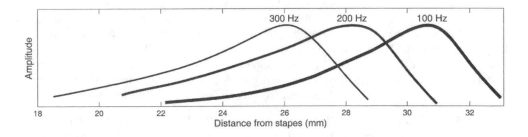

FIG. 13.9.   Illustration of the relationship between the frequency of a sound and the point of maximum displacement along the basilar membrane. After part of figure in von Békésy (1960).

membrane. So frequency is encoded according to the origin of the stimulation along the row of inner hair cells. This explanation, in which frequency is encoded according to location, is called the *place theory.*

The alternative explanation is called the *temporal theory.* If one or more hair cells responds to the *period* of each sine wave component of a sound wave then its frequency could be directly encoded. There is good evidence that this does indeed happen. Recording electrical activity in hair cells reveals that they "lock on" to a particular point in the cycle of a periodic wave and their associated neurons fire at the same point in successive cycles. Thus the interval between neural firings yields the period of the sine wave component.

The place theory and the temporal theory might better be called the place mechanism and the temporal mechanism, nowadays, because there seems little doubt that both apply. The ear's response to frequency is discussed in more detail in chapter 15.

Active Role of the Cochlea in its Response to Frequency and Amplitude

Von Békésy's measurements were performed on cadaver cochleas. Subsequent research has confirmed his basic findings but among more recent elaborations and qualifications is the finding that there are differences in the response of the basilar membrane of a live animal in good physiological condition, as compared with one that is in poor physiological condition, or dead. The frequency peaks of Fig. 13.9, are narrower and steeper in a healthy, live animal (or, presumably, human) than in a dead animal. The conclusion drawn from this is that there is an active element that performs fine tuning of the cochlear response. Evidence supporting this interpretation comes from the existence of efferent (i.e., transmitting), as well as afferent (receiving), neurons in the organ of Corti, implying that the basilar membrane–organ of Corti complex is not merely a passive device; it includes neurally driven modifications to its response. The three rows of *outer hair cells*, which, like the inner hair cells, also run the length of the organ of Corti, are thought to play a significant role in refining the response of the basilar membrane.

An active element has also been identified in the basilar membrane's response to differences in amplitude. As might be expected, a sound of greater amplitude produces a bigger traveling wave along the basilar membrane. The active element increases the ear's response to weak sounds, but not equally so across the input amplitude range. At intermediate input levels (from about 30 up to at least 80 dB), the basilar membrane displacement does not increase proportionally with increase in input level. It compresses this range, in contrast to the ranges below 30 dB and somewhat above 80 dB, which remain linear. In a dead animal, the response remains linear over the whole range. These differences are not just observed between life and death. They also occur to some extent according to the general physiological condition of the animal. An interesting implication of these findings is that state of health affects the processing of sound by the cochlea.

Otoacoustic Emissions.   Startling confirmation that the response of the cochlea to sound is not just passive, but active as well, comes from the phenomenon of *otoacoustic emissions.* A sensitive microphone placed near the tympanic membrane can record acoustic signals coming *from* the cochlea after it has received stimulation by a sound (and sometimes even in the absence of any sound stimulation). Otoacoustic emissions tend to be weak or absent when the auditory apparatus is in an unhealthy physical condition. Testing for otoacoustic emissions does not rely on the active cooperation of the subject and it can therefore be a useful technique in assessing hearing in babies and infants.

EXERCISES

1. The ear can be divided into three parts. What are they?
2. Which part of the ear contains fluid rather than air?
3. The transfer function of the outer ear produces a gain which is largest in the range:

   A. 200 Hz to 600 Hz.
   B. 500 Hz to 2000 Hz.
   C. 2 kHz to 5 kHz.
   D. 3 kHz to 8 kHz.

4. A pure tone of 3 kHz entered a person's right ear from an angle of 45°. When it reached the tympanic membrane, it had an amplitude of 50 dB SPL. What would its amplitude have been, at the same point in space, if the person had not been there?
5. Sound A was a 3 kHz pure tone that approached a listener's right ear directly from the side (an angle of 90°). Sound B was another 3 kHz pure tone and it had the same amplitude as sound A, but it approached the listener from directly behind. How many decibels greater would sound A have been than sound B, on arrival at the tympanic membrane?
6. If a wave front approaches a listener at an angle of 2°, then it must travel 0.006 meters further to reach the left ear, compared with the right. What is the interaural time difference? (Assume the speed of sound is 340 meters/second.)
7. At what other angle of source will the right-to-left interaural time difference be the same as that in question 6?
8. At what other angles of source will the interaural time difference be the same as that in question 6, but left-to-right?

14
Loudness

Loudness is a listener's sensation of the strength of a sound. Loudness forms a continuum from, at one end, sounds that are so quiet they are only just detectable by a listener to, at the other end, sounds that are so loud as to be painful. As one would expect, the sensation of loudness is associated with the sound pressure amplitude of a sound. An increase in sound pressure amplitude will result in an increase in loudness, other things being equal. However, it is important to remember that the sensitivity of hearing differs according to frequency. So a sound of 50 dB SPL will not necessarily be louder than a sound of 40 dB SPL, if the frequency composition of the two sounds is different.

Above about 20 kHz, the word "sound" becomes a misnomer. An air pressure wave of 50 kHz, for example, of whatever amplitude, is inaudible to humans. A wave of 20 kHz would be audible to many (young) humans so long as it had a sound pressure level of a least 60 dB SPL. Considerable research has been directed toward discovering the precise relationships between loudness and sound pressure amplitude, across the relevant frequency range. The results are used in the assessment of hearing loss in people with impaired hearing and in the design of hearing aids to alleviate such loss. This chapter includes a brief account of different types of hearing impairment and a description of how reduced sensitivity to sound pressure amplitude is recorded.

The rule that loudness refers only to a psychological sensation is generally very well observed throughout the speech and hearing science literature. Loudness should not be used to mean the physical magnitude of a sound. A lot of research into loudness (and other aspects of hearing) uses sine waves, which in this context are called pure tones. *Pure tones* are sine waves that are (or might conceivably be) audible (although the "pure" is sometimes omitted when it is clear from the context that the tone is sinusoidal).

LIMITS OF HEARING

Threshold of Hearing

In chapter 10, where the decibel scale was described, the reference level for the dB SPL scale (recall that 0 dB SPL is a sound pressure of 0.00002 Pascals) was said to be at the threshold of human hearing. The concept of the threshold of human hearing must now be examined more closely. For one thing, the threshold differs according to frequency, because the sensitivity of the ear is different at different frequencies. (The reference sound pressure of 0.00002 Pascals was chosen because it was thought to be the threshold at 1000 Hz; actually, according to modern estimates, the threshold at 1000 Hz tends to be slightly greater than this, as we later see.) For another, the threshold varies somewhat from one person to another, as you might expect. Some people have more acute hearing than others. However, it is useful, especially for the purpose of assessing problems with hearing, to have a standard reference threshold with which to make a comparison. Because the threshold of hearing varies with frequency, it should be defined across a wide frequency range and it should reflect as accurately as possible the average threshold of the normally hearing population. An International Standard has in fact been established, which is used in audiological assessment and that is described later in this section.

A listener's threshold of hearing, for any given frequency, is the minimum sound pressure amplitude at which a pure tone of that frequency produces a sensation. The response of the listener does not require any special interpretation; they need only report whether or not they heard a sound. Indeed, hearing thresholds of animals can be determined, by using techniques of behavioral conditioning (associating a pleasant or unpleasant stimulus with the hearing of a tone, for example). Exercise 1, at the end of this chapter, provides an example.

Pure tones are used for determining the threshold of hearing across a frequency range. One technique is to bring a person into an anechoic chamber and play a pure tone of, for example, 100 Hz, at a very low level. The sound pressure amplitude is gradually increased, until the person is able to report hearing a sound. The person is then removed from the chamber and the sound that they could just detect is played again. Its sound pressure level is measured, in dB SPL, at the point that had been occupied by the middle of the person's head. This measurement represents this person's threshold of hearing at 100 Hz. The procedure is repeated for pure tones across a large range of frequencies. The results are plotted on a graph of sound pressure amplitude over frequency. Threshold measured in this way is called the minimum audible field (MAF).

Figure 14.1 shows the human hearing threshold, according to the current International Standard, for the frequency range 20 Hz to 12500 Hz, in dB SPL. The curve of Fig. 14.1 represents average values from a large number of subjects between 18 and 25 years of age, when listening binaurally and facing the sound source. It is important to bear in mind the average nature of these values and the fact that the subjects were young adults. Hearing thresholds can differ from one ("normal") person to another, by as much as 20 dB (Moore, 2003) and hearing usually deteriorates with age. The subjects were tested in "free field" (i.e., using a technique like that described in the previous paragraph, as opposed to using earphones) and the curve of Fig. 14.1 therefore defines the minimum audible field (MAF). The graph of Fig. 14.1 shows that normal human hearing is most sensitive in the range 2 kHz to 5 kHz. At 1000 Hz, the threshold is 2 dB SPL. Below 1000 Hz, the threshold rises with increasing steepness. Likewise, the threshold rises steeply at much higher frequencies as it approaches the limit of 20 kHz, although the higher end of the range is not shown on Fig. 14.1.

Ear's Response to Large Sound Magnitudes

An upper amplitude limit of hearing cannot be defined with similar precision to the lower limit (threshold) of hearing. There is not a well-defined point at which the sensation of hearing disappears as the sound pressure amplitude is increased. However, three kinds of higher thresholds have been described: the loudness discomfort level, the threshold of feeling, and the threshold of pain. Determining these relies on subjective reporting. The first and the last are more or less self-explanatory. The threshold of feeling refers to a level at which the sound causes a tactile sensation in addition to an auditory sensation. None of these upper limits changes with frequency as much as does the threshold of hearing. The loudness discomfort level (LDL) for a person of normal hearing is usually somewhere around 110 dB SPL. Certainly, continued

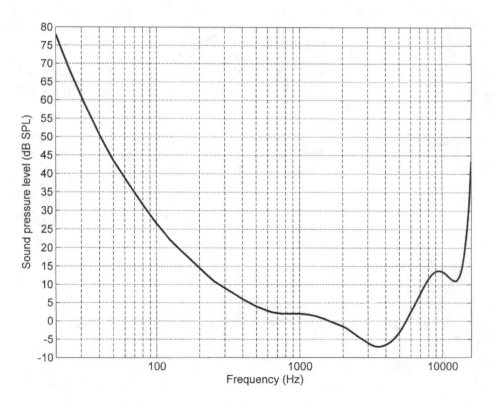

FIG. 14.1.   The human threshold of hearing in free field. The graph is based on values in Table 1 of ISO 389-7 (1998).

Practice 14.1

These questions all relate to Fig. 14.1.

1. At what frequency is human hearing least sensitive, within the 20 Hz to 10000 Hz range?
2. Greatest sensitivity, measured by the MAF, occurs within the range:

    A. 1000 Hz to 2000 Hz
    B. 2000 Hz to 3000 Hz
    C. 3000 Hz to 4000 Hz
    D. 4000 Hz to 5000 Hz

3. Estimate, in dB SPL, the sound pressure level of a 1000-Hz pure tone that would be at the threshold of audibility for an individual whose hearing was 10 dB *better* than average.
4. Estimate, in dB SPL, the sound pressure level of a 6000-Hz pure tone that would be at the threshold of audibility for an individual whose hearing was 10 dB *worse* than average.

Answers. 1. 20 Hz 2. C 3. –8 dB SPL (the average threshold, at 1000 Hz, is 2 dB SPL) 4. 13 dB SPL

---

exposure to this level of sound causes damage to hearing (cf. chap. 10, The Decibel Scale section). Above a frequency of about 100 Hz, there is little variation in LDL across the frequency range, except that it is likely to dip to around 100 dB in the 2 kHz to 5 kHz range (see later, Loudness Scales section, for more detail). A threshold of pain at around 140 dB SPL does not vary much across frequency. Therefore the response of the ear to very large sound pressure levels is much flatter than its response to smaller sound pressure levels. Laboratory experiments on the upper limits of hearing are obviously and rightly constrained by ethical considerations.

Audiograms

Hearing impairments have different causes and there are different types, which show different patterns of impairment. However, virtually all types of hearing impairment include raised thresholds of hearing. An *audiogram* is a graph used by audiologists for recording how a client's hearing thresholds, for a series of pure tones, compare to the norm. In hearing assessment using pure tones, sound pressure levels are referenced to the hearing threshold for each tone. The hearing threshold usually used in audiological assessment is *not* that shown in Fig. 14.1. The audiologist usually tests for the threshold in each ear separately, the tones being delivered through earphones. Therefore the relevant threshold is that for tones delivered through earphones to a single ear. However, for the purposes of exposition, we ignore this complication here and proceed as if the threshold of Fig. 14.1 were the correct one in all cases.

Suppose, for example, that a client is played a pure tone of 500 Hz and that they only manage to detect the presence of this tone when it reaches a level of 21 dB SPL. The normal threshold for this frequency is 6 dB SPL (see Fig. 14.1). Their threshold is therefore 15 dB above the norm. This is recorded as 15 dB HL (HL = Hearing Level). 15 dB HL means 15 dB above the average threshold level for normally hearing young adults at this frequency. The dB HL scale therefore has a reference that varies according to frequency: The value of 0 dB HL, for any given frequency, is the level of the normal threshold at that frequency. It therefore does not make any sense to give a value in dB HL without stating the frequency.

Figure 14.2 shows the audiogram of a person with a mild hearing loss. The vertical scale of an audiogram is in dB HL. Notice that the scale is the "wrong way up," in that the decibel level increases from the top downward. So the amount of hearing loss, at each frequency, corresponds to how far *down* from 0 dB HL the symbol is drawn. A cross is used for hearing in the left ear and a circle for the right ear. The audiogram of Fig. 14.2 shows a similar reduction in hearing sensitivity across the frequency range. This pattern is typical of a conductive hearing loss. A *conductive hearing loss* is one that results from problems with the outer ear or the middle ear that reduce the efficient transmission of sound. If earwax accumulates in the outer ear, for example, or if the middle ear is filled with fluid, then sound will not be conducted so efficiently through the outer and middle ear to the cochlea. In a conductive loss, the amount by which the threshold is raised, in dB, tends to be similar across the frequency range. So if, for example, someone's threshold at 1000 Hz is 40 dB HL, then their threshold at 3000 Hz is also likely to be approximately 40 dB HL. (There are, however, some conditions that are exceptions to this general rule.) Another feature of a conductive hearing loss is that the reduction in sensitivity at threshold can be used to predict reduction in sensitivity at all other

---

Practice 14.2

1. Following are some sound pressure level values, in dB SPL, of some pure tones. Convert each dB SPL value into dB HL. (For this exercise, use the threshold in Fig. 14.1 as the reference for dB HL.)

   a. A 70-Hz tone with a sound pressure level of 55 dB SPL
   b. A 200-Hz tone with a sound pressure level of 30 dB SPL
   c. A 1000-Hz tone with a sound pressure level of 60 dB SPL
   d. A 1000-Hz tone with a sound pressure level of –5 dB SPL
   e. A 5000-Hz tone with a sound pressure level of 0 dB SPL

2. Following are some amplitude values, in dB HL, of some pure tones. Convert each dB HL value into dB SPL. (For this exercise, use the threshold in Fig. 14.1 as the reference for dB HL.)

   a. A 400-Hz tone of amplitude 30 dB HL
   b. A 500-Hz tone of amplitude 15 dB HL
   c. A 3000-Hz tone of amplitude 40 dB HL
   d. A 5000-Hz tone of amplitude –8 dB HL

Answers. 1. a. 20 dB HL b. 16 dB HL c. 58 dB HL d. –7 dB HL e. 3 dB HL   2. a. 36 dB SPL b. 19 dB SPL c. 34 dB SPL d. –10 dB SPL

sound pressure amplitudes, at the same frequency. So if, for example, some-one's hearing threshold is 40 dB HL at 1000 Hz, then for this person any 1000-Hz sound is likely to have to be raised by 40 dB in order to give it a loud-ness equivalent to normal. This may seem unsurprising. However, as de-scribed in a later section, in some other types of hearing loss the reduction in sensitivity is not the same at all sound pressure amplitudes.

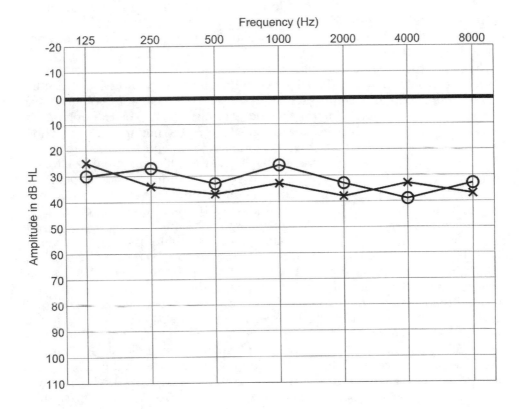

FIG. 14.2.   Audiogram showing a pattern of mild conductive hearing loss, in both ears. Crosses represent hearing thresholds in the left ear, and circles represent the right ear.

Practice 14.3

1. Suppose a person has a hearing threshold of 30 dB HL at 200 Hz, in free field. Using the threshold displayed in Fig. 14.1 as a guide, estimate the sound pressure, in dB SPL, at which a 200-Hz tone would be just audible.
2. Suppose a person has a hearing threshold of 33 dB HL at 4000 Hz. Using the threshold displayed in Fig. 14.1 as a guide, estimate the sound pressure, in dB SPL, at which a 4000-Hz tone would be just audible.

Answers. 1. 44 dB SPL 2. 26 dB SPL

LOUDNESS SCALES

Above the threshold of hearing, sounds have different loudnesses, which can be described by phrases like "very quiet," "quite loud," "extremely loud," and so on. However, actually quantifying such differences in an accurate *scale* of loudness is problematic. It requires listeners to give consistent judgments of the sort: "Sound A is twice as loud as sound B," "sound B is half as loud as sound C," "sound C has the same loudness as sound D." Large numbers of subjects, large numbers of trials, and controls on reliability, are all necessary for devising a valid scale. Two scales are in use, the sone scale and the phon scale. Only the latter is described here.

In one method used in devising the *phon* scale of loudness, listeners were played a reference tone and then asked to adjust the level of another tone until it had the same loudness as the reference tone. The reference tones all had a frequency of 1000 Hz, with different sound pressure levels. For example: A listener is played a 1000-Hz reference tone of 10 dB SPL. They are asked to adjust the level of an 800-Hz comparison tone until it has the same loudness as the reference tone. At this point, the level, in dB SPL, of the 800-Hz comparison tone is recorded. The procedure is repeated with a 600-Hz comparison tone, a 400-Hz comparison tone, and so on. In this way, the sound pressure level that produces a loudness equivalent to the loudness of a 1000-Hz tone of 10 dB SPL can be determined, for tones of all frequencies. The results can be plotted as an *equal loudness contour*. The 10 dB equal loudness contour shows the level, in dB SPL, of all tones that have a loudness that is the same as the loudness of a 10 dB SPL tone of 1000 Hz. All sounds that lie along the 10 dB equal loudness contour have a loudness level of 10 phons. Using a similar procedure, the 20 phon, 30 phon, and so on, equal loudness level contours were determined. In each case, a tone of 1000 Hz is used as the reference. So a 1000-Hz tone with a level of *n* dB SPL has a loudness level of *n* phons. Figure 14.3 shows the series of equal loudness contours from 10 phons to 110 phons, at intervals of 10 phons. The threshold of hearing, which is the 2 dB equal loudness contour (because 2 dB SPL is the threshold at 1000 Hz), is also shown on Fig. 14.3. The loudness discomfort level will probably be in the region of the 100 to 110 phon contours.

Sensorineural Hearing Loss

Sensorineural hearing loss is a hearing loss that arises from impairment of the cochlea or the auditory nerve or an impairment at higher levels of the auditory nervous system. When the hearing loss stems from impairment of the cochlea, it is called *cochlear loss*. Hearing loss stemming from impairment of neural transmission along the auditory nerve or beyond is called *retrocochlear loss.*

Figure 14.4 shows an audiogram with a pattern that is typical after damage to the cochlea resulting from continued exposure to high levels of noise. In such cases, sensitivity in the region 3 kHz to 5 kHz is relatively badly affected.

Loudness Recruitment.   Most cases of cochlear loss result in loudness recruitment. *Recruitment* is an abnormal response to sound level, which can be socially awkward. If you raise your voice for the benefit of someone who can't hear you and meet with the complaint that you are now speaking at an uncomfortably loud volume, the chances are that this is the result of recruitment. In this condition, the threshold of hearing is raised, so that sounds of low amplitude are not heard. However, above the raised threshold, sensitivity increases so steeply that high amplitude sounds may be heard with normal (or near normal) loudness. Perception of speech can be quite badly affected by this condition because in speech there is frequent alternation of low and high amplitude sounds. Vowels and sibilant fricatives may be heard clearly whereas nasals and liquids, for example, are not heard at all, with the result that many syllables are only partly audible.

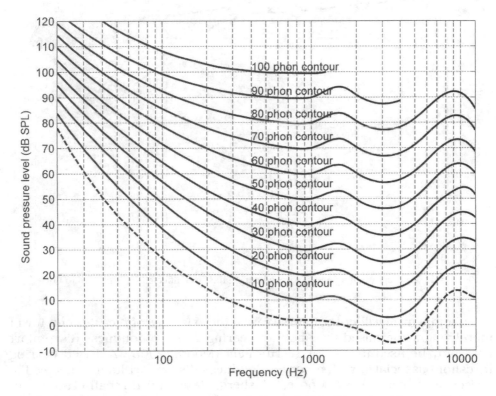

FIG. 14.3.   Equal loudness contours for adults aged 18 to 25 years, with normal hearing, based on values in Table B.1 of ISO 226 (2003). The dashed line is the threshold of hearing in free field, which corresponds to a loudness level of 2 phons. The 90-phon and 100-phon contours are comparatively incomplete and the 10-phone and 100-hone contours are constructed from comparatively sparse data.

Practice 14.4

1. What is the sound pressure, in dB SPL, of a 40-Hz tone of 70 phons?
2. What is the sound pressure, in dB SPL, of a 2000-Hz tone of 70 phons?
3. What is the sound pressure, in dB SPL, of a 4000-Hz tone of 90 phons?

Answers. 1. 100 dB SPL   2. 70 dB SPL   3. 89 dB SPL

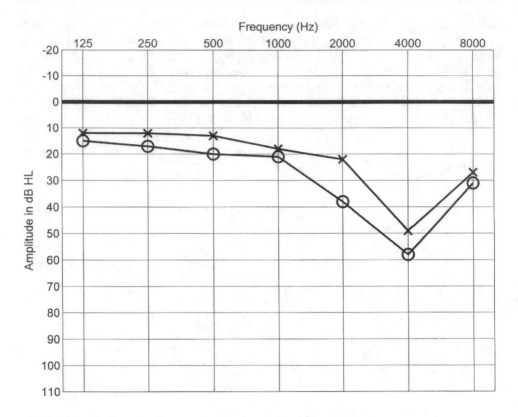

FIG. 14.4.   Audiogram of a person whose hearing has been affected by exposure to noise.

An audiogram will not of course reveal the existence of recruitment; it will merely show the raised threshold of hearing. A test of loudness discomfort level may be used to test for recruitment (Moore, 2003). A raised hearing threshold associated with a *normal* loudness discomfort level indicates the presence of recruitment. Moore, Glasberg, Hess, and Birchall (1985) provided a quantification of recruitment, which was achieved by testing people who had one normal ear and one ear affected by recruitment resulting from a cochlear hearing loss. They played a 1 kHz tone of fixed sound pressure level to the impaired ear and asked the subject to adjust a tone (of the same frequency) played to the normal ear, until it had the same loudness. This technique allowed them to quantify, in dB, the difference in level required for equal loudness between the impaired ear and the normal ear, for sound levels of increasing magnitude. Figure 14.5 shows a graph of the results. The horizontal axis shows the level of the fixed tone played to the impaired ear and this is plotted against the level in the normal ear (vertical axis) that had the same loudness. Of course, in a person with normal hearing, sounds of similar level and frequency should produce the same loudness in both ears. The dashed line of Fig. 14.4 shows the results for normal listeners. For the most part, this shows similar levels in both ears. However, at higher levels of the fixed tone (above about 75 dB SPL), subjects tended not to adjust the tone in the other ear quite high enough. The authors interpret this as a reluctance on the part of the subjects to suffer very high levels of sound input. Likewise, the procedure was abandoned with the hearing impaired subjects for levels of the fixed tone above 90 dB SPL, because of the discomfort caused.

Something akin to this loudness recruitment is found by comparing sensitivity at low and higher frequencies in normal hearing. As Fig. 14.3 shows, the threshold of hearing is comparatively high at low frequencies. However, loudness grows very rapidly with increasing sound pressure level at these low frequencies, so that it catches up, so to speak, with the loudness sensations at higher frequencies.

DIFFERENTIATING CONDUCTIVE AND SENSORINEURAL LOSS

Audiologists use a clever and simple technique to determine whether a patient has a conductive loss or a sensorineural loss. In addition to testing the person's hearing threshold for airborne sounds, the audiologist tests their threshold sensitivity to signals transmitted by a vibrator attached to some part of the bone of the skull. This is called *bone conduction.* Signals transmit-

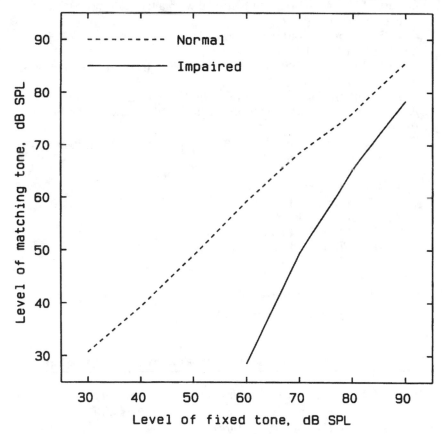

FIG. 14.5.   Loudness recruitment in subjects with one impaired cochlea and one normal cochlea (solid line, average results of five subjects). The solid line shows the level, in dB SPL, of tones played to the normal ear that matched in loudness the level of tones played to the impaired ear. The dashed line shows the results of a similar matching procedure for subjects with two normal ears. From Moore (2003, p. 153, Fig. 4.9).

ted through the bone of the skull stimulate the cochlea directly, bypassing the outer and middle ear. Therefore, if the hearing loss is just a conductive loss then bone conduction thresholds should be the same as for normal hearing. If, on the other hand, bone conduction thresholds are raised, then the conclusion to be drawn is that there is impairment of the cochlea, auditory nerve, or the higher auditory nervous system. Table 14.1 summarizes the characteristics of sensorineural and conductive hearing loss.

EXERCISES

1. Figure 14.6 is a graph of the average hearing threshold of the big brown bat, across the frequency range 850 Hz to 120 kHz ("big brown bat" is the name of the species), based on results reported by Koay, Heffner, and Heffner (1997). Note that the frequency scale of Fig. 14.6 is labeled in *kilo*hertz.

   a. Could a big brown bat hear a sound with a frequency of 10 kHz at a level of 70 dB SPL?
   b. Could a big brown bat hear a sound with a frequency of 2 kHz at a level of 70 dB SPL?
   c. Could a big brown bat hear a sound with a frequency of 100 kHz at a level of 70 dB SPL?
   d. What is the big brown bat's hearing threshold at 1 kHz?
   e. At approximately what frequency is the big brown bat's hearing most sensitive?
   f. Suppose an individual big brown bat, with a hearing loss, has thresholds as follows:

      i. 110 dB SPL at 1 kHz;
      ii. 80 dB SPL at 4 kHz;
      iii. 74 dB SPL at 6 kHz;
      iv. 38 dB SPL at 20 kHz;
      v. 45 dB SPL at 60 kHz;
      vi. 93 dB SPL at 90 kHz.

   Convert each of these dB SPL values into dB HL, where HL = Hearing Level of the big brown bat.

TABLE 14.1   **Comparison of Characteristic of Conductive and Sensorineural Hearing Loss**

	Raised Airborne Thresholds	Raised Bone Conduction Thresholds	Amount of Loss Differs With Frequency	Recruitment
Conductive	Yes	No	Rarely	Rarely
Sensorineural Loss (cochlear)	Yes	Yes	Often	Often

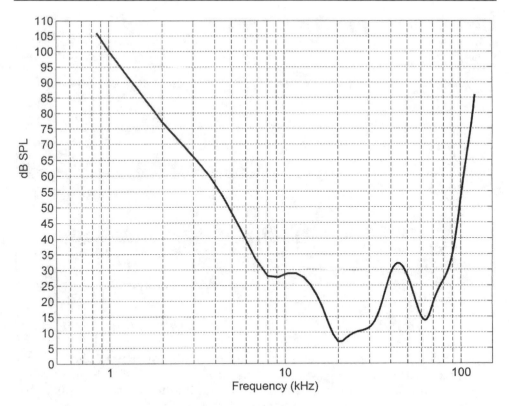

FIG. 14.6.   Hearing threshold of the big brown bat. Based on Koay, Heffner, and Heffner (1997).

2. True or False?

a. The upper limit of the ear's sensitivity to sound can be determined with more certainty than the threshold of hearing.
b. The threshold of hearing varies with age.
c. Exposure to noise typically results in an approximately equal reduction of sensitivity across frequencies.
d. A hearing threshold of –10 dB HL implies a better sensitivity than average.
e. A sound with a loudness level of 40 phons is equal in loudness to that of a 1-kHz pure tone with a level of 40 dB SPL.
f. Bone conduction levels are not affected by fluid in the middle ear, whereas air conduction levels are.
g. Recruitment is an impairment in which a series of distinct sounds over a short time span are collected together and heard as one.

3. For a tone of 4000 Hz, the average threshold of hearing of 70-year-old females is 24 dB higher than the average threshold of normal 18- to 25-year-old listeners at this frequency (ISO 7029, 2000). What is the average threshold of a 4000-Hz tone for 70-year-old females, in dB SPL?

15

Pitch and Quality

Pitch is primarily associated with the fundamental frequency of a sound. It is discussed in the following section. This section includes a description of phase-locking, a phenomenon that helps to explain the precision of pitch discrimination. Quality is primarily associated with the ear's response to the shape of the spectrum and it is discussed in the section after Pitch. For the most part, the ear's response to frequency is explained on the basis of the relationship between an acoustic frequency and a location along the basilar membrane. The frequency-resolving abilities of the ear (its ability to respond separately to signals of different frequency, presented simultaneously) have been established by masking experiments, which are described in the third section. The theory of auditory filters, described in the last section, is designed to explain the ear's frequency-resolving abilities. This theory provides a powerful explanation of many experimental findings, not only those related to pitch and quality but also those relating to loudness (although applications to loudness are not covered here). It is therefore basic to an explanation of human hearing.

PITCH

Completing the sentence "Pitch is our sensation of the _____ of a sound" is difficult to do without using the word "pitch" itself. "Musical note" (references to ordering on a musical scale are common in textbook definitions) has a meaning that is narrower than that of pitch and it leaves the pitch of speech out of account. "Height" is probably the best word available. Although "height" and related words are strongly linked to the spatial dimension, voices, and also musical notes of course, are commonly compared using phrases like "higher pitched" and "lower pitched," in English. Fortunately, pitch is easier to recognize than it is to describe! Pitch has a very strong relationship with the fundamental frequency of a sound. A change in f_0 nearly always produces a change in pitch. Only to a minor extent can other factors affect pitch; for example, a large variation in amplitude can sometimes produce a small variation in pitch, in the absence of a change in fundamental frequency.

Lower and Upper Limits of the Ear's Response to Frequency

There is no sharp cut-off in the range of frequencies that evoke a pitch sensation, at either the lower or upper end of the scale. Indeed, for any frequency of a stimulus, pitch is not necessarily an all-or-none sensation. Various factors (one example would be a degree of irregularity in the length of the period, from one cycle to the next) may make the sensation more or less strong, more or less certain. A common convention is that the lower limit of the pitch scale corresponds to a frequency of 16 Hz (four octaves below middle C, in musical terms). Large organs include a pipe that produces a note with a f_0 of 16 Hz. However, Pressnitzer, Patterson, and Krumbholz (2001) conducted an experiment in which listeners had the task of identifying changes of one semitone in one of the notes of a four-note melody. Judgments were unreliable for notes with a f_0 below about 30 Hz, which suggests that a more realistic lower limit would be 30 Hz.

At the upper end of the range, it has been established that humans make consistent and reliable judgments about pitch for f_0 s up to about 5 kHz. For sounds with f_0 above about 5 kHz, pitch is less clearly identifiable and judgments about it become erratic. A piano keyboard normally extends no higher than 4186 Hz (four octaves above middle C). The weakening of pitch-frequency relationships above 5 kHz has significance for explaining the mechanism of pitch detection, as described later in this section.

Frequency Discrimination

For frequencies below 5 kHz, fine discriminations in frequency are possible. In the region of 1000 Hz, a difference of 2 or 3 Hz can be detected, at least by trained listeners. Fineness of discrimination depends on the absolute frequencies involved, as well as the interval between them. So it is possible to detect a difference between 100 Hz and 103 Hz but not between 4000 Hz and 4003 Hz. In other words, the ratio of two frequencies is a better guide to their discriminability than the difference between them. Another interesting finding is that pitch discrimination is better when the stimuli are complex periodic sounds than when they are pure tones.

The Pitch of Complex Tones

Much of the research on the ear's response to frequency has been carried out using pure tones, despite the fact that most natural, periodic sounds—and all periodic speech sounds—are complex. Where a complex periodic sound and a pure tone have the same pitch, then we would expect the first harmonic of the complex periodic sound to have the same frequency as the frequency of the pure tone. In general, this prediction is borne out. Of course, it is difficult for listeners to compare pure tones with (parts of) intonation contours of speech. Directly investigating the pitch of speech introduces a further level of difficulty, because as soon as the f_0 of a speech sound is held constant for an appreciable duration, it ceases to sound speechlike. The complex periodic sounds used in pitch experiments tend to be of a musical sort and are called *complex tones*. Listeners usually describe the pitch sensation evoked by a complex tone as being stronger, and more definite, than that evoked by a pure tone. Also, when presented with a complex tone, listeners sometimes report being able to hear separately one or two higher harmonics, in addition to the fundamental.

Virtual Pitch or the Case of the Missing Fundamental.   A case of particular interest, in relation to the question of the nature of the pitch-determining mechanism, is that in which a sound is constructed by combining a series of sine waves that are all whole-number multiples of a first harmonic ($= f_0$) that is not itself present. For example, a complex tone can be synthesized by combining sine waves of 400 Hz, 600 Hz, 800 Hz, and 1000 Hz. What pitch would it have? If a listener is played this tone, and asked to adjust the frequency of another, pure tone so that it has the same pitch as the complex tone, they adjust the second tone so that it has a frequency of 200 Hz. In other words, the pitch of the complex tone is 200 Hz. Although a tone consisting of 400-, 600-, 800-, and 1000-Hz harmonics is unnatural from the point of view of speech *production*, it is not such an unnatural stimulus from the point of view of the listener to speech. The presence of low frequency background noise could obscure the lower harmonics in a speech signal, so that the listener would be presented with exactly this problem of reconstructing the f_0 from hearing just the higher harmonics. The phenomenon is known as *virtual pitch* or *the case of the missing fundamental.*

Two Pure Tones Very Close in Frequency.   Howard and Angus (2001) described as "rough" the auditory sensation produced by two sine waves (pure tones) that are very close together in frequency. For example, two tones, one of 120 Hz and the other of 150 Hz, do not evoke the sensation of a sound having a f_0 of 30 Hz, even though they could be the fourth and fifth harmonics of a complex tone with a f_0 of 30 Hz. Instead, what is heard is a sound with a rough quality, of uncertain pitch. (For even closer frequencies, e.g., 120 Hz and 130 Hz, a periodic swelling and fading of amplitude, known as beats, is heard.) Such sounds are not a feature of speech, in which adjacent harmonics of a periodic sound would not be so close together. Their auditory characteristics, however, provide support for the theory of auditory filters, which will be discussed later. The amount of separation that is required between the two harmonics, before a tone of this sort becomes audibly smooth, depends on the absolute frequencies of the two sine waves: the higher the frequency, the wider apart must the two tones be in order to eliminate roughness in the perceived quality of the sound.

The Mechanism of Pitch Detection

What is the mechanism by which the ear detects pitch? Chapter 13 described how the frequency of a tone determined the location of a peak on the traveling wave along the basilar membrane. For example, a tone of 200 Hz always produces a peak at the same point along the basilar membrane. So neural activity derived from the hair cells in this region could form the basis for pitch detection. This is the so-called place theory, described briefly in chapter 13. Chapter 13 also mentioned the temporal theory. It does seem unlikely that place of origin along the basilar membrane could, alone, account for the precision with which humans can make pitch distinctions. Neural firings from auditory nerve fibers at the relevant location have been observed to coincide with a particular phase of the period of the sine wave—firing only at positive peaks, for example. This phenomenon is known as *phase locking* and it could indeed account for the precision of human pitch perception.

One possibility, then, might be a mechanism that involved, firstly, the location of the furthest peak on the basilar membrane toward the apical end. (Remember that the basilar membrane is widest at this end, i.e., the end farthest from the oval window, and the lower the frequency, the nearer is the peak to the wider end.) Phase locking of the neural firings from this location would provide the observed precision of response. However, this simple mechanism could not account for all the findings reported earlier. For example, it could not account for the more definite sensation of pitch from a complex tone as compared with a pure tone and (most notably) it could not account for the case of the missing fundamental. Clearly, pitch is a sensation that involves (where available) information from a number of harmonics. The best explanation is that it arises from a computation of the highest common factor of the harmonic frequencies. Further support for this explanation comes from the fact that phase locking is observed on higher harmonics, not just the lowest. Interestingly, though, the phase locked neural firings can be somewhat haphazard: They do not occur on every single cycle. Despite this, pitch does not suddenly sink in frequency when a neural firing is missed, presumably because of the location of origin of the neural firings in question and because of information coming from other harmonic locations and other neurons from the same location. Thus, both the place mechanism and the temporal mechanism are necessary to an explanation of pitch. However, phase locking ceases to operate above about 5 kHz and this coincides with the fact that the sensation of pitch becomes uncertain from about this frequency.

Practice 15.1

A complex tone consisting of four sine wave components, at 250 Hz, 375 Hz, 500 Hz, and 625 Hz, respectively, would have a virtual pitch of:

    A. 25 Hz
    B. 125 Hz
    C. 250 Hz

Is it A, B or C?

Answer. B (Not A, because although 25 is a factor of all the frequencies, it is not the highest factor; not C, because neither 375 Hz or 625 Hz are whole number multiples of 250.)

Scaling of Pitch of Speech

Most studies of speech intonation that have included frequency analysis have used a linear, hertz scale (see, e.g., Beckman, 1996, who explicitly supports the use of a linear scale for analyzing intonation). f_0 contours using such a scale were illustrated in chapter 9 (see Fig. 9.3). A hertz scale has the virtue that the relationship with the production side remains transparent, because number of hertz is equal to the number of cycles of the vocal folds per second. The semitone scale, which is a logarithmic scale, was also described in chapter 9. It has been used for centuries to capture the perceptual relationships among musical notes and it is also sometimes used in the analysis of speech f_0. To a smaller extent, psychoacoustic scales have also been used. A psychoacoustic scale is one that is constructed from the results of experiments with hearing.

The *mel scale* (Stevens & Volkman, 1940) is a psychoacoustic scale of pitch derived from an experiment that tried to determine "equal sense-distances." Listeners were played two pure tones, one of 200 Hz and the second of 6500 Hz, and they were asked to adjust the frequency of another pure tone until it had a pitch midway between these two. The procedure was repeated until the 200 Hz to 6500 Hz range was divided into four perceptually equal intervals. A similar test was done over other frequency ranges. In the scale drawn up from the results, a pure tone of 1000 Hz was arbitrarily assigned a value of 1000 mels. Figure 15.1 is a graph of the mel scale. It shows the relationship between mels and hertz.

At higher frequencies (above 1000 Hz), the mel scale is quite logarithmic in character. If it was perfectly logarithmic, then every doubling of frequency, in hertz, would result in an equal step in mels. The perceptual difference between 2000 Hz and 1000 Hz is 550 mels and the difference between 4000 Hz and 2000 Hz, at 625 mels, is not a great deal more than this. Up to at least 700

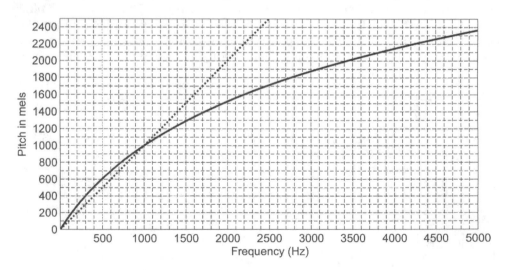

FIG. 15.1.   The mel scale. The solid line shows pitch, in mels, plotted against frequency, in hertz, over the range 100 Hz to 5000 Hz.

Practice 15.2

For each pair of values, in Hz, in the following questions, (a) state the difference between them in hertz, and (b) estimate the difference between them in mels.

1. 200 Hz, 100 Hz
2. 500 Hz, 300 Hz
3. 600 Hz, 300 Hz
4. 1700 Hz, 1000 Hz
5. 2000 Hz, 1000 Hz
6. 4600 Hz, 3900 Hz

Answers. 1. a. 100 Hz b. about 130 mels 2. a. 200 Hz b. about 200 mels 3. a. 300 Hz b. about 300 mels 4. a. 700 Hz b. about 400 mels 5. a. 1000 Hz b. about 550 mel. 6. a. 700 Hz b. about 200 mels

---

Hz, however, a linear scale provides a better approximation of the mel scale (although, admittedly, below about 200 Hz, the graph falls more steeply). The dotted line of Fig. 15.1 represents a linear relationship between the hertz scale and pitch, for comparison.

Because the f_0 of speech would not usually go much above 700 Hz, the shape of the mel scale would imply that a linear scale is more appropriate than a logarithmic scale for displaying and analyzing the intonation contours of speech. In this case, perception of the f_0 of speech must be different from perception of the f_0 of music. However, since the mel scale was introduced, two alternative psychoacoustic scales, the ERB scale and the Bark scale, have been proposed. Like the mel scale, both these scales span a much wider range of frequencies than speech f_0; in fact, both the ERB and the Bark scales were constructed with a view to explaining the human response to spectral information rather than f_0. (ERBs—equivalent rectangular bandwidths—are described later in this chapter.) Over the range of interest for speech intonation (up to about 700 Hz), the Bark scale is quite linear in character, whereas the ERB scale is more logarithmic.

Some researchers claim that a purely logarithmic scale is in fact the most appropriate scale for speech, as well as music. Traunmüller and Eriksson (1995), reporting their results of liveliness estimations of male and female speakers (described in chap. 9), used their results to support the use of a logarithmic scale of pitch. They argued explicitly against the position of Hermes and van Gestel (1991), who found that an ERB scale was the most appropriate of the three alternatives (out of linear, logarithmic, and ERB) for modeling subjects' responses to different pitch contours. Further support for a logarithmic scale comes from Nolan (2003). He asked male and female subjects to reproduce intonation contours modeled by both a male and a female speaker. He tested the results with all the available scales (hertz, semitone, mel, Bark, and ERB) to discover which recorded the most similar pitch excursions between the model contours and their reproductions by the different subjects. The logarithmic (semitone) scale performed best, just ahead of the ERB scale.

In summary, there are five competing scales for analysis of the intonation of speech. Three (mel, Bark, and ERB) are psychoacoustic, one (hertz) is linear, and one (semitone) is logarithmic. There is conflicting evidence as to which provides the best match to the human perception of speech intonation. It is worth pointing out that none of the psychoacoustic scales is based on experiments focused mainly on the f_0 range of speech or including speech sounds in the data. Also, it is just possible that different aspects of intonation (linguistic vs. emotional, for example) are perceptually decoded according to different scales.

QUALITY

A difference in the auditory effect of two sounds, which have identical pitch, overall loudness, and duration, is a difference in the sensation of *quality.* In music, a difference in quality allows us to distinguish, for example, a note on the piano from the same note on the violin. The word *timbre* is commonly used to describe quality in music (and sometimes in phonetics as well). In speech, a difference in quality is the largest factor in most phonemic distinctions; for example, in distinguishing an /ɑ/ sound from an /u/ sound, or an /s/ sound from an /ʃ/ sound. It also plays a large role in distinguishing one speaker from another. The sensation of quality is associated mainly with the spectral composition of a sound. This follows from the description offered in the opening sentence of this section. However, f_0, amplitude, and duration (and interactions among these) cannot be entirely ruled out as contributors to the sensation of quality. For example, the phonemes /i/ and /ɑ/, in English, are differentiated by spectral composition. However, other things being equal, /i/ is likely to have a slightly higher f_0 than /ɑ/, because its forward tongue position tends to produce increased tension in the laryngeal muscles. And, other things being equal, /ɑ/ is likely to have greater amplitude than /i/, because the vocal tract is more open. It is possible that these factors may be integrated into the sensation of the quality of /ɑ/ compared with the quality of /i/. Certainly, dynamic factors, that is, *changes* in spectrum and/or f_0 and/or amplitude over time, are perceptually important. This also holds for the perception of timbre in music. Howard and Angus (2001, p. 221) reported that, for example, a note played on an open string of a violin cannot be reliably distinguished from the same note played on a trumpet, in the absence of the onset and offset of the sounds.

The focus here is on the ear's ability to distinguish the pattern of relative amplitudes in the components that make up a spectrum. Crucial to an explanation of the mechanism involved is the question of the ear's ability to resolve (i.e., to hear separately) energy at different frequencies. If the resolving ability of the ear is as good as that of a good electronic spectrum analyzer then we could assume that a line spectrum of a vowel, for example, could give a good indication of the pattern of the sensation experienced by human hearing. If, on the other hand, the frequency components within some range, say 1900 Hz to 2100 Hz, went into the same perceptual bin, so to speak, then some of the detailed pattern seen in a line spectrum would be inaccurate as a representation of the corresponding auditory sensation. An understanding of the perception of quality requires a closer look at the place mechanism for sensing frequency.

Formant Matching Experiments

The formant matching experiment is a well-established paradigm in research on vowel perception. The technique involves the subject being able to control the frequency of the second formant of a synthetic vowel (by turning a knob, for example). The second formant of this experimental vowel is called F2'. The subject adjusts the frequency of F2' until they feel it best matches the quality of another stimulus, for example the recording of a natural (or natural-sounding) vowel of their language. A much quoted early experiment was that of Carlson, Granström, and Fant (1970), using nine Swedish vowels. They synthesized excellent versions of all these vowels (with carefully controlled f_0), containing formants F1 to F4. They then used experimental stimuli containing F1 of each vowel together with an adjustable F2'. The task of the subjects was to adjust F2' until the stimulus best matched the corresponding, full, four-formant vowel. The results are shown in Fig. 15.2. In the case of the three back vowels, /ɑ, o, u/, F2' was placed at the same frequency as the F2 of the full vowel. The rest of the vowels were all front vowels. In all cases except /i/, F2' was placed somewhere between F2 and F3. In the case of /i/, F2' was placed even higher, between F3 and F4.

Whereas the back vowels have a low F2, well separated from F3, the front vowels have a high F2, which is quite close to F3 (except for /i/, in which F3 and F4 are closer together). These results suggest that at higher frequencies the formant peaks make some kind of combined contribution to the perception of the quality of the vowel, whereas at lower frequencies the formants are well distinguished from each other.

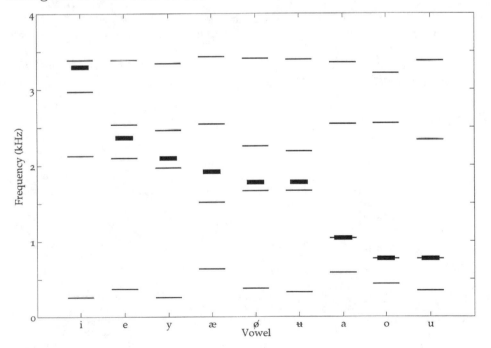

FIG. 15.2.   F2' matches to nine Swedish vowels. After Carlson, Granström, and Fant (1970).

MASKING

Masking means rendering a tone or other sound inaudible by introducing some noise or a second tone. This noise (or the second tone) is called the *masker* (and the first tone is then the *maskee*, or signal). One experimental paradigm for masking is illustrated in Fig. 15.3. Suppose a 1000 Hz pure tone is played in the presence of noise. The frequencies that make up the noise cover a wide range (i.e., the noise has a wide *bandwidth*; e.g., from 50 Hz to 10000 Hz). The level of the noise is adjusted so that it just (and only just) renders the pure tone inaudible (masks it). Then the bandwidth of the noise is gradually narrowed, keeping it centered around the frequency of the pure tone. Narrowing the bandwidth of the noise makes no difference at first: The pure tone remains masked. However, when the noise is narrowed sufficiently, the tone will be unmasked. The significance of this result is that only energy within a certain *critical bandwidth* competes effectively with the tone of interest. Noise outside this critical bandwidth makes little difference to the audibility of the tone. Figure 15.3 shows the breakpoint occurring when the noise range is reduced to 935 Hz to 1065 Hz, a bandwidth of 130 Hz. This value was chosen for the illustration because 130 Hz is approximately the critical bandwidth at 1000 Hz, according to one method of calculation (the ERB method, described in the next section). As the bandwidth of the noise continues to be narrowed, the pure tone is increasingly easily heard. The critical bandwidth represents the frequency region within which different frequencies are not resolved by the ear. Figure 15.3 also illustrates the same scenario with a target tone of 3000 Hz. In this case, the critical bandwidth is much wider, around 350 Hz. As frequency increases, the critical bandwidth widens. A variety of masking experiments have been carried out, using a number of different techniques, and the amplitude and frequency relationships between maskers and maskees have been well mapped, across the frequency range.

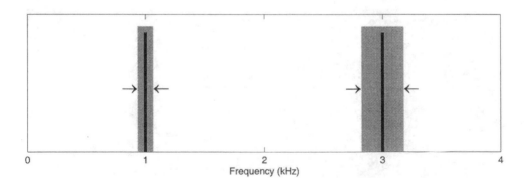

FIG. 15.3.   Cartoon of masking by a band of noise. The dark vertical lines represent pure tones, of 1 kHz and 3 kHz. The surrounding gray rectangles represent bands of noise, which just mask the respective pure tones. The bands of noise are being gradually narrowed and they are just reaching the point where the pure tone will, in each case, become audible.

THE THEORY OF AUDITORY FILTERS

Relevant findings described in previous sections can be summarized as follows:

- The frequency response of the ear to a pure tone, or to a sine wave component that is widely separated in frequency from its neighbors, is very precise, at least up to about 5 kHz.
- At higher frequencies there is a tendency for adjacent formants to be perceived in a holistic fashion. At lower frequencies, adjacent formant peaks (or even harmonics) are resolved.
- A pure tone is only masked by neighboring frequencies. The bandwidth within which masking occurs widens with increasing frequency.

These findings are explained by a model of hearing in which frequency analysis depends, primarily, on frequency-place coding on the basilar membrane. Each of the thousands of auditory neurons is linked to a particular point on the basilar membrane. Each neuron has a *characteristic frequency*, a frequency to which it responds best, because of the point along the basilar membrane with which it is associated. As the frequency of the stimulus moves further away from the neuron's characteristic frequency, the excitation of that neuron progressively reduces. The response of each neuron can be modeled as a *band-pass filter*, that is, a filter that allows frequency components within a certain range of frequencies to pass through it. The gain it confers on input stimuli across this frequency range can be graphed by its transfer function (cf. Chap. 13). Figure 15.4, from Moore and Glasberg (1983), illustrates the model. The upper figure shows a selection from the sequence of overlapping filters (in reality, there will be a great many more filters within the frequency range shown). The center frequency (peak) of each filter is the characteristic frequency of the corresponding neuron. Notice that the filters broaden with increasing center frequency. An input sine wave component of 1000 Hz (represented by the vertical dashed line) will most greatly excite the neuron associated with the point corresponding to 1000 Hz. Neurons associated with adjacent locations will also be excited, but to a lesser extent. This is represented by the overlap from nearby filters. The lower graph of Fig. 15.4 shows the neural excitation pattern resulting from the 1 kHz input. The "1 kHz neuron" is most greatly excited (represented by the fact that energy passes through the filter centered at 1 kHz without loss). The "850 Hz neuron" and the "1300 Hz neuron," at either side, are also somewhat excited. Those yet further away (represented by filters a and d) are excited to only a small extent. Beyond, excitation falls to negligible levels.

Two adjacent frequency components will fail to be resolved if they both excite the same neuron, to a significant degree. Or, in terms of Fig. 15.4, if they both "inhabit" the same filter, with significant amplitude. But how are we to interpret "significant amplitude?" In other words: "What is the critical bandwidth of each filter?" or "How broad, for practical purposes, is each filter?" The approach taken to this problem was to calculate how wide, in hertz, the filter would be if its sides were vertical (i.e., if the filter had a rectangular shape instead of a triangular one) and it passed exactly the same amount of

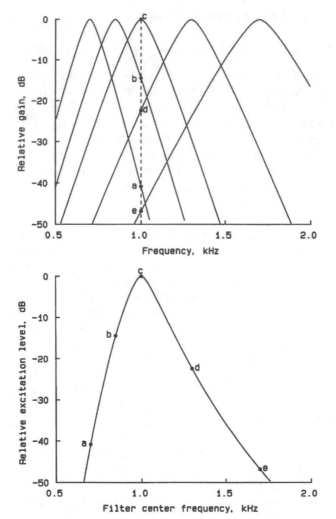

FIG. 15.4. Auditory filters (top and bottom) the pattern of excitation provoked by a 1-kHz pure tone. Reprinted with permission from B. C. J. Moore & B. R. Glasberg, *The Journal of the Acoustical Society of America*, 74, 752 (1982). Copyright 1983, Acoustical Society of America.

power (for a noise input that has the same amplitude at all frequencies) as the original, more triangular-shaped shaped filter. This calculated width, in hertz, is known as the *equivalent rectangular bandwidth* and it forms the basis for an auditory frequency scale that has been extensively used in speech perception research. The earlier version of the scale, which is still quite commonly used, is the Bark scale (Zwicker, 1961; Zwicker & Fastl, 1999). A later version, which is said to give a more accurate representation of the ear's response, is known simply as the ERB (Equivalent Rectangular Bandwidth) scale (Moore & Glasberg, 1983). Of course, as with any aspect of the ear's response, the critical bandwidth for frequency resolution may vary from one person to another. The notation ERB_N is used to denote the average ERB of young adults with normal hearing. The ERB_N, in hertz, at a given frequency, f, can be calculated from the equation:

$$ERB_N = 24.7(0.00437f + 1) \qquad (15.1)$$

where f is the frequency, in hertz (see Glasberg & Moore, 1990; Moore, 2003). From considering this equation, it can be appreciated that as frequency rises, the bandwidth rises too.

Example 1

Calculate the bandwidth (ERB_N) of a neuron whose characteristic frequency is 120 Hz.
$ERB_N = 24.7(0.00437 \times 120 + 1) = 38$ Hz

Example 2

Calculate the bandwidth (ERB_N) of a neuron whose characteristic frequency is 3.4 kHz.
$ERB_N = 24.7(0.00437 \times 3400 + 1) = 392$ Hz

In order to estimate whether two adjacent frequency components might be resolved, it is necessary to find out whether or not there is a filter that contains them both. For example, suppose we are interested in two adjacent components, one of 800 Hz and one of 900 Hz. Choose the filter centered at 850 Hz, which is halfway between them (filters can be imagined as being spaced at 1 Hz intervals) because this has the most likelihood of being able to contain both. The ERB_N of this filter is:

$$\mathbf{ERB_N = 24.7(0.00437 \times 850 + 1) = 116 \ Hz}$$

So the bandwidth of the filter centered at 850 Hz extends 58 Hz above 850 Hz and 58 Hz below 850 Hz (a range from 792 Hz–908 Hz) and therefore the two components in question, at 800 Hz and 900 Hz, would not be resolved. The implications for the perception of speech sounds are quite significant. Suppose, for example, that these 800-Hz and 900-Hz components were the eighth and ninth harmonics of a vowel sound with a f_0 of 100 Hz. The frequency information from at least 800 Hz upward would be somewhat "smeared," compared to the information as portrayed in a line spectrum of the acoustic signal, for example. Pitch perception would not normally be affected because there are plenty of lower harmonics that would be resolved. However, if the energy below 800 Hz was obliterated by noise, then pitch could be affected because cues from both place and temporal information would be degraded (the occurrence of the two harmonics within the same filter would presumably compromise the process of phase locking).

Practice 15.3

"The fourth and fifth harmonics of a vowel with a f_0 of 200 Hz will not be resolved." True or false?

Answer. False. The fourth and fifth harmonics are at 800 Hz and 1000 Hz, respectively. The filter centered at 900 Hz is halfway between them. Its ERB is 122 Hz, which means that the filter bandwidth extends from 839 Hz to 961 Hz. The two harmonics in question fall outside this range.

The implication of the answer to Practice 15.3 is that there is no single neuron that is simultaneously excited by harmonics of 800 Hz and 1000 Hz (or not to a similar extent, at least), whereas the previous example showed that there *is* a single neuron that is simultaneously excited, and to a similar extent, by harmonics of 800 Hz and 900 Hz.

We have tacitly assumed (in the discussion of Practice 15.3 and in Exercises 3 and 4, at the end of this chapter) that if two adjacent harmonics do *not* lie within the same critical band then they *will* be resolved. The results of masking experiments provide indirect support for this assumption. Is there any direct evidence for it? It is indeed possible for a listener to "hear out" an individual sine wave component within a complex tone, if it is sufficiently separated from its neighbors. "Hear out" means the ability to single out the individual component in a conscious way, so as to be able to make accurate judgments about it. Results of experiments on the hearing out of individual sine wave components suggest a similar relationship of bandwidth with frequency to that defined by the ERB_N equation, except that the bandwidths are consistently wider (i.e., in order to be heard out, a component must be separated from its neighbors by more than the ERB_N). Moore (2003, p. 85) suggested that "a partial [that is, a sine wave component] can be heard out from neighboring partials when it is separated from those partials by 1.25 times the ERB_N." The wider bandwidth implied by these results might be accounted for by the more demanding nature of the task, which typically involves making pitch comparisons between an individual component of a complex tone and a pure tone played before or after it. It seems significant that (unlike masking experiments) trained musicians perform much better on these hearing out tasks than untrained listeners.

It is not surprising that critical band theory accounts well for the evidence from masking experiments, because it was constructed based on information from the results of these experiments. However, it also gives a good explanation of the subjective effects of trying to determine the pitch of a sound consisting of two pure tones close in frequency, described in the section Pitch, earlier. It is also broadly supported by the results of "hearing out" experiments, as just discussed. It does not provide an immediate explanation of the formant matching evidence described in the Quality section, earlier, because the formants that F2' forms a compromise between, so to speak, are often considerably further apart than the relevant ERB_N. However, we are dealing here not with individual harmonics but with spectral peaks, which may themselves vary in width. Higher level factors of phonetic perception may also be involved, although the implied pattern of lower resolution at higher frequencies is at least suggestive of the role of auditory filters like those modeled by ERB_Ns.

Hearing Impairment Involving Loss of Frequency Resolution

The outer hair cells of the organ of Corti are responsible for fine tuning the response of the basilar membrane, that is, increasing its frequency resolution (frequency resolution is also called frequency selectivity). Damage to the cochlea usually includes damage to the outer hair cells, leading to a reduction in resolution. Figure 15.5, from Glasberg and Moore (1986) contrasts the response of a number of normal ears (top) with that of a number of ears that have suffered cochlear damage (bottom), for a point centered on 1 kHz. The normal ears are more sharply tuned and therefore have more effective frequency resolution. Some types of hearing loss involve what is in effect a broadening of the auditory filters, which results in a reduction of frequency resolution. Figure 15.5 (bottom) shows the shape of the auditory filters, centered on 1 kHz, of a number of hearing-impaired subjects with cochlear damage in one ear only. These may be compared with the corresponding filter shapes for the other (nondamaged) ears, in Fig. 15.5 (top). One consequence of this type of loss would be a reduced ability on the part of the listener to distinguish the quality of a sound; distinctions between one vowel and another, for example, would be reduced. Another consequence would be a reduced ability to distinguish a signal from background noise.

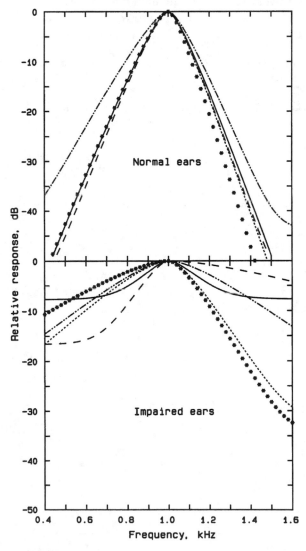

FIG. 15.5. The shape of the auditory filter for a number of normal ears (top) and a number of ears that have suffered cochlear damage. Reprinted with permission from B. R. Glasberg & B. C. J. Moore, *The Journal of the Acoustical Society of America*, 79, 1027 (1986). Copyright 1986, Acoustical Society of America.

EXERCISES

1. "On large organs, some stops can have pipes whose f_0 exceeds 8 kHz, but these are provided to be used in conjunction with other stops" (Howard & Angus, 2001, p. 133). Why would notes at such frequencies not be played alone?
2. A noisy environment made the lowest harmonics of a vowel inaudible. A listener heard successive harmonics of the vowel at 345 Hz, 460 Hz, 575 Hz, and so on. What f_0 did the listener perceive the vowel to have?
3. "A vowel was produced with a f_0 of 110 Hz. According to the ERB_N equation, a listener with normal hearing would fail to resolve its eighth and ninth harmonics." True or false? "A listener would also fail to resolve its ninth and tenth harmonics." True or false?
4. Work out, and state, the lowest pair of adjacent harmonics that a normal listener would fail to resolve, according to the ERB_N equation, in each of the following cases:

    a. A vowel with a f_0 of 150 Hz.
    b. A vowel with a f_0 of 180 Hz.
    c. A vowel with a f_0 of 208 Hz.
    d. A vowel with a f_0 of 280 Hz.
    e. A vowel with a f_0 of 340 Hz.

16

Speech Perception

Speech perception is the process whereby a listener interprets a stream of sound as a sequence of linguistic units. There are two major problems that confront the investigation of speech perception:

1. The process is a mental one, so it is not directly observable.
2. We don't know what the linguistic units are, that is, the units that form the immediate objects of perception in speech. They could be phonemes, or they could be smaller phonetic "building blocks" (known as distinctive features), like "nasal," "fricative," and "voiced." Or perhaps the listener immediately perceives the stream of sound as a sequence of syllables, or even whole words.

The first problem is addressed by setting up laboratory experiments in which acoustic signals are precisely controlled and manipulated and listeners are asked questions about them. In this respect they are like many of the experiments used in the investigation of hearing, but in speech perception experiments listeners are usually asked to identify what they hear as linguistic items, by answering questions like "What word did you hear?" or "Was that 'sew' or 'show'?"

The second problem is the one that, above all, divides one theory from another in the field of speech perception. Frustratingly, the question of what the linguistic units are is not at all accessible to self-enquiry. If in ordinary circumstances someone hears an acoustic signal that they identify as the word "sheep," for example, they are likely to be focused on the identity and meaning of the word, not its form. When questioned about its form, literate people most often describe it in terms of letters of the alphabet, as consisting of the letters "s," "h," "e," "e," and "p." This is not very helpful because we can be sure that the spoken word "sheep" is *not* represented in our minds as a spelling—you don't have to be literate to use spoken language. On the other hand, letters of the alphabet are roughly "phoneme-sized," and this type of response (together with the very existence of alphabetic writing) might be taken as evidence in favor of the validity of assuming a phoneme-sized unit. Certainly, it seems fair to say that perceptionists, and phoneticians generally, seem to find it most convenient to discuss speech in terms of phonemes, whatever their theoretical positions on the issue. To date, much of the work on speech perception has been carried out under an assumption, explicit or implicit, that the units involved are phonemes. Under this assumption, when a listener hears an utterance of the word "sheep," they first decode it into a sequence of three phonemes, /ʃip/. Such an assumption encourages researchers to ask questions like "What is the perceptual boundary between 'sheep' and 'seep' (or 'sheep' and 'sheet,' or 'sheep' and 'ship')?" and to address them by focusing on the acoustic structure of short (phoneme-sized) chunks in the signal. This has proved a fruitful approach.

Notice that our ignorance extends not just to the *size* of the perceptual units of language but to their *content* as well. What do the units "look like?" Do they correspond to aspects of the acoustic signal? Or articulations of the speech organs? Or are they abstract bits of neural code, each with an articulatory interpretation and an acoustic–auditory interpretation? This is a much debated issue, which arises in speech production theory as well as in speech perception.

We do not attempt anything like a definitive account of the field in the following sections but we illustrate the experimental approach and the findings. An accessible introduction to speech perception is Ryalls (1996).

ACOUSTIC CUES

Some aspect of the acoustic signal counts as an *acoustic cue* if it has a role in distinguishing between one phoneme and another. The first step in identifying an acoustic cue is to identify some aspect of the acoustic signal that changes significantly between one sound category and another, for example an acoustic parameter that has a different value in /b, d, g/ as compared with /p, t, k/. The second step is to prepare a series of test stimuli to play to listeners with a view to discovering whether, and in what way, changing the values of the parameter in question brings about a change in the listener's perception. The stimuli for such experiments are created by speech synthesis, that is, machine production of a speech signal. This is the only way of guaranteeing that the acoustic parameter of interest varies systematically, while all other parameters remain constant. For example, the acoustic parameter of VOT can be systematically increased in a syllable that starts off sounding like /da/. When the VOT gets long enough, the syllable (so to speak) turns into /ta/.

Figure 16.1 shows the result of an actual experiment of this sort, reported by Sharma and Dorman (1999). In this experiment, 16 listeners listened to stimuli consisting of an alveolar plosive sound followed by /a/. The VOT of the initial plosive was changed from 0 ms to 80 ms, in steps of 10 ms, and the listeners were asked to judge each stimulus as being either "DA" or "TA." As Fig. 16.1 shows, the results of this experiment confirm that VOT is indeed a significant cue to the voicing status of a plosive. At low VOTs (up to 30 ms), the stim-

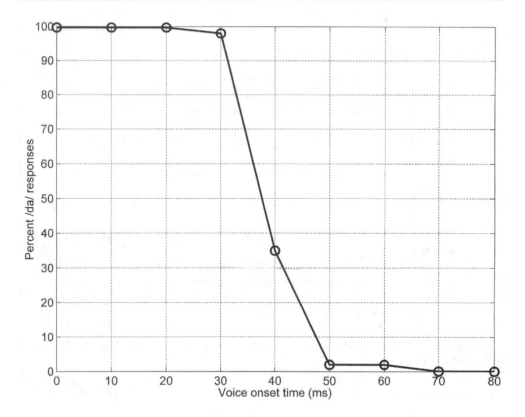

FIG. 16.1.   The acoustic cue of voice onset time (VOT). Listeners were played stimuli that all sounded the same (an alveolar stop followed by /a/) except that the VOT varied, in steps of 10 ms, between 0 ms and 80 ms. Each of the nine stimuli was played 10 times, giving a total of 90, played in random order. The listeners were asked to judge, in each case, whether the stimulus was "DA" or "TA." Figure redrawn from Figure 1 of Sharma and Dorman (1999, p. 1079).

uli were nearly always identified as /da/; at higher VOTs (50 ms and above) the stimuli were nearly always identified as /ta/. Note that the graph only plots the /da/ responses; so if, for example, 2% of the responses were /da/, this implies that the remaining 98% were /ta/.

This experiment confirms that a difference in VOT can indeed make the difference between perceiving a /t/ and perceiving a /d/ and that the continuum represented along the horizontal axis of Fig. 16.1 represents a "t-d continuum." The results suggest that alveolar plosives with VOTs below about 20 ms are likely to be perceived as /d/ whereas those with VOTs above about 40 ms will be unambiguously perceived as /t/; those with VOTs between about 20 ms and 40 ms tend to be ambiguous between /t/ and /d/. It should be emphasized that such inferences can be drawn only for the language spoken by the listeners in the experiment because the perceptual boundary between /t/ and /d/ is liable to differ from one language to another. Indeed, to be on the safe side, the listeners in such experiments should speak with a similar accent because the t–d boundary in English, for example, may differ with accent.

Practice 16.1

All these questions refer to Fig. 16.1.

1. When the VOT was 0 ms, what was the percentage of "/da/" judgments?
2. When the VOT was 0 ms, what was the percentage of "/ta/" judgments?
3. When the VOT was 60 ms, what was the percentage of "/da/" judgments?
4. When the VOT was 60 ms, what was the percentage of "/ta/" judgments?
5. When the VOT was 40 ms, what was the percentage of "/da/" judgments?
6. When the VOT was 40 ms, what was the percentage of "/ta/" judgments?
7. On the graph of Fig. 16.1, the data points are joined by straight lines, giving interpolated (as they are called) values. According to this graph, at what VOT would 50% of judgments be"/da/" and the other 50% be "/ta/?"

Answers. 1. 100% 2. 0% 3. 0% 4. 100% 5. About 35% 6. About 65% 6. About 38 ms

Multiple Acoustic Cues

Most (probably all) phonemic distinctions are signaled by several different acoustic cues. In cases where one cue is obviously the most important, it is called the primary cue. For example, VOT is the primary cue to the voicing status of an initial stop. However, secondary cues that have been identified include:

- *amplitude of aspiration*: higher amplitude of aspiration promotes the perception of a voiceless stop
- *first formant onset frequency*: a higher frequency of F1 at the onset of the vowel promotes perception of a voiceless stop
- f_0 *at the onset of the vowel*: a higher f_0 (relative to the middle of the vowel) promotes the perception of a voiceless stop

The existence of a secondary cue is confirmed if it induces a shift in the perceptual boundary between the two phonemes, in a perception experiment. In this case, the experiment requires two tests of the sort just described and illustrated in Fig. 16.1, with the (hypothesized) secondary cue being set at a different value in each test. Figure 16.2 shows the results of an experiment that, like that of Fig. 16.1, tested listeners' perceptions of plosives with different VOTs. In this case, however, the figure shows the responses to two tests: In one test there was comparatively low aspiration noise during the VOT; in the other, the aspiration noise was greater. As Fig. 16.2 shows, where the aspiration noise is greater, VOT does not have to increase so much before listeners judge the initial stop to be voiceless. Relationships like this, in which a greater amount of one cue compensates for a lesser amount of another, are called *trading relations* (there is a "trade-off" between one cue and another).

Some speech perception experiments include rather unnatural tokens. For example, in another experiment on trading relations, Liberman, Fitch, Halwes, and Erikson (1980) investigated the difference between the words "split" and "slit." If you take the word "lit" and then place an "s" at the beginning of it, you get "slit." Now if you insert a silent gap between the "s" and the "l," you get "s[GAP]lit." As there are no words "stlit" or "sklit" in English, listeners tend to perceive this signal as being the word "split"—at least they do when the gap gets long enough. The effect is shown on Fig. 16.3. The line with the crosses on Fig. 16.3 shows how the percentage of "split" responses increased with increasing length of the silent gap. By the time the gap was 128 ms, "split" perceptions reached 100%.

However, a silent interval between the "s" and the "l" is not the only thing that distinguishes "split" from "slit." After a /p/, there are typically rising formant transitions into the /l/. The other line on Fig. 16.3 (with circles) shows

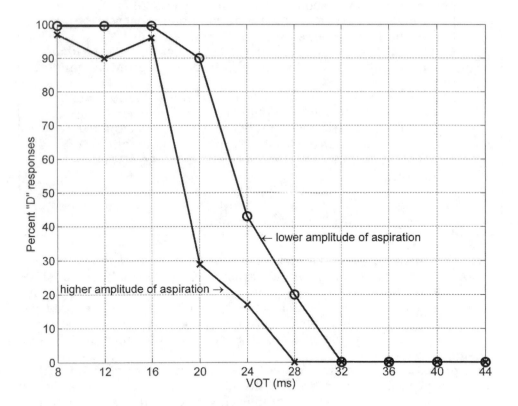

FIG. 16.2.   An example of trading relations. The graph shows percentage of "D" responses (the listeners were asked to label each stimulus as beginning with either a "D" or a "T") as a function of VOT, in two different conditions. The line on the left (with crosses) shows responses to stimuli that had greater aspiration noise; the line on the right (with circles) shows responses to stimuli that had lesser aspiration noise. Figure redrawn from Figure 2 (bottom panel) of Repp (1979, p. 178).

Practice 16.2

These questions all refer to Fig. 16.2.

1. In the higher amplitude of aspiration condition, what was the percentage of "D" responses when the VOT was 8 ms?
2. In the higher amplitude of aspiration condition, what was the percentage of "T" responses when the VOT was 8 ms?
3. In the higher amplitude of aspiration condition, what was the percentage of "D" responses when the VOT was 40 ms?
4. In the higher amplitude of aspiration condition, what was the percentage of "T" responses when the VOT was 40 ms?
5. In the lower amplitude of aspiration condition, what was the percentage of "D" responses when the VOT was 8 ms?
6. In the lower amplitude of aspiration condition, what was the percentage of "T" responses when the VOT was 8 ms?
7. In the lower amplitude of aspiration condition, what was the percentage of "D" responses when the VOT was 20 ms?
8. In the higher amplitude of aspiration condition, what was the percentage of "D" responses when the VOT was 20 ms?
9. At approximately what VOT does the graph cross the 50% identification point, in the higher amplitude of aspiration condition?
10. At approximately what VOT does the graph cross the 50% identification point, in the lower amplitude of aspiration condition?
11. At the 50% identification point, what is the approximate difference, in milliseconds of VOT, between the lower amplitude of aspiration condition and the lower amplitude of aspiration condition?

Answers. 1. 98%   2. 2%   3. 0%   4. 100%   5. 100%   6. 0%   7. 90%   8. 30%   9. About 17 ms   10. About 23 ms   11. About 6 ms

listeners' responses to the same series of signals, except this time the beginning of the "l" was given rising formant transitions. In this condition, the silent interval did not need to be so long before the listeners started hearing "split." There is therefore a trading relation between silent interval and formant transitions: In order to induce the switch from perceiving "slit" to perceiving "split," more of one cue (silent interval) is needed if the other cue (formant transitions) is absent.

It is probably quite valid to draw inferences, from an experiment like this, about how people actually perceive speech in natural, everyday situations. It is worth pointing out, however, that in each version of the experiment (i.e., with and without the formant transitions) some unrealistic signals are included—that is, signals that could not be produced by a human speaker. Consider those tokens that have a long silent interval but no formant transitions at the beginning of the "l." In normal speech the silent interval would always contain a stop articulation, which would produce formant transitions at the beginning of the "l." Conversely, consider the tokens with no silent in-

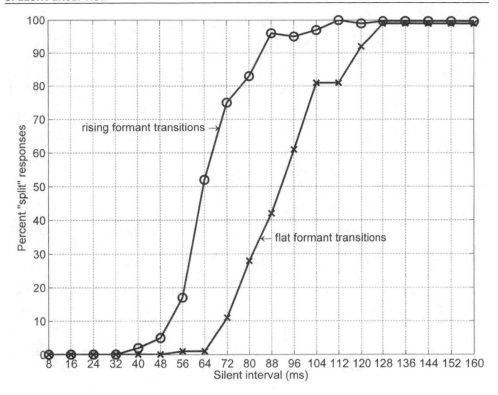

FIG. 16.3.   Listeners' identifications of synthesized syllables as either "split" or "slit." The duration of the silent interval was systematically varied. In one condition (line with crosses) the formant transitions into the "l" were appropriate for the word "slit"; in the other condition (line with circles), the formant transitions into the "l" were appropriate for the word "split." Adapted from Liberman, Fitch, and Erickson (1980), reprinted in Liberman (1996, p. 378, Fig. 20.4).

terval between the "s" and the "l," but that *do* have formant transitions at the beginning of the "l." In these cases, there is no sign of a p-closure, but the after-effects of a "p"-closure are nevertheless present. It is a bit like an auditory version of the Cheshire cat's grin in the story of Alice in Wonderland. In the story, the cat disappeared but its grin remained!

CATEGORICAL PERCEPTION

In a classic case of *categorical perception* of a series of stimuli, listeners are:

- able to *categorize* the stimuli consistently
- unable to *discriminate* between stimuli in the same category

In the experiments described in the previous section, listeners were asked to label a stimulus (as being either a "slit" or "split," for example). These were therefore categorization tasks (each stimulus must be assigned to one or the other category). Notice that in all the graphs of Fig. 16.1 to Fig. 16.3, the labeling functions are quite steep; that is, there is a sudden and decisive switch from one category to the other, at a certain point along the continuum. This in itself suggests a "categorical" mode of perception. In order to count truly as categorical perception, however, a certain outcome is also required from a test of discrimination.

In a discrimination test the subject is asked to judge whether two stimuli are the same or different. In the ordinary way, people can usually make very fine discriminations between pairs of stimuli, even though they cannot reliably label (categorize) each stimulus in isolation. An example from vision would be color: We can discriminate reliably among thousands of different shades of color, when they are presented in pairs, although we can't name them all reliably when each shade is presented in isolation (even if we invent a sufficient number of names). The same is presumably true of triangles, sheep, textures of surfaces, and so on. The phenomenon can be summarized by saying "discrimination is better than categorization."

For some speech sound contrasts, however, discrimination is hardly any better than categorization. This is the case with the VOT continuum. Figure 16.4 illustrates the results of a discrimination test on "/da/-ta/" stimuli varying in VOT. The stimuli were actually the same as those of Fig. 16.1, described earlier. In this case, however, the listeners were played pairs of stimuli and asked to judge each pair as being either "same" or "different." The members of each pair of stimuli were either identical to each other or they differed by 20 ms. Figure 16.4 shows that the 30 ms-50 ms pair were very successfully discriminated. However, the listeners performed only at around chance on the 60 ms-80 ms pair. The explanation is that the 30 ms-50 ms pair were an "across-category" pair; 30 ms to 50 ms was the interval during which the switch occurred from /da/ responses to /ta/ re-

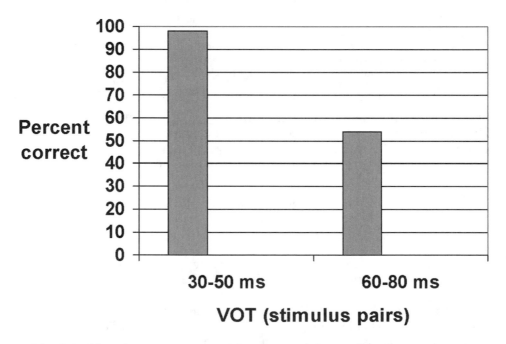

FIG. 16.4.   Mean discrimination scores for two stimulus pairs, from the stimuli used in the experiment on the acoustic cue of VOT described earlier (see Fig. 16.1 and the associated text). The 30-50 ms pair were an across-category pair and the 60-80 ms pair were the within-category pair.

sponses (see Fig. 16.1). However, the 60 ms-80 ms pair were a "within-category" pair; during the interval 60 ms to 80 ms, nearly all responses were /ta/.

Taken in conjunction, Fig. 16.1 and Fig. 16.4 demonstrate that perception of the voiced–voiceless distinction is categorical. Figure 16.1 shows that listeners can consistently and reliably label most of the stimuli as either /da/ or /ta/ and the region of ambiguity is quite small. Figure 16.4 shows that their discrimination among the different stimuli is poor, *except* across the category boundary. What this amounts to is that listeners are sensitive to differences that matter for distinguishing one word from another and insensitive to differences that don't.

The theoretical significance of categorical perception has been much discussed and the phenomenon has therefore been quite extensively researched, with a view to answering such questions as: Does categorical perception really only apply to speech sounds or does it occur with some nonspeech sounds as well? Does it apply to all speech sound contrasts? Does it apply only to human perception or do animals show it as well? Nonspeech sounds, like a series of pure tones changing in f_0, are perceived normally; that is, discrimination is better than categorization. Many phoneme distinctions in speech are typically perceived categorically; categorical perception, however, is much more characteristic of consonant perception than vowel perception. Moreover, experiments have shown evidence of some animals having a categorical perception of some speech sounds.

EXERCISES

1. Table 16.1 shows the results of an experiment in which listeners were asked to label stimuli as being either the word "rapid" or the word "rabid" (the data are based on a figure in Liberman, Harris, Eimas, Lisker, & Bastian 1961 [1996, p. 172]). The only difference among the stimuli was the length of the silent interval in the middle of the word, corresponding to the labial plosive. This was systematically varied, from 20 ms to 130 ms, in steps of 10 ms.

    a. Draw a graph (either by hand or using a computer) showing how percentage of "rabid" responses varied as a function of length of silent interval.
    b. When the silent interval was 60 ms, what percentage of the responses were "rapid?" (Note: "rapid" not "rabid!")
    c. According to the graph, at approximately what silent interval would 50% of the responses have been "rabid" and 50% "rapid?"
    d. Do these results suggest that length of silent interval is a significant acoustic cue to the distinction between /b/ and /p/ in intervocalic (i.e., between vowels) position?
    e. Choose two stimulus pairs, in which the members of each pair differ from each other by 30 ms of silent interval, to use in a discrimination test. One pair should be across-category, the other within-category.
    f. Draw a graph of the imaginary results of such a discrimination test, modeled on Fig. 16.4. The results should be such as to lead to the conclusion that this was a case of categorical perception.

g. Draw a graph of alternative imaginary results of the discrimination test. This time, the results should be such as to lead to the conclusion that this was *not* a case of categorical perception.

TABLE 16.1	Percentage of "Rabid" Responses to Stimuli
Length of Silent Interval (ms)	*Percent "Rabid" Responses*
20	95
30	98
40	98
50	91
60	72
70	52
80	16
90	6
100	7
110	3
120	0
130	0

Note. Stimuli consists of /ra[bilabial plosive]id/, in which the silent interval corresponding to the bilabial plosive differed, in steps of 10 ms, from 20 ms to 130 ms.

IV

Speech Production

17
The Vocal Tract as a Resonator

The vocal tract is a fleshy tube, the shape of which can be altered by the actions of the speech organs. A sound is created by the vibrating vocal folds and it is then modified by passing through the tube. This, in essence, is the *source-filter model* (or theory) of speech production. Source is a good name for the role of the sound made by the vocal folds, but the term filter may seem obscure. It refers to the role of the vocal tract in modifying the sound created by the vocal folds. The difference between the sound created by the vocal folds and the corresponding sound that emerges into the open air is explained by the "filtering" action of the vocal tract, which determines the amount of energy allowed to pass through, at different frequencies. The most notable modification made by the vocal tract is the introduction of formants (see chap. 11), that is, peaks in the spectrum. This chapter is concerned with the relationship between vocal tract shape and formant frequencies.

The description in the previous paragraph is written with vowels in mind. Actually, the source-filter model does apply to the production of all speech sounds, including obstruent consonants, which have sources other than the vibrating vocal folds. These other sources are discussed briefly at the end of the chapter. However, the source-filter model is most appealing as a model for the production of periodic sounds. In the production of such sounds, source and filter are separate in location and distinct in anatomy. The character of a vowel, in particular, can largely be captured by stating the frequencies of its formants, with other aspects of the shape of its spectrum being treated as matters of detail. The source-filter model is therefore described here with reference only to the formants of vowels. Vowel formants are created by resonances of the vocal tract, which explains the title of the chapter. The source is described only briefly and in an idealized form. It is, for the most part, held constant in order to make easier the explanation of the effect of vocal tract shape. (Vocal fold vibration is the subject of chap. 18.)

This chapter relies on facts and concepts introduced in Parts I and II of this book. It explains the link between vocal tract shapes (described in Part I) and the acoustic structure of speech sounds (described in Part II). Chapters 3 and 11 are especially relevant. Two major works, Fant (1960) and Stevens (1998), have been extensively consulted in the writing of this chapter. Other useful sources include Borden, Harris, and Raphael (2003), Johnson (2003), Kent and Read (1992), and Lieberman (1977).

SOURCE AND FILTER

Vocal fold vibration produces a complex periodic wave, which has a fundamental frequency and harmonics that are multiples of the fundamental (see chap. 11). Figure 17.1(a) shows a spectrum of vocal fold vibration, which is often called the *glottal spectrum*. The fundamental frequency of this sound (the one in Fig. 17.1) is 100 Hz. There is a *roll-off* of 12 dB/octave, that is, the harmonics reduce in amplitude by 12 dB with every successive octave. This is the only variation of amplitude with frequency; there are no peaks or troughs in this spectrum. The sound with this spectrum forms the input to the vocal tract tube, at the larynx. It is modified by passing through the vocal tract: notably, a series of peaks and troughs are formed. Figure 17.1(b) shows the transfer function (cf. chap. 13) of the vocal tract when it forms a relatively open tube but with a constriction in the palatal region. Given an appropriate input (such as that of Fig. 17.1[a]), this transfer function produces the vowel [i], with its low first formant and high second formant. The output spectrum is shown in Fig. 17.1(c). This output spectrum reproduces the shape of the transfer function quite well. The harmonics of the source are close together and so the peaks in the output spectrum replicate the peaks of the transfer function faithfully. (If the f_0 had been 400 Hz, say, the situation would be different: The first peak would not appear in the output spectrum and the higher peaks would be less well defined.) The peaks in the output spectrum reduce in amplitude with increasing frequency, as would be expected given the roll-off in the input spectrum. Actually, the output spectrum suggests a less severe roll-off than would be expected from looking at the glottal spectrum of Fig. 17.1(a). This is because a further factor has been taken into account in Fig. 17.1(c), namely the effect of an amplitude enhancement that occurs as the sound wave radiates from the lips. The size of the effect increases with frequency and therefore moderates the roll-off due to the source spectrum.

The following two sections discuss how resonance occurs in vocal tract-like tubes. *Resonance* is the amplification that is created at certain frequencies, due to the dimensions of the tube. It is probably more appropriate to use the term resonance for a peak in the transfer function, as distinct from a peak in the output spectrum; the term formant, on the other hand, is routinely used to refer to either a peak in the transfer function or a peak in the output spectrum (cf. Fant, 1960, p. 20). In the ideal scenario, the peaks in the transfer function are well reproduced in the output spectrum, because the harmonics of the source are sufficiently closely spaced.

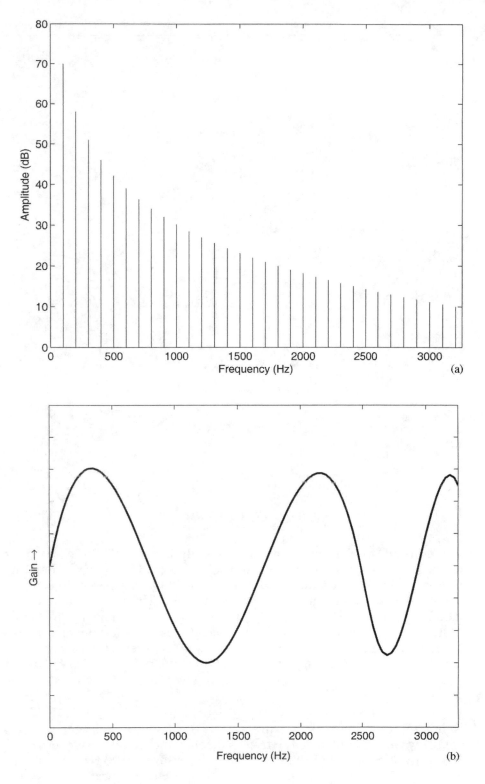

FIG. 17.1.   Elements in the production of an [i] vowel: (a) Source spectrum, (b) vocal tract transfer function, and (c) output spectrum.   (*continued*)

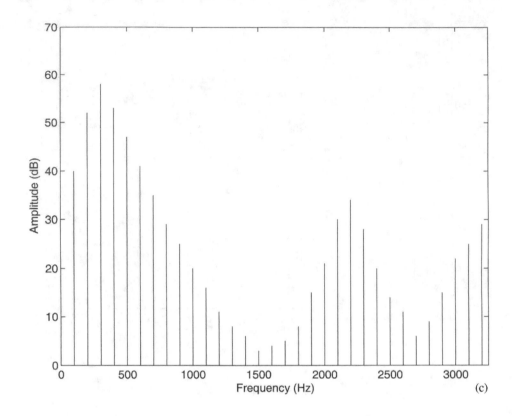

FIG. 17.1.   *continued*

HOW [ə] GETS ITS FORMANTS

Descriptions of vocal tract resonances usually begin with the case of the schwa vowel, [ə]. During [ə], the vocal tract shape is said to approximate a uniform tube, that is, a tube with the same cross-sectional diameter along its entire length. The tube is open at one end (the lips) but when the vocal folds are vibrating, it is effectively closed at the glottis end. When a longish tube of uniform diameter is excited by a suitable source, its resonant frequencies are determined by its length. To explain the relationship between a tube's length and its resonances, it is necessary first to introduce the property of wavelength.

Wavelength

The *wavelength* of a sound pressure wave is the distance over which one period of the wave is completed, as it travels through the air. So wavelength is the spatial equivalent of period. Take, for example, a wave of 100 Hz, which has a period of 0.01 seconds. At a certain point in space it achieves its maximum positive pressure and 0.01 seconds later, at a further point in space, the maximum positive pressure occurs again. How far apart are these two points? In other words, what distance has the wave traveled in 0.01 seconds? That depends on the speed at which sound travels through the air. If the speed of sound is 354 meters/second, then in 0.01 seconds, the wave will travel 354 × 0.01 = 3.54 meters. So the wavelength of a 100 Hz sound wave is 3.54 meters. Generally:

$$\text{Wavelength} = cT \qquad (17.1)$$

where c is the speed of sound and T is the period. In chapter 13, we assumed a speed of 340 meters/second (m/s) but 354 m/s is more appropriate for the warm, humid conditions inside the human vocal tract. Also, because vocal tract dimensions are given in centimeters (cm) in later sections (it makes the numbers involved easier to handle), it will be as well at this point to change from meters to centimeters and quote the speed of sound as 35,400 cm/s. So the foregoing calculation becomes 35,400 × 0.01 = 354 cm. Table 17.1 gives some examples of the relationships among frequency, period and wavelength. (The relationship between frequency and period is explained in chap. 9.) Notice that wavelength shortens with increasing frequency.

TABLE 17.1   **The wavelengths of the first five harmonics of a complex periodic wave with a f_0 of 125 Hz, assuming a speed of sound of 35400 cm/s**

f (Hz)	T (seconds)	Wavelength (cm)
125	0.008	283.2
250	0.004	141.6
375	0.0026667	94.4
500	0.002	70.8
625	0.0016	56.64

Practice 17.1

State the period and the wavelength of :

1. a sine wave of 1500 Hz.
2. a sine wave of 2500 Hz
3. a sine wave of 3500 Hz

Assume a speed of sound of 35400 cm/s and give your answers to six decimal places.
Answers. 1. T = 0.000667 s, wavelength = 23.600000 cm 2. T = 0.000400 s, wavelength = 14.160000 cm 3. T = 0.000286 s, wavelength = 10.114286 cm

Resonances of the Vocal Tract When It Is Approximately a Uniform Tube

Figure 17.2 is a drawing, based on an X-ray image, of the vocal tract during the production of the vowel [ə]. It is obviously not perfectly uniform. There is a right-angled bend in it, between the pharynx and the oral cavity, but this feature has virtually no acoustic effect. There are other features that may have more effect. The epiglottis, uvula, and teeth protrude into the tube, for example. The section immediately above the larynx is narrower and there are spaces to the side (the piriform sinuses) just near this section. Nevertheless, the tongue does not significantly narrow the tube at any point and the lips are in a neutral position. This vocal tract shape may be roughly approximated by a tube of uniform diameter, which is closed at one end (the glottis) and open at the other (the lips), as shown in Fig. 17.3.

A wave is generated by a pulse of the larynx and it advances along the vocal tract. It consists of many sine wave components. It is best to think of the description that follows as applying to an individual sine wave component. When it reaches the open end, it is *reflected*: It reverses direction and travels back toward the closed end. The sudden change from the relatively dense tube to the wide open air creates a boundary, which causes the reflection. (Not all the energy is reflected back; some of it is transmitted onward into the air.) A boundary of this sort (where the wave encounters a less dense medium) has an additional effect, namely *inversion*: Pressure peaks become pressure troughs, and vice versa. As the reflected wave travels back down the vocal tract, it encounters later phases of the original wave (called the *incident* wave)

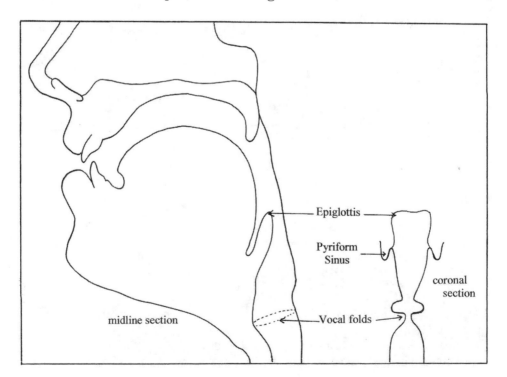

FIG. 17.2.   Mid-sagittal section of the vocal tract during [ə].

FIG. 17.3.   Tube model of vocal tract shape during [ə].

coming from the opposite direction. The two waves add together at each point but pass on through each other. When the reflected wave reaches the closed end again, it is reflected back. At the closed end, the wave encounters a much denser medium, so no pressure inversion occurs. The process continues. The reflected wave travels up and down the tube. Every time it reaches the closed end it undergoes reflection and every time it reaches the open end it undergoes both reflection and inversion. Resonance occurs if the reflected wave combines constructively with the incident wave, such that pressure peaks combine to produce larger peaks and pressure troughs combine to produce deeper troughs. Instead of examining in detail the pressure variations along the length of the vocal tract, we focus on one of the conditions of resonance, namely that the reflection of a pressure peak at the glottis occurs just as a new pressure peak is produced.

After leaving the glottis, a pressure peak is reflected up and down the tube, as peak or trough. We are searching for the first occasion when it coincides with a new pressure peak. If the reflected peak is in inverted form (i.e., it is a trough) when this happens, this creates a situation in which a trough combines with the new peak and therefore no resonance occurs. If the reflected peak is actually a peak when the new peak is produced, then the reflected peak combines with the new peak and resonance occurs.

In order for this resonance condition to be achieved, a reflected pressure peak must arrive back at the glottis after a whole number of periods. Therefore, whether or not a particular sine wave resonates depends on its wavelength relative to the length of the tube. The tube length:wavelength relationship is explored in the next few paragraphs, using a trial and error approach for the purpose of exposition, but we reveal the answer in advance: Resonance occurs if the tube is one quarter the length of the wavelength of the sine wave, if it is three quarters of the length, if it is one and a quarter times the length, and so on. The focus here is on exploring the *relationship* (ratio) between tube length and wavelength, thus it is not necessary to consider particular values, either of sine wave frequency or vocal tract length. However, in a real case there are lots of sine wave components but only one vocal tract, the length of which cannot be altered (much). So in the following description, it is best to imagine the ratio being altered by choosing a different wavelength rather than by choosing a different tube length.

Suppose tube length and wavelength are the same, that is, a ratio of 1:1. It will take exactly one period for the pressure peak to reach the open end. It undergoes reflection and inversion and travels back to the glottis as a trough. Exactly two periods have now elapsed. The trough reflects from the glottis at exactly the moment that the larynx produces another pressure peak. A trough combines with a peak, which is destructive. So a tubelength:wavelengh ratio of 1:1 will not produce resonance.

Consider a wave that is twice the length of the tube, that is, a tube length:wavelength ratio of 1:2. The pressure peak travels down to the open end in half a period and undergoes reflection and inversion. It arrives back at the glottis just as a new pressure peak is produced. But again this is a trough combining with a peak, which is destructive. So a tubelength:wavelengh ratio of 1:2 will not produce resonance.

Consider a wave that is four times the length of the tube, that is, a tube length:wavelength ratio of 1:4. The pressure peak takes one quarter of a period to travel to the open end and after a further quarter of a period (one half of a period altogether), it is back at the glottis again, as a trough. After yet a further quarter of a period (three quarters of a period altogether) the trough reaches the open end and undergoes reflection and inversion again, so now it is a peak. This peak reaches the glottis again after another quarter of a period. One period has elapsed altogether, so the glottis is just producing a new peak. The two peaks combine and so there is resonance. This resonance is in fact the first formant of [ə]. Figure 17.4 illustrates stages of the process.

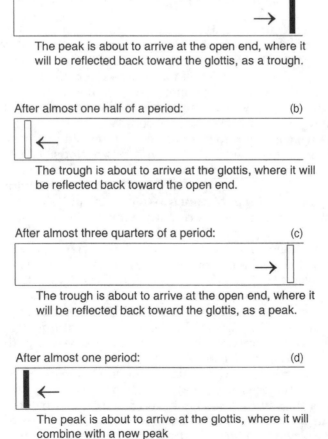

After almost one quarter of a period: (a)

The peak is about to arrive at the open end, where it will be reflected back toward the glottis, as a trough.

After almost one half of a period: (b)

The trough is about to arrive at the glottis, where it will be reflected back toward the open end.

After almost three quarters of a period: (c)

The trough is about to arrive at the open end, where it will be reflected back toward the glottis, as a peak.

After almost one period: (d)

The peak is about to arrive at the glottis, where it will combine with a new peak

FIG. 17.4. The quarter-wavelength resonance. The length of the tube is one quarter of the wavelength of the sine wave. A pressure peak (represented by a filled bar), starting from the closed end of a tube, travels toward the open end (a). Reflected and inverted, and so now a trough (represented by an unfilled bar), it travels back toward the closed end (b). It is reflected back toward the open end (c). At the open end it undergoes reflection and inversion again and travels toward the closed end (d), where it will combine with the next pressure peak produced by the larynx.

Practice 17.2

One and a quarter wavelengths of a sine wave fits into the vocal tract.

1. How long (in periods) will a pressure peak take to travel from the glottis to the open end?
2. At the open end, reflection occurs and what else?
3. How much time (in periods) will have elapsed when the trough arrives back at the glottis?
4. How much time (in periods), will have elapsed when the trough reaches the open end again?
5. What will happen to the trough at the open end?
6. How much time (in periods), will have elapsed when the peak reaches the glottis?
7. Will the glottis be producing another peak at this time?

Answers. 1. One and a quarter periods 2. Inversion 3. Two and a half periods 4. Three and three quarter periods 5. Reflection and inversion occur 6. Five periods 7. Yes

---

What about the other formants, the second, third, and so on? Shorter wavelengths will have to be considered. The shorter the wavelength, the more of it will fit into the vocal tract. We have already tried two possibilities, namely, where exactly half a wavelength fits into the vocal tract and where a whole wavelength does, without success. Try the situation in which three quarters of the wavelength fits into the vocal tract, a tube length:wavelength ratio of 3:4. The pressure peak reaches the open end after three quarters of a period, undergoes reflection and inversion and travels back to the glottis, to arrive there after one and a half periods in total, as a trough. It is reflected back to the open end and inverted to a peak. Two and a quarter periods have elapsed now. The peak travels back to the glottis, taking a further three quarters of a period. Exactly three periods have now elapsed, so the glottis is just producing a new pressure peak. The two pressure peaks combine.

Tube length:wavelength ratios of 1:4 and 3:4 worked, so it seems worth trying 5:4. In this case one and a quarter wavelengths will fit inside the vocal tract.

The answers in Practice 17.2 demonstrate that a ratio of 5:4 works, as well. The first three formants occur at tube length:wavelength ratios of 1:4, 3:4, and 5:4. The pattern continues, so that 7:4 is the ratio corresponding to the fourth formant, 9:4 the fifth, and so on. (In speech analysis, formants above the third are rarely considered. However, in theory, there are an endless number.)

All that is now needed, in order to discover which sine wave components will resonate during [ə], is the vocal tract length of the person concerned. It is useful to choose, as an example, a length that yields round figures for the formant frequencies. The formant frequencies of [ə] are reference points with which the formants of other vowels are compared, so it is good to have a set of frequencies that are easy to remember. A legitimate way of achieving this is to use the average male vocal tract length of 16.9 cm (according to Goldstein, 1980, cited in Stevens, 1998) and then to add on an end correction. The *end correction* is a notional addition to the length of the tube, which takes account of the fact that reflection at the open end in fact occurs a little way beyond the actual end of the tube. Stevens suggested an end correction of 0.8 cm for an adult male vocal tract. Adding the end correction to the actual vocal tract length gives 16.9 + 0.8 = 17.7 cm.

The effective tube length is 17.7 cm and this is one fourth of the wavelength of the first formant. So the wavelength of the first formant is 4 × 17.7 = 70.8 cm. To calculate the corresponding period, it is necessary to manipulate the formula for wavelength, given earlier. So:

$$T = \frac{\textbf{\textit{wavelength}}}{c} \tag{17.2}$$

which in this case gives:

$$T = \frac{70.8}{35400} = 0.002s$$

Since $f = 1/T$, the corresponding frequency is 1/0.002 = 500 Hz. The wavelengths, periods, and frequencies of higher formants can be calculated similarly. For example, the wavelength of the second formant is (4 × 17.7)/3 = 23.6 cm; the wavelength of the third is (4 × 17.7)/5 cm; and so on.

It would be fortunate if this man's vocal tract was excited by a source with the spectrum of Fig. 17.1, because it supplies sine wave components (harmonics) that coincide exactly with each formant frequency. For example, the fifth harmonic coincides exactly with F1 and the fifteenth harmonic does likewise with F2. If harmonics did not occur at exactly these frequencies, the consequences would not be too serious. Harmonics with wavelengths near to a resonant wavelength will still receive some gain in amplitude.

A formula for obtaining the formant frequencies of [ə] from the vocal tract length is:

$$F = n\frac{c}{4L} \tag{17.3}$$

where n = 1, 3, 5, 7, 9, ... and L is the effective vocal tract length (i.e., the actual vocal tract length plus the end correction factor). F1 is obtained from n = 1, F2 from n = 3, F3 from n = 5, and so on. The LPC spectrum of an actual schwa vowel can be seen in Fig. 11.8. Its formant frequencies (at least the lower ones) conform reasonably well to the predicted frequencies for an average male vocal tract.

Practice 17.3

1. What are the frequencies of F1, F2, and F3 of [ə], pronounced by a male speaker with an average length vocal tract?
2. Without doing any actual calculation, guess the frequency of F4.

Answers. 1. F1 = 500 Hz, F2 = 1500 Hz, F3 = 2500 Hz   2. F4 is 3500 Hz

> *Practice 17.4*
>
> Using the given formula, state the frequencies of F1, F2, and F3 of [ə], pro-
> duced by a woman with a vocal tract length of 14.1 cm. Assume the end
> correction = 0.7 cm and c = 35400 cm/s.
>
> *Answer.* F1 = 1 × 35400/(4 × 14.8) = 598 Hz F2 = 1794 Hz F3 = 2990 Hz

OTHER VOWELS

The schwa vowel, [ə], is the only one for which the vocal tract approximates a
uniform tube. However, the principles of resonance in a uniform tube form
the basis of all attempts to explain the resonances created by the non-uni-
form tube shapes of other vowels. The following description gives an indication of how the first two formants of [ɑ] can be modeled by a tube made up of
subsections of different diameter. A similar approach is taken to explaining
F1 and F2 of the vowels [i] and [u]. In this section, we ignore the end correction (calculation of which is anyway more complicated in the case of more
complex tube shapes).

The First Two Formants of [ɑ]

The vowel [ɑ] has a high first formant and a low second formant, compared
with [ə]. The shape of the vocal tract during [ɑ], in mid-sagittal section, can be
seen in Fig. 5.5. The pharynx is narrow and the oral cavity is wide. Figure 17.5
shows a tube model of it. The overall length of the tube is 17 cm. It has a narrow section, corresponding to the pharynx, which opens onto a wide section,
corresponding to the oral cavity.

The narrow section of the tube in Fig. 17.5 behaves like a uniform tube
closed at the glottis end and open at the other (where it gives onto the wide
tube). The wider section also behaves like a uniform tube closed at one end
(the junction with the narrow tube) and open at the other (the lips). The formant frequencies of each tube, considered for the moment as separate tubes,
can be calculated using the formulas for the resonances of a uniform tube
closed at one end, described in the previous section. Assume that the two
tubes are equal in length (which is a reasonable assumption). In a vocal tract
17 cm long, the pharynx tube and the oral cavity tube are both 8.5 cm long. As
the resonances of a uniform tube depend only on its length, the resonance frequencies of these two tubes are the same. Using Equation 3, the first formant
of each tube, considered separately, can be calculated:

$$F1_{sep} = \frac{c}{4L} = \frac{35400}{34} = 1041 Hz$$

where "F1$_{sep}$" symbolizes the first formant of each tube, each considered as a
separate tube.

However, the tubes are not in fact separate, but coupled together. Coupling
together two tubes of very different diameter has the effect of driving the reso-

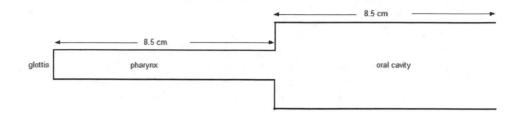

FIG. 17.5.   Tube model of vocal tract shape during [ɑ].

nances apart. Therefore in the coupled system, $F1_{sep}$ becomes two resonances, the lower of which is F1 and the higher is F2, in the coupled system.
The formulas for calculating F1 and F2 are:

$$F1 = F1_{sep}\left(1 - 0.637\frac{D_b}{D_f}\right)$$ (17.4)

$$F2 = F1_{sep}\left(1 + 0.637\frac{D_b}{D_f}\right)$$ (17.5)

where D_b is the diameter of the back (pharynx) cavity and D_f is the diameter of
the front (oral) cavity. The diameter of the pharynx during [ɑ] is approximately
one third the diameter of the oral cavity. Say D_b/D_f is 0.3. Then F1 and F2 can
be calculated as follows:

F1 = 1041(1 – 0.637(0.3)) = 842 Hz

F2 = 1041(1 + 0.637(0.3)) = 1240 Hz

Refinements to the model could be introduced to make it more realistic, at
the price of complicating the calculation of formant frequencies. For example, the change in diameter at the junction between the pharynx tube and the
oral cavity tube is nothing like as abrupt in reality as it is in the model. However, the model described here does produce the high F1 and low F2, characteristic of [ɑ].

Practice 17.5

Calculate F1 and F2 of [ɑ], pronounced by a person with a vocal tract 16
cm long. Assume c = 35400 cm/s, D_b/D_f = 0.3 and the lengths of the pharynx and oral cavity are equal.

Answer. $F1_{sep}$ = 1106 Hz therefore F1 = 895 Hz and F2 = 1317 Hz

---

The First Two Formants of [i]

The vowel [i] has a low first formant and a high second formant. The shape of the vocal tract during [i] can be seen in Fig. 5.5. The tongue is raised close to the hard palate, forming a quite long and very narrow constriction at that point. Behind this constriction, the pharynx is wide. In front of it, the oral cavity widens again, ending at the spread lips. Figure 17.6 shows a tube model of [i]. It has been given an overall length of 16.5 cm, a bit shorter than for [ɑ], which reflects the effect of the spread lips.

The lowest resonance (first formant) of [i] is created by the relatively large back cavity giving onto the very narrow constriction. This sort of configuration produces a *Helmholtz resonance*. The air in the narrow constriction acts like a piston, driving the relatively large mass of air in the cavity connected to it. The frequency of the resonance depends on the cross-sectional area and length of the constriction and the volume of the cavity, according to the formula:

$$R_{Helmholtz} = \frac{c}{2\pi}\sqrt{\frac{A_c}{VL_c}} \tag{17.6}$$

where V is the volume of the cavity and A_c and L_c are the cross-sectional area and length, respectively, of the constriction. ($\pi = 3.1416$)

The following values apply to a Helmholtz resonance of the back cavity in the model of Fig. 17.6: $A_c = 0.3$ cm^2, $V = 28.2$ cm^3, and $L_c = 5$ cm. So:

$$R_{Helmholtz} = \frac{35400}{2\pi}\sqrt{\frac{0.3}{(28.2)(5)}}$$

$$= (5634)(0.046)$$

$$= 260\,Hz$$

This gives the required low frequency for F1 of [i].

It is tempting to think of [i]'s high F2 as being associated with the small size of the oral cavity in front of the tongue constriction. However, Fant (1960, p. 121) said "F2 of [i] is clearly a half-wavelength resonance of the back cavity" and Stevens (1998) seemed also inclined to ascribe F2 of [i] to the back cavity.

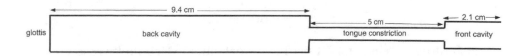

FIG. 17.6. Tube model of vocal tract shape during [i].

In this case, the back cavity is behaving as a tube that is closed at *both* ends. The resonances of such a tube are given by the formula:

$$F_n = n\frac{c}{2L}$$

(17.7)

where n = 1, 2, 3, 4, ...

The length of the back cavity is 9.4 cm, therefore the first resonance is:

$$F1_{back\ cavity} = \frac{35400}{18.8} = 1883\,Hz$$

This is higher than the Helmholtz resonance, therefore it is the F2 of [i]. 1883 Hz seems a little low for the F2 of [i] (see chap. 11). However, Stevens (1998, p. 279) remarked that a more realistic back cavity shape, which narrowed more gradually toward the pharyngeal constriction, would result in a higher F2. Also, some coupling between the back and front cavities might raise it further (cf. Stevens, 1998, p. 146).

The First Two Formants of [u]

In the vowel [u], F1 and F2 are both low (see chap. 11). The back of the tongue is raised toward the soft palate (velum), creating a short, narrow constriction, and the lips are rounded (see Fig. 5.5). Figure 17.7 shows a tube model of [u]. The overall length of the vocal tract model of Fig. 17.7 is 19 cm, that is, 2 cm longer than that for [ɑ], to allow for the effect of lip-protrusion. We have chosen lengths of 7.5 cm and 8.5 cm for the back and front cavities, respectively, a 2-cm tongue constriction and a 1-cm long lip aperture.

Fant (1960) described the vocal tract configuration of [u] as that of a double Helmholtz resonator, that is, two Helmholtz resonators coupled together. To work out the Helmholtz resonance of the back cavity, we need to know the cross-sectional area of the tongue constriction, A_c, which is 0.3 cm^2, the volume V of the back cavity, which is 22.5 cm^3, and the length of the tongue constriction, L_c, which is 2 cm. So the Helmholtz resonance of the back cavity is:

$$R_{Helmholtz} = \frac{35400}{2\pi}\sqrt{\frac{0.3}{(22.5)(2)}}$$

$$= (5{,}634)(0.0816)$$

$$= 460\ \text{Hz}$$

which is rather too high for F1 of [u]. To work out the Helmholtz resonance of the front cavity, we use the same formula but in this case A_c is the cross-sectional area of the lip constriction, which is 0.3 cm^2, V is the volume of the front cavity, which is 25.5 cm^3, and L_c is the length of the lip constriction, which is 1 cm. So the Helmholtz resonance of the front cavity is:

$$R_{Helmholtz} = \frac{35400}{2\pi} \sqrt{\frac{0.3}{(25.5)(0.1085)}}$$

$$= (5,634)(0.1085)$$

$$= 611 \text{ Hz}$$

which is a bit *too* low for F2 of [u]. However, the effect of coupling the two Helmholtz resonators is (according to a complicated formula) to lower the lower resonance and raise the higher one, which is the adjustment required in order to bring the theoretical prediction in line with the experimental results for the frequencies of F1 and F2 of [u].

APPLICATION OF SOURCE-FILTER MODEL TO OTHER SOUNDS

All speech sound sources are powered by a flow of air through the vocal tract. This flow is provided by air expired from the lungs, except in the few, relatively rare, cases described in the section More Places of Articulation, in chapter 6. In the case of vocal fold vibration, the source described in this chapter's first section, the air flow is interrupted at the larynx. Vocal fold vibration is also the sound source for nasals and approximants, to which the source-filter model applies in much the same way as for vowels. If the vocal folds are held open, no vibration occurs at the larynx. Instead, a sound source is created by means of an interruption or blockage created higher up in the vocal tract. This applies to many consonant sounds. As with vowels, the end result relies on the acoustic quality of the source, as modified by the shape of the vocal tract. The source-filter model therefore applies to these sounds as well. In the case of most nonperiodic consonants, however, the place of articulation of the consonant is also the location of the source. Among these consonants, therefore, there is less scope for independent variation of source and filter. This section briefly reviews nonperiodic sound sources.

Fricative Sound Sources

Fricative noise results from turbulent flow created by an airstream being forced through a narrow constriction. An air flow can be measured in terms of its volume velocity, that is, the volume of air that passes a fixed point in a unit of time. Production of a fricative consonant requires an airflow of something of the order of 600 cm^3/s (Shadle, 1997, p. 38) flowing through a space of something like 0.1 cm^2. A suitable constriction may be made at more or less

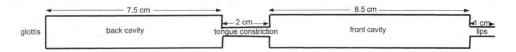

FIG. 17.7.   Tube model of vocal tract shape during [u].

any point in the vocal tract, from glottis to lips. A flow of 600 cm³/s is quite a considerable requirement (it is about three times what is required in the production of a normal vowel, for example). This probably accounts for the rarity of nasalized fricatives in human language. If the velum is open, much of the air flow will escape through the nasal cavity, compromising the creation of a noise source within the mouth. In lingual fricatives, the position of the tongue is critical for production of the source. However, there is some scope for modification of the spectrum from lip position (rounded or spread). Likewise, in the case of labial fricatives, there is some scope for modification due to the position of the tongue to the rear of the sound source, although the acoustic effects are minor.

[h] Sounds and Whispered Speech.   [h] is an exception to the generalization made in the previous paragraph. The sound source of [h] is fricative noise created at the glottis and therefore supralaryngeal tract shape is as free to vary as it is for vowels and other sonorant sounds. In fact, [h] usually occurs either as a singleton consonant at the syllable onset, or preceding a sonorant consonant, and amounts to a voiceless version of the following vowel or other sonorant. Frication created at the glottis is also responsible for the aspiration phase of aspirated voiceless plosives like [pʰ, tʰ].

In a rather different category is whispered speech. In whisper, the source provided by vocal fold vibration in normal speech is replaced by a fricative sound source similar to that of [h]. As with vowels (and [h] itself), vowel-like formants are created according to the shape of the vocal tract. The formants of a whispered vowel will be very similar in frequency to those of the corresponding voiced vowel (as would be expected, because formant frequencies are determined by vocal tract shape). However, in the case of whisper the glottis is more open, allowing an influence on resonances from an additional tube section below. The effect may be to raise formant frequencies slightly.

Transient Sources

As the name implies, transients (see chap. 8) are very short sounds, which typically occur at the release of a consonant closure. They are created when a buildup of pressure behind a closure is suddenly released with a consequent rush of air, as occurs, for example, at the release of the alveolar closure in a [t] or [d] sound. Possible places of articulation are limited by the requirement of a complete closure in order to create the necessary buildup of pressure. Thus plosives occur at the lips ([p, b]) and at all locations along the hard and soft palate, where a seal can be made by raising the tongue, as in [t, g], for example. For all the sounds cited so far, the buildup of pressure is provided by the compression of a column of air in the vocal tract that is continuous with the trachea and lungs. However, transients also occur at the release of ejectives (see chap. 6), like [p', k'], the compression behind the closure being provided by closing the glottis and driving the larynx upward. The mechanism for the production of clicks (see chap. 6), like [ǁ,ʘ], involves a *decrease* in pressure behind the closure, resulting in an inward rush of air on release.

EXERCISES

Note. In answering all these questions, assume a speed of sound of 35,400 cm/s.

1. Draw up a table showing the tube length:wavelength ratio, the wavelength, the period, and the frequency corresponding to each of the first six resonances of the vowel [ə]. Assume a vocal tract length of 16.9 cm, with an end correction of 0.8 cm.
2. A child with a vocal tract length of 11 cm produced a [ə] vowel. Construct a table showing the tube length:wavelength ratio, the wavelength, the period, and the frequency of F1, F2, and F3. Assume an end correction of 0.6 cm.
3. Suppose the f_0 of the vowel described in question 2 was 200 Hz. State which harmonic (first, second, third, etc.) will inhabit (or most nearly inhabit):

    a. F1
    b. F2
    c. F3

4. The external auditory canal (see chap. 13) is, more or less, a uniform tube closed at one end and open at the other. Assuming it has an effective length of 2.7 cm, what would be the frequency of its lowest frequency resonance?
5. Using a tube model of the sort shown in Fig. 17.5, state the frequencies of F1 and F2 of [ɑ], in the case of a tube with the following dimensions:

    overall length L = 16 cm
    back cavity length L_b = 8 cm
    back cavity diameter D_b = 1.5 cm
    front cavity length L_f = 8 cm
    front cavity diameter D_f = 4.8 cm

6. Using a tube model of the sort shown in Fig. 17.6, state the frequencies of F1 and F2 that would be predicted for [i], if the relevant tube dimensions were:

    overall length L = 16 cm
    back cavity length L_b = 9 cm
    back cavity volume V = 27 cm^3
    tongue constriction length L_c = 4.9 cm
    tongue constriction cross-sectional area A_c = 0.3 cm

18

Phonation

The importance of phonation as a principal sound source for speech has been highlighted in the previous chapter, and its function in differentiating between voiced and voiceless sounds was introduced in chapter 4. This chapter examines the anatomical and physiological bases of phonation in a bit more detail, and introduces a range of relevant analysis techniques. As we show, phonation is much more than a simple on–off phenomenon, whereby voiced sounds involving vocal fold vibration contrast with voiceless sounds that do not. There is, in fact, considerable variation in the pattern of vocal fold vibration associated with voiced sounds, and this chapter introduces a number of different types of phonation.

Further study of phonation may be prompted by a number of different motivations. One might be a wish to understand the complex associations between laryngeal structure and function, acoustic output, and auditory quality. Another is an interest in the influence of phonation in social interaction, and a brief exploration of this area may help to set the scene for this chapter.

THE ROLE OF PHONATION IN SOCIAL INTERACTION

Phonation, together with other aspects of voice quality, plays a role in spoken communication that goes far beyond its linguistic function in differentiating between voiced and voiceless segments. Speech output, as a whole, potentially conveys a large amount of information. Some of this is directly communicative, in the sense that the speaker adjusts speech output with the intention of conveying information, whereas some features are simply informative, in that they are not consciously manipulated by the speaker, but allow the listener to glean information (Lyons, 1977). Phonation is a particularly rich source of information about a speaker, in addition to its directly communicative function. Figure 18.1 summarizes some of the functions of phonation, indicating the time-scale of the phonatory adjustments involved, along a continuum from short-term segmental adjustments to long-term habitual patterns of phonation. The most obvious communicative function is at a segmental level, in the differentiation of voiced and voiceless segments, but adjustments of phonation pattern that extend over more than one segment or utterance are also important. Adjustments of the frequency of vocal fold vibration are a key means of signaling intonation and tones, and adjustments of phonation quality may play a part in regulating discourse. Longer term adjustments of the pitch and quality of phonation may also be used to express emotional state or attitude. Individual habitual patterns of phonation reflect not only the speech norms of a speaker's sociolinguistic community, but also the physical state of the speaker. Phonation is thus a powerful informative feature of speech, which listeners may use quite confidently to make judgments about a speaker, including judgments about social and geographical background, personality, overall size and physique, mental state, and state of health.

The use of phonation as an indicator of physical state may be of particular interest to speech and language therapists/pathologists and laryngologists. This is because any speaker's potential pattern and range of vocal fold vibration is determined by the physical state of his or her larynx. The overall size and shape of the larynx and vocal folds, the elasticity of the cartilaginous framework, the physiological state of the muscles involved in phonation, and the state of the tissues covering the vocal folds will all influence phonation. Laryngeal function may also be affected by seemingly unrelated factors, such as

Timescale		Examples of phonation behavior	Function (C) = communicative + Informative (I) = informative only
SHORT TERM	segment-to-segment adjustments	voiced versus voiceless	signal linguistic contrasts between segments (C)
	adjustments within utterances / speech turns	adoption of creak at end of turn	may contribute to control of discourse (C)
	adjustments lasting for several turns or whole social interactions	adoption of whisper	may be used as a paralinguistic signal of confidentiality (C)
		adoption of tense, harsh phonation	may be a paralinguistic signal of anger (C) or the result of muscle tension caused by emotional disturbance (I)
LONG TERM	habitual adjustments that characterize an individual	habitual use of any phonation type	usually an extralinguistic indicator of age, physique, personalty, sociolinguistic background (I) May be part of a consciously selected style of presentation (C)

FIG. 18.1. Communicative and informative functions of phonation.

overall bodily posture and bodily tension, because these have an effect on the muscles supporting the larynx (Lieberman, 1998).

One of the interesting phenomena that arise from the complicated communicative and informative functions of phonation is the possibility of misattribution of purely informative aspects of phonation as being communicative, and vice versa. For example, if a speaker addresses someone in a whisper, the listener may assume that the speaker is intending to signal secrecy or confidentiality and respond appropriately. Problems of misattribution may arise if the whisper phonation is, in fact, the result of acute laryngitis, and similar misinterpretations are not uncommon experiences for people with voice disorders.

ANATOMY OF THE LARYNX

The larynx is a complex piece of biological engineering. Access to relevant anatomical models or multimedia materials relating to the anatomy of the larynx may be helpful as an adjunct to the following description. The account given here focuses on phonation, although this is only one of the three key functions of the larynx, which are: (a) to protect the airway during swallowing, so that food does not enter the lungs; (b) to act as a pressure valve; When the larynx is closed to block airflow in or out of the lungs, air pressure within the chest and abdomen can be used to support activities such as lifting heavy weights, defecation, or child birth; (c) phonation.

The larynx consists of a protective framework of cartilages, enclosing the internal muscles and soft tissues of the vocal folds and adjacent parts of the airway. Although the cartilages of the larynx are bound tightly to each other, they have no connecting joints with the rest of the skeleton. The larynx itself sits on top of the trachea (or wind pipe) and is supported within a web of ligaments, membranes, and muscles. As shown in Fig. 18.2, it is suspended from the jaw, hyoid bone, and base of the skull above, and is braced down by muscles connecting to the sternum (breast bone), clavicles, and scapulae. The hyoid bone itself is also free from direct attachment to any other part of the skeleton, and forms part of the suspension system, lying between the tongue and the larynx. Activity of muscles within this supporting web allows both the hyoid bone and the larynx a considerable range of vertical movement, which is involved both in swallowing and, to a lesser extent, in speech. The phonatory function of the larynx as a whole relies on an appropriate balance of tension between the muscles.

Laryngeal Framework

The largest cartilage of the larynx is the thyroid cartilage, which surrounds the front and sides of the airway. Its name is derived from the Greek word for shield, which is an appropriate description both of its shape and its function in protecting the larynx. It takes the form of two quadrilateral plates of cartilage (the laminae), which join at the front to form the thyroid angle. At the top of the thyroid angle there is a small notch, where the two laminae are incompletely joined. At the two back corners of each lamina are two protruding points of cartilage, the superior and inferior horns. The inferior horns curve downward and forward, and form the points of articulation with the cricoid cartilage. The cricoid cartilage is partly enclosed by the thyroid cartilage but is slightly lower. It is located just above the trachea and is often described as being somewhat like a signet ring, as it completely encircles the airway, and is enlarged at the back.

The much smaller arytenoid cartilages articulate with the upper border of the cricoid cartilage, sitting one on each side, close to the back of the ring. They are usually described as being pyramid shaped, although it has to be said that insofar as they do resemble pyramids, they are rather distorted and curvaceous examples. One surface of each cartilage articulates with the cricoid cartilage, with the apex of the pyramid pointing upward. The most acutely angled corner of the base points forward and joins with the vocal fold, which is described further later. Two other sets of tiny cartilages need only brief mention here, and are not discussed further. The paired corniculate cartilages are roughly cone shaped, and sit on the upper apex of the arytenoid cartilages, whereas the cuneiform cartilages are tiny cartilagenous rods embedded in the

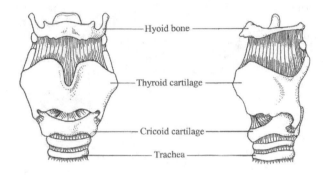

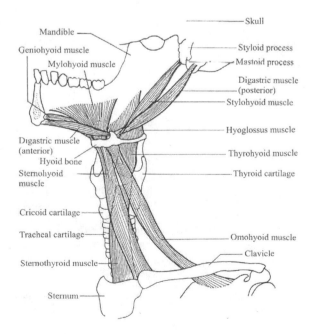

FIG. 18.2. A schematic view of the larynx and surrounding structures: (a) from the front; (b) from the side; (c) to show relationships with head, neck, and chest.

fold of tissue that runs from the arytenoid cartilages to the epiglottis (the aryepiglottic fold). The cartilages of the larynx are shown in Fig. 18.3.

Internal Structure

As the airway passes through this laryngeal framework, from the trachea below to the pharynx above, its internal walls are modified to create two pairs of tissue folds, as shown in Fig. 18.4, which is a diagram of a vertical section of the larynx. The upper pair, the ventricular folds, are rich in glandular tissue, and can be brought together to close the airway, but have little potential for fine adjustment. The vocal folds, by contrast, are largely muscular, and are capable of very finely tuned adjustments, as a result of the large number of muscles within and around the larynx. The main bulk of each vocal fold consists of the vocalis muscle, which attaches to the front of the thyroid cartilage and runs back to the arytenoid cartilage. Rocking and lateral movements of the arytenoid cartilages control the rear portions of the vocal folds so that they can be pulled apart (*abducted*), allowing free passage of air through the larynx, or brought together (*adducted*), so as to impede airflow. When they are

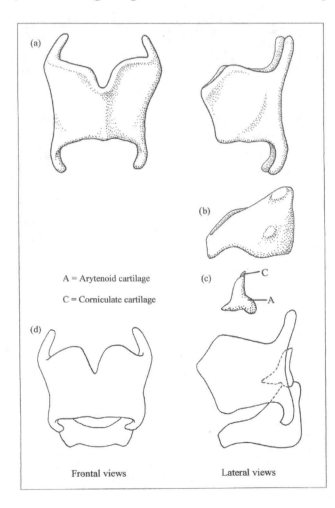

A = Arytenoid cartilage

C = Corniculate cartilage

Frontal views   Lateral views

FIG. 18.3. The principal cartilages of the larynx: (a) the thyroid cartilage (from the front and from the side); (b) the cricoid cartilage; (c) one of the paired arytenoid cartilages with a corniculate cartilage; (d) shows the cartilages assembled.

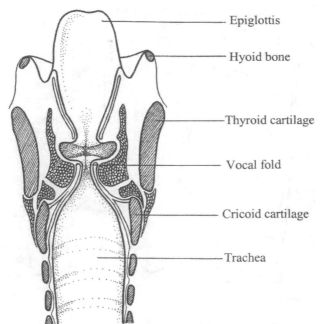

Epiglottis

Hyoid bone

Thyroid cartilage

Vocal fold

Cricoid cartilage

Trachea

FIG. 18.4. A vertical section
of the larynx.

abducted, the glottis (i.e., the space between the vocal folds) is approximately triangular shaped. The precise manner of adduction can vary in a number of ways, with consequent effects on phonatory quality, which is discussed in more detail later in this chapter. A schematic view of the vocal folds is shown in Fig. 18.5. The labeling follows Laver (1980) in describing the anterior two thirds of the vocal fold, where the glottal edge is formed by the vocal ligament, as the ligamental portion. The posterior third, where the glottal edge is formed by the arytenoid cartilage, is described as the cartilaginous portion of the vocal fold.

Detailed studies of the tissues of the vocal folds have led to major advances in understanding of vocal fold mechanics. Pioneering work in this area from the 1970s and 1980s is well summarized in Hirano (1981). Prior to that time the ligamental portion of each vocal fold was typically described as being composed simply of the muscular body of the vocal fold and the vocal ligament, with an overlying layer of mucosa. The ligament runs along the free edge of the vocal fold, and extends from the inner side of the thyroid cartilage at the front to the arytenoid cartilage at the back, as shown in Fig. 18.5. This gross description of the structure overlooks the importance of the internal structure of the vocal ligament, which seems to be crucial for efficient vocal fold vibration.

A diagrammatic view of the tissue layers of a vocal fold, as it appears in cross section, is shown in Fig. 18.6. The body of the vocal fold is formed by the vocalis muscle, also known as the thyroarytenoid muscle. The fibers of this muscle are arranged in parallel, running from the thyroid cartilage to the arytenoid cartilage. The connective tissue that overlies this muscle is thickened and fibrous at the vocal fold edge, and it is this band of connective

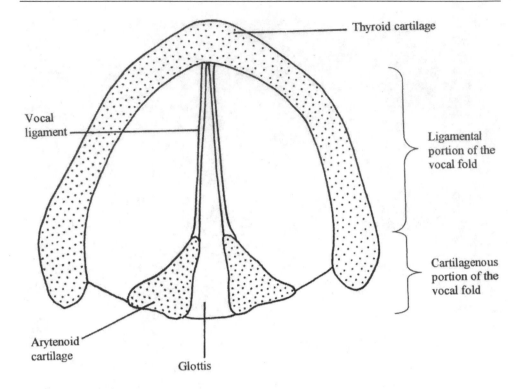

FIG. 18.5.   A schematic view of the vocal folds as seen from above.

tissue that is known as the vocal ligament. In adults it is quite clearly delin-
eated into three layers, which together make up the lamina propria. The
deep layer, immediately overlying the vocalis muscle, is densely packed with
bundles of collagen fibers, arranged in parallel with both the vocal fold edge
and the muscle fibers of the vocalis muscle. The intermediate layer of the
lamina propria is rich in elastin fibers, which again are organized so that
they lie parallel to the vocal fold edge. The superficial layer of the lamina
propria has both collagen and elastin fibers, but at a much lower density
than the underlying layers, and they are in a much looser, haphazard
arrangement. The whole of the surface of the vocal fold is covered by a thin
layer of epithelium (covering tissue). The lamina propria and the epithelial
layer are collectively described as the cover. An expanded view of these tissue
layers is shown in Fig. 18.7.

   The mechanical properties of the vocal fold are easily grasped from
Hirano's description (1981, p. 5). He described the epithelium as being "... a
thin and stiff capsule, whose purpose is to maintain the shape of the vocal
fold" and the superficial layer of the lamina propria as being "... somewhat
like a mass of soft gelatine." These two layers together behave rather like a
thickish fluid with a very high surface tension. Hirano then likened the intermediate layer of the lamina propria to a bundle of soft rubber bands, and the
deep layer to a bundle of cotton thread. He described the vocalis muscle as re-
sembling a bundle of rather stiff rubber bands, but the mechanical properties

of this layer will of course depend on whether the muscle is actively contracted or not.

The relative thickness of the layers of the lamina propria varies along the length of the vocal ligament. The superficial layer is thinner at the ends than in the middle, whereas the intermediate layer is thicker at the ends, forming cushions of elastic material that probably give some protection against impact during adduction and vocal fold vibration.

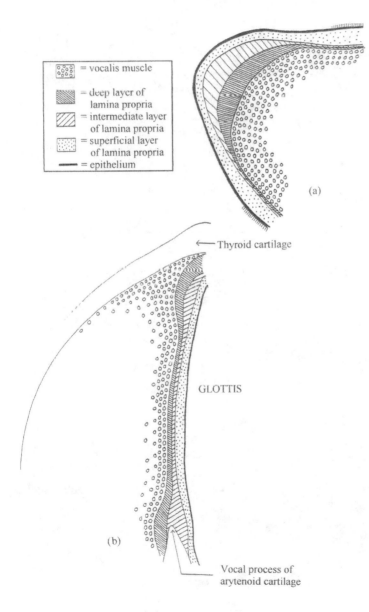

FIG. 18.6. The tissue layers of the vocal folds: (a) a vertical section of one vocal fold, showing the tissue layers; (b) a transverse section of one vocal fold showing variation in tissue thickness (adapted from Hirano, 1981).

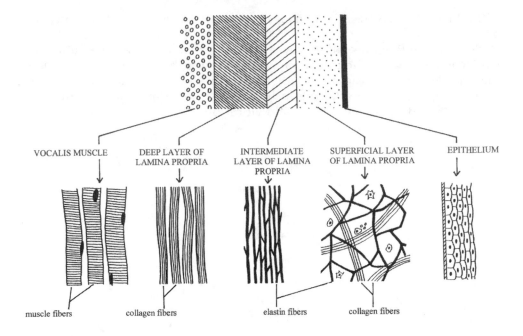

FIG. 18.7.   An exploded view of the tissue layers within the lamina propria and epithelial covering of the vocal fold.

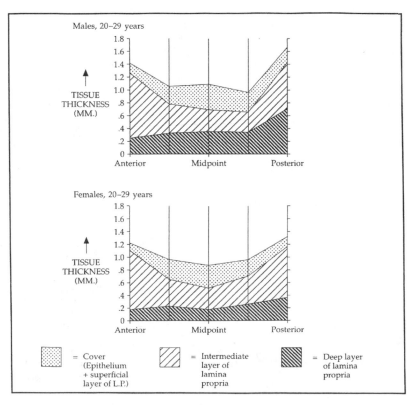

FIG. 18.8.   A graphic representation of the relative thickness of the tissue layers of the vocal fold along its length (based on data from Hirano et al., 1982, p. 274).

HOW THE VOCAL FOLDS VIBRATE

Vibration of the Vocal Folds

The folds are set into vibration when they are placed close together and a flow of air is driven between them from below. Vibration implies rapid and repeated opening and closing movements of the folds and this is shown in Fig. 18.9, as observed from above and in cross section. The vibratory pattern is quite complex, involving both vertical and lateral movement of the folds. In order to sustain vibration, an appropriate balance is required between the muscular tension that the folds are under and the pressure of air from beneath them. If the muscular tension is too great (relative to the air pressure) it will

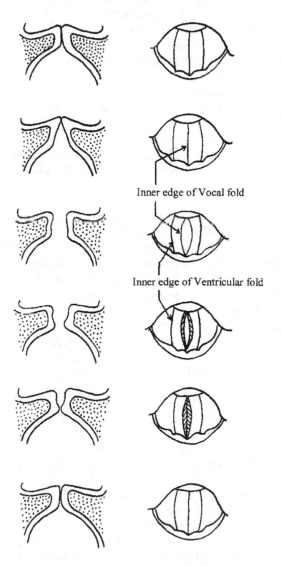

Inner edge of Vocal fold

Inner edge of Ventricular fold

FIG. 18.9. A schematic representation of the sequence of vocal fold vibrations as see (a) in cross section, and (b) from above (adapted from Hirano, 1981, p. 44).

not allow the folds to be parted; on the other hand, if the air pressure is too great (relative to the muscular tension of the folds) then it will not allow the glottis to close. A description of the forces operating to produce vocal fold vibration is provided in the "myoelastic-aerodynamic theory" originally proposed by van den Berg (1958); a more recent account can be found in Titze (1994).

Myoelastic-Aerodynamic Theory of Vocal Fold Vibration.   The myoelastic element referred to in this theory is the elasticity of the paired vocalis muscles, which, under appropriate tension, tend to bring the folds together. The main aerodynamic element is the airflow from the lungs; this opposes the myoelastic force of the vocalis muscles by exerting a build-up of pressure beneath the closed folds until it is strong enough to force them apart. Once this happens, the release of air results in a pressure drop across the folds, the myoelastic forces cause the vocal folds to snap together, whereupon the subglottal pressure builds up again, initiating another cycle. In this way, the opening and closing of the folds is achieved as the result of two sets of opposing forces alternately gaining predominance.

A second aerodynamic element is said to aid the myoelastic forces of the vocalis muscles in bringing about the closure phase. This is the *Bernoulli effect*, whereby pressure is exerted upon the walls of an aperture, tending to bring them together and close that aperture, when there is a drop in pressure resulting from a flow of air through the aperture. Although the Bernoulli effect no doubt plays some role, its importance in effecting the closure of the glottis is currently a matter of debate.

The Mucosal Wave.   A traveling wave on the surface of the vocal folds, which spreads outward from the point of contact of the two vocal folds during vibration, was observed and reported as long ago as 1940 (Farnsworth, 1940). Similar early reports (van den Berg, Vennard, Berger, & Shervanian, 1960; Hiroto, 1966; Perelló, 1962) have been followed by many detailed observations of this ripple-like wave. It seems to be an essential feature of normal phonation (Harris, Harris, Rubin, & Howard, 1998, p. 278). Observation of this wave is taken as an indication that the outer two layers of the vocal fold (the fluid-like superficial layer of the lamina propria together with the epithelium) are acting relatively independently of the deeper tissue layers, and is a useful clinical indicator of vocal fold health. Absence of the mucosal wave is usually interpreted as being the result either of excessive muscular tension or of increased stiffness or scarring of the vocal folds or some type of pathological tissue disruption (Colton & Casper, 1996; Hirano & Bless, 1993).

Supply of Subglottal Pressure for Vocal Fold Vibration

What is required of the breathing mechanism in order to keep the vocal folds vibrating, more or less uniformly, for a reasonable amount of time? In order for the vocal folds to vibrate, the pressure beneath them (the subglottal pressure) must be greater than the pressure above them, resulting in a flow of air through them. The pressure above the vocal folds (i.e., the pressure within the supralaryngeal vocal tract) will be influenced by the extent to which it is obstructed. If a complete closure occurs, as in a plosive consonant, the pressure above the larynx will quickly become equal to that below, as air flows in from the lungs, bringing vocal fold vibration to a stop. In sounds requiring sustained vocal fold vibration, the supralaryngeal vocal tract tends to be relatively open and so the pressure is near to the atmospheric pressure outside. In order to create vocal fold vibration for an utterance at normal conversational loudness, a subglottal pressure of the order of 0.7 Pascals is required. In order to maintain the same loudness, this subglottal pressure must be kept more or less constant over the duration of the utterance. The problem is that the lungs are steadily emptying over the course of expiration and, other things being equal, the air pressure delivered to the larynx would be reducing all the time. This would result in a continuous sharp fall in f_0 and in amplitude. For example, at inspiration (i.e., an intake of breath), the pressure created by the lungs might be 1 Pascal. The lungs would then empty until the pressure reached 0 Pascals (i.e., the same pressure as that above the glottis). Only at one instant would the desired pressure of 0.7 Pascals occur. The problem is solved by the action of the respiratory muscles. The muscles of inspiration can be exerted in order to reduce the pressure created by the lungs and the muscles of expiration can be exerted in order to increase it. Over the course of an utterance, continuous adjustment of these muscular forces is required in order to modify the pressure provided by the elastic recoil of the lungs.

MUSCULAR CONTROL OF PHONATION

Clear descriptions of muscle action within the larynx are available in a number of specialist texts, including Hardcastle (1976), Laver (1980), Dickson and Maue-Dickson (1982), and Seikel, King, and Drumright (2000). Phonation relies on the coordinated activity of a large number of muscles, including those involved in respiration as well as those within and around the larynx itself. In the interest of simplicity, we concentrate here on the muscular control of *adduction* (closing) and *abduction* (opening) of the vocal folds and on the control of pitch.

Key Muscle Actions

Pulling the vocal folds apart so as to open the glottis, for breathing or for voiceless sounds, is achieved by contraction of the posterior cricoarytenoid muscles (see Fig. 18.10). The process of adducting the vocal folds for phonation is a bit more complicated, however. Laver (1980, pp. 108–109) offered a useful summary of muscle activity involved in adduction, showing how a number of muscle groups act in concert to produce three parameters of muscular control. These three parameters, adductive tension, medial compression, and longitudinal tension, are shown schematically in Fig. 18.11. The specific muscles involved in each parameter are:

1. Adductive tension: The interarytenoid muscles bring the arytenoid cartilages together.
2. Medial compression: The lateral cricoarytenoid muscles, aided by the lateral parts of the thyroarytenoid muscles, bring the ligamental portion of the vocal folds together.

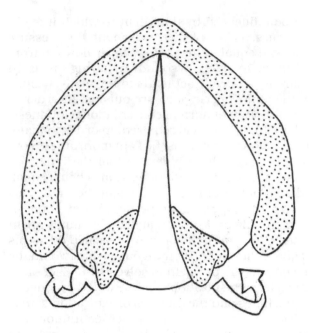

FIG. 18.10. A schematic representation of posterior cricoarytenoid muscle activity during vocal fold abduction.

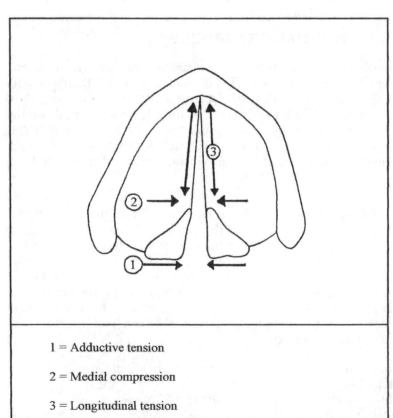

1 = Adductive tension

2 = Medial compression

3 = Longitudinal tension

FIG. 18.11. A schematic representation of the muscle forces acting on the vocal folds during phonation.

3. Longitudinal tension: Vocalis (the main body of the thyroarytenoid muscle) may contract the vocal fold itself (active longitudinal tension) or the vocal fold may be stretched by contraction of the cricothyroid muscles (see following).

Both adductive tension and medial compression are involved in adducting the vocal folds, but they can be controlled independently. These three parameters are referred to later in the chapter to explain different phonation types that may occur during speech.

Control of f_0

f_0 (see chap. 9), of which pitch is the perceptual correlate (see chap. 15), directly reflects the rate of vocal fold vibration. f_0 depends largely on the degree of tension, the mass, and the length of the vibrating vocal folds. For any speaker at a given time the overall mass will be invariable, so the key to voluntary control of pitch is the manipulation of vocal fold tension. The control of vocal fold tension may involve a number of interacting mechanisms, but two key elements can be identified. These two frequently act in combination, so that adjustments of f_0 are often highly complex. The most obvious way of tensing the vocal folds is to contract the vocalis (thyroarytenoid) muscles. If the arytenoid cartilages are braced in position, then contraction of this muscle will increase the tension of the vocal folds without altering their length, and f_0 will increase. Of course, if the arytenoids are not braced, then contraction of the vocalis muscle will reduce the length of the vocal folds, and increase their cross-sectional thickness. The other, and probably more important mechanism for changing f_0 involves adjustments of the cricothyroid joint. Although the arytenoids have some freedom to slide and rock sideways relative to the cricoid cartilage, they are nonetheless bound quite tightly to the cricoid cartilage and will tend to move with it. Because the vocal folds run from the front of the thyroid cartilage to the back of the cricoid cartilage, it follows that if the back of the cricoid is pulled away from the thyroid cartilage then the vocal folds will be stretched. To understand how this may happen, it may be useful to envisage the front of the thyroid and cricoid cartilages as being somewhat like the visor of a helmet, which hinges at the side, toward the back of the two cartilages. Contraction of the thyroarytenoid muscle pulls the visor closed, and as it does so, the back of the cricoid cartilage tilts downward, stretching the vocal folds so that they are tighter and thinner and vibrate more rapidly. The cricothyroid visor is shown schematically in Fig. 18.12.

Practice 18.1: Pitch Control

1. To get a feel for the general relationship between vocal fold tension and pitch, try prolonging a vowel, first of all at a comfortable pitch for your normal speaking style and then while tightening up all of the muscles in the neck region. Notice what happens to the pitch. It is quite likely that it will rise automatically as you tense up, due to the fact that increasing tension in the whole of the neck region is likely to boost tension in the muscles within the larynx as well. Now try yawning, stretching and relaxing as much as you can, and

then produce the same prolonged vowel again. Notice what happens to the pitch. For most speakers, as soon as you relax the muscles in your neck and larynx the pitch will automatically fall.

2. Using your fingers fairly firmly but gently, feel the structures in your neck. Locate the thyroid cartilage, which is recognizable as the largest cartilage. You should be able to feel how the two flattish laminae meet in an angle at the front. If you move down from this cartilage, you may be able to feel a soft area between the lower border of the thyroid cartilage and the cricoid cartilage sitting at the top of the trachea. Place a finger lightly just below the lower border of the thyroid cartilage and say a very low, relaxed [ɑ], followed by a high-pitched squeak and feel what happens. Many people will find that the whole larynx moves, but in addition, you may be able to feel that the space between the two cartilages expands for the low note, and contracts for the high-pitched squeak. This is the cricothyroid visor opening and closing. Do not worry if you find this difficult to feel, as some people have much more prominent cartilages than others and there is a lot of variability in the ease with which this visor movement can be felt.

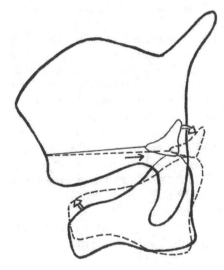

FIG. 18.12. A schematic representation of cricothyroid visor control of vocal fold tension.

TECHNIQUES FOR ANALYZING PHONATION

Techniques for examining laryngeal function fall into three main categories: those that directly examine physiological function of the larynx, those that record acoustic output, and those that are based on perceptual analysis. The following section describes some of the more widely available measurement tools. A fuller review of techniques for voice analysis can be found in Kent and Ball (2000).

Techniques for Examining Physiological Aspects of Phonation

Laryngoscopy.   Laryngoscopy includes any method for visual inspection of the larynx. Laryngoscopy has been greatly enhanced by the development of fiberoptic technology, and modern equipment allows video recordings of laryngeal movement to be made. Stroboscopic light sources give the illusion of slowing down the rapid vibration sufficiently to observe the pattern of vibration. Two types of fiberoptic probe may be used. A rigid probe, which usually gives a clearer image, has an angled end so that when it is slid over the tongue the operator is able to see down into the pharynx. Flexible probes are passed through the nasal cavity, and have the advantage that the speaker is able to articulate normally while the larynx is being observed. Figure 18.13 shows these two techniques and a typical laryngeal image.

Electrolaryngography. Electrolaryngography (also known as electroglottography) is a relatively simple, robust, and noninvasive method for investigating vocal fold vibration. It involves the placement of two surface electrodes either side of the larynx, between which a small current is passed. When the folds are pressed together, as occurs during the closure phase of vibration, the current passes easily, but as the folds are pushed apart, during the open phase, the resistance to current flow progressively increases. The instrument, by recording variations in the level of current passing between the electrodes, thus produces a fair representation of each cycle of opening and closing. On a laryngographic waveform an amplitude peak represents maximum closure (coinciding with maximum current) and a trough represents the open phase. Figure 18.14 shows the waveform of glottal opening and closing (and thus the waveform of vocal fold vibration) obtained using a laryngograph. This technique is a very useful source of information about f_0 perturbation of f_0 and amplitude, and relative speeds of closing and opening phases of vocal fold vibration. The opening and closing phase ratios give useful information about the detailed pattern of vibration and are good indicators of muscle tension and laryngeal efficiency.

Air Flow/Pressure. Hirano (1981, p. 25) stated that "the aerodynamic aspect of phonation is characterized by four parameters: subglottal pressure, supraglottal pressure, glottal impedance, and the volume velocity of the airflow at the glottis." The techniques and equipment used to measure these parameters are beyond the scope of this chapter, but further information can be found in many specialist texts. For a helpful review, see Hillman and Kobler (2000).

Acoustic Measurement of Phonation

Whereas it is not possible, of course, to actually record the sound made by the vocal folds in isolation from the rest of the vocal tract (not in a live subject anyway), we can derive a glottal waveform by applying inverse filtering to the speech signal. This indicates the pattern of acoustic energy produced by vocal fold vibration, and is somewhat similar to the laryngographic waveform described earlier. We can also get a good idea of the spectral composition of the sound created by the folds by preparing a spectrum from the waveform of glottal vibration. Such a spectrum, in idealized form, was described in chapter 17 (see Fig. 17.1). Key parameters derived from the glottal waveform include:

- f_0, which reflects speed of vocal fold vibration and correlates with the perceptual impression of pitch.
- Amplitude, as the amplitude of speech is to a large extent determined by the amplitude of glottal vibration. (Amplitude correlates with the perceptual impression of loudness.)
- Perturbation of f_0 (jitter) and amplitude (shimmer), which reflect irregularity of vocal fold vibration.

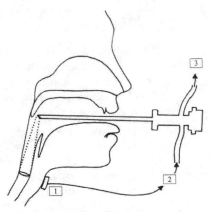

a) Rigid endoscope fiberoptic laryngoscopy

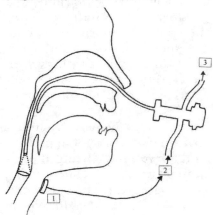

b) Flexible nasendoscopic laryngoscopy

1 Throat microphone

2 Light source (continuous or stroboscopic). Frequency of stroboscopic light is adjusted in accordance with frequency recorded at throat microphone.

3 Video monitoring/recording of observed images

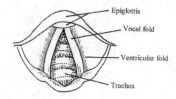

c) A typical view of the larynx

FIG. 18.13. A diagrammatic representation of fiberoptic laryngoscopy using (a) rigid endoscope fiberoptic laryngoscopy; and (b) flexible nasendoscopic laryngoscopy. (c) shows a typical view of the larynx (adapted from Mathieson, 2001, p. 429).

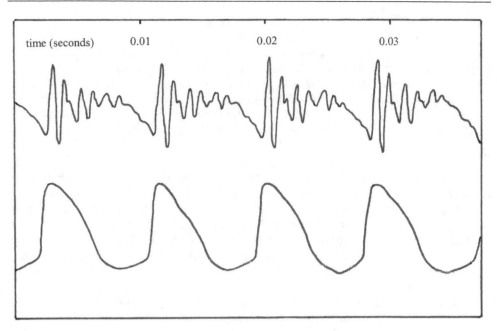

FIG. 18.14. Audio waveform (top) and laryngographic waveform (bottom) of a male speaker producing a sustained vowel. The laryngographic waveform shows how the amplitude of the current across the electrodes varies with time. A peak signifies maximum closure of the vocal folds.

In addition, some useful measures can be derived from the unfiltered speech waveform, including:

- Interharmonic noise, which indicates fricative air flow at the glottis (or elsewhere in the vocal tract);
- Spectral tilt, as the balance between high and low frequency energy within the spectrum may indicate the level of tension within the vocal tract.

Perceptual Analysis of Phonation

Physiological and acoustic aspects of phonation do, of course, have a direct impact on the sound we hear. The labeling conventions for describing phonation vary somewhat within phonetics, depending partly on whether segmental contrasts or longer term phonation qualities are the focus of interest. Descriptions of phonation at a segmental level most often rely on a simple distinction between voiced (vocal folds adducted and vibrating) and voicelessness (vocal folds abducted and not vibrating), although more detail may be required for a small number of languages where different patterns of voicing signal linguistic contrasts at a segmental level. For example, some languages of West Africa have been reported to have a linguistic contrast between normally voiced and creaky voiced vowels, and some Indo-European languages exploit a contrast between normal voicing and whispery voice (or murmur) (Laver, 1994, pp. 196–200). Creakiness and whisperiness are explained in the next section.

PHONATION TYPES

The vocal folds are able to produce a wide range of phonatory qualities, depending on the balance of muscle tension within the larynx and the extent of vocal fold adduction. It is convenient to differentiate between a number of phonation types, and the description given here draws heavily on the principles for voice quality analysis developed by Laver (1980) and the three-parameter model of laryngeal control that was described in the first section of this chapter.

Modal Voice

Modal voice, or modal phonation, is a term used to describe the type of phonation that is produced when there is a moderate degree of longitudinal tension, adductive tension, and medial compression. Vocal fold vibration is regular and periodic, and the vocal folds are adducted along their full length so that there is no fricative airflow between the vocal folds. Figure 18.15(a) shows a laryngographic trace for modal phonation. The laryngographic trace is characterized by a very regular waveform, with minimal cycle-to-cycle variation in period or peak height.

Modal voice is sometimes interpreted as meaning "normal" voice, but this is not entirely accurate and it is better to view it as a convenient baseline against which to compare other types of phonation. Language communities vary considerably in terms of the typical phonation types used and, as we see later, evidence from a range of subject groups suggests that modal voice is usually found in combination with one or more of the other phonation types described later. The practice activities are intended to encourage readers to experiment with a wider range of phonation types than they would normally use. Most people, when they try these exercises, initially find it difficult to predict just what sounds they will produce. The best piece of advice is to treat these activities as an opportunity for laughter and experimentation, while persevering long enough to succeed in producing at least most of the phonation types described. Figure 18.15 shows laryngographic waveforms for some of the phonation types and Fig. 18.16 shows the laryngeal and muscle tension balance of each type.

Falsetto

Falsetto phonation contrasts with modal voice in terms of the longitudinal tension of the vocal folds, which is much greater in falsetto. This is passive tension, in the sense that the vocalis muscles within the vocal folds are not themselves contracted, but the vocal folds are stretched, so that they have a rather thinner cross section than in modal voice. The resultant phonation is typically high pitched, although the pitch range may overlap with the upper part of the modal pitch range, and has a characteristically "pure" or "thin" quality.

Falsetto is most striking when used by men, as when they are imitating women or children. It is also adopted by some male popular singers. In some cultures falsetto may also have a paralinguistic function; Brown and Levinson (1987) described the use of falsetto in the Mayan language Tzeltal as an honorific signal.

Creak

Creak is a very distinctive phonation type in which high levels of adductive tension and medial compression, in combination with low levels of longitudi-

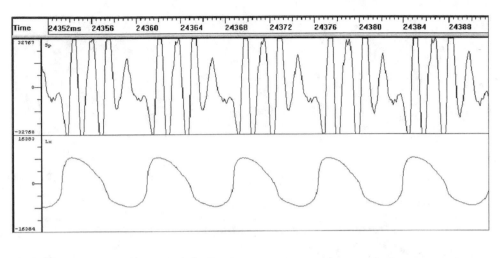

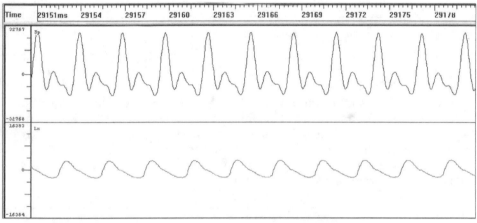

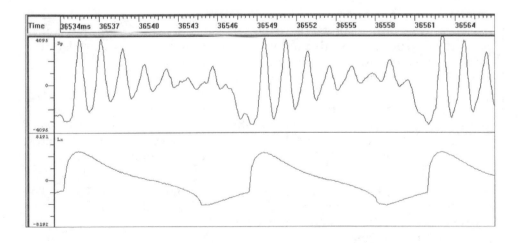

FIG. 18.15. Laryngographic waveforms of: (a) modal voice; (b) falsetto; (c) creak; (d) whispery voice (note that whisper in isolation would show a flat trace because there is no vocal fold vibration).   *(continued)*

275

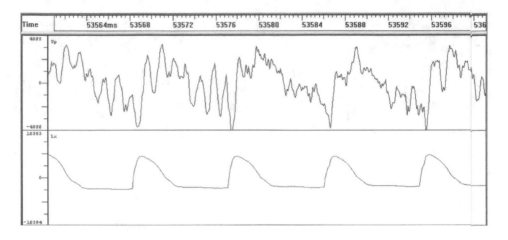

FIG. 18.15.   *continued*

Practice 18.2: Modal Voice and Falsetto

Try producing modal phonation and then falsetto. If you don't find it easy
to produce falsetto, think of it as a fairly quiet, high-pitched "child-like"
voice, which should not involve undue tension. Another method that
sometimes helps is to start with a high-pitched cat's "miaow" and then
speak around that same kind of phonation. Once you are confident that
you can feel and hear the difference between modal voice and falsetto, try
raising the pitch in modal voice, and then lowering the pitch in falsetto.
For many people the top of the modal pitch range overlaps with the lower
part of the falsetto pitch range, which shows that these phonation types
are different in quality and not just in pitch.

Practice 18.3: Creak

To produce creak, keep fairly relaxed, and try to produce a very
low-pitched voice, experimenting until you can hear individual pulses of
creak phonation. Keeping the chin slightly tucked in toward the chest
sometimes makes it easier to get the right tension balance for creak. Some
people may find it easier just to try imitating a creaky door, or something
similar. Another approach is to try sliding from a normal pitch to the lowest
possible pitch. Try maintaining creak throughout an extended utterance,
or while counting up to 10. Note that the pitch range of creak is very limited,
so that creak phonation interferes with natural intonation patterns.

---

nal tension, result in a very thick cross section, as shown in Fig. 18.16. This
results in a very low f_0 (in the region of 50 Hz to 90 Hz), which allows each cycle
to be heard as a discrete sound. The auditory effect of creak is often described
as being somewhat robotic or mechanical, like a ratchet, or the noise made
when a stick is pulled along a set of railings.

Intermittent creak, or creak combined with voice (see later section on combined phonation types) is quite characteristic of some accents of English, no-

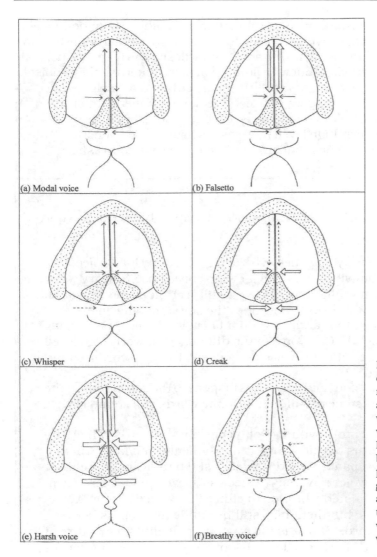

FIG. 18.16. Larynx configuration and muscle tension balance for: (a) modal voice; (b) falsetto; (c) whisper; (d) creak; (e) harsh voice; (f) breathy voice. The upper part of each diagram shows the larynx as viewed from above; the lower part shows a vertical section of the vocal folds.

tably in some areas of North America and in Received Pronunciation. It also functions in some cultures as a signal of boredom or tiredness. Many speakers use creak intermittently, most often on falling intonation contours at the end of utterances. It appears to be involved in signaling the end of a turn in interactions (Laver, 1994, p. 196).

Whisper

Whisper, when it occurs in isolation, does not involve any vibration of the vocal folds, but is simply the creation of fricative noise (see chap. 13) within the glottis. Figure 18.16 shows the typical configuration of the larynx in whisper, where high medial compression and low adductive tension cause tight adduction of the ligamental portion of the vocal folds and a posterior chink between the arytenoids. A stream of turbulent airflow through this small space thus creates an aperiodic sound source, with energy right across the spectrum.

Whisperiness may also occur in combination with other phonation types if the vocal folds are vibrating without being fully adducted, so that some fricative leakage of air occurs. In this case, the spectrum will show evidence of periodic glottal pulses and harmonics, but with additional noise (interharmonic noise).

Whisper functions paralinguistically in many cultures as a signal of confidentiality or secrecy. In whispered speech the usual phonetic differentiation between voiced and voiceless segments is, of course, lost. Intelligibility is usually maintained at a fairly high level, however, as listeners are generally able to use alternative phonetic cues to identify voiced/voiceless contrasts.

Practice 18.4: Whisper

Place your fingers fairly firmly against your larynx, with the finger tips on the thyroid cartilage.

1. Try saying "many young men are leaving" in a fairly loud voice. Can you feel a slight vibration through your finger tips? Now try whispering the same utterance. Do you still feel the same sensation through your finger tips? How does the sound quality change?
2. Say the words "zoo" and "Sue" in a fairly loud voice, prolonging the words slightly. Can you feel the difference between the voiced fricative onset and the voiceless onset? Do the words sound clearly different?
3. Say the words "zoo" and "Sue" in whisper. Do the sensations at the larynx feel the same or different? Do the words still sound clearly different?
4. Repeat steps 2 and 3 with the following pairs of words, which differ only in terms of voiced/voiceless segments: van/fan, pan/ban, toe/doe, badge/patch. Would a listener still be able to differentiate between the "voiced" versus "voiceless" segments? There is, of course, no vocal fold vibration in either the "voiced" or the "voiceless" segments, but there may still be subtle differences between the pairs of words. If this is the case, try to identify the nature of any differences between the pairs of words. Subtle differences may be apparent just on the target segments, or may affect the whole word.

Harshness

Harshness is the auditory effect of irregular vocal fold vibration, which is evident in the laryngeal waveform as cycle-to-cycle variations in either amplitude or period (i.e., shimmer or jitter). Harshness is somewhat different from the previous phonation types, because it does not occur in isolation, but only as a modification of either modal voice or falsetto. In speakers with normal laryngeal structure, harshness is typically associated with excessive levels of muscular tension, with adductive tension and medial compression being most marked. There is often additional adduction of the ventricular folds, as shown in Fig. 18.16 (e). Depending on the balance between longitudinal tension and medial compression, harshness may be perceived as a modification of either modal voice (in which case it is described as harsh voice) or of falsetto (harsh falsetto). Harshness is often interpreted as a signal of aggression or anger, although it has also been identified as a normal feature of certain accents, (Esling, 1978; Stuart-Smith, 1999). Perceived harshness and perturbation of the glottal waveform in the absence of excessive tension may indicate abnormalities of the vocal fold structure, but this is discussed further at the end of this chapter.

Practice 18.5: Harsh Voice

Warning: You shouldn't repeat this activity more than once or twice at a time, and you should stop at once if you experience any throat discomfort or coughing. This is important, as prolonged excessive tension during phonation may traumatize the edges of the vocal folds and cause inflammation.

Sit on a sturdy, hard chair, with your hands positioned as if you were trying to lift the chair underneath you. Count from one to five, with a break between each number, using a loud phonation at a relatively low pitch. As you say each number, simultaneously pull forcefully against the seat of the chair, as if you were trying to lift the chair underneath you, or pull yourself down into the seat. Are you aware of muscular tension around your neck and throat? Notice what happens to your phonation. The physical effort often causes exactly the right laryngeal conditions for harsh voice, in which case your voice will sound quite "rough." Alternatively, just trying to sound very angry or aggressive, while keeping the pitch of your voice quite low, may result in harsh voice.

Breathiness

Like harshness, *breathiness* cannot occur in isolation, but only as a modification of modal voice or falsetto. In terms of muscle tension, it could hardly be less like harshness, as it is characterized by rather low levels of adductive tension, medial compression, and longitudinal tension. The vocal folds are brought toward each other, but do not make complete closure, so that there is a lot of air leakage, but with rather lower amplitude of vibration and less fricative energy than in whispery voice. Whereas whisperiness is used as a signal of confidentiality, breathy voice seems to function as a signal of intimacy (Laver, 1980).

Practice 18.6: Breathy Voice

Take a fairly deep breath, relax your neck and shoulders, and make a gentle, voiced sigh. You will probably find that you use a lot of air, but that the volume and pitch are quite low. Now try to count, using the same kind of voicing. It may help to aim at sounding like Marilyn Monroe in an intimate film scene, or a mother soothing a sleepy baby. You will probably find that you can only manage a few numbers on each breath.

Combined Phonation Types

The simple phonation types just described commonly co-occur, and Fig. 18.17 shows some of the possible combinations. Note that falsetto and modal voice cannot occur simultaneously, because of their incompatible tension requirements, although they may alternate in some speakers, especially under conditions of heightened emotion or during laughter. Note, too, that harshness cannot occur as a simple phonation type, for the reasons discussed earlier. The table only shows binary combinations, but more complex phonation types are also common. Common examples include harsh + whisperiness + (modal) voice (harsh whispery voice), or whisper + creak + (modal) voice (whispery creaky voice).

The term "modal voice" is used only when modal voice occurs in isolation. When it is a component of a complex phonation type, it is described simply as "voice."

Phonation in Normal Speech

Perceptual studies of phonation types used in normal speech suggest a wide range of variation within and between speech communities. Table 18.1 shows

	MODAL	FALSETTO	CREAK(Y)	WHISPER(Y)	HARSH
MODAL	modal voice				
FALSETTO	falsetto and modal voice cannot co-occur	falsetto			
CREAK(Y)	creaky voice	creaky falsetto	Creak		
WHISPER(Y)	whispery voice	whispery falsetto	whispery creak	whisper	
HARSH	harsh voice	harsh falsetto	only if also combined with (modal) voice or falsetto	only if also combined with (modal) voice or falsetto	harshness occurs only as a modification of either voice or falsetto
BREATHY	breathy voice	breathy falsetto			

FIG. 18.17.   Combined phonation types. Shaded boxes indicate combinations that are prohibited.

Practice 18.7: Combined Phonation Types

1. *Whispery Voice.* Count from one to 10, first using modal voice alone and then using whisper alone. In modal voice, it should be easily possible to identify fluctuations in the fundamental pitch that results from vocal fold vibration. There is not true of whisper, where there is no vocal fold vibration. Now try adding a quiet voice component to whisper, as if you were producing a "stage whisper." Notice that as soon as voice is added to the whisper, a fundamental pitch becomes discernible, but without the fricative quality being lost. Try varying the balance between the voice and whisper components. In extremely whispery voice, the voice element will be almost masked by the fricative whisper component. In slightly whispery voice, the voice component will be perceptually more prominent, but overlaid with a minimal fricative component.

2. *Whispery Falsetto.* Repeat the previous activity, but use falsetto in place of modal voice.

3. *Creaky Voice.* Count from one to 10, first using creak alone and then using creaky voice. If the combination doesn't immediately seem easy, then try just thinking about pitch variation. You will probably notice that when you use creak alone, the pitch range is severely limited and it is not possible to introduce very much intonational movement. If you aim to produce creak, but with some clear pitch variation, you may find that you automatically begin to combine creak and voice. To start with the creak and/or the voice component may be intermittent, but as long as you can begin to combine both components for brief stretches of speech then you should find that a little practice makes this combination easier.

4. If you find that you can control these combinations successfully, you could try some more difficult combinations, such as harsh whispery voice, or harsh creaky voice.

5. Having practiced these combined phonation types, listen analytically to your own habitual voice, and to the voices of people you hear around you or on film, television, or radio. Try to identify examples of compound phonation types. Varying balances of whisper, creak, and voice are especially common.

---

the results of a study of young adult speakers (18–40 years) in Scotland (Mackenzie Beck, 1988). The numbers within each cell indicate the number of subjects who were judged to have a phonation type at that scalar degree. All speakers used modifications of (modal) voice, which is scored simply as being present or absent. The scalar degrees assigned to harshness, creakiness, and whisperiness indicate their perceptual prominence relative to the voice component. Scalar degree 1 of whisperiness + voice would thus indicate that the voice component was much more prominent, whereas scalar degree 6 + voice would indicate that the whispery component was so marked that the voice component was only just audible. None of these speakers used falsetto. In both male and female groups, all subjects had some degree of whisperiness, but creakiness was significantly more frequent in males. Note

TABLE 18.1   Phonation Types Used by Normal Scottish Speakers (18–40 years)

Phonation Type	Scalar Degree					
	1	2	3	4	5	6
Harshness (present in 8% of subjects)	2	2				
Whisper(iness) (present in 100% of subjects)		14	9	2		
Creak(iness) (present in 64% of subjects)	2	9	5			
Voice (present in 100% of subjects)	25					

(a) Female subjects (N=25)

Phonation Type	Scalar Degree					
	1	2	3	4	5	6
Harshness (present in 28% of subjects)	3	4				
Whisper(iness) (present in 100% of subjects)		19	6			
Creak(iness) (present in 92% of subjects)		11	9	3		
Voice (present in 100% of subjects)	25					

(b) Male subjects (N=25)

that where harshness and creakiness were judged to be present, they were often intermittent, rather than being constant throughout the speech sample.

Stuart-Smith (1999) also found whisperiness, and to a lesser extent creakiness, to be characteristic of speakers from Glasgow. An earlier study by Esling (1978) showed a clear difference between the characteristic phonation types adopted by speakers from two areas of Edinburgh with contrasting socioeconomic profiles. In males, at least, creaky voice seemed to be associated with higher socioeconomic status, whereas whisperiness and harshness seemed to be associated with lower socioeconomic status. When different languages are compared, even greater discrepancies in phonation type may be apparent, and this may cause real difficulties for clinical assessment or cross-linguistic studies of normal phonation. For example, an evaluation in Scotland of a French system for clinical assessment of voice (using acoustic parameters) found that when French norms were applied to data from normal Scottish speakers, almost all Scottish men were classified as having disordered voices (Mackenzie Beck, 1996). The most likely explanation for this was that higher f_0 perturbation levels recorded for the Scottish speech samples was largely due to the creakiness that is a normal feature of Scottish speech, but that is much rarer in French male speakers. Such studies support the view stated earlier that modal voice cannot be taken as a normal baseline. Phonation norms clearly vary according to age, gender, social status, and linguistic background.

SOURCES OF VARIATION IN PHONATION

Organic Versus Phonetic Factors

As the foregoing sections have shown, when phonatory behavior is examined in detail, considerable variation is seen both within speakers and between speakers. Some of this variation arises from phonetic adjustments of the larynx, but organic factors are also important in determining an individual's habitual phonatory pattern and in governing the phonatory changes that occur during the life cycle. There is an extensive literature on the nature and causation of organic variations in phonation, and it would not be appropriate to explore this in detail here. A few illustrations may, however, serve to illustrate some of the general principles that need to be taken into account when considering phonation.

Mechanical Consequences of Variations in Vocal Fold Structure

Useful, if somewhat simplistic, models of the effects of variations in vocal fold structure have been proposed by a number of authors as an aid to predicting the consequences of vocal fold pathology (Hirano & Bless, 1993; Mackenzie, Laver, & Hiller, 1991), but the same principles can be applied to the range of normal, nonpathological variation. Mackenzie et al. (1991) based predictions on four parameters: vocal fold mass, vocal fold stiffness; symmetry/asymmetry of the vocal folds, and protrusion of any mass into the glottis so that it interferes with vocal fold closure. Stiffness encompasses both rigidity (i.e., resistance to bending) and tensile stiffness (i.e., resistance to stretching). The changes in vibratory pattern that might be expected to result from these types of change are summarized in Fig. 18.18.

One important factor that has been included in the table in order to capture differences between speakers, as well as changes within a speaker, is vocal fold length. Vocal fold length has a direct impact on f_0, and f_0 itself is a key feature in differentiating between speakers. The marked differences between the typical f_0 of phonation of children versus adults, or women versus men, are straightforwardly explained by this table. There is a general developmental tendency for increasing laryngeal size to be associated with lowering f_0, and the f_0 difference between men and women is largely explained by the differential increase in vocal fold length that occurs in boys at puberty.

STRUCTURAL FACTOR	VIBRATORY CONSEQUENCE	ACOUSTIC CONSEQUENCE	PERCEPTUAL CONSEQUENCE
Vocal fold mass ↑	rate of vibration ↓ amplitude ↓	lower F0	lower pitch, less loud
Stiffness↑	rate of vibration ↑ amplitude ↓	higher F0	higher pitch, less loud
Asymmetry of mass, configuration or consistency	irregular rate and amplitude of vibration	F0 perturbation (jitter and shimmer)	harshness
Protrusion of any mass into the glottis	incomplete adduction of the vocal folds with air leakage during vibration	interharmonic noise	whisperiness
Vocal fold length ↑	rate of vibration ↓ amplitude ↑	lower F0	lower pitch, louder

FIG. 18.18. Effects of organic variation on phonation.

Vocal fold length is only one factor among many that may affect phonation, however. The detailed structure of the vocal folds undergoes quite marked changes as part of the normal life cycle, and it is these changes that are largely responsible for the normal age- and sex-related differences in phonation quality. In addition to these changes, most people, at some point in their lives, will experience phonation changes that are associated with pathological changes within the larynx. Fortunately, such changes are usually transient, and have no long-term consequences for vocal quality. One common example of a temporary change in vocal fold structure is the type of vocal fold inflammation that often accompanies an upper respiratory tract infection such as a "common cold." Similar inflammation may also result from short bursts of excessive vocal use, such as shouting at a football match or talking over loud music at a party. The inflamed vocal folds become thicker and heavier, so that they vibrate more slowly, and the f_0 of the voice is hence lower. If the swelling is asymmetrical, the vibratory pattern may also become rather irregular and harsh, and it is not unusual for such harshness to be exacerbated as the sufferer boosts muscular tension in an attempt to compensate for their phonatory difficulties. More permanent lowering of f_0 may result from disorders such as Reinke's oedema, a chronic inflammation of the vocal folds that is often associated with smoking.

CONCLUSION

Phonation is a complex process, which can be affected by a whole constellation of phonetic and organic factors. When you add to this the importance of phonation in realizing linguistic contrasts, signaling communicative intent, regulating interactions, expressing emotion, and generally conveying information about a speaker, it is not surprising that phonation has been the focus of a diverse range of research. For example, phonetic analysis of phonation has been applied to topics such as expression and recognition of emotion (e.g., van Bezooyen, 1984), mother–child interaction (Marwick, Mackenzie, Laver, & Trevarthen, 1984), characteristics of speech disorder (van Erp, 1991), and forensic phonetics (Nolan, 2005). A particularly fertile area of research has developed around the analysis of phonation in the assessment of voice disorder. A useful overview of relevant analysis techniques and applications is available in Kent and Ball (2000).

19

Articulation

The division of content between this chapter and the previous one follows a traditional division between "phonation" (i.e., production of a sound source by vocal fold action, the subject of chap. 18) and "articulation" (in this context, the actions of the speech organs above the larynx). The division is useful in that the larynx works in a different way from the supralaryngeal organs. The primary contribution of the larynx to the speech production process comes from the workings of its internal mechanism. A supralaryngeal organ usually makes its contribution by the shape or position it adopts. However, when it comes to explaining the motor control of speech production, the division is not always relevant. For example, the important phenomenon of coarticulation, which is discussed in this chapter (in Dynamics of Speech), includes the larynx just as much as the other speech organs. Ultimately, a theory of speech production must explain how all components of the system, from the lungs to the lips and nose, work together in concert.

The first section extends the description of the supralaryngeal speech organs, which were introduced in chapter 3. There are also some practice exercises that explore the phonetic function of each organ, through a scenario in which each in turn is disabled. The second section describes some techniques used for measurement and direct observation of supralaryngeal articulatory gestures. The last section addresses speech dynamics, in particular coarticulation.

The word gesture, as it was used in the preceding paragraph, is now common in the literature on speech production. A movement of a single speech organ in the production of a speech sound is sometimes called an *articulatory gesture.* The raising of the blade of the tongue in the production of a [ʃ] sound would be an example of a lingual gesture; the rounding of the lips, which also usually occurs in the production of this sound, would be a labial gesture. It can also be used to describe the coordinated actions of different articulators in the production of a single speech sound; for example, the lip closure combined with velar lowering and vocal fold vibration, which together form the production of a [m] sound. The term gesture gained in popularity following its use in the influential theory of articulatory phonology (Browman & Goldstein, 1989), which claims that speech sounds are mentally represented as instructions for articulatory action.

THE SUPRALARYNGEAL SPEECH ORGANS

Above the larynx, the speech organs are the lips, tongue, and velum. To these may be added the lower jaw, which assists with lip positioning and tongue positioning. The organs interrupt the flow of air through the vocal tract in various ways and modify its shape and dimensions. The cavities of the vocal tract are the pharynx, the oral cavity, and the nasal cavity. They were described in chapter 3 and in chapter 17. The posture of the lower part (root) of the tongue modifies the shape of the pharynx (although the pharynx itself has muscular walls and these muscles can also alter the shape and size of the pharynx to some extent). The forward part of the tongue, in conjunction with the lips and lower jaw, modifies the shape of the oral cavity. The position of the velum determines whether the vocal tract forms a single tube or has a side branch through the nasal cavity (see chap. 3). The focus of the account that follows is on the speech organs, that is, the main moving parts of the system. More detailed descriptions than that offered here can be found in Hardcastle (1976), Kent (1997), and Atkinson and McHanwell (2002). UCLA Phonetics Laboratory (2002) is an illustrated guide to a dissection of the speech production mechanism.

The Tongue

The forward part of the tongue (approximately the front two thirds of its entire length) moves about with great rapidity within the oral cavity during speech and it can be formed into a large variety of shapes. Much of this forward part can be seen by looking into the mouth. The rear portion extends down into the pharynx. This rear portion is not so flexible.

The tongue is a muscular hydrostat. A *hydrostat* is a body of fluid enclosed by a flexible membrane. Fluid is not compressible, so its volume remains constant even though its shape changes. Consequently, if the object is squashed in one place, it will bulge elsewhere. The tongue contains some fat, blood vessels, and other tissue and it is well supplied with nerves; however, it consists mainly of muscles, which contain a high percentage of water. A *muscular hydrostat*, that is, a hydrostat containing muscles, need not rely on external forces to change its shape. Contraction of its own muscles does this. Longitudinal contraction has the effect of bunching up the tongue. Transverse contraction has the effect of lengthening it. The direction in which the tongue expands is always orthogonal (at right angles) to the direction of muscle contraction. The flexibility of the tongue partly derives from the large number of different muscles contained within it and the variety of their orientation. Collectively, these muscles are known as the *intrinsic muscles* of the tongue. There are four intrinsic muscles: the superior longitudinal muscle, the inferior longitudinal muscle, the transverse muscle and the vertical muscle. Atkinson and McHanwell (2002) referred to these as "muscle groups," which suggests complexity in their arrangement, and Kent (1997) warned that dif-

ferent authorities give conflicting descriptions of the details of tongue muscu-
lature. The intrinsic muscles can be seen in Fig. 19.1.

Although it is true that the volume of one part of the tongue affects the volume
of the rest, as just described, it is also possible to move one part of the tongue to
some extent independently of the rest. The tongue tip and blade, in particular,
can perform the same action more or less regardless of how the rest of the
tongue is positioned. The extrinsic muscles of the tongue (which are described
in the next paragraph) doubtless have something to do with this. However, this
facility is also due to how the intrinsic muscles themselves are physically inter-
laced (interdigitated being the technical term) and how they work together.
When one muscle is tensed, other muscles can brace against it. In this way, the
tongue can provide its own, varying, internal "skeleton."

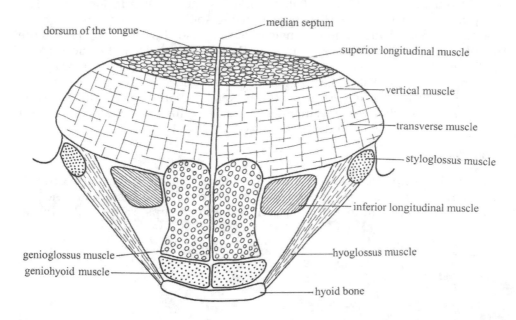

FIG. 19.1.   A transverse (coronal) section of the tongue. Adapted from Hardcastle (1976).

Practice 19.1

Use the statement in the preceding paragraph (that the direction of expansion is always orthogonal to the direction of contraction) to match the intrinsic muscles of the tongue named here on the left (the two longitudinal
muscles are counted as one) with their functions, listed on the right.

    A. longitudinal muscle   D. widens and flattens the tongue
    B. transverse muscle   E. bunches and shortens the tongue
    C. vertical muscle   F. elongates and narrows the tongue

Answer. A→E, B→F, C→D

Worms and slugs are examples of muscular hydrostats that are whole organisms. The tongue, however, like an elephant's trunk (another example of a muscular hydrostat), is attached to the rest of the body. Some of the muscles that make up the tongue originate from bones outside it. They are known as the *extrinsic muscles.* When an extrinsic muscle contracts, it pulls the relevant part of the tongue toward the bone from which it (the muscle) originates. The extrinsic muscles include the genioglossus, the hyoglossus, the palatoglossus, and the styloglossus. The genioglossal muscles originate from the inside edges of the lower jaw. The hyoglossus originates from the hyoid bone, down in the pharynx. The palatoglossal muscles run laterally and upward to join the soft palate, forming the anterior palatoglossal arches. The styloglossal muscles also run laterally, to attach to the styloid process, which is a protruberance of bone from the skull. These extrinsic muscles can be seen in Fig. 19.2. The shaping and positioning of the tongue during speech is achieved through the cooperation of intrinsic and extrinsic muscles. Also shown on Fig. 19.2 is the mylohyoid muscle, which plays a minor role in raising and fronting the tongue.

Tongue lowering and tongue raising are usually facilitated by the action of the lower jaw. For example, from a position of rest, the oral cavity can be enlarged simply by opening the jaw, without exertion of the tongue muscles. During speech, coordinated movements of the tongue and jaw adjust the size and shape of the oral cavity and the pharynx.

The Lips

The speaker's lips are visible in face to face conversation and they can provide additional cues to a listener about the identities of speech sounds. The glabrous portions are quite distinctive, and sometimes "lips" refers just to these.

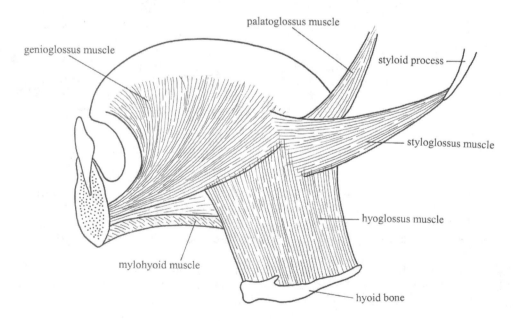

FIG. 19.2.   The extrinsic muscles of the tongue.

Practice 19.2

Try reading the following sentence without moving your tongue. You will find this difficult. Try fixing it approximately in the posture for the vowel [ə].

When the sunlight strikes raindrops in the air, they act like a prism and form a rainbow.

If you did manage to keep your tongue completely still, you may well have found it almost impossible to make appropriate, synchronized movements with the remainder of the speech organs, including the larynx. In any case, the result will have been unintelligible. Further practice exercises in this section will ask you to hold the lips, jaw, or velum stationary, while pronouncing a sentence. You will find them easier to perform and the results more intelligible. The sentence used here is the first sentence of the Rainbow Passage, from Fairbanks (1960), a passage that has often been used in phonetic research. Later practice exercises in this section use sentences from the same passage.

They are the parts immediately around the mouth opening, on which no hairs grow. They seal against each other to close off the vocal tract in the production of bilabial stops. The lips are a complex of muscles (see Fig. 19.3), the main one being orbicularis oris. Orbicularis oris is a ring of muscle that forms a sphincter around the opening of the mouth. Contraction of the inner part of orbicularis oris has the effect of protruding the lips and thus elongating the vocal tract, which has the acoustic effect of lowering its resonant frequencies (see chap. 17). The upper and lower parts can also be contracted independently. Other muscles, from above and below and either side, merge into orbicularis oris. One of these, risorious (based on a Latin word meaning "smile"), is especially important for lip spreading.

For the achievement of lip closure, there is a trade off between action of the lip muscles and upward movement of the lower jaw. At one extreme, a complete closure of the lips can be achieved just by raising the lower jaw, with the lips remaining largely passive; at the other extreme, the jaw stays down and the closure is achieved entirely by the muscular action of the lips themselves. Protrusion of the lower lip is commonly assisted by protrusion of the lower jaw. Retrusion (a rare word, meaning the opposite of protrusion) of the lower lip is required for labiodental fricatives, for which, according to Atkinson and McHanwell (2002, p. 295), retrusion of the lower jaw is also necessary. (It certainly seems difficult to achieve a full and careful labiodental articulation while holding the lower jaw still.) Lip "rounding" normally involves both rounding and protrusion, using orbicularis oris and the depressor labii inferior (Honda, Kurita, Kakita, & Maeda, 1995). Lip rounding is required, notably, for the rounded vowels (see chap. 5), the consonant /w/, and also, in English, /ʃ/.

The Lower Jaw (Mandible)

The lower jaw, or mandible, is a horizontal U-shape, with processes that run vertically and end in front of each ear, at the temporomandibular joint. The jaw is lowered, raised, retracted, and protruded from this joint, by the action

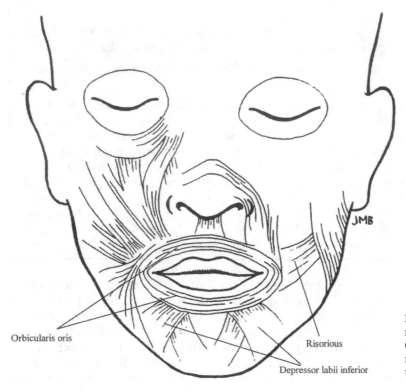

Orbicularis oris

Risorious

Depressor labii inferior

FIG. 19.3. The muscles of the lips. Only the muscles mentioned in the text are named.

Practice 19.3

Hold the lips in a neutral position (like in the vowel [ə]), while you read the following sentence out loud:
The rainbow is a division of white light into many beautiful colors

Words without labial consonants or rounded vowels, like "the," "light," and "colors," sound normal. Those with labial closures, namely "rainbow," "many," and "beautiful," are inevitably distorted. People tend to resort to some kind of palatal or velar lingual gesture in their attempts to convey the presence of these labials. The /w/ in "white" is a little easier. This is a labiovelar sound and the velar element can be exaggerated to compensate for the lack of lip protrusion. Velar raising of the tongue and protrusion of the lips have a similar acoustic effect because both increase the effective length of the oral cavity.
"Division" contains a labiodental target, which is impossible to attain, and a voiced post-alveolar fricative. The latter is not much compromised, but native English speakers will find it an effort of will to suppress the labial gesture that normally accompanies [ʒ].
Ventriloquists, who try to speak without visibly moving lips or jaw, tend to adopt a smiling posture. In this way, labiodentals can be produced more or less normally and a substitute for a labial stop can be achieved by surreptitiously pushing the bottom lip against the upper teeth.

of a number of muscles that attach to it. Notable among these are the masseter, the temporalis, and the pterygoid muscles. Figure 19.4 shows, in schematic form, the attachment of these muscles to the jaw. The jaw cooperates both in lingual and labial gestures and so it moves more or less continuously in the normal production of speech. Normally, during speech, the jaw remains slightly open throughout, although it is possible to produce intelligible speech even through tightly clenched teeth (cf. Practice 19.4, in which the scenario is less extreme than this). The extent of the jaw's movement during speech normally remains well within its maximum range.

The Velum or Soft Palate

The soft palate continues from the end of the hard palate, to which it is attached, toward the back of the pharynx. It ends in the uvula, which is easily seen when looking into the mouth. It also continues around and down at either side of the mouth, to form the faucal pillars. As the name implies, the soft palate contains no bone. It is composed of connective tissue and muscles. When relaxed, it hangs down toward the root of the tongue, allowing an opening (the velopharyngeal port) between the nasal cavity and the pharynx. Complete closure of the velopharyngeal port is important in the creation of sounds like [θ] and [s], which require a build-up of pressure behind the point of stop closure or fricative stricture (if the velopharyngeal port was open, air would leak out through the nose and it would be difficult to build up sufficient pressure to create turbulence in the fricative, or plosion at the release of the stop).

The levator veli palatini muscles originate from the outer wall of the Eustachian tube and travel down to insert into the soft palate. Contraction of these

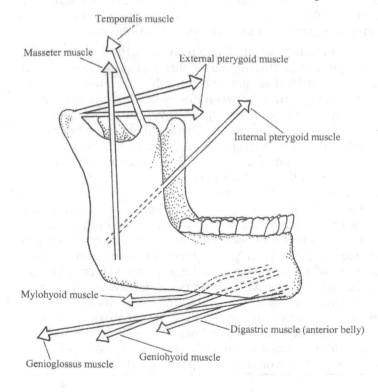

Temporalis muscle

Masseter muscle

External pterygoid muscle

Internal pterygoid muscle

Mylohyoid muscle

Digastric muscle (anterior belly)

Genioglossus muscle

Geniohyoid muscle

FIG. 19.4. Lower jaw, showing, schematically, the muscles that attach to it and move it. Dashed lines indicate attachment to the inner side of the bone. After Hardcastle (1976).

Practice 19.4

Clamp the end of a pencil firmly between your front teeth and read the following sentence out loud:
These take the shape of a long round arch, with its path high above and one end apparently beyond the horizon

It may have sounded a bit odd, but it should have been perfectly intelligible. "Bite-block," as it is called, is actually a well-known experimental procedure in phonetics. It has been used to study the ability that humans have to compensate for a change to one part of the vocal tract by modifying the movements of other parts, in such a way as to produce a similar acoustic signal. This ability (called *articulatory compensation* or *motor equivalence*) is used frequently in everyday life (speaking while eating or smoking, e.g.) and it is an ability that becomes particularly important for people who have suffered paralysis or loss through surgery to some part of the vocal apparatus.

---

muscles, assisted by forward movement of the pharyngeal wall and lateral stretching of the tensor palatini muscles, combine to seal the soft palate against the pharyngeal wall and so close the velopharyngeal port. Figure 19.5 shows the hard and soft palates and the insertion of the levator veli palatini muscles into the soft palate.

Practice 19.5

Try reading the following sentence while keeping the velum closed (if you are not aware whether your velum is open or closed, pinch your nose instead).
There is, according to legend, a boiling pot of gold at one end

The effect will be something like that of speaking with a heavy cold. Speech should remain largely intelligible in this condition, although it sounds abnormal. Obviously, it is nasal sounds that are affected. However, the means for distinguishing between, for example, a /d/ and an /n/ are not entirely lost. A /d/ tends to have little or no vocal fold vibration during the closure in English (see chap. 8, Waveform Types), whereas /n/ has strong vocal fold vibration during the closure; so an alveolar stop produced with strong vocal fold vibration still has a chance of conveying the presence of an /n/, even if the velum is closed.
Reading the sentence with the velum *open* can also be done with little loss of intelligibility, although again it will sound abnormal. (Try it.) Nasalization of the vowel sounds doesn't have a serious effect on intelligibility, as there are no phonemic distinctions between nasalized and non-nasalized vowels in English. However, the /p/ in "pot" will be awkward to pronounce. A plosive requires a build-up of pressure in the oral cavity during the closure and this is difficult to achieve when there is a leak through the nose.
Hypernasality (i.e., unwanted nasality, during sounds that should be exclusively oral) sometimes occurs because the speaker has an abnormally short soft palate, which has difficulty reaching the back wall of the pharynx. Lack of nasality (hyponasality) is most commonly due to enlarged adenoids and/or tonsils, which inhibit air from flowing up through the nasal cavities.

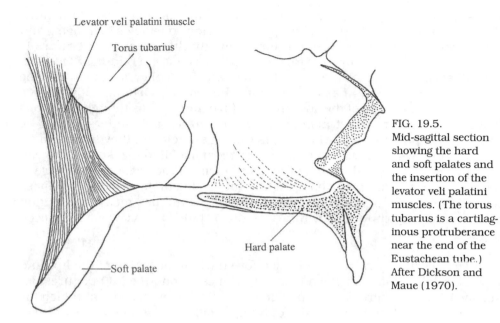

Levator veli palatini muscle

Torus tubarius

Hard palate

Soft palate

FIG. 19.5. Mid-sagittal section showing the hard and soft palates and the insertion of the levator veli palatini muscles. (The torus tubarius is a cartilaginous protruberance near the end of the Eustachean tube.) After Dickson and Maue (1970).

IMAGING AND MEASUREMENT TECHNIQUES

We can make ourselves consciously aware of the postures of our own speech organs during the production of speech sounds (although this is most true of the lips and of the forward part of the tongue and least true of what goes on in the pharynx). This ability has been immensely useful for describing the different speech sounds of languages but it has obvious limitations. Experimental techniques have been developed for imaging and measuring the articulatory gestures of speech. Many of these allow measurement and imaging of continuous speech.

Some experimental research into speech production relies solely on acoustic analysis. An estimate is made of the probable position or movement of a speech organ, or of the overall shape of the vocal tract, from a spectrum or spectrogram of the sound that was produced, based on knowledge of articulatory–acoustic relationships of the sort described in chapter 17. However, it is preferable to investigate articulatory gestures directly. The acoustic signal is the end result of the combination of movements of all the speech organs and identification of movements of individual speech organs from the acoustic signal alone is inevitably uncertain. Another indirect method is airflow measurement. Devices are available that can measure the volume velocity of airflow (in liters/second, e.g.). Precise conclusions about articulatory action are difficult to draw. However, if the apparatus records nasal airflow and oral airflow separately, it gives useful evidence about the action of the velum in closing and opening the velopharyngeal port.

Preferable though it may be to use direct methods, easy it isn't. Most of the speech apparatus is hidden from view, including the most important organ, the tongue. It is three dimensional, which complicates both imaging and measurement. And most of its moveable parts are moving most of the time, during an utterance. These factors present serious obstacles to imaging and measurement. It is therefore not surprising that the relevant literature is almost as much preoccupied with techniques as it is with findings. This section describes some of the available techniques. Fuller accounts can be found in, for example, Lass (1996), and Baken and Orlikoff (2000). It is useful to see an image of the speech organ(s) of interest, as though any intervening structures were transparent. Such images aid understanding of articulatory postures and movements during speech and they inform judgments about which parameters would be most useful to measure. They can also provide the actual means of measurement, if the scale of the image is known. Dynamic imaging, that is, a fast succession of images that produces a motion picture, is especially useful. Other techniques measure position and movement, without providing a photographic-style view of the speech organs.

Video. Ordinary video can be used for studying the action of the lips and jaw. Standard American video takes 30 frames/second (i.e., 30 pictures per second), and standard European video takes 25 frames/second, although the rate may be doubled at a sacrifice of image quality. These rates are sufficient for the human eye, in the sense that they make the action on the screen appear continuous, although ideally they would be faster for speech analysis. In analysis, videos are viewed frame by frame. Video was used, for example, both by Demolin and Teston (1996) and Olson and Hajek (1999) to study the labial flap, a sound used in a number of African languages. The flap involves a swift movement in which the lower lip is drawn back and then bats against the upper lip or teeth in passing.

X-ray. X-ray, a well known medical imaging system, has proved valuable because it can image the whole vocal tract at once and because of the clarity of its image. X-ray films of the vocal tract during speech, involving multiple X-ray exposures per second, have also been made. Extensive exposure to X-ray was found to be a serious health risk and it is no longer a routine technique in speech research. However, the X-ray films of speech collected some years ago are still available (see Munhall, Vatikiotis-Bateson, & Tohkura, 1995). Precise interpretation of an X-ray image is complicated by the fact that it is the result of a beam passing all the way through the head and it can be difficult to estimate the depth of a feature under consideration. This complication is overcome by the use of computed tomography (CT), in which the image is a composite of a number of thin X-ray slices. However, this technique does not allow dynamic imaging and it has the same health risks.

X-ray microbeam (see Westbury, 1991) is a point tracking technique that has been used quite extensively in speech production research. Gold pellets are fixed in strategic places in the vocal tract and their movements are tracked by a narrowly focused X-ray beam. Radiation exposure is considerably reduced in this technique. Another example of a point tracking technique (electromagnetic articulography) is described later in this chapter.

Videofluoroscopy is a dynamic X-ray technique that is able to use much lower dosage rates. It is frequently used, for example, in the assessment of children who were born with a cleft palate (a fissure in the hard palate).

Magnetic Resonance Imaging. Magnetic Resonance Imaging (MRI) provides excellent imaging of soft tissue. Bones and air spaces show as a uniform black. The technique works by detecting the density of hydrogen protons and these are mostly confined to soft tissue, which is watery. The disadvantages of MRI are that frame rates of dynamic imaging are low, the experimental conditions are quite demanding (the subject must lie immobile in a very confined space), and it is expensive. All these disadvantages may be overcome in time. Figure 19.6 shows an MRI image.

Ultrasound. Ultrasound is being used increasingly for investigating speech production. Gick (2002) described the use of ultrasound in field recordings of speech data. Maureen Stone and her colleagues have pioneered the laboratory use of ultrasound for precise imaging and measurement of the tongue and have recently developed three dimensional models of the tongue, based on ultrasound data (see Stone, 1999, and the references cited there). The image quality is not as clear as that of X-ray or MRI and the range of structures that can be viewed is more limited. However, it has some considerable advantages. It is considered very safe (so much so that it is used routinely for imaging the fetus in the womb). It is easy to use and undemanding of the subject. Ultrasound systems are also comparatively cheap and are widely available. Frame rates vary between about 20 and 120 frames/second. However, ultrasound was developed primarily for static imaging and currently in speech research the dynamic image is usually exported to video, which limits the frame rate to 25 or 30 frames/second (see foregoing).

The crucial component of an ultrasound system is the probe. The probe is a sender/receiver unit. It emits pressure waves of very high frequency, far above

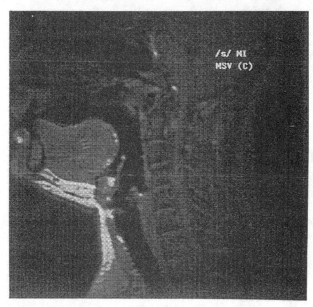

FIG. 19.6. An MRI image of the vocal tract during /s/. Reprinted with permission from S. Narayanan, A. Alwan, and K. Haker, *The Journal of the Acoustical Society of America*, 98, 1325 (1995). Copyright 1995, Acoustical Society of America.

the limit of human hearing. When a wave encounters a "surface" (i.e., any change in impedance of the medium through which it is traveling), some or all of the signal is reflected back to the probe. The system uses the time that elapses between the wave leaving the probe and arriving back again to compute the distance from probe to surface. The information from a number of waves, each one closely following the last in time and space, is used to construct a realistic picture of the surfaces encountered, by displaying surfaces as lines of brightness on the screen.

For imaging the tongue, the probe is placed against the skin under the jaw, as shown in Fig. 19.7. Waves are transmitted upward into the flesh of the tongue. They encounter muscle surfaces inside the tongue, and these form part of the image. When the waves arrive at the tongue surface, virtually all of the signal is reflected back (or scatters) because ultrasound waves at these frequencies do not travel through air. Therefore the surface of the tongue shows up strongly, as a bright line. However, where the tongue makes contact against the hard palate, as in a lingual stop closure, its surface outline may be lost.

An ultrasound image of the tongue, in mid-sagittal view, can be seen in Fig. 19.8. It is one frame from an ultrasound film taken during a pronunciation of the /a/ phase of the diphthong /aɪ/. This frame comes from early in the vowel, shortly after the release of the alveolar closure.

Electromagnetic Articulography. Electromagnetic articulography (EMA) is an example of a point tracking system. It involves gluing sensors at various locations within the vocal tract, using medical glue, and tracking their movements. The focus of interest is on movements of the speech organs. Sensors are usually glued at two or three points along the center line of the tongue and at the midpoint of the

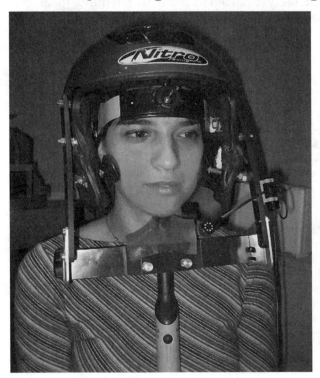

FIG. 19.7. Ultrasound probe fixed beneath a subject's chin, by means of a holder attached to a helmet, for the collection of speech data. The head of the probe is covered with a sheet of jelly-like material, which aids efficient transmission of the signal.

Practice 19.6

Ultrasound waves travel through flesh at a speed of 1540 meters/second. An ultrasound wave took 0.0649 ms (0.0000649 seconds) to travel from the probe to the tongue surface and back again. What was the distance of the tongue surface from the probe?

Answer. The distance there and back was $0.0000649 \times 1540 = 0.1$ meters, so the distance was $0.1/2 = 0.05$ meters $= 5$ cm.

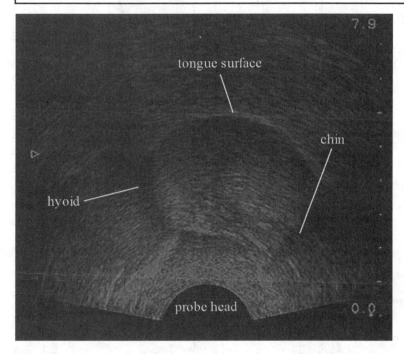

FIG. 19.8. Ultrasound image of the tongue during the /a/ phase of the diphthong /aɪ/. Shadows created by the hyoid bone and the chin are indicated. The scale on the right is in centimeters. The air above the tongue surface does not transmit ultrasound; the speckled markings here are just "noise."

glabrous border of the upper lip and the lower lip. (Few subjects are able to tolerate a sensor glued to the velum and it is impossible to reach into the pharynx, because of an inevitable gag reflex.) Sensors are also glued to the forehead and upper teeth, to provide immobile reference points. A helmet is worn, to which is attached three electromagnetic coils. The electromagnetic field created by these coils enables the position of the sensors to be tracked continuously over time. The system measures the displacement, in both the vertical and horizontal dimensions, and calculates the velocity and acceleration, of each sensor. By these means, a fairly comprehensive idea can be gained of how the forward part of the tongue, and the lips, change in shape and position over the course of an utterance. Figure 19.9 shows the movement of the tongue-tip coil (horizontal and vertical movement are shown on separate lines), and also its speed of movement, during the utterance "Why yell or worry?"

Electropalatography.   Electropalatography (EPG) monitors the contact made by the tongue with the hard palate. The speaker wears an artificial palate that has a number of electrodes embedded in it (see Fig. 19.10). When the speaker's

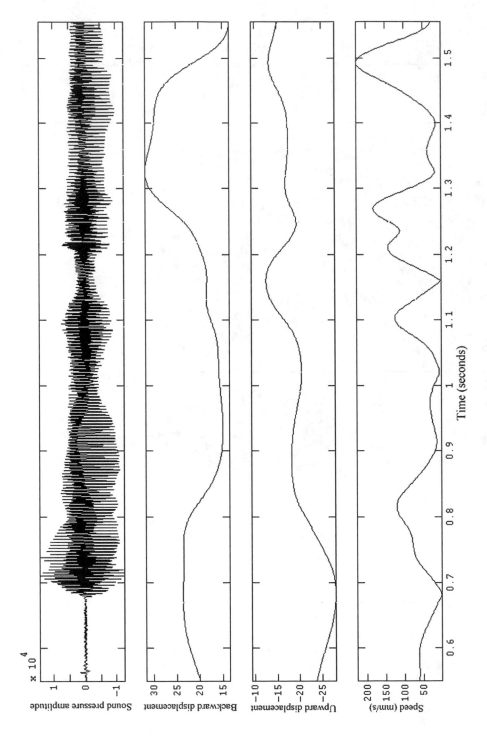

FIG. 19.9. Tongue tip movement recorded using electromagnetic articulography. The utterance was "Why yell or worry?" /waɪ jɛl ɔ wʌrɪ/, by a non-rhotic speaker. The audio waveform is at the top. The lower three traces are waveforms of the coil glued to the tip of the tongue. The lowest shows how its speed of movement varies over the utterance. The one above this shows movements in the vertical dimension (up and down movement). The next one above shows movements in the vertical dimension (up and down movement). The next one above shows back and forward movement (a rise in the line of the graph denotes a backward movement of the tongue tip). Courtesy of James M. Scobbie.

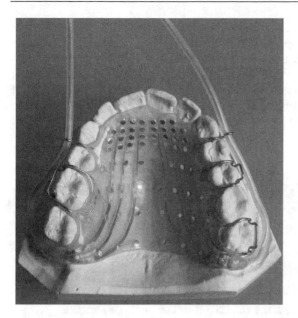

FIG. 19.10. Photograph of an EPG artificial palate. Notice that the electrodes at the alveolar ridge are more closely spaced than those further back.

tongue makes contact with an electrode, a signal is sent to the processor. The system described and illustrated here is the most recent of a number of versions of EPG developed by Bill Hardcastle and colleagues. Hardcastle and Gibbon (1997) gave a description of the principles and operation of EPG, including an account of its use in the analysis and treatment of speech disorders. The artificial palate contains 62 electrodes, arranged in eight rows. The pattern of contacts is displayed schematically on a computer screen. The rows of electrodes are represented as rows of squares. A filled square represents tongue–palate contact at that point. Figure 19.11 shows a succession of EPG frames during the final /ts/ cluster in a pronunciation of the word "sweets." In the first frame, all the first three rows are filled, indicating complete tongue contact across the alveolar ridge. By the third frame, one of the electrodes in the third row is no longer contacted, suggesting that the tongue is already beginning to peel away from the alveolar ridge. The tenth frame shows a loss of contact at the midline, suggesting a narrow gap through which the air could flow, as required for an /s/.

EPG is a reliable and robust technique that causes little inconvenience to the subject and it has been widely used. The technique is limited to information on tongue–palate contact, and is therefore mainly of use for investigating lingual consonant articulations. (In fact, it can only record contact as far back as the end of the hard palate, as subjects cannot tolerate wearing an artificial palate that extends onto the soft palate.) Also, although the system itself is comparatively cheap, the artificial palate must be custom-made for each subject, because there can be large differences in the shape of the palatal arch and in dental formation between one person and another.

Strain Gauge Measurement. Measurements of lip and jaw action can be made using a strain gauge device (Barlow, Cole, & Abbs, 1983). The device consists of a light metal strip, one end of which is attached to a place on the lips or the jaw. The measuring instrument (i.e., the strain gauge itself) is mounted on the strip. The measurements that it provides include the force exerted by the relevant articulator, its displacement (i.e., the extent of its movement) and its velocity of movement. Such a device can be used to measure both up-and-down (inferior/superior) and forward-and-back (anterior/posterior) movements of the upper lip, the lower lip, and the jaw. Figure 19.12 shows an output of the device, in the form of a graph of inferior/superior displacement over time and anterior/posterior displacement over time, for each of the upper lip, lower lip, and jaw.

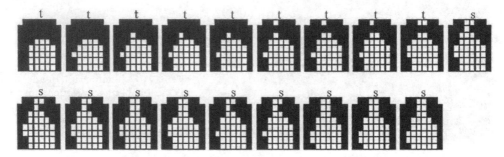

FIG. 19.11.   Nineteen successive EPG frames showing tongue–palate contact during the /ts/ of "sweets." Frames are at 10 ms intervals. In each block of squares, the alveolar ridge is at the top and the velum is at the bottom. A filled square indicates that the corresponding electrode was contacted. The frames are all labeled "t" up to the frame at which an open channel appears; thereafter they are labeled "s."

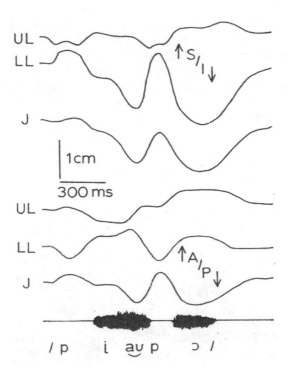

FIG. 19.12.   Strain gauge record during the utterance of a nonsense word "peeowpaw." The upper three traces show up–down (superior/inferior) movements of the upper lip, lower lip, and jaw. The lower three traces show forward-and-back (anterior/posterior) movements. The trace at the bottom is the acoustic waveform. Reprinted with permission from E. M. Müller & J. H. Abbs, *The Journal of the Acoustical Society of America*, 65, 485 (1979). Copyright 1979, Acoustical Society of America.

Hinton and Arokiasamy (1997) used strain gauge measurement to measure the pressures exerted by adult subjects when they pressed their lips together as hard as they could (without clenching their teeth) and they compared these with the pressures used to form bilabial closures during speech. They found that pressures during speech never reached more than 20% of maximum pressure. This finding reflects a general truth, that the demands of speech production remain well within the maximum muscular capabilities of the speech organs (see Perkell, 1997, pp. 355–356, and the references cited there). Speech production requires rapid, precise movements and it sometimes continues for hours on end, so the muscles must be able to operate well within their maximum capacities.

Optical tracking.   More recent alternatives for studying lip and jaw movement include the tracking by camera of markers attached to the jaw and fixed to the lips. Use of multiple cameras and sophisticated software enables measurement of the displacement of each marker, in three dimensions, during speech. Vatikiotis-Bateson and Ostry (1995) defined six different ways in which the jaw can move, three of which involve rotation about the joint at which the jaw is attached to the skull and three that involve translation (i.e., movement of the entire jaw with respect to the skull). The rotational movements are pitch (vertical rotation), roll (rolling rotation), and yaw (sideways rotation). The translational movements are vertical (up and down), lateral (side to side), and horizontal (forward and backward). (In visualizing these movements, it may be helpful to think of the motion of a boat on the water. For example, when it is caught from behind by a wave, a boat is liable to be tipped nose-down and at the same time be propelled forward; in other words, it undergoes pitch rotation and horizontal translation.) They used the optical tracking technique to measure all six sorts of movement during repetitions of the syllables /asasa/. Their results are illustrated in Fig. 19.13. They confirm that the major movements of the jaw that occur when the mouth opens during, in this case, the transition from a /s/ to a /a/, are a pitch rotation in a downward direction and a horizontal translation in a forward direction. In other words, the jaw moves forward as it rotates downward. The remaining four movement types show much lesser excursions.

Practice 19.7

   1. Müller and Abbs (1979, p. 483) said "Movements of the lips and jaw seldom if ever exceed the 2-cm range." Do any of the movements of Fig. 19.12 contradict this?
   2. Describe the lower lip gesture, in moving from the diphthong [au] to achieving a bilabial closure.
   3. Describe the movements of all the articulators in achieving the configuration for the final vowel, /ɔ/, following the bilabial closure.

Answers. 1. No. 2. It rises and retracts. 3. The upper lip rises and the lower lip and jaw both descend. The descent of the lower lip cannot have been entirely the result of jaw lowering, because it moves more than the jaw. The upper and lower lips protrude, while the jaw retracts.

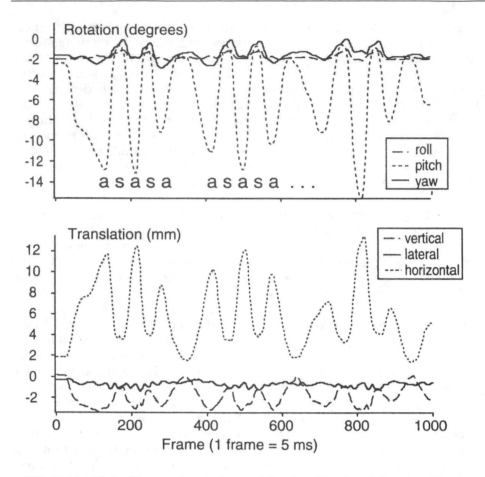

FIG. 19.13.   Plots of jaw rotation, in degrees (above) and jaw translation, in millimeters (below) during pronunciations of /asasa/. From Vatikiotis-Bateson and Ostry (1995, p. 108, Fig. 5).

The optical tracking technique has also been used to study the development of control, by young children, of the jaw, upper lip, and lower lip in the achievement of a consonant closure (Green, Moore, Higashikawa, & Steeve, 2000; Green, Moore, & Reilly, 2000). Among other things, Green and his associates found that young children tend not to be able to control the upper and lower lips separately, but to treat them as a single unit (Gibbon, 1999, proposed a similar pattern of development with respect to control of the front and back of the tongue.) And Harrington, Fletcher, and Roberts (1995), used the technique in a study of coarticulation, which is the topic of the next section.

DYNAMICS OF SPEECH: COARTICULATION

In speech, as in any well-learned physical activity, the articulators move smoothly and fluently, rather than lurching in a staccato fashion from one target to the next. This is achieved by the overlapping of gestures. While implementing the current target, the articulators are still finishing the previous one and they are also getting ready for the next one. This overlapping is called *coarticulation*.

Describing and explaining coarticulation lies at the heart of an explanation of the process of speech production. Speech without any coarticulation would not sound much like speech at all. Speech with too much coarticulation would lose intelligibility. However, the nature and extent to which any particular sequence of gestures overlaps is liable to vary from one language/accent to another, from one speaker to another, and from one speaking style to another.

Measurement of airflow through the nose and through the mouth has been used in several studies to investigate nasal coarticulation. Zajac et al. (1998), for example, used a divided face mask, with airflow measurement instrumentation mounted on it, to measure the airflow through the nose and compare it with the airflow through the mouth. Twenty American English-speaking subjects pronounced the nonsense word /ini/. All but one subject showed significant nasal airflow by the midpoint of the first vowel. This demonstrates *anticipatory coarticulation*; in this case anticipation of the velar lowering gesture required for the /n/ was made during the preceding vowel. In all subjects, air was still flowing through the nose at the midpoint of the second vowel. This is an example of *carryover coarticulation*. Many studies of coarticulation have included the investigation of factors such as language or accent differences or speaking rate or syllable stress or speaker age or speaker sex. The Zajac et al. study found no significant difference in nasal coarticulation between the men and women among their subjects. However, the subjects were also asked to stress the word /ini/ in two different ways: with equal stress on the two syllables and with greater stress on the second syllable. Their results showed evidence that when the second vowel was stressed there was less coarticulation, both anticipatory and carryover.

Nasal coarticulation, of the sort just described, is a cost-free means of making the process of speech production easier, for English speakers. Unlike French, for example, which has nasalized versus non-nasalized vowels, there are no nasalized vowel phonemes in English, to contrast with non-nasalized vowels. Therefore, by opening the velum during a vowel, there is no danger of signaling to the listener a different word to that which the speaker intends. Many English speakers obviously feel that some nasalization doesn't much compromise the "i-ness of /i/." However, absence of contrast is apparently not a reliable predictor of presence of coarticulation, among speakers of different languages (see Manuel, 1999, for a review of the evidence on this).

In the production of some consonants, the precise posture of the lips is not crucial. For a /s/, for example, as in "sun," it is necessary for the lips to be open sufficiently for the air to flow freely through them. Beyond that, they are fairly free to adopt a shape convenient to the wider phonetic context. In a syllable /si/, for example, as in "sea," they can start moving to the spread position required for the following /i/. In a syllable /su/, on the other hand, as in "Sue," they can start adopting the protruded and rounded posture required for the following /u/. There is little risk of a listener failing to identify the /s/ correctly as a result of the modest acoustic modifications that result from lip rounding/spreading. A similar observation might be made for nasalization of the /s/. If, in the word "snow," for example, the velum were to open during the /s/, in anticipation of the /n/, this would be unlikely to interfere with the perception of an /s/ by the listener. However, in this instance, anticipatory nasal coarticulation would be a disadvantage to the speaker. It is difficult to sustain enough airflow through the mouth to maintain frication, when air is leaking through the nose. And frication may be considered an essential characteristic of an /s/ sound and so it cannot be sacrificed (although the phonetics literature does not provide well-established criteria for distinguishing "essential" from "nonessential" phonetic characteristics of different phonemes).

Anticipatory coarticulation in a consonant–vowel sequence in which the consonant is a bilabial stop is a prime example of convenient and cost-free coarticulation. In the sequence /ipi/, for example, as might occur in the word "sleepy," during the closure of the /p/, there is no sound and the tongue is not involved, because it is a bilabial consonant. So during the closure, the tongue is free to adopt any position. Figure 19.14 shows tongue shapes during pronunciations of the nonsense forms /ipi/ and /apa/, extracted from ultrasound images. They confirm that, during the bilabial consonant, tongue posture remains similar to that for the vowel either side.

Sometimes, coarticulation produces a compromise between the gesture for one sound and the gesture required for the next, where both gestures involve the same articulator. The sequence /sʃ/, as in "this shoe," /ðɪs ʃu/, is an example. To make a good /s/, the tip or blade of the tongue moves near the alveolar ridge to create a narrow slit, with the body somewhat grooved along its length. Then, for the /ʃ/, it retracts and the body is raised and flattened. Nolan, Holst, and Kühnert (1996) analyzed a number of /sʃ/ sequences, by two speakers,

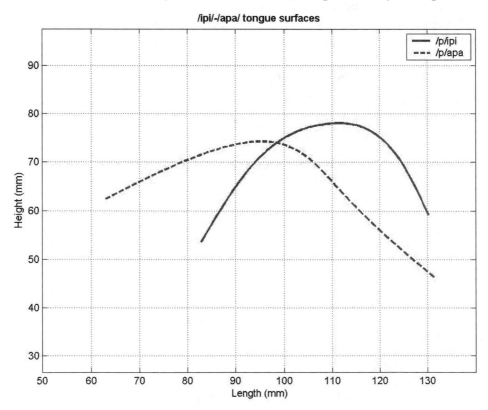

FIG. 19.14.   Tongue surface shapes during the /p/ of /ipi/ (solid line) and /apa/ (dashed line).

using a combination of acoustic and EPG analysis. In some cases, there were two distinct phases to be observed, the first corresponding to the /s/ and the second to the /ʃ/. In others, the two gestures overlapped, to a greater or lesser extent, with a place of articulation that was a compromise between the two. This type of coarticulation is often called *blending*. However, in yet other cases there was no evidence of any s-like articulation: [ðɪʃ ʃu]. Where, as in this latter example, one sound becomes completely identical to another, the process is more often called *assimilation*, rather than coarticulation. Transcribing the utterance [ðɪʃu] (usually on the basis of short fricative duration) would imply that there is no phonetic evidence of the /s/, transformed or not, which is a case of *deletion*. Alveolar consonants, given an appropriate context, are particularly prone to these processes and EPG has proved useful for investigating them (see, e.g., Ellis & Hardcastle, 2002).

We have probably given the impression that coarticulation is confined to adjacent pairs of sounds but this is not the case. In a classic early work on coarticulation, from which many further investigations have followed, Öhman (1966) demonstrated that one vowel may influence another vowel across an intervening consonant, in a sequence of vowel-consonant-vowel. And several studies (e.g., Sussman & Westbury, 1981) have shown that in a syllable that contains a rounded vowel and begins with a consonant cluster, as in "screw," lip-rounding in anticipation of the vowel may be observed even on the first consonant.

We may also have given the impression that coarticulation is solely an advantage for the speaker and detrimental to the interests of the listener. Certainly, insofar as coarticulation reduces the contrastiveness among speech sounds, it seems unhelpful to a listener (indeed, the opposite interests of listener and speaker, in this respect, form the basis of Lindblom's, 1990, theory of speech production). However, in an example like the one of anticipatory labial coarticulation, just described, the rounding of the preceding consonants can provide a useful cue to the listener about the identity of the upcoming vowel.

This issue in turn prompts consideration of the nature of the units that form the input to the speech production process, in the speaker's brain. We have assumed that they correspond in size to the segments symbolized in a phonetic transcription (although what their content is is another question). Most people (especially those who have used an alphabetic writing system) seem to feel comfortable with the notion of segment- or phoneme-sized units but it must be admitted that positive, hard evidence to support it remains sparse. As in chapter 16 (see its introductory section), we merely identify this issue, without pursuing it further.

EXERCISES

1. Six muscles are listed. State the organ (lips, tongue, or soft palate) to which each belongs.

   a. superior longitudinal
   b. orbicularis oris
   c. genioglossus
   d. levator veli palatini
   e. risorius
   f. hyoglossus

2. State the approximate, probable time-point of (a) the /l/ of "yell," and (b) the /w/ of "worry," on Fig. 19.9. In each case, give reasons for your answer.
3. Figure 19.15 shows EPG records taken from Recasens, Pallares, and Fontdevila (1997). In the left column of the figure, the EPG frames are from the middle of the consonant closure/constriction when the consonant was uttered between two /i/ vowels. In the right column, the records are from the middle of the consonant closure/constriction when the consonant was uttered between two /a/ vowels. For example, the frame at the top of the right-hand column shows the EPG contact pattern during the /l/ in /ala/.

   a. Compare the EPG pattern in the /i/ context and the EPG pattern in the /a/ context, for each consonant, and explain the differences as being coarticulation with the adjacent vowels, where possible. (Look ahead to question 3b before answering this question.)
   b. In the case of one consonant, the differences between the /i/ context and the /a/ context cannot be explained by the articulatory characteristics of the vowels. Which consonant is this?

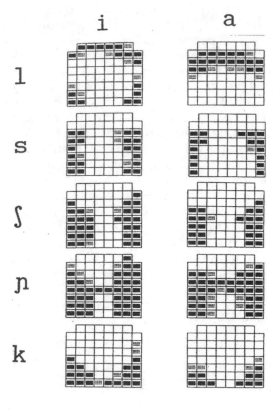

FIG. 19.15. Electropalatographic records showing the pattern of contact of the tongue against the hard palate during the consonant closure in utterances of /ili/, /ala/; /isi/, /asa/; /ishi/, /asha/; /inji/, /anja/; /iki/, /aka/. Reprinted with permission from D. Recasens, M. D. Pallares, & J. Fontdevila, *The Journal of the Acoustical Society of America*, 102, 547 (1997). Copyright 1997, Acoustical Society of America.

Appendix A
The International Phonetic Alphabet

THE INTERNATIONAL PHONETIC ALPHABET (revised to 1993)

CONSONANTS (PULMONIC)

	Bilabial	Labiodental	Dental	Alveolar	Postalveolar	Retroflex	Palatal	Velar	Uvular	Pharyngeal	Glottal
Plosive	p b			t d		ʈ ɖ	c ɟ	k g	q ɢ		ʔ
Nasal	m	ɱ		n		ɳ	ɲ	ŋ	N		
Trill	ʙ			r					R		
Tap or Flap				ɾ		ɽ					
Fricative	ɸ β	f v	θ ð	s z	ʃ ʒ	ʂ ʐ	ç ʝ	x ɣ	χ ʁ	ħ ʕ	h ɦ
Lateral fricative				ɬ ɮ							
Approximant		ʋ		ɹ		ɻ	j	ɰ			
Lateral approximant				l		ɭ	ʎ	ʟ			

Where symbols appear in pairs, the one to the right represents a voiced consonant. Shaded areas denote articulations judged impossible.

CONSONANTS (NON-PULMONIC)

Clicks		Voiced implosives		Ejectives	
ʘ	Bilabial	ɓ	Bilabial	'	as in:
ǀ	Dental	ɗ	Dental/alveolar	p'	Bilabial
ǃ	(Post)alveolar	ʄ	Palatal	t'	Dental/alveolar
ǂ	Palatoalveolar	ɠ	Velar	k'	Velar
ǁ	Alveolar lateral	ʛ	Uvular	s'	Alveolar fricative

SUPRASEGMENTALS

ˈ	Primary stress	ˌfoʊnəˈtɪʃən
ˌ	Secondary stress	
ː	Long	eː
ˑ	Half-long	eˑ
˘	Extra-short	ĕ
.	Syllable break	ɹi.ækt
|	Minor (foot) group	
‖	Major (intonation) group	
‿	Linking (absence of a break)	

TONES & WORD ACCENTS

	LEVEL			CONTOUR	
e̋	or ˥	Extra high	ě	or ˄	Rising
é	˦	High	ê	˅	Falling
ē	˧	Mid	e᷄		High rising
è	˨	Low	e᷅		Low rising
ȅ	˩	Extra low	e᷈		Rising-falling
					etc.
↓	Downstep		↗	Global rise	
↑	Upstep		↘	Global fall	

VOWELS

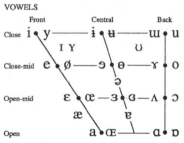

Where symbols appear in pairs, the one to the right represents a rounded vowel.

OTHER SYMBOLS

ʍ Voiceless labial-velar fricative
w Voiced labial-velar approximant
ɥ Voiced labial-palatal approximant
ʜ Voiceless epiglottal fricative
ʢ Voiced epiglottal fricative
ʡ Epiglottal plosive

ɕ ʑ Alveolo-palatal fricatives
ɺ Alveolar lateral flap
ɧ Simultaneous ʃ and x

Affricates and double articulations can be represented by two symbols joined by a tie bar if necessary.

k͡p t͡s

DIACRITICS

Diacritics may be placed above a symbol with a descender, e.g. ŋ̊

̥	Voiceless	n̥ d̥	̤	Breathy voiced	b̤ a̤	̪	Dental	t̪ d̪
̬	Voiced	s̬ t̬	̰	Creaky voiced	b̰ a̰	̺	Apical	t̺ d̺
ʰ	Aspirated	tʰ dʰ	̼	Linguolabial	t̼ d̼	̻	Laminal	t̻ d̻
̹	More rounded	ɔ̹	ʷ	Labialized	tʷ dʷ	̃	Nasalized	ẽ
̜	Less rounded	ɔ̜	ʲ	Palatalized	tʲ dʲ	ⁿ	Nasal release	dⁿ
̟	Advanced	u̟	ˠ	Velarized	tˠ dˠ	ˡ	Lateral release	dˡ
̠	Retracted	i̠	ˤ	Pharyngealized	tˤ dˤ	̚	No audible release	d̚
̈	Centralized	ë	̴	Velarized or pharyngealized	ɫ			
̽	Mid-centralized	e̽	̝	Raised	e̝ (ɹ̝ = voiced alveolar fricative)			
̩	Syllabic	l̩	̞	Lowered	e̞ (β̞ = voiced bilabial approximant)			
̯	Non-syllabic	e̯	̘	Advanced Tongue Root	e̘			
˞	Rhoticity	ɚ	̙	Retracted Tongue Root	e̙			

309

Appendix B
The International Phonetic Alphabet:
Extended Set of Symbols

ExtIPA SYMBOLS FOR DISORDERED SPEECH
(Revised to 1997)

CONSONANTS (other than those on the IPA Chart)

	bilabial	labiodental	dentolabial	labioalv.	linguolabial	interdental	bidental	alveolar	velar	velophar.
Plosive		p̪ b̪	p̪ b̪	p̪ b̪	t̼ d̼	t̪ d̪				
Nasal			m̪	m̪	n̼	n̪				
Trill					r̼	r̪				
Fricative: central		f̪ v̪	f̪ v̪	θ ð	θ̪ ð̪	ħ ħ				ʩ
Fricative: lateral+central								ʪ ʫ		
Fricative: nareal	m̰							n̰	ŋ̰	
Percussive	w̰ w					n̰				
Approximant: lateral					l̼	l̪				

DIACRITICS

↔	labial spreading	s̫		strong articulation	f̎		⌁ denasal		m̃
″	dentolabial	v̼	˻	weak articulation	v̠		⌁ nasal escape		v̰
″	interdental/bidental	n̪	\	reiterated articulation	p\p\p		˷ velopharyngeal friction		s̰
=	alveolar	t̲	◆	whistled articulation	s̍		↓ ingressive airflow		p↓
˷	linguolabial	d̼	→	sliding articulation	θs̠		↑ egressive airflow		ǃ↑

CONNECTED SPEECH

(.)	short pause
(..)	medium pause
(...)	long pause
f	loud speech [{f lɑʊd f}]
ff	louder speech [{ff lɑʊdə ff}]
p	quiet speech [{p kwaɪət p}]
pp	quieter speech [{pp kwaɪətə pp}]
allegro	fast speech [{allegro fɑːst allegro}]
lento	slow speech [{ lento slɔʊ lento}]
crescendo, ralentando, etc. may also be used	

VOICING

ˬ	pre-voicing	ˬz
ˬ	post-voicing	zˬ
(ₒ)	partial devoicing	(z̧)
(ₒ	initial partial devoicing	(z̧
ₒ)	final partial devoicing	z̧)
(ᵥ)	partial voicing	(s̬)
(ᵥ	initial partial voicing	(s̬
ᵥ)	final partial voicing	s̬)
=	unaspirated	p=
ʰ	pre-aspiration	ʰp

OTHERS

(‾) indeterminate sound	(( )) extraneous noise ((2 sylls))
(V̄), (Pl) indeterminate vowel, plosive, etc.	¡ sublaminal lower alveolar percussive click
(Pl,vls) indeterminate voiceless plosive, etc.	ǃ¡ alveolar & sublaminal click ('cluck-click')
( ) silent articulation (ʃ), (m)	* sound with no available symbol

© 1997 ICPLA   Reproduced by permission of the International Clinical Phonetics & Linguistics Association.

Appendix C
Answers to Exercises

Note. For those exercises that involve measurements on figures, the answers given here should be regarded as approximate.

Chapter 6

1. See Table E.1.

2.
    a. = b);
    b. = a);
    c. = c);
    d. = b);
    e. = c);
    f. = a)

3.
    a. [l̪];
    b. [s̺];
    c. [B];
    d. [ħ];
    e. [b̪];
    f. [n̪];
    g. [ʁ];
    h. [ɽ]

4.
    a. a voiced pharyngeal fricative
    b. a voiced uvular implosive
    c. a bilabial click
    d. A voiced pharyngeal plosive
    e. a voiced linguolabial nasal (stop)
    f. a voiceless palatal ejective
    g. a voiced bilabial fricative
    h. a voiced palatal nasal stop

Chapter 8

2. 460 ms (tie), 530 ms (die).

TABLE E.1

Place of Articulation	Active Articulator	Passive Articulator
a) Labiodental	lower lip	upper teeth
b) Pharyngeal	root of tongue	pharyngeal walls
c) Linguolabial	tip or blade of tongue	upper lip
d) Dentolabial	upper lip	lower teeth
e) Retroflex	under-surface of tongue	front of hard palate
f) Labioalveolar	lower lip	alveolar ridge
g) Bidental	lower teeth	upper teeth

3. 30 ms.

4. 20 ms.

5.
    a. w = periodic, i = periodic, s = random, k^h = quiescent + transient + random.
    b. 200 ms.
    c. 80 ms.
    d. 80 ms.
    e.
        i. 2.6 words/second.
        ii 2.6 syllables/second.
        iii 5.8 segments/second.

6. Yes.

Chapter 9

1.
    a. 100 Hz.
    b. 500 Hz.
    c. 111 Hz.
    d. 67 Hz.
    e. 77 Hz.
    f. 125 Hz.
    g. 250 Hz.
    h. 105 Hz.
    i. 1000 Hz.
    j. 154 Hz.

2. Male.

3.
    a. The first vowel, [i], must have had the higher f_0, because the periods of the cycles are shorter.
    b. 170 Hz. (There are 17 cycles in the interval of 100 ms. Therefore $T = 100/17 = 5.9$ ms and $f_0 = 1000/5.9 = 170$ Hz.)
    c. Female.

4.
    a. 0.0056 s.
    b. 0.0111 s.
    c. 0.0048 s.
    d. 0.0067 s.
    e. 0.0020 s.
    f. 0.0125 s.
    g. 0.0027 s.
    h. 0.0081 s.
    i. 0.0019 s.
    j. 0.0010 s.

    k. 0.0021 s.
    l. 0.0118 s.

5.
    a. 200 Hz (P).
    b. 1 Hz (I).
    c. 0.5 Hz (I).
    d. 2 Hz (I).
    e. 385 Hz (P).
    f. 111 Hz (P).
    g. 1000 Hz (P).
    h. 1250 Hz (P).
    i. 10000 Hz (I).
    j. 0.2 Hz (I).
    k. 20000 Hz (I).
    l. 67 Hz (P).

6. 53 semitones.

7. The female group (male range = 33.89 semitones, female range = 33.99 semitones).

Chapter 10

1. See Table E.2.

2. 140 dB SPL.

3.
    a. You would expect to see less rapid deterioration in the child's performance as the S/N ratio reduces.
    b. B.

TABLE E.2   **Pressure Ratios and Corresponding Decibel Values**

P/Po	dB
1	0
2	6
10	20
20	26
100	40
50000	94
178000	106
14200000	144
0.5	–6
0.00023	–72

   c. No, it wasn't carelessness. In the case of a decibel value expressing a Signal-to-Noise ratio, the reference amplitude is the amplitude of the noise.

   d. It means the signal had an amplitude 1.8 times less than the noise.

Chapter 11

1.
   a. F.
   b. T.
   c. F.
   d. T.
   e. T.
   f. T.
   g. T.
   h. F.
   i. F.
   j. F.
   k. F.
   l. T.
   m. F.
   n. T.
   o. F.

2. 590 Hz.

3. 100 Hz.

4. 279 Hz.

5. See Fig. E.1.

6. 185 Hz.

7. See Fig. E.2.

Chapter 12

1. Figure 12.11, Macbeth [məkbɛθ]. Figure 12.12, Hamlet [hamlɪt]. Figure 12.13, Romeo and Juliet [roʊmioʊndʒuliɛt]. Figure 12.14, Julius Caesar [dʒuliəssizə]. Figure 12.15, The Merchant of Venice [ðəmɜtʃəntʰəvvɛnɪs].

2. 20 ms.

3. 128 Hz.

4. 2050 Hz and 1150 Hz, respectively.

5. F3 remains high.

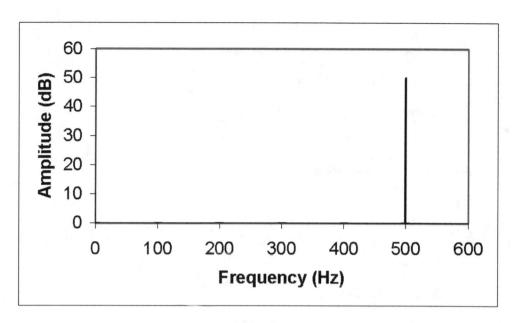

FIG. E.1.   Line spectrum of a sine wave of frequency 500 Hz and amplitude 50 dB.

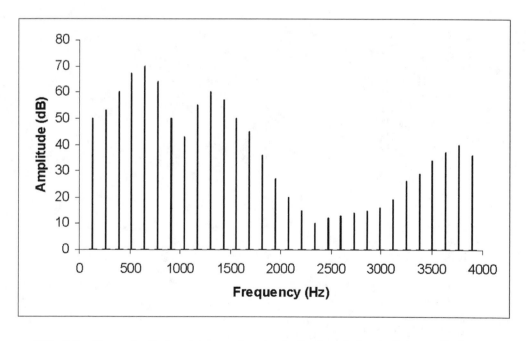

FIG. E.2.   Example of a spectrum conforming to the description in Exercise 7 of chapter 11.

6. The presence of a voice bar.

Chapter 13

1. Outer ear, middle ear, inner ear.

2. The cochlea.

3. C.

4. 30 dB SPL (see Fig. 13.3).

5. 6 dB.

6. 0.0176 ms.

7. 178 degrees.

8. 358 degrees and 182 degrees.

Chapter 14

1.
   a. Yes.
   b. No.
   c. Yes.
   d. 100 dB SPL.
   e. 20 kHz.
   f.
      i. 10 dB HL;
      ii. 23 dB HL;
      iii. 34 dB HL;
      iv. 31 dB HL;
      v. 30 dB HL;
      vi. 58 dB HL.

2.
   a. F.
   b. T.
   c. F.
   d. T.
   e. T.
   f. T.
   g. F.

3. About 17 dB SPL.

Chapter 15

1. Pitch detection by the human hearing system is uncertain and unreliable above about 5 kHz.

2. 115 Hz.

3. Both statements are true.

4.
   a. H8, H9.
   b. H8, H9.
   c. H8, H9.
   d. H8, H9.
   e. H9, H10.

Chapter 16

1.
   a. See Fig. E.3.
   b. 28%.
   c. About 71 ms.
   d. Yes.
   e. For example, the pair 20ms, 50 ms (within-category) and the pair 50 ms, 80 ms (across-category), would be suitable.
   f. See Fig. E.4.
   g. See Fig. E.5.

Chapter 17

1. See Table E.3.

2. See Table E.4.

3.
   a. Fourth.
   b. Eleventh.
   c. Nineteenth.

4. 3278 Hz.

5. F1 = 886 Hz, F2 = 1326 Hz.

6. F1 = 255 Hz, F2 = 1967 Hz.

Chapter 19

1.
   a. Tongue.
   b. Lips.
   c. Tongue.
   d. Soft palate.
   e. Lips.
   f. Tongue.

2.

  a. 1.16 seconds. Reasons: The tongue tip is stationary at this moment and it is at its highest point. This suggests it is raised momentarily against the alveolar ridge, as for an /l/.

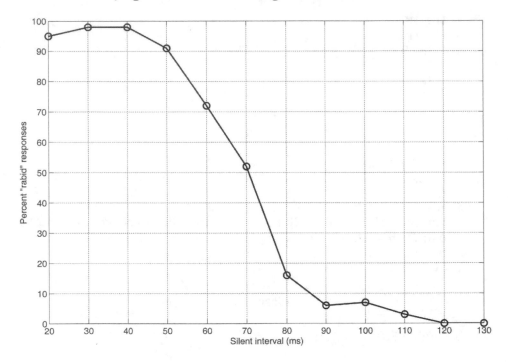

FIG. E.3.   Number of "rabid" responses plotted against duration of silent interval.

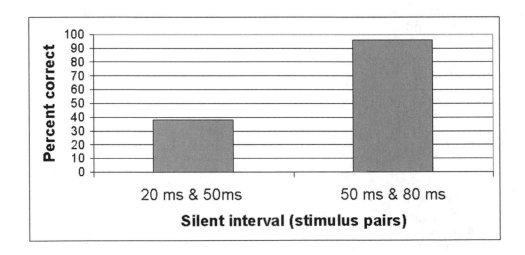

FIG. E.4.   Example of hypothetical results of a discrimination test between stimulus pairs, suggesting categorical perception.

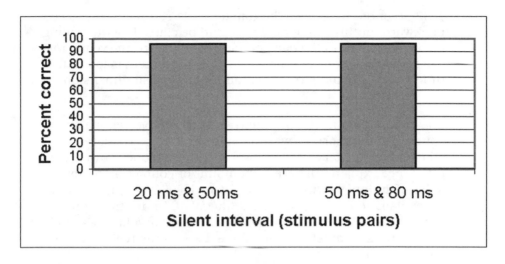

FIG. E.5. Example of hypthetical results of a discrimination test between stimulus pairs, suggesting non-categorical perception.

TABLE E.3   First Six Resonances of the Vowel [ə]

Formant number	Tube length: wavelength	Wavelength (cm)	Period (s)	Frequency (Hz)
1	1:4	70.8	0.002	500
2	3:4	23.6	0.0006667	1500
3	5:4	14.16	0.0004	2500
4	7:4	10.11429	0.0002857	3500
5	9:4	7.86667	0.0002222	4500
6	11:4	6.43636	0.0001818	5500

TABLE E.4   First Three Resonances of the Vowel [ə] (child's vocal tract)

Formant number	Tube length: wavelength	Wavelength (cm)	Period (s)	Frequency (Hz)
1	1:4	46.4	0.0013107	763
2	3:4	15.466667	0.0004369	2289
3	5:4	9.28	0.0002621	3815

b. 1.32 seconds. Reasons: The tongue tip is retracted (displaced backward) at this moment. This could be caused by the pulling back and raising of the back of the tongue toward the velum (/w/ is a labial-velar sound). The speed of its movement is low at this time and it is in a neutral position in the vertical dimension.

3.

a. /ili/, /ala/: /i/ is a front vowel and /a/ is a back vowel, which accounts for the more forward closure in /ili/ as compared with /ala/. /isi/, /asa/: /i/ is a close vowel and /a/ is an open vowel. This difference explains the greater amount of contact made by the sides of the tongue with the hard palate, in /isi/. /iʃi/, /aʃa/: A similar explanation as for /isi/, /asa/. /iki/, /aka/: Under the influence of the back vowel, /a/, the closure for the /k/ in /aka/ was made further back, against the soft palate, beyond the region covered by the EPG palate.

b. /ɲ/.

GLOSSARY

abduction (abducted) Pulling apart (of the vocal folds)

acoustic cue A term in speech perception. An acoustic property of a phoneme that appears to be important for its identification by listeners.

adduction (adducted) Bringing together (of the vocal folds).

airstream mechanism Method for generating a flow of air through the vocal tract.

allophone A member of a set of sounds that all belong to the same phoneme. For example, in English, the sound [pʰ] as in "pill" and the sound [p] as in "spill," are allophones of the same phoneme, written /p/.

anechoic A very well sound-insulated studio with no internal sound reflections.

aperiodic Waveforms that have no repeating cycle. Cover term for all **random, transient**, and **quiescent** waves.

articulation The actions of the speech organs, above the larynx, during speech.

articulation rate Quantity of speech per unit time, excluding pauses. Usually measured in syllables/second.

articulatory gesture A movement made by a speech organ in the pronunciation of a phoneme. Alternatively, a combination of movements of several speech organs in the pronunciation of a phoneme.

assimilation A substitution of one phoneme by another, under the influence of an adjacent phoneme.

audiogram A graph for recording a person's hearing thresholds, in decibels referenced to **Hearing Level**, across a range of frequencies.

bandwidth The range of frequencies passed by a **filter**.

Bernoulli effect Pressure upon the walls of an aperture, resulting from a pressure drop within the aperture, as caused by a flow of air through the glottis.

binaural hearing Hearing with two ears.

bone conduction Transmission of sound through the bones of the skull.

breathiness Vocal fold vibration with incomplete closure of the folds, allowing air leakage.

Cardinal vowel A vowel quality used as a reference, according to the Cardinal Vowel system.

categorical perception A number of stimuli, lying along a continuum, are each consistently and strongly perceived as belonging to either one or another of two categories. Within the same category, discrimination among the stimuli is poor.

characteristic frequency The **frequency** to which a given auditory neuron is most sensitive.

coarticulation Overlap in the articulation of adjacent, or near-adjacent, phonemes.

complex tone A term used most often to describe complex periodic sounds when these are used as stimuli in experiments on hearing.

complex wave A wave containing energy at more than one **frequency**, that is, any wave that is not a **sine wave**.

conductive hearing loss Hearing loss resulting from problems in the outer or middle ear.

creak Very low frequency vocal fold vibration. Each cycle can be heard separately.

decibel The logarithm, multiplied by 20, of the ratio of two **sound pressure amplitudes**. (Alternatively: The logarithm, multiplied by 10, of the ratio of two sound **intensities**.)

declination A tendency for **fundamental frequency** to fall over the time-course of an utterance.

dynamic range (of voice) The range from greatest to least sound pressure amplitudes.

end correction A term from the theory of tube **resonance**. The effective length of the tube is slightly longer than the actual length, for the purpose of calculating resonant frequencies.

equal loudness contour A graph of amplitude over frequency, for a series of sounds, all of which have been judged of similar **loudness** in perception experiments.

equivalent rectangular bandwidth (ERB) A device used for expressing the **bandwidths** of auditory **filters**. The bandwidth of a rectangular filter, which has the same center frequency as the auditory filter of interest and that passes the same power.

extrinsic muscles (tongue) Muscles of the tongue that attach to structures outside the tongue.

falsetto High pitched vibration, in which the vocal folds are under high longitudinal tension.

filter A device (natural or artificial, mechanical or electrical) that suppresses energy outside a certain range (band) of frequencies.

formant A **resonance** of the vocal tract.

frequency Property of **periodic waveforms**, namely the rate at which the cycle repeats in time. Usually measured in cycles/second, for which the standard term is Hertz (Hz).

fundamental frequency The frequency at which the cycle of a complex wave repeats in time.

General American An accent of the United States, with wide geographic distribution across that country.

glottal spectrum Spectrum of the sound made by the action of the vocal folds, in isolation.

harmonic A **sine wave** component of a complex periodic wave.

harshness Irregular vocal fold vibration.

hearing level (HL) The average threshold of hearing (at the frequency of interest) of young adults, according to an internationally agreed standard.

hydrostat A volume of water contained by a flexible skin.

incident wave Wave traveling outward, away from its source.

intensity Power per unit area, usually measured in watts/m^2. The power delivered to a "window" positioned at right angles to the direction of propagation of the wave.

interaural level difference A term from the study of hearing. The difference in the sound pressure amplitude of a sound wave between one ear and the other.

interaural time difference A term from the study of hearing. The difference in time of arrival of a sound wave between one ear and the other.

intrinsic muscles (tongue) Muscles that are contained within the body of the tongue.

inversion An important feature of tube **resonance**. A switch from positive to negative pressure, or vice versa, which occurs at the open end of a tube.

lateral (sound) Speech sound in which air flows around the sides of the tongue, as in [l].

locus The apparent frequency origin of a formant, judged from its trajectory.

logarithm The logarithm of a number is the power to which 10 must be raised in order to equal that number. For example, the logarithm of 100 is 2, because $100 = 10^2$. (Note. Other bases besides 10 are sometimes used.)

loudness Perceptual property, related (mainly) to the **sound pressure amplitude** of a sound.

manner of articulation Degree of constriction and/or configuration of the tongue, during the production of a speech sound.

masking Experimental technique used in the study of hearing. Rendering one sound (usually a **pure tone**) inaudible due to the introduction of another sound.

mel scale A scale of **pitch**, constructed from the results of an experiment using **pure tone** stimuli.

middle ear reflex A tightening of the muscles of the middle ear in response to a sound of large magnitude.

modal voce Full vocal fold vibration, with the vocal muscles under moderate tension.

nasal (sound) A sound produced with the velum open, so that air may flow through the nose.

nasal stop A **stop** produced with the velum open.

octave A doubling of frequency.

oral stop See **plosive**.

oro-nasal process Opening and closing action of the soft palate, which determines whether or not air flows though the nose.

period The duration of a single cycle of a periodic wave.

periodic A type of waveform that has a repeating cycle.

phase The time alignment of a wave. Two sine waves may have identical frequency and peak amplitude but still differ in phase, in which case their positive amplitude peaks, for example, will never coincide.

phase locking Property of the hearing mechanism, in which a neuron fires at the same point in successive cycles of a stimulus sound.

phon scale A scale of loudness, constructed from **equal loudness contours**.

phonation The action of the vocal folds in generating a sound source for speech.

phoneme A sound-type that acts as a contrastive unit in the language under consideration. For example, [t] sounds and [d] sounds are used to distinguish one word from another in English (compare "tie" and "die"), so the sounds belong to different phonemes, written /t/ and /d/.

phonetogram A graph showing the **dynamic range** of a person's voice, across their **fundamental frequency** range.

phonology The study of sound patterns of individual languages. An area of linguistics.

pitch Perceptual property, related (mainly) to the fundamental frequency of a sound.

place of articulation Location of a stricture between two articulators, in the production of a speech sound.

place theory A theory of hearing in which frequency is resolved according to the location of a peak of displacement along the basilar membrane.

plosive A **stop** produced with **velic closure**.

psychoacoustics Study of the auditory effects resulting from modulations of the acoustic signal.

pure tone A **sine wave**, used as a stimulus in a hearing experiment.

quality Perceptual property, related (mainly) to the shape of the spectrum of a sound.

quiescent A term used in this book to describe a straight-line waveform, which occurs during a silent interval.

random A type of waveform that has chaotic variations of high and low pressure, with no repeating cycle.

recruitment Clinical condition of hearing, in which the threshold of hearing is raised but, above threshold, sensitivity increases very rapidly with increasing amplitude.

resonance Enhancement of the amplitude, at a certain frequency or frequencies, of a sound wave, due to its encounter with a structure in its path. See also **formant**.

roll-off Property of a spectrum: a reduction in amplitude with rising frequency. Typically measured in dB/ocatve.

RP Received Pronunciation. An accent of the United Kingdom, especially England, mainly associated with high social class.

segment A speech sound within a continuous utterance. Use of the term implies no commitment on the question of the status of the stretch of sound concerned but it usually corresponds in size to a phoneme.

semitone The twelfth part of an octave. An octave is divided into 12 semitones.

sensorineural hearing loss Hearing loss resulting from problems in the cochlea or the auditory brainstem.

signal-to-noise-ratio The **sound pressure amplitude** of the signal divided by the sound pressure amplitude of the noise, where the noise is unwanted sound and the signal is wanted sound.

sine wave A wave in which the sound pressure amplitude varies over time in a sinusoidal fashion. A sine wave has energy at only a single **frequency**. (cf. **complex wave**.)

sound pressure amplitude Usually measured in Pascals (Pa). The sound pressure amplitude of a sound pressure wave is constantly varying, so measurement is made either of the instantaneous pressure or the root mean square (RMS) pressure, that is, the pressure averaged over time.

sound pressure level (SPL) A pressure of 0.00002 Pascals. A standard reference in the measurement of sound magnitude.

sound wave Alternations of pressure, transmitted through a medium (air, in the usual case), which are audible to the human ear.

source-filter model Model of speech production. Vocal fold or other action provides a source of sound energy, which is modulated according to the shape and dimensions of the vocal tract.

speaking rate Quantity of speech per unit time, including pauses. Usually measured in syllables/second.

spectrogram A three-dimensional graph of frequency, time, and amplitude, the latter being represented by degree of darkening on the page/screen.

spectrum A graph of amplitude over **frequency**.

stop (sound) A sound produced with a complete closure such that air is prevented from flowing out from the mouth.

temporal theory A theory of hearing in which frequency is resolved according to the rate of firing of an auditory neuron.

timbre Perceptual property, related (mainly) to the shape of the spectrum of the sound. Used exclusively of periodic sounds and especially of musical notes. See also **quality**.

tone A pitch phoneme. When two words, otherwise similar in form, are distinguished by the pitch on which they are spoken, the pitches are called tones.

(Note: In this usage, tone has a different meaning from that in **pure tone** and **complex tone**.)

trading relations A feature of speech perception. A reduction in the value of one **acoustic cue** may be compensated by an increase in the value of another.

transfer function Specification of the changes made by a system to sound waves that enter it.

transient A sound that occurs at the release of a stop closure. It has a waveform that decays rapidly.

virtual pitch Pitch of a sound that has a missing fundamental.

voice onset time (VOT) The interval between the release of a stop consonant closure and the onset of vocal fold vibration, where the sound following the stop is voiced.

voicing Vibration of the vocal folds.

waveform A graph showing how the amplitude of a wave varies with time. The waveform is the graph and the wave is the physical event. Where the distinction is not crucial, the two terms are sometimes used interchangeably (i.e., inconsistently!) in this book.

wavelength The distance, in space, over which a single cycle of a periodic waveform is completed. For example, if the wave cycle contains a single pressure peak, the wavelength could be measured as the distance between two successive peaks.

whisper Fricative noise created at the vocal folds.

REFERENCES

Abercrombie, D. (1967). *Elements of general phonetics*. Edinburgh, Scotland: Edinburgh University Press.

Aibara, R., Welsh, J. T., Puria, S., & Goode, R. L. (2001). Human middle-ear sound transfer function and cochlear input impedance. *Hearing Research, 152,* 100–109.

Atkinson, M., & McHanwell, S. (2002). *Basic medical science for speech and language therapy students*. London: Whurr.

Awan, S. N. (1991). Phonetographic profiles and the F0-SPL characteristics of untrained versus trained vocal groups. *Journal of Voice, 5,* 41–50.

Baken, R. J., & Daniloff, R. G. (1991) (Eds.). *Readings in clinical spectrography of speech*. San Diego, CA: Singular.

Baken, R. J., & Orlikoff, R. F. (2000). *Clinical measurement of speech and voice*. San Diego, CA: Singular.

Barlow, S. M., Cole, K. J., & Abbs, J. H. (1983). A new head mounted lip–jaw movement transduction system for the study of motor speech disorders. *Journal of Speech and Hearing Research, 26,* 283–288.

Bauer, L. (1985). Tracing phonetic change in the Received Pronunciation of British English. *Journal of Phonetics, 13,* 61–81.

Beckman, M. (1996). The parsing of prosody. In P. Warren (Ed.), *Prosody and parsing* (pp. 17–67). Hove, England: Psychology Press. (Special edition of *Language and Cognitive Processes, 11,* issues 1 and 2.)

van den Berg, J. (1958). Myoelastic-aerodynamic theory of voice production. *Journal of Speech and Hearing Research, 1,* 227–244.

van den Berg, J., Vennard, W., Berger, D., & Shervanian, C. C. (1960). *Voice production. The vibrating larynx*. [Film]. Utrecht, Netherlands: SFW-UNFI.

von Békésy, G. (1960). *Experiments in hearing*. New York: McGraw-Hill.

van Bezooyen, R. (1984). *Characteristics and recognisability of vocal expressions of emotion*. Dordrecht, Netherlands: Foris.

Borden, G. J., Harris, K. S., & Raphael, L. J. (2003). *Speech science primer: Physiology, acoustics and perception of speech* (2nd ed.). Philadelphia: Lippincott, Williams & Wilkins.

Bronkhurst, A. W., & Plomp, R. (1988). The effect of head-induced interaural time and level differences on speech intelligibility in noise. *Journal of the Acoustical Society of America, 83,* 1508–1516.

Browman, C. P., & Goldstein, L. (1989). Articulatory gestures as phonological units. *Phonology, 6,* 151–201.

Brown, G. (1990). *Listening to spoken English* (2nd ed.). London: Longman.

Brown, P., & Levinson, S. C. (1987). *Politeness: Some universals in language usage.* Cambridge, England: Cambridge University Press.

Bruel & Kjaer. (1984). *Measuring sound* [Manufacturer's handbook]. Naerum, Denmark: Bruel & Kjaer.

Bryson, B. (2003). *A short history of nearly everything.* London: Transworld.

Carlson, B., Granström, B., & Fant, G. (1970). *Some studies concerning perception of isolated vowels.* (STL Quarterly Progress and Status Report 2–3). Stockholm: Royal Institute of Technology (KTH), Department of Speech Communication.

Carr, P. (1999). *English phonetics and phonology.* Oxford, England: Blackwell.

Coleman, R. F. (1993). Sources of variation in phonetograms. *Journal of Voice, 7,* 1–14.

Colton, R. H., & Casper, J. K. (1996). *Understanding voice problems: A perspective for diagnosis and treatment.* Baltimore: Williams & Wilkins.

Cruttenden, A. (1997). *Intonation* (2nd ed.). Cambridge, England: Cambridge University Press.

Delattre, P. C., Liberman, A. M., & Cooper, F. S. (1955). Acoustic loci and transitional cues for consonants. *Journal of the Acoustical Society of America, 27,* 769–773.

Demolin, D., & Teston, B. (1996). Labiodental flaps in Mangbetu. *Journal of the International Phonetic Association, 26,* 102–111.

Dickson, D. R., & Maue, W. M. (1970). *Human vocal anatomy.* Springfield, IL: Thomas.

Dickson, D. R., & Maue-Dickson, W. M. (1982). *Anatomical and physiological bases of speech.* Boston: Little, Brown.

Docherty, G. J. (1992). *The timing of voicing in British English obstruents.* Berlin, Germany: Foris.

Durrant, J. D., & Lovrinic, J. H. (1995). *Bases of hearing science* (3rd ed.). Baltimore: Williams & Wilkins.

Ellis, L., & Hardcastle, W. H. (2002). Categorical and gradient properties of assimilation in alveolar and velar sequences: Evidence from EPG and EMA data. *Journal of Phonetics, 30,* 373–396.

Engstrand, O., & Krull, D. (1994). Durational correlates of quantity in Swedish, Finnish and Estonian: Cross-language evidence for a theory of adaptive dispersion. *Phonetica, 51,* 80–91.

van Erp, A. J. M. (1991). *The phonetic basis of personality ratings, with specific reference to cleft-palate speech.* Nijmegen, Netherlands: KUN.

Esling, J. H. (1978). *Voice quality in Edinburgh: A sociolinguistic and phonetic study.* Unpublished doctoral dissertation, University of Edinburgh, Scotland.

Esling, J. H. (1999). Voice quality settings of the pharynx. *Proceedings of the 14th International Congress of Phonetic Sciences: Vol. 3* (pp. 2449–2452). Berkeley, CA: University of California.

Fairbanks, G. (1960). *Voice and articulation drillbook* (2nd ed.). New York: Harper.

Fant, G. (1960). *Acoustic theory of speech production.* The Hague, Netherlands: Mouton.

Farnsworth, D. W. (1940). High speed motion pictures of the human vocal cords [and film]. *Bell Laboratories Record, 18,* 203–208.

Fox, C. M., & Ramig, L. O. (1997). Vocal sound pressure level and self-perception of speech and voice in men and women with idiopathic Parkinson disease. *American Journal of Speech-Language Pathology, 6,* 85–94.

Fry, D. B. (1979). *The physics of speech.* Cambridge, England: Cambridge University Press.

Gibbon, F. (1999). Undifferentiated lingual gestures in children with articulation/phonological disorders. *Journal of Speech, Language and Hearing Research, 42,* 382–397.

Gibbon, F. E., & Crampin, L. (2002). Labial-lingual double articulations in speakers with cleft palate. *The Cleft Palate and Craniofacial Journal, 39,* 40–49.

Gick, B. (2002). The use of ultrasound for linguistic phonetic fieldwork. *Journal of the International Phonetic Association, 32,* 113–121.

Glasberg, B. R., & Moore, B. C. J. (1986). Auditory filter shapes in subjects with unilateral and bilateral cochlear impairments. *Journal of the Acoustical Society of America, 79,* 1020–1033.

Glasberg, B. R., & Moore, B. C. J. (1990). Derivation of auditory filter-shapes from notched-noise data. *Hearing Research, 47,* 103–138.

Goldman-Eisler, F. (1956). The determinants of the rate of speech output and their mutual relations. *Journal of Psychosomatic Research, 1,* 137–143.

Green, J. R., Moore, C. A., Higashikawa, M., & Steeve, R. W. (2000). The physiologic development of speech motor control: Lip and jaw coordination. *Journal of Speech, Language and Hearing Research, 43,* 239–255.

Green, J. R., Moore, C. A., & Reilly, K. J. (2000). The physiologic development of speech motor control: Lip and jaw coordination. *Journal of Speech, Language and Hearing Research, 45,* 66–79.

Handbook of the International Phonetic Association (1999). *Handbook of the International Phonetic Association: A guide to the use of the international phonetic alphabet.* Cambridge, England: Cambridge University Press.

Hardcastle, W. J. (1976). *Physiology of speech production.* London: Academic Press.

Hardcastle, W. J., & Gibbon, F. (1997). Electropalatography and its clinical applications. In M. J. Ball & C. Code (Eds.), *Instrumental Clinical Phonetics* (pp. 151–195). London: Whurr.

Harrington, J., Fletcher, J., & Roberts, C. (1995). Coarticulation and the accented/unaccented distinction: Evidence from jaw movement data. *Journal of Phonetics, 23,* 305–322.

Harris, J. (1994). *English sound structure.* Oxford, England: Blackwell.

Harris, T., Harris, S., Rubin, J. S., & Howard, D. M. (1998). *The voice clinic handbook.* London: Whurr.

Hartmann, W. M. (1997). *Signals, sound and sensation.* New York: Springer.

Henton, C. G. (1983). Changes in the vowels of Received Pronunciation. *Journal of Phonetics, 11,* 353–371.

Hermes, D. J., & van Gestel, J. C. (1991). The frequency scale of speech intonation. *Journal of the Acoustical Society of America, 90,* 97–102.

Hewlett, N., & Rendall, M. (1998). Rural versus urban accent as an influence on the rate of speech. *Journal of the International Phonetic Association, 28,* 63–71.

Hillman, R. E. & Kobler, J. B. (2000). Aerodynamic measures of voice production. In M. J. Ball & R. D. Kent (Eds.), *Voice quality measurement* (pp. 245–256). San Diego, CA: Singular.

Hinton, V. A., & Arokiasamy, W. M. C. (1997). Maximum interlabial pressures in normal speakers. *Journal of Speech, Language and Hearing Research, 40,* 400–404.

Hirano, M. (1981). *Clinical examination of voice.* Vienna: Springer-Verlag.

Hirano, M., & Bless, D. (1993). *Videostroboscopic examination of the larynx.* San Diego, CA: Singular.

Hiroto, I. (1966). Patho-physiology of the larynx from the standpoint of vocal mechanism. *Practica Otologica Kyoto, 59,* 229–292.

Honda, K., Kurita, T., Kakita, Y., & Maeda, S. (1995). Physiology of the lips and modeling of lip gestures. *Journal of Phonetics, 23,* 243–254.

Howard, D. M., & Angus, J. (2001). *Acoustics and psychoacoustics* (2nd ed.). Oxford, England: Focal Press.

Hughes, A., & Trudgill, P. (1996). *English accents and dialects: An introduction to social and regional varieties of English in the British Isles.* London: Arnold.

International Phonetic Association (1999). *Handbook of the International Phonetic Association.* Cambridge, England: Cambridge University Press.

ISO 226. (2003). *Acoustics—Normal equal-loudness-level contours.* Geneva, Switzerland: International Organization for Standardization.

ISO 389-7. (1998). *Acoustics—Reference zero for the calibration of audiometric equipment: Part 7. Reference threshold of hearing under free-field and diffuse-field listening conditions.* Geneva, Switzerland: International Organization for Standardization.

ISO 7029. (2000). *Acoustics—Statistical distribution of hearing thresholds as a function of age.* Geneva, Switzerland: International Organization for Standardization.

Johnson, K. (2003). *Acoustic and auditory phonetics* (2nd ed.). Cambridge, MA: Blackwell.

Jones, D. (1947). *An outline of English phonetics.* (4th ed.). Cambridge, England: Heffer.

Kahane, J. C. (1988). Anatomy and physiology of the organs of the peripheral speech mechanism. In J. Lass, L. V. McReynolds, J. L. Northern, & D. E. Yonder (Eds.), *Handbook of speech-language pathology and audiology* (pp. 109–155). Toronto/Philadelphia: Decker.

Kent, R. D. (1997). *The speech sciences.* San Diego, CA: Singular.

Kent, R., & Ball, M. J. (Eds.) (2000). *Voice quality measurement.* San Diego, CA: Singular.

Kent, R., Kent, J., & Rosenbeck, J. (1987). Maximum performance tests of speech production. *Journal of Speech and Hearing Disorders, 52,* 367–387.

Kent, R. D., & Read, C. (1992). *The acoustic analysis of speech.* San Diego CA: Singular.

Koay, G., Heffner, H. E., & Heffner, R. S. (1997). Audiogram of the big brown bat (*Eptesicus fuscus*). *Hearing Research, 105,* 202–210.

Krook, J. (1988). Speaking f_0 characteristics of normal Swedish subjects obtained by glottal frequency analysis. *Folia Phoniatrica, 40,* 82–96.

Ladd, D. R. (1996). *Intonational phonology.* Cambridge, England: Cambridge University Press.

Ladefoged, P. (1971). *Preliminaries to linguistic phonetics.* Chicago: University of Chicago Press.

Ladefoged, P. (1972). Phonological features and their phonetic correlates. *Journal of the International Phonetic Association, 2,* 2–12.

Ladefoged, P. (2000). *A course in phonetics* (4th ed.). Fort Worth, TX: Harcourt College.

Ladefoged, P., & Maddieson, I. (1996). *The sounds of the world's languages.* Oxford, England: Blackwell.

Lass, N. J. (Ed.). (1996). *Principles of experimental phonetics.* St Louis, MO: Mosby.

Laver, J. (1980). *The phonetic description of voice quality.* Cambridge, England: Cambridge University Press.

Laver, J. (1994). *Principles of phonetics.* Cambridge, England: Cambridge University Press.

Laver, J., Wirz, S., Mackenzie, J., & Hiller, S. M. (1981). A perceptual protocol for the analysis of vocal profiles. *Edinburgh University Department of Linguistics Work in Progress, 14,* 139–155.

Li Wei, Zhu Hua, & Dodd, B. (2002). Phonological saliency and phonological acquisition by Putonghua-speaking children: A cross-populational study. In F. Windsor, M. L. Kelly, & N. Hewlett (Eds.), *Investigations in clinical phonetics and linguistics* (pp. 169–184). Mahwah, NJ: Lawrence Erlbaum Associates.

Liberman, A. M. (1996). *Speech: A special code.* Cambridge, MA: MIT Press.

Liberman, A. M., Fitch, H. L., Halwes, T., & Erickson, D. M. (1980). Perceptual equivalence of two acoustic cues for stop consonant manner. *Perception and Psychophysics, 27,* 343–350.

Liberman, A. M., Harris, K. S., Eimas, P., Lisker, L., & Bastian, J. (1961). An effect of learning on speech perception: The discrimination of durations of silence with and without phonemic significance. *Language and Speech, 4,* 175–195. Reprinted in Liberman (1996, pp. 165–182).

Liberman, P. (1977). *Speech physiology and acoustic phonetics*. New York: MacMillan.

Lieberman, P. (1998). *Eve spoke: Human language and human evolution*. London: Picador.

Lindblom, B. (1990). Explaining phonetic variation: A sketch of the H and H theory. In W. J. Hardcastle & A. Marchal (Eds.), *Speech production and speech modeling* (pp. 403–439). Dordrecht: Kluwer.

Lyons, J. (1977). *Semantics*. Cambridge, England: Cambridge University Press.

Mackenzie, J., Laver, J., & Hiller, S. M. (1991). Structural pathology of the vocal folds and phonation. In J. Laver (Ed.), *The gift of speech* (pp. 281–318). Edinburgh, Scotland: Edinburgh University Press.

Mackenzie Beck, J. (1988). *Organic variation and voice quality*. Unpublished doctoral dissertation, University of Edinburgh, Scotland.

Mackenzie Beck, J. (1996). *Clinical evaluation of EVA: Preliminary report for EC-VALUE Programme: "Valorisation d'une station d'aide au diagnostic et à la rééducation des pathologies de la parole."* Unpublished manuscript, Queen Margaret University College, Edinburgh, Scotland.

Mackenzie Beck, J. (2003, August). Is it possible to predict students' ability to develop skills in practical phonetics? In M. J. Solé, D. Recasens, & J. Romero (Eds.), *Proceedings of the 15th International Congress of Phonetic Sciences*, 2833–2836.

Magnan, P., Dancer, A., Probst, R., Smurzynski, J., & Avan, P. (1999). Intracochlear acoustic pressure measurements: Transfer functions of the middle ear and cochlear mechanics. *Audiology and Neuro-otology, 4*, 123–128.

Manuel, S. (1999). Cross-language studies: Relating language-particular coarticulation patterns to other language-particular facts. In W. J. Hardcastle & N. Hewlett (Eds.), *Coarticulation: Theory, data and techniques* (pp. 229–245). Cambridge: Cambridge University Press.

Marwick, H., Mackenzie, J., Laver, J., & Trevarthen, C. (1984). Voice quality as an expressive system in mother-to-infant communication: A case study. *Edinburgh University Department of Linguistics Work in Progress, 17*, 85–97.

Mathieson, L. (2001). *Greene and Mathieson's The voice and its disorders* (6th ed.). London: Whurr.

Moore, B. C. J. (2003). *An introduction to the psychology of hearing* (5th ed.). San Diego, CA: Academic Press.

Moore, B. C. J., & Glasberg, B. R. (1983). Suggested formulae for calculating auditory-filter bandwidths and excitation patterns. *Journal of the Acoustical Society of America, 74*, 750–753.

Moore, B. C. J., Glasberg, B. R., Hess, R. F., & Birchall, J. P. (1985). Effects of flanking noise bands on the rate of growth of loudness of tones in normal and recruiting ears. *Journal of the Acoustical Society of America, 77*, 1505–1515.

Müller, E. M., & Abbs, J. H. (1979). Strain gauge transduction of lip and jaw motion in the mid-saggital plane: Refinement of a prototype system. *Journal of the Acoustical Society of America, 65*, 481–486.

Munhall, K. G., Vatikiotis-Bateson, E., & Tohkura, Y. (1995). X-ray film database for speech research. *Journal of the Acoustical Society of America, 98*, 1222–1224.

Narayanan, S., Alwan, A., & Haker, K. (1995). An articulatory study of fricative consonants using MRI. *Journal of the Acoustical Society of America, 98*, 1325–1347.

Nolan, F. (2003, August). Intonational equivalence: An experimental evaluation of pitch scales. *Proceedings of the 15th International Congress of the Phonetic Sciences*, 771–774.

Nolan, F. (2005). Forensic speaker identification and the phonetic description of voice quality. In W. J. Hardcastle & J. Mackenzie Beck, J. (Eds.), *A figure of speech: A festschrift for John Laver*. Mahwah, NJ: Laurence Erlbaum Associates.

Nolan, F., Holst, T., & Kühnert, B. (1996). Modelling [s] to [ò] accommodation in English. *Journal of Phonetics, 24*, 113–137.

Official Journal of the European Communities. (1986). Council Directive 86/188/EEC of 12 May 1986 on the protection of workers from the risks related to exposure to noise at work. *Official Journal of the European Communities,* Volume L, 28–34.

Öhman, S. E. G. (1966). Coarticulation in CVC utterances: Spectrographic measurements. *Journal of the Acoustical Society of America, 39,* 151–168.

Olson, K. S., & Hajek, J. (1999). The phonetic status of the labial flap. *Journal of the International Phonetics Association, 29,* 104–114.

Pemberton, C., McCormack, P., & Russell, A. (1998). Have women's voices lowered across time? A cross-sectional study of Australian women's voices. *Journal of Voice, 12,* 208–213.

Perelló, J. (1962). The muco-undulatory theory of phonation. *Annals of Otolaryngology, 79,* 722–725.

Perkell, J. S. (1997). Articulatory processes. In W. J. Hardcastle & J. Laver (Eds.), *Handbook of the phonetic sciences* (pp. 333–370). Oxford, Egland: Blackwell.

Perkins, W. H., & Kent, R. D. (1986). *Functional anatomy of speech, language, and hearing: A primer.* San Diego, CA: College-Hill Press.

Peterson, G. E., & Barney, H. L. (1952). Control methods used in a study of the vowels. *The Journal of the Acoustical Society of America, 24,* 175–184. (Reprinted in Baken & Daniloff (Eds.) (1991, pp. 124–133).

Pickles, J. O. (1988). *An introduction to the physiology of hearing* (2nd ed.). London: Academic Press.

Potter, R. K., Kopp, G. A., & Green, H. C. (1947). *Visible speech.* New York: Van Norstrand.

Pressnitzer, D., Patterson, R. D., & Krumbholz, K. (2001). The lower limit of melodic pitch. *Journal of the Acoustical Society of America, 109,* 2074–2084.

Rammage, L. A., Morrison, M., Nichol, H. Pullan, B. Salkeld, L., & May, P. (2001). *Management of the voice and its disorders* (2nd ed.). New York: Thomson-Delmar Learning.

Recasens, D., Pallares, M. D., & Fontdevila, J. (1997). A model of lingual coarticulation based on articulatory constraints. *Journal of the Acoustical Society of America, 102,* 544–561.

Reich, A. R., Frederickson, R. R., Mason, J. A., & Schlauch, R. S. (1990). Methodological variables affecting phonational frequency range in adults. *Journal of Speech and Hearing Disorders, 55,* 124–131.

Repp, B. H. (1979). Relative amplitude of aspiration noise as a voicing cue for syllable-initial stop consonants. *Language and Speech, 22,* 173–189.

Ryalls, J. (1996). *A basic introduction to speech perception.* San Diego, CA: Singular.

Scobbie, J. M., Hewlett, N., & Turk, A. (1999). Standard English in Edinburgh and Glasgow: The Scottish vowel length rule revealed. In P. Foulkes & G. Docherty (Eds.), *Urban voices: Accent studies of the British Isles* (pp. 230–245). London: Arnold.

Seikel, J., King, D., & Drumright, D. (2000). *Anatomy and physiology for speech, language and hearing* (8th ed.) San Diego, CA: Singular.

Shadle, C. (1977). The aerodynamics of speech. In W. J. Hardcastle & J. Laver (Eds.), *Handbook of the phonetic sciences* (pp. 33–64). Oxford: Blackwell.

Sharma, A., & Dorman, M. (1999). Cortical evoked potential correlates of categorical perception of voice onset time. *Journal of the Acoustical Society of America, 106,* 1078–1083.

Shaw, E. A. G. (1974). Transformation of sound pressure level from the free field to the eardrum in the horizontal plane. *Journal of the Acoustical Society of America, 56,* 1848–1861.

Shoup, J. E., & Pfeifer, I. L. (1976). Acoustic characteristics of speech sounds. In N. Lass (Ed.), *Contemporary issues in experimental phonetics* (pp. 171–224). New York: Academic Press.

Sihvo, M., Laippala, P., & Sala, E. (2000). A study of repeated measures of softest and loudest phonations. *Journal of Voice, 14,* 161–169.

Speaks, C. E. (1996). *An introduction to sound* (2nd ed.). San Diego, CA: Singular.

Stevens, K. N. (1998). *Acoustic phonetics.* Cambridge, MA: The MIT Press.

Stevens, S. S., & Volkman, J. (1940). The relation of pitch to frequency: A revised scale. *The American Journal of Psychology, 53,* 329–353.

Stone, M. (1999). Imaging techniques. In W. J. Hardcastle & N. Hewlett (Eds.), *Coarticulation: Theory, data and techniques* (pp. 246–259). Cambridge, England: Cambridge University Press.

Stuart-Smith, J. (1999). Glasgow: Accent and voice quality. In G. Docherty & P. Foulkes (Eds.), *Urban voices: Accent study in the British Isles* (pp. 203–222). London: Arnold.

Sussman, H., & Westbury, J. (1981). The effects of antagonistic gestures on temporal and amplitude parameters of anticipatory labial coarticulation. *Journal of Speech and Hearing Research, 16,* 16–24.

Titze, I. R. (1994). *Principles of voice production.* Englewood Cliffs, NJ: Prentice-Hall.

Traunmüller, H., & Eriksson, A. (1995). The perceptual evaluation of F_0 excursions in speech as evidenced by liveliness estimations. *Journal of the Acoustical Society of America, 97,* 1905–1915.

Truax, B. (Ed.). (1999) *Handbook for acoustic ecology* (2nd ed.). Burnaby, Canada: Cambridge Street Publishing.

Turner, J. D., & Pretlove, A. J. (1991). *Acoustics for engineers.* Basingstoke, UK: MacMillan.

UCLA Phonetics Laboratory. (2002). Dissection of the speech production mechanism. *UCLA Working Papers in Phonetics, 102.* Available from http://www.linguistics.ucla.edu/people/ladefoge/anatomy/Preface.pdf

Vatikiotis-Bateson, E., & Ostry, D. J. (1995). An analysis of the dimensionality of jaw motion in speech. *Journal of Phonetics, 23,* 101–117.

Wells, J. (1982). *Accents of English. Vol. 1. Accents of English 1: An Introduction. Vol. 2. Accents of English 2: The British Isles. Vol. 3. Accents of English 3: Beyond the British Isles.* Cambridge: Cambridge University Press.

Wells, J., & House, J. (1995). *The sounds of the International Phonetic Alphabet.* London: University College London.

Westbury, J. R. (1991). The significance and measurement of head position during speech production experiments using the X-ray microbeam system. *Journal of the Acoustical Society of America, 89,* 1780–1791.

White, F. A. (1975). *Our acoustic environment.* New York: Wiley.

Yavas, M. (2002). VOT patterns in bilingual phonological development. In F. Windsor, L. Kelly, & N. Hewlett (Eds.), *Themes in clinical linguistics* (pp. 341–349). Mahwah, NJ: Lawrence Erlbaum Associates.

Yip, M. (1994). Tone in East Asian languages. In J. A. Goldsmith (Ed.), *The handbook of phonological theory* (pp. 476–494). Cambridge, MA: Blackwell.

Yost, W. A. (2000). *Fundamentals of hearing* (4th ed.). San Diego, CA: Academic Press.

Zajac, D. J., Mayo, R., & Ryuta, K. (1998). Nasal coarticulation in normal speakers: A reexamination of the effects of gender. *Journal of Speech, Language, and Hearing Research, 41,* 503–510.

Zraick, R. I., Nelson, J. L., Montague, J. C., & Monoson, P. K. (2000). The effect of task on determination of maximum phonational frequency range. *Journal of Voice, 14,* 154–160.

Zwicker, E. (1961). Subdivision of the audible frequency range into critical bands. (Frequenzgruppen). *Journal of the Acoustical Society of America, 33,* 248.

Zwicker, E., & Fastl, F. (1999). *Psychoacoustics: Facts and models* (2nd ed.). Berlin, Germany: Springer.

Author Index

Subject Index